A
DURABLE
PEACE

BOOKS EDITED BY BENJAMIN NETANYAHU

International Terrorism: Challenge and Response

Terrorism: How the West Can Win

Self-Portrait of a Hero: The Letters of Jonathan Netanyahu
(with Iddo Netanyahu)

BOOKS WRITTEN BY BENJAMIN NETANYAHU

Fighting Terrorism

BENJAMIN NETANYAHU

A
DURABLE PEACE

ISRAEL AND ITS PLACE AMONG THE NATIONS

WARNER BOOKS

A Time Warner Company

The song, "Jerusalem of Gold," on page 195 is printed by permission of Naomi Shemer

Warner Books Edition
Copyright ©1993, 2000 by Benjamin Netanyahu
All rights reserved.

This Warner Books edition is published by arrangement with Bantam Books, New York, NY

Warner Books, Inc., 1271 Avenue of the Americas, New York, NY 10020

Visit our Web site at www.twbookmark.com

A Time Warner Company

Printed in the United States of America
First Warner Books Printing: January 2000
10 9 8 7 6 5 4 3 2 1

Library of Congress Cataloging-in-Publication Data

Netanyahu, Binyamin.
    A durable peace : Israel and its place among the nations / Benjamin Netanyahu.
        p.   cm.
    Rev. ed. of : A place among the nations. 1993.
    Includes bibliographical references and index.
    ISBN 0-446-52306-2
    1. Arab-Israeli conflict.   2. Arab-Israeli conflict—1993—Peace.   3. Zionism—
History.   [1. Israel—Foreign relations.]   I. Netanyahu, Binyamin.   Place among the
nations.   II. Title.
DS119.6.N48   1999
327.5694—dc21   99-22713
                                                                                         CIP

Book design by H. Roberts Design

TO YONI

I grieve for thee, my brother Jonathan;
A great comfort hast thou been to me.
Thy love to me was wonderful. . . .

II SAMUEL 1:26

CONTENTS

LIST OF MAPS

PREFACE

Writing anything while you are still in office is a hazardous task. Writing anything after leaving office can be equally hazardous. For one is supposed to have the perspective of detachment and introspection to secure the desired objectivity. I profess at the outset: While I have done a great deal of thinking since leaving office, I am neither detached nor objective when it comes to securing the future of the Jewish state. In fact, I plead unabashed and passionate partisanship in seeking to assure the Jewish future. This is the conviction that guided me as the Prime Minister of Israel between 1996 and 1999, and this is the conviction that will guide me for the rest of my life.

The historical imperative of preserving the Jewish state was reinforced on a visit to China in 1999. The President of China, Jiang Zemin, expressed to me his great admiration for the legacy of the Jewish people, who produced such geniuses as Albert Einstein. "The Jewish people and the Chinese people are two of the oldest civilizations on earth," he said, "dating back four thousand and five thousand years respectively."

I concurred, adding India to the list.

"But there are one or two differences between us," I said. "For instance, how many Chinese are there?"

"1.2 billion," replied Zian Zemin.

"How many Indians are there?" I pressed on.

"About 1 billion."

"Now how many Jews are there?" I queried.

No answer.

"There are 12 million Jews in the world," I said.

Several Chinese jaws dropped in the room, understandably, given that this number could be contained in an enlarged suburb of Beijing.

"Mr. President," I said, "since the Jews have been around for thousands of years that is a remarkably low number. Two thousand years ago the Jews constituted ten percent of the population of the Roman Empire. Today there should have been 200 million Jews."

"What happened?" asked the Chinese president.

"Many things happened," I replied. "But they all boil down to one big thing. You, the Chinese, kept China; the Indians kept India; but we Jews lost our land and were dispersed to the four corners of the earth. From this sprang all our calamities, culminating in our greatest catastrophe in the twentieth century. This is why for the last two thousand years we have been trying to re-trieve our homeland and re-create our independent state there."

I was trying to impress upon the Chinese leadership the impor-tance of refraining from supplying Iran with nuclear weapons tech-nology. That would jeopardize not merely the modem State of Israel but threaten to wipe out forever an ancient and admired civilization. (Jiang Zemin assured me that China was not selling such technol-ogy to Iran, something I verified with our intelligence just in case.)

This, then, is the perspective that guided me as Israel's Prime Minister and that ought to guide anyone concerned with the future of the Jewish State: assuring that the people of Israel have what they need to survive and thrive in the next millennium, the fifth of their existence. I am convinced of one thing: The Jewish people will not get another chance. There are only so many miracles that history can provide a people, and the Jews have had more than their share. After unparalleled adversity, the Jews came back to life in the modern State of Israel. For better or worse, the Jewish future is centered on the future of that state. Therefore we must be extra careful not to toy with Israel's security or jeopardize its defenses, even as we pursue peace with our neighbors, for what is at stake is the destiny of an entire people.

In the long run, what will stand are not the passing praises of those who seek a quick fix for the Middle East's problems, but the bulwarks of a durable peace—one that can be credibly defended by a strong Israel. Any other kind of peace will not last. Achieving peace treaties with the Arabs is relatively easy. All you have to do is give in to the Arab demands. Achieving peace agreements that will stand the test of time is much harder to do.

This is what I set out to achieve as Prime Minister. I insisted on a secure peace, stressing the fundamental principle that in the Middle East peace and security are intertwined. A peace that undermines Israel's defenses and leaves unresolved central issues, such as the fate of Jerusalem and the Arab refugees, is one that is sure to crumble over time. It should be passed over until a more sustainable, more realistic peace is achieved.

This "stubbornness" in defense of a tough-minded peace did not make me, nor would it make any leader of Israel, popular in the diplomatic and press salons of the world. But it is the right policy and it is worth fighting for. If one possesses a millennial perspective, the slings and arrows of criticism are meaningless compared to the awesome responsibility of protecting the Jewish people and their one and only state.

I am confident that such persistence will pay off. The Jewish people have shown a remarkable capacity to overcome hardship, and surely they have the will and intelligence to pursue a genuine peace. The second half of the twentieth century offers indubitable proof of this.

•   •   •

Neither the present nor the future are free of problems. But they pale compared to those that faced the Jewish people in the ghettos of Europe just a few decades ago. This tells us how far the Jewish people have traveled and it fires our imagination and infuses us with hope as we begin the next fifty years.

This was the central fact of Jewish existence as Israel celebrated its first half-century. In the ancient Jewish traditions, jubilees were a time for both celebration and reflection. Indeed, there is much to celebrate. Half a century ago, at the close of World War II, it was not clear at all that the Jewish people would survive. A third of all Jews were consumed in the fires of the Holocaust, and the remaining two-thirds faced the dual threat of persecution and relentless assimilation. Stalin targeted the Jews of the Soviet Union as class enemies, and the Jews of America and Europe were rapidly embracing assimilation and intermarriage. Absent a vital center, Jewish numbers would have shrunk further, and the Jewish people, after four millennia of unparalleled struggle for their place under the sun, would have finally yielded to the forces of history and disappeared.

This has not happened. The pivotal change in Jewish destiny occurred with the founding of the Jewish state. This seminal event of reestablishing Jewish sovereignty in the ancient Jewish homeland was preceded by nearly a hundred years of renewed Jewish settlement activity in the Holy Land and by over fifty years of Zionist agitation, heralded by the prophetic and inspired genius of Theodor Herzl. Indeed, the Jewish state changed everything for the Jewish people. From a fledgling beachhead on the Mediterranean coast, struggling to survive the Arab onslaughts aimed at exterminating the Jewish presence in the land, the Jews were able to repel the attack; build a state; create one of the world's finest armies; defeat the much larger Arab forces in successive wars forced on Israel; unite their ancient capital, Jerusalem; bring in millions of immigrants and refugees, including a million beleaguered Jews from the former Soviet Union and the imperiled Jewish community of Ethiopia; revive an ancient language; build an astonishing scientific and technological capability; develop the most thriving economy in the Middle East, and one of the most advanced in the world; create a vibrant cultural life, which includes some of the leading artists and musicians of the world; and maintain a staunchly democratic ethos amidst a sea of despotic regimes.

By any criteria, these achievements are nothing short of miraculous. But they are all subsumed under the one greater accomplishment: The Jewish people, after long centuries of exile, has once again seized control over its destiny. And within the next decade or two it will realize the dream of ages, the Ingathering of the Exiles. For the first time since the era of the Second Temple two thousand years ago, the majority of the Jewish people will live in the Jewish homeland. This is a momentous development, the one guarantor of the Jewish future. For it is also true that in the last fifty years, a significant threat to Jewish survival has been the accelerating rate of intermarriage, assimilation, and loss of identity among Jews of the Diaspora, especially the Jews of the West. While the Jewish population of Israel grew from 600,000 in 1948 to five million in 2000, the population of American Jewry stayed flat and is beginning to show alarming signs of steady decline. In Israel itself the threat of assimilation is nonexistent. And to the extent that Jewish identity has been maintained and strengthened in important parts of American Jewry, this is due to the strong identification that these Jews have with the State of Israel. In simple terms, the future of the Jewish people depends on the future of the Jewish state.

For the Jewish people, therefore, the history of the twentieth century may be summed up thus: If there had been a Jewish state in the first half of the century, there would have been no Holocaust. And if there had not been a Jewish state after the Holocaust, there would have been no Jewish future. The State of Israel is not only the repository of the millennial Jewish hopes for redemption; it is also the one practical instrument for assuring Jewish survival.

Assuring that survival is not free of problems. Israel has yet to complete the circle of peace around its borders, a peace that must be based on security if it is to last. I view this as the first task facing the country, and any prime minister must dedicate himself to its completion. This of course does not depend on Israel alone, but on the willingness of its Arab neighbors to forge a true compromise with Israel and genuinely accept its right to exist. Perhaps the most difficult agreements to be completed are the Oslo Accords with the Palestinians. This will require the Palestinians to keep their commitments, especially to fight terror, and Israel to maintain adequate security defenses. Much of this book was written before the Oslo Accords, and I have amended and added a few segments to indicate how I believe the Oslo process could be completed so as to provide Israel with peace and security.

During my three years as Prime Minister (1996–1999), I firmly pursued these principles for a realistic peace, despite a torrent of criticism and abuse from those who cavalierly refuse to understand that in the volatile Middle East, peace without security is a sham. Such shortsightedness ought not to deflect Israel from pursuing a lasting peace that will endure not a flicker of time but for generations to come.

Assuring its security will also require Israel to address new threats on the horizon, presented by radical regimes developing fearsome weapons and the means to deliver them. Even if Israel completes the circle of peace with its immediate neighbors, and it should strive to do so, this threat will loom large in the coming decades. What if Iraq or Iran detonates nuclear devices? This will send infinitely greater shockwaves around the world than the addition of India and Pakistan to the league of nuclear nations. The possession of atomic bombs by Saddam Hussein or the Ayatollas of Teheran is not merely a mortal threat to Israel's existence. It is a threat to the peace of the world. The community of responsible nations will have to make every effort to contain or eliminate this threat. But surely for Israelis, once again they recognize that the one guarantor of their survival against these dangers is their own strength and capacity to deter and punish aggression directed against the state.

The transformation of the Jewish condition from one of utter powerlessness to one of effective self-defense marks the great change that the founding of Israel introduced into Jewish life, in fact making that life possible. As Herzl and the founding fathers of Zionism foresaw, the founding of the Jewish state would not necessarily stop the attacks on the Jewish people, but would assuredly give the Jews the means to resist and repel those attacks.

Naturally, such a momentous change in the life of a nation does not occur without internal turbulence and turmoil. Israel is undergoing the adjustment pains as it moves from adolescence to maturity. If initially its governing socialist class wanted to straitjacket all Israelis into one European socialist prototype, they have had a hard time accepting the fact that this will not happen, that the currents of life and the natural desire for unrestricted diversity and pluralism are more powerful than any rigid ideological construct. Israel after half a century is a rich tapestry of Jews from a hundred lands, each bringing to the national fabric its own unique strands of culture, folklore, and memory. Modern Hebrew is laced with Russian, Arabic, and English slang, and with expressions liberally borrowed from the Jews of Poland and Morocco alike. Each community affects the other, creating a dynamic synthesis that enhances the national culture. There are of course some lingering sharp divides, as between Israel's Jewish majority and its non-Jewish minority and, in the Jewish population, between the secular majority and an ultra-orthodox minority. It takes a crisis in the Persian Gulf to remind Israelis that inflying Iraqi missiles do not distinguish between religious and non-religious Jews, and, in fact, between any of the groups that make up Israel's population. Yet I believe that despite the inevitable frictions that accompany this extraordinary maturation of an immigrant nation, the forces that unite the people of Israel are infinitely greater than those that divide them: a common past in a sacred ancestral homeland, and a millennial desire to return to this land and forge in it a common future.

This of course is not the picture of Israel presented by many observers, as Israel celebrated its jubilee. The foreign press amplified the Israeli press, which regularly amplifies the grievances of the old elites that complain of giving way to the new realities. This chorus of gloom is an episodic and irrelevant footnote in the larger tale of Jewish revival in the last fifty years. After all that we have struggled against, and all that we have achieved, I have no doubt that Israel can meet with equal success the remaining challenges of external and internal peace.

Israel at the start of the twenty-first century is undoubtedly one of the greatest success stories of the twentieth century. Communism, fascism, socialism, and so many other "isms" have crumbled into dust. But Zionism, the national liberation movement of the Jewish people, the one true liberation movement amidst so many false ones, has far from crumbled. It has fended off powerful foes, and is on the verge of creating the second most successful technological society on earth, the "Silicon Wadi," as it is becoming known. In a profound sense, Zionism has achieved its central purpose of securing Jewish independence in the Jewish land, and it can look to the future and its challenges with confidence.

It can do so with the remarkable kinship and support of the American people. The friendship of the United States of America has been a cornerstone of Israel's modern history. It is a partnership based on common values and common ideals, and it remains constant. *The New York Times*, which affords ample space for the discontent of the Israeli left, expressed in noteworthy honesty its surprise at a Jubilee year poll commissioned by the newspaper, which showed that instead of waning, American support for Israel had reached a twenty-year high. Non-Jewish Americans from every part of that great land identified with Israel and not with its adversaries. They deeply valued the special relationship between Israel and the United States. Many thought of Israel as the biblical promised land upon which America was modeled. They saw Jerusalem as the original city on the hill and strongly believed that it must never be divided again. They viewed Israel's struggle as one of a solitary democracy surrounded by dictatorships, resolutely fighting terrorism. Beyond the swirl of daily events and the often tendentious coverage of Israeli affairs, this is what emerges in the American mind when the name of Israel is evoked. It need not surprise anyone for a simple reason: It is true.

Yet the truth has often eluded discussions about modern Israel. Israel has been portrayed as an aggressive obstacle to peace, a force bent on physically and economically colonizing its neighbors, a twister and bender of the Jewish soul. I believe that all of these slanders, like so many others that afflicted the Jewish people down the ages, will also pass in due time. I wrote this book not only to help accelerate their demise, but to express my boundless faith in the Jewish future, my unreserved confidence that the last fifty years have shown that the Jewish people will survive, and that against all obstacles the Jewish state will prevail.

• • •

During the Gulf War, Israel sustained thirty-nine Scud missile attacks that rained down on its cities. Deafening sirens warned Israelis to don their gas masks in the tense minutes as the missiles headed for their targets. In the course of one such alert I was being interviewed, with a gas mask on, at the CNN television headquarters in Jerusalem. After the alert subsided, the CNN bureau chief, evidently moved by the experience, asked me to show the network's viewers Israel's position on the map of the Middle East.

"Show them what you showed me in your office the other day," he said, producing a map of the Middle East in front of the camera.

"Here's the Arab world," I said, "walking" across the map with my hands open wide. It took me a number of handbreadths to span the twenty-one Arab countries.

"And here is Israel," I added, easily covering it with my thumb.

The results of this simple demonstration were astonishing. For months after the war, I received hundreds of letters from around the world expressing sympathy and support for Israel. But the one thing that repeatedly appeared in many of those letters was the shock experienced by viewers from as far afield as Minnesota and Australia concerning the walk I took across the map. One viewer wrote: "Most

Americans, myself included, have little real knowledge of the kind of danger and turmoil that confronts your part of the world." But when presented with the simple geographic facts, she said, "suddenly the picture came into focus for me—and I think for many Americans." In other interviews I used the opportunity to spell out the basic facts of Israel's predicament, prompting a viewer from Britain to confess that this "changed my way of thinking. . . . I went to the library to find out more about the Arab-Israeli problem and realized I knew very little about it." A third said these facts represented "the first real view I've had of the Jewish side to all this. . . . I began to feel with you."[1] This was the refrain I heard again and again as the letters filled one binder, then a second, then a third.

I had been aware of the general lack of familiarity with the facts of Israel's physical circumstances, but this torrent of mail brought home to me, as nothing else had, the gaping void in the world's knowledge of my country and its struggle. Here were people who clearly wished Israel well, yet who did not know something so elementary as the fact that the Arab world is more than five hundred times the size of the Jewish state. (See Maps 1 and 2.) They did not realize that the Israel they were incessantly hearing about and seeing every day on their television screens is all of forty miles wide (*including* the West Bank), and that if it were to give up the entire West Bank, it would be ten miles wide.

If an image of a country, its scenery, and its history is repeatedly implanted in people's minds, it tends to assume overblown dimensions. Contrary to the common view, this is not just the result of the distorting prism of television. Sunday-school instruction a hundred years ago had a similar effect. Here is what Mark Twain wrote of his visit to the Holy Land in 1869:

> I must studiously and faithfully unlearn a great many things I have somehow absorbed concerning Palestine. . . . I have got everything in Palestine on too large a scale. Some of my ideas were wild enough. The word Palestine always brought to my mind a vague suggestion of a country as large as the United

States. . . . I suppose it was because I could not conceive of a small country having so large a history.[2]

These lingering misimpressions are not limited to the geographic realities of Israel's existence. They are matched by a widespread lack of familiarity with the political and historical circumstances of Israel's birth and its efforts to achieve peace with its Arab neighbors. Twain, at least, knew the history of the land in considerable detail, and he was up to date on the contemporary conditions of the Jewish people. This is not the case with many of those who shape, and receive, opinions about Israel today.

Over the last twenty-five years, since my days as an Israeli student in an American university following the Yom Kippur War, I have had no choice but to engage in the Sisyphean labor of trying to roll back this boulder of ignorance, which has grown increasingly heavy each year. For with each passing season, the facts of Israel's emergence as a modern state, although readily ascertainable in any library, recede further and further from memory. What has been inserted in their place is a facile misrepresentation of reality. Moreover, there has been a growing tendency in the United States and in the West to use this distorted view of Israel to explain away the region's complicated conflicts. Many people have come to believe that all the turbulence of the Middle East is somehow associated with the Jewish state. This is dangerous on two counts: It is losing Israel's vitally needed support abroad, and it has skewed Western policy away from a sober appraisal of Middle Eastern politics and of the danger that this region's endemic instability poses for the peace of the world.

This book is an attempt to restore to public awareness what were once evident truths to all fair-minded students of the region. I have tried to focus on the main assumptions concerning the Arab-Israeli conflict and to analyze their truthfulness. I have also concentrated on Israel's current predicament—its position in the world, its internal administration, and its relationship to the Jewish people worldwide—which is often glossed over in public discourse. Though I have used available historical material, I do not intend this to be a comprehensive chronicle of events. Nor is this a personal narrative, notwithstanding the references to my family that appear in the text; in its own way, each Israeli household tells the story of Zionism, the movement for Jewish statehood, and gives testimony to its unfolding saga. In the same vein, I have included experiences from my military service, diplomatic postings, and work in government that can help the reader better understand why many Israelis have come to hold views similar to my own.

The fact that they do hold such views may have been obscured by the victory of the opposition Labor party in the 1992 elections over the Likud government, in which I served, and by the vocal opposition from the left to my own government, which came into power in 1996. The ebb and flow of Israeli politics creates an impression of a great divide in Israel over every aspect of national life. Nevertheless, the differences that divide Israelis on political matters are dwarfed by the enormous areas of agreement that bind them together. The attentive reader will find that these disagreements over policy represent only a small part of what is covered in this book. On most of the subjects, I believe my approach is representative of the views of the majority of Israelis, wherever they fall on the political spectrum.

I write as an Israeli who wishes to see a secure Israel at peace with its neighbors, and who profoundly believes that peace cannot be conjured up out of vapid pronouncements. Unless it is built on a foundation of truth, peace will founder on the jagged rocks of Middle Eastern realities. Indeed, the Arab world's main weapon in its war against the Jewish National Home has been the weapon of untruth. For many people around the world, and for some in Israel itself, the fundamental facts of this conflict have been distorted and obfuscated—about the nature of Zionism, the justice of its cause, the sources of the Arabs' intractable hostility to the Jewish state, and the barriers that have locked peace out of a violent region.

The Jewish people has had to contend with defamation for generations. But the scale of this century's slanders against it and

against Israel, their reach, effectiveness, and devastating consequences, have far exceeded anything seen before. Nevertheless, I
am convinced that these slanders can be refuted and the battle for
truth can be won—that open-minded people *can* tell the difference
between the endless calumnies leveled against the Jewish state and
the unvarnished truth, when the facts are presented before them.

When the battle for truth is won, it will open the way for an enduring peace between Arab and Jew. That such a peace can be
achieved I have no doubt. It will necessitate an understanding of
the special conditions required to sustain peaceful relations in the
Middle East. I have attempted to spell out what such a peace
would be like, and what changes are needed to produce it—
changes in Western policies toward the region, in Arab approaches to Israel, and in Israel's own attitudes.

We are entering a historical period that portends both threat
and promise. The old order has collapsed, and the new one is far
from established. The final guarantor of the viability of a small nation in such times of turbulence is its capacity to direct its own
destiny, something that has eluded the Jewish people during its
long centuries of exile. Restoring that capacity is the central task
of the Jewish people today.

No one yet knows what awaits the Jews in the twenty-first century, but we must make every effort to ensure that it is better than
what befell them in the twentieth, the century of the Holocaust.
The rebirth of Israel, its development and empowerment, is ultimately the only assurance that such will be the case. More is at
stake than the fate of the Jewish people alone. Since biblical times
civilization has been riveted by the odyssey of the Jews. If after all
their fearful travails the Jewish people will have rebuilt a permanent and secure home in their ancient corner of the earth, this will
surely give meaning and hope to all of humanity.

1. Israel and the Arab World

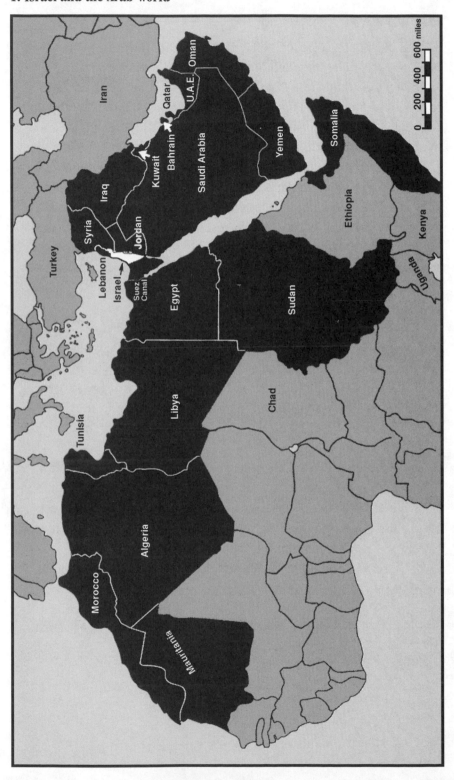

2. Israel's Relative Size

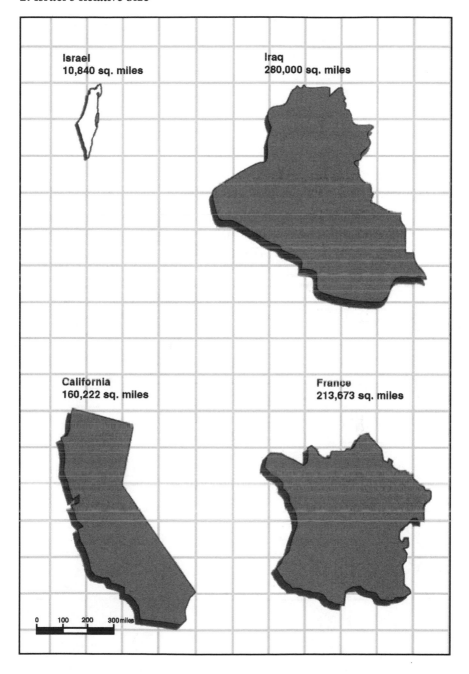

Israel
10,840 sq. miles

Iraq
280,000 sq. miles

California
160,222 sq. miles

France
213,673 sq. miles

0   100   200   300 miles

A
DURABLE
PEACE

Introduction

The reemergence of the Jews as a sovereign nation is an unprecedented event in the history of mankind. Yet for all its uniqueness, one cannot truly understand the struggle of the Jewish people to bring the State of Israel into existence in isolation from the universal longings of nations to be free. The rise of the Zionist movement to restore a Jewish state can be comprehended only with reference to the more universal conflicts between nations and empires, between demands for self-determination and the supranational ideologies of colonialism and Communism that have characterized the history of the last two centuries. It is for this reason that the cataclysmic events at the close of the twentieth century will have a profound impact on Israel's future.

Seldom has the world witnessed such a spectacular disintegration as that of the Soviet Union. Shredded to confetti are the Soviet dreams of global grandeur to be acquired through the assimilation of provinces from Eastern Europe to Latin America. Equally remarkable has been the evaporation of the belief in Communism as the great organizing principle for world order and human justice—a principle in which millions had vested a faith bordering on the religious. Such a dual collapse of the greatest empire in history (in terms of territory) and the greatest "church" in history (in terms of the number of people under its sway) cannot occur without unleashing political tidal waves that will wash over every nation and state in the world. It will be impossible to make any sense of events without paying due attention to the unfolding search for a new organizing principle, or principles, with which to assist in settling an unsettled world. Obviously, the focus of this search will first be on the newly liberated Soviet republics and the countries of the former Communist bloc. But the arrangements that are devised to meet the needs of these newly freed peoples will have far-reaching consequences for the rest of the world and for the ways in which it will resolve its various disputes.

In the search for a new order, the international community is going back, almost against its will, to where it was before it was so rudely interrupted by the rise of Communism. For the spread of Soviet totalitarianism and the resulting Cold War was a glacier that buried beneath itself, in a state of invisible but perfect preservation, many of the great unresolved problems of the nineteenth century. Of course, to some the nineteenth century did not seem problematic at all. After the decisive defeat of Napoleon in 1815, it was perhaps the most peaceful century in two millennia—since the Pax Romana. The world was nicely divided up among rival empires: no major wars, no major calamities. But underneath the calm surface of empire there was great ferment. Historical tribal groupings, regional duchies, and medieval city-states were coalescing into nations across Europe, and millions of people were moving from the hinterland to the rapidly industrializing and politically conscious metropolises, processes that were to ripple from Europe into Asia and Africa in our own century.

The rise of nationalism in the nineteenth century clashed with the world order of the day, and the resultant national uprisings were summarily put down in 1848, the brief Spring of Nations. But when the old order finally did collapse after World War I, the various and often competing demands of nations for self-determination, and the problem of nationalism as a whole, required an immediate solution. Thus, following their victory in World War I, the Allied powers convened to launch a "new world order," signing the Treaty of Versailles, establishing the League of Nations, and promulgating President Woodrow Wilson's doctrine of self-determination.

The Versailles Conference was actually only the first in a seemingly interminable series of international conferences held between 1919 and 1923 to determine the "outcome" of World War I. Britain's prime minister, David Lloyd George, one of the chief architects of the postwar settlement, himself attended no fewer than thirty-three such conferences, the most significant of which (for the Jews) were Versailles (beginning in January 1919), the First Conference of London (February 1920), the San Remo Conference in Italy (April 1920), and the Sèvres Conference in France (August 1920).[1] For simplicity, I will refer to the decisions taken by the nations of the world at these various conferences as the Versailles settlement.

Versailles and the series of conferences that followed it produced a blueprint, however imperfect, for determining who got what and why. It was generally predicated on Wilson's premise that distinct national groups were entitled to countries of their own and to the freedom to pursue their own destinies according to their own lights. In some cases, as in what became Czechoslovakia and Yugoslavia, several nations were clustered together in a single state where this was deemed practicable. But such cases were more the exception than the rule. Thus, the Baltic nations of Estonia, Latvia, and Lithuania, each with a unique language, history, and culture, received independent national domains. So did Poland, which for over a century had been divided among Russia, Prussia, and Austria. So did Hungary, which like Czechoslovakia had hitherto been controlled by the Austro-Hungarian Empire. By the same token, Armenia, Georgia, and Azerbaijan were supposed to be free from the Russian yoke. Largely Greek portions of western Anatolia were to be transferred to Greece, Albania was to be given independence, and Kurdistan was to be granted autonomy. For the first time, Australia, Canada, and South Africa received recognition as sovereign nations. And similar recognition was also accorded to one more nation: the Jews.[2]

The case of the Jews was unique because, unlike the other peoples, they were a scattered nation, exiled for many centuries from their homeland. But this in no way affected the judgment of the civilized world at the beginning of this century that the Jews were entitled to a land of their own. Moreover, it was widely recognized that they were entitled to restore their national life in their ancient homeland, Palestine,* which up to 1918 was controlled by the crumbling Ottoman Empire. If anything, the tragic dispersion of the Jews through the centuries *strengthened* rather than diminished the belief that they deserved a state of their own—and an end to their wanderings. Zionism was accorded the kind of consideration given to other national movements seeking to realize their national goals.

Now that the ice of the Cold War has melted, the world of Versailles that was buried underneath is being revealed once again. The tenets of Versailles are being dusted off, its arrangements reinstated, and its unsolved problems (as in the Balkans) are erupting, as though the intervening century had not intervened. Baltic independence has been restored, as has the freedom Versailles

---

*The name Palestine is derived from the Philistines, a seafaring people that invaded the coast of the land of Canaan from the sea around 1200 B.C.E., shortly after the Jewish conquest overland from the east. The main Philistine dominions never extended much farther than the coastal strip between Gaza and today's Tel Aviv, and the Philistines disappeared as a people under the heel of the Babylonians. It was the Roman Empire, bent on destroying every vestige of Jewish attachment to the land, that invented the name Palestine to replace Judea, the historic name of the country.

Thus according to Professor Bernard Lewis:

> The official adoption of the name Palestine in Roman usage to designate the territories of the former Jewish principality of Judea seems to date from after the suppression of the great Jewish revolt of Bar Kochba in the year 135 C.E. . . . it would seem that the name Judea was abolished . . . and the country renamed Palestine or Syria Palestine, with the . . . intention of obliterating its historic Jewish identity.[3]

While this Roman name disappeared in the land itself shortly after the conquest by the Moslems,[4] Christian cartographers kept the name alive in their own lands and eventually bequeathed it to the Allied negotiators at Versailles and the inhabitants of the land, who adopted it only after the British took control. According to Professor Lewis:

promised to the peoples of Central and Eastern Europe. The passage of time appears to have made little difference. Even the much-celebrated and anticipated monetary union of Western Europe, meant by some to erase national allegiance, shows no sign of achieving such a radical shift away from basic national loyalties. The relevance of nationalism as a central driving force in global affairs is being demonstrated daily, as is the durability of many, though not all, of the arrangements conceived at the beginning of the century in response to the demands for independence of diverse peoples. Most of these arrangements have endured and gained the world's acceptance.

But this has not been the case with the Jewish national restoration. For what was accepted at Versailles as a just solution to the question of Jewish nationhood is today shunned by governments and chancellories the world over. They accept, most of them, that the Jewish people is entitled to a state. But they reject the Versailles conception of the size and viability of that domain, preferring to toss the Jews a scrap at best from the original offering. The promise of Versailles to the Jewish people was that it would be allowed to build a nation in the land of Palestine—understood then to comprise both sides of the Jordan River (see Map 3). This area, now referred to as Mandatory Palestine (the area in which Britain was charged in 1920 to secure a Jewish national home), included the territory of the present-day states of

By the early twentieth century, with the predominance of European influence . . . the name Palestine came to be used even in the country [i.e., in Palestine]. This use was, however, in the main confined to Christians and to a very small group of westernized Muslims. The name was not used officially, and had no precise territorial definition until it was adopted by the British to designate the area which they acquired by conquest at the end of World War I.[5]

Thus, up until the twentieth century, the name Palestine referred exclusively to the ancient land of the Jews—as did the names Judea, Judah, Zion, and Israel. It had never yet been argued that there existed a "Palestinian people" other than the Jews. The Arabs who lived there were called Arabs, just as the Armenians, Turks, Druze, and Circassians who migrated into Palestine were then still called Armenians, Turks, Druze, and Circassians. With the exception of the Jews, who called the land Eretz Yisrael (the Land of Israel) and viewed it as their national home, all of these groups considered themselves as living in the realm of Southern Syria.

Jordan and Israel. In fact, many people now argue that the Jews do not deserve even 20 percent of this territory (that is, present-day Israel, including the West Bank), and they demand that the Jewish people be satisfied with a mere 15 percent of the original Mandate (Israel minus the West Bank, which comprises the heart of the country). This would leave the Jews with a state ten miles wide, its cities crowded along the Mediterranean, with radical leaders peering down at them from the Samarian and Judean mountains that dominated the country. All that would be left of the Versailles promise to the Jewish people, of a small but nonetheless viable country capable of accommodating fifteen million Jews and their descendants, would be a truncated ghetto-state squeezed onto a narrow shoreline.

What a curious transformation: Versailles promised the Jewish people a national home in its historic land, five times the size of the present-day State of Israel. This promise was given as a result of the universal recognition of the Jews' right to be restored to the land from which they had been forcibly exiled, a recognition reinforced by the knowledge of the extent of Jewish suffering over the centuries as a result of that exile. No one gave more eloquent expression to this direct relationship between the removal of the Jews from their land and their subsequent suffering than Lord Byron in his melancholy "Hebrew Melodies," and at Versailles the whole world echoed his sentiments.

Yet today, nearly eighty years after Versailles, after the destruction of six million Jews in the Holocaust, a horror that Byron could not possibly have imagined, and after five wars launched by the Arabs to annihilate the survivors who had gathered in a fraction of the land promised to the Jews, the Jewish people are now being told that this is still too much. Worse, they are told that the desire to have a country not ten but forty miles wide is proof that they are expansionist, aggressive, and unreasonable.

How is it that Zionism, which enjoyed such universal goodwill at the beginning of the century, is under such relentless attack at its close? How is it that a movement that was enthusiastically supported by the leading statesmen of the day, such as Woodrow Wilson, David Lloyd George, Georges Clemenceau, and Tomáš Masaryk, has come under increasing criticism and pressure from today's world leaders? How is it that the very word *Zionist*, once proudly espoused by Christian and Jew alike, has acquired an odious or at least suspect connotation? How did these transformations come about? To answer these questions, we must examine Zionism's spectacular rise, assisted by the foremost powers of the world, and its equally spectacular betrayal by these very powers.

THE RISE OF
ZIONISM

I n the autumn of 1895, Theodor Herzl, the Paris correspondent
of the influential Viennese newspaper *Neue Freie Presse*, called
on his friend, the eminent writer Max Nordau. Herzl wanted to
hear Nordau's reaction to his thesis that the Jews of Europe were
being placed in unprecedented danger by the rise of anti-Semitism.
This would produce Jewish activists for Communism, he sus
pected, and further grist for the anti-Semites. Such developments,
Herzl believed, would lead to catastrophe, not only for the Jews but
for Europe as a whole. The only solution was the immediate estab
lishment of a Jewish state and the exodus of the persecuted Jews
to it.

Herzl was candid with Nordau about the reception that established quarters of European Jewry were giving his ideas. One of
his friends had suggested that he explain his project to Nordau because Nordau was a psychiatrist. "Schiff says that I'm insane,"
Herzl said, leaving the obvious question unasked. Nordau, who
had written extensively about the decline of European civilization,
turned to his friend and said, "If you are mad, then I am mad as
well. I'm behind you, and you can count on me."[1]

Herzl's recruitment of Nordau began a unique partnership between two of Europe's leading Jewish intellectuals, combining prophetic genius with pragmatic purpose, which was to found political Zionism, the movement that revolutionized modern Jewish history. To these men, Mount Zion in the heart of Jerusalem symbolized the reestablishment of a Jewish state in which the scattered Jewish people would reassemble and begin anew its national life. Herzl's Zionism, of course, had many antecedents, from the continuous longings of Jews since ancient times to restore their sovereign life in their homeland, to the aspirations for national salvation of Rabbi Yehudah Alkalai in Serbia of the 1840s and of Rabbi Zvi Hirsch Kalischer in Prussia in the 1860s, to the yearnings for Jewish redemption of the secularist Moses Hess. Hess had begun his quest by inventing Communism, which he instilled in his ungrateful student Karl Marx, only to end up discarding it in favor of the idea of a Jewish national home.[2]

Above all, Herzl's Zionism was preceded by the Jewish national movement that emerged in Russia in the 1880s under the leadership of M. L. Lillienblum and Leo Pinsker. Pinsker's short but powerful tract, *Auto-Emancipation*, published in 1882, one year after a wave of pogroms in Russia, touched on most of the major themes that Herzl later developed. It galvanized the dormant Jewish national consciousness in a large segment of Russian Jewry, and it made a mass movement of the drive toward settlement in Palestine that had begun as a trickle around 1800. Herzl had not read Pinsker before he wrote *The Jewish State* in 1896, but he arrived at the same conclusions independently, much as in the seventeenth century Leibniz and Newton had both invented calculus without knowledge of each other's work. Nor did Herzl know, when he put forth his ideas, that a fertile field had already been prepared to receive them in the Jewish communities of Eastern Europe. But he soon became acquainted with this movement as his ideas reverberated throughout the Jewish world.

Yet Herzl was unlike any Jewish idealist or dreamer before him. Prompted into action by the spectacle of the anti-Semitic Dreyfus trial in Paris in 1894, which he covered as a reporter, Herzl was soon able to offer a concrete program to solve a real problem: a series of practical steps to establish a modern Jewish nation-state in Palestine as a haven and a home for the millions of Jews whose life in Europe, Herzl knew, was rapidly drawing to a disastrous end. Herzl sought to obtain commitments from the leading powers of the world to support an autonomous Jewish settlement in Palestine, to be protected by its own military force. He sought to harness Jewish financial resources around the world to this goal, and he founded the Jewish Colonial Trust (today Israel's Bank Leumi) and the Jewish National Fund for the purchase and restoration of the Land of Israel.

It was the political nature of Herzl's version of the age-old Jewish dream of returning to the land that ignited the imagination of millions of Jews and non-Jews around the world. One of the innumerable spirits moved to action by Herzl's message was my grandfather Rabbi Nathan Mileikowsky, who was converted to Zionism as a youth in the 1890s and became one of its foremost orators, spreading its message to Jews from Siberia to Minnesota. Later, in 1920, he followed his own exhortations and, sailing from Trieste to Jaffa, took his large family to settle in Palestine. I have a photograph of him as a delegate to one of the early Zionist Congresses originated by Herzl. The photo is from the congress of 1907, one of the first to be convened after Herzl's premature death. For my grandfather, then a young man of twenty five, this was the first congress. Not so for Chaim Weizmann, who later led the liberal General Zionists and who would become the first president of Israel; nor for the gifted author and orator Vladimir Jabotinsky, who later led the Revisionist movement in the campaign for Jewish independence under the British Mandate. Over the next three decades these two men were to clash over the destiny and direction of the Zionist movement, but in 1907 they were still united on many of the issues. The congress drew not only political activists; Haim Nahman Bialik, the great Hebrew poet of modern times, attended the same gathering.

Such was the brilliance and power of Herzl's idea that within a

few years many of the best Jewish writers, scholars, and artists in
Europe had dedicated themselves to the cause—winning sympathizers in every civilized nation and in every humane government,
founding the institutions of the Jewish national government, and
inspiring the mass resettlement of the barren and broken Jewish
homeland.

Initially, Herzl found greater receptiveness among non-Jews
than among his own people. He succeeded, for example, in obtaining an audience with Kaiser Wilhelm II of Germany. (It would
perhaps be easier today for a private person from an unimportant
country to get an audience with the leader of China than it was for
a young Jewish journalist to receive an audience with the Kaiser a
hundred years ago.) Herzl's secret was that he was the first Jew in
modern times to rediscover the art of politics and the idea of co-
hering interests. To the Kaiser he described Zionism as a plan that
would not only divert the energy of some of Germany's young
radicals but create a Jewish protectorate allied with Germany at
the crossroads of the Middle East, thus opening a pathway to the
East for the Kaiser. (Herzl made the case for German sponsorship
of Zionism on the basis of political gain for Germany, but the
Kaiser was also interested in ridding his realm of some of its "radicals.") Appealing again to self-interest, Herzl was able to secure
another unimaginable audience with a world potentate of the day,
this time with the Ottoman sultan, in Constantinople in May 1901.
Invoking the story of Androcles, who removed the incapacitating
thorn from the lion's paw, Herzl told the bankrupt sultan: "His
Majesty is the lion, perhaps I am Androcles, and perhaps there is
a thorn that needs pulling out. The thorn, as I see it, is your public debt." And this thorn Herzl proposed to remove with the help
of the great Jewish financiers.[3]

The remarkable speed with which world leaders hastened to
give a hearing to Herzl's unfamiliar, fledgling cause demonstrates
the success of his approach and the power of his personality. By
October 1898, only a year after Zionism had made its debut at the
First Zionist Congress, he had met with the Kaiser three times.

The receptivity that the great courts of the day accorded him in no way blinded Herzl to the primacy of winning Jewish adherents to Zionism. After Nordau, his greatest conquest among Jewish intellectuals was the celebrated English writer Israel Zangwill, who used his talents and influence to spread the creed of Zionism in Britain, which at the time was the foremost world power. Yet his most fervent support came not from the comfortable Jewish salons of Central and Western Europe but from the multitudes of impoverished Jews in the East—in Poland and Russia. There he found an emerging Jewish intelligentsia that embraced Zionism with the enthusiasm of youth, rebelling as they were against the cloistered ghettos in which most of their people still lived.

Herzl began his public campaign when he was thirty-six years old. He died only eight years later, at the age of forty-four. But in those brief eight years he wrought a revolution without parallel in the history of nations. Indeed, Herzl's clairvoyance was anything but mad. Within five decades, both the horror and the triumph of his stunning vision had come to pass. The separate anti-Semitic fires were collected into one vast conflagration that destroyed the millennia-old Jewish communities of Europe. At the same time the Jewish people, again precisely as Herzl foresaw, stood on the threshold of the creation of the State of Israel.

Why was international opinion so ready to receive Herzl's ideas? At the beginning of the twentieth century, the widespread support for Zionism in the leading countries of the world was grounded in a view of the Jews that had developed in the wake of the European Enlightenment two centuries earlier, a movement that stressed the natural rights and liberties of all mankind. Many, though by no means all, of the Enlightenment's leading thinkers (Voltaire being a conspicuous exception) believed that the Jews had been unjustly condemned to suffer an unparalleled deprivation of these rights, with all the misery that this deprivation entailed; hence the Jewish people were entitled to be reinstated to a position of dignity and equality among the nations.

It was Jean-Jacques Rousseau, the father of so many of the

most powerful ideas of the Enlightenment, who put his finger on
the uniqueness of the Jewish situation:

> The Jews present us with an outstanding spectacle: the laws of
> Numa, Lycurgus, and Solon are dead; the far more ancient ones
> of Moses are still alive. Athens, Sparta and Rome have perished
> and their people have vanished from the earth; though de-
> stroyed, Zion has not lost her children. They mingle with all na-
> tions but are not lost among them; they no longer have their
> leaders, yet they are still a nation; they no longer have a country,
> and yet they are still citizens.[4]

The solution to the problem of the Jews initially seemed obvious. The Jews would be granted civic and religious equality in the
societies in which they lived. In America, where a new society was
being created according to the principles of Enlightenment,
Thomas Jefferson wrote with considerable satisfaction that he was
"happy in the restoration of the Jews to their social rights."[5] Similar advances were being made in Europe. The Jewish problem was
well on the way to being solved.

Or was it? Rousseau, at once arch-revolutionary and arch-skeptic,
also sounded one of the earliest chords of skepticism. After the
legacy of "tyranny practiced against them," he was not at all sure the
Jews would be allowed or able to partake of the new liberties envisioned in the new society, including the most basic one, freedom of
speech:

> I shall never believe I have seriously heard the arguments of the
> Jews until they have a free state, schools, and universities [of
> their own], where they can speak and dispute without risk. Only
> then will we be able to know what they have to say.[6]

In this, Rousseau was among the first to condition personal
freedom on national freedom. Although in our century of dictatorships, many have wrongly believed that national freedom can

happily exist without individual freedom,[7] Rousseau was hinting here at a contrary idea: that the Jews could never be truly free as individuals unless they possessed a free state of their own.

This idea was later developed and modified by the Zionists, who said that the Jews would never be equal unless their persecuted members came to live in a state of their own, and that even those who were left behind as fully enfranchised minorities would suffer from a sense of inferiority unless they too had somewhere a sovereign homeland that would bolster their sense of identity and to which they could choose to go—much as the Irish in America had Ireland, the Italians had Italy, the Chinese had China.

But the fact was, and it was plainly evident to the leading thinkers of the Enlightenment, that the Jews did *not* have such a homeland to which they could return. As Byron evocatively captured it in his "Hebrew Melodies":

> The wild dove hath her nest
> The fox his cave
> Mankind their country
> Israel but the grave.[8]

Slowly at first, then with great rapidity, the idea began to take hold that civic equality was necessary but insufficient as a remedy for the Jewish problem. Only a Jewish national restoration in the Jewish homeland would produce a satisfactory solution. It would restore the Jews to a condition of normalcy not only as a nation but as individuals as well, much as Rousseau had intimated. As U.S. President John Adams put it, "I really wish the Jews again in Judea an independent nation, for as I believe . . . once restored to an independent government and no longer persecuted, they would soon wear away some of the asperities and peculiarities of their character."[9] The need of the Jews to be reinstated in Israel was recognized by Napoleon, who apparently understood that extension of citizenship to the Jews of France could not substitute for Jewish national restoration. In 1799, when his army was twenty-five miles from Jerusalem, he proclaimed: "Israelites arise! Now is the moment . . . to claim your political existence as a nation among nations!"[10]

The stream of sympathy for the Jews grew progressively stronger in the nineteenth century. The increasing frequency of Western travel to the Holy Land, the emergence of a small but growing movement for Jewish immigration, and the appearance of concrete plans for large-scale Jewish settlement of Palestine all contributed to the rapid growth of non-Jewish support for Jewish national restoration. Just as the romance of renascent Greek nationalism elicited enthusiastic support from Byron, and just as the Italian national revival excited many of the greatest minds in Europe, the prospect of the rebirth of Jewish nationhood had a similar effect. British, American, and French writers, journalists, artists, and statesmen all became ardent proponents of facilitating the return of the Jews to their desolate homeland.

There was, for example, Lord Shaftesbury, who wrote in 1838 that he was

> anxious about the hopes and destinies of the Jewish people. Everything [is] ripe for their return to Palestine. . . . the inherent vitality of the Hebrew race reasserts itself with amazing persistence . . . but the great revival can take place only in the Holy Land.[11]

In 1840 the British foreign minister, Lord Palmerston, offered protection to the Jews in Palestine and undertook to convince the Ottoman sultan that it would be to his advantage if "the Jews who are scattered throughout other countries in Europe and Africa should be induced to go and settle in Palestine."[12] Lord Lindsay, too, wrote in 1847 that the "Jewish race, so wonderfully preserved, may yet have another stage of national existence open to them, may once more obtain possession of their native land."[13] And in 1845, Sir George Gawler, a governor of southern Australia and the founder of the Palestine Colonization Fund, urged: "Replenish the farms and fields of Palestine with the energetic people whose warmest affection are rooted in the soil."[14] British statesmen who declared their support for Jewish national restoration were a "who's who" of prime ministers and elder statesmen, including not only Palmerston and Shaftesbury but Disraeli, Lord Salisbury, and Lord Manchester. In the United States, successive presidents made declarations of sympathy for Zionism, including William McKinley, Theodore Roosevelt, and William Howard Taft.[15]

From the nineteenth century on, modern Zionism thus enjoyed long, intimate, and ultimately successful support from powerful forces working within the non-Jewish world, support that expressed itself in the literature of the day in passages that are hauntingly prophetic of the ideals that would later be espoused by the Zionist movement. In 1876 the great English author George Eliot foresaw in these terms the rebirth of Israel in her influential novel of Zionism, *Daniel Deronda*:

> There is a store of wisdom among us to found a new Jewish polity, grand, simple, just, like the old—a republic where there is equality of protection, an equality which shone like a star on the forehead of our ancient community, and gave it more than the brightness of Western freedom amid the despotisms of the East. . . . For there will be a community in the van of the East which carries the culture and the sympathies of every great nation in its bosom.[16]

With this humanist stream converged another important current that became ascendant in the last century—that of Christian Zionism, a movement that promoted the belief that the spiritual redemption of mankind could occur only if it were preceded by the ingathering of the Jewish exiles, as foretold in the Bible. After all, to both Christians and Jews, Zionism was the fulfillment of ancient prophecy. "[He] will assemble the outcasts of Israel and gather together the dispersed of Judea from the four corners of the earth," said Isaiah. "He that scattered Israel will gather him," promised Jeremiah. "For I will take you from among the nations and gather you out of all countries and will bring you into your own land," Ezekiel foretold.[17]

Christian clergymen's application of these verses antedates the modern Zionist movement by at least half a century. As early as 1814, a New York pastor named John MacDonald published a famous sermon demonstrating the central role that Isaiah had envisioned for the new American state in restoring the Jews to their land. "Rise, American ambassadors," called the pastor, "and prepare to carry the tidings of joy and salvation to your Savior's kinsmen in disgrace. . . . send their sons and employ their substance in his heaven-planned expedition." In 1821, the missionary Levi Parsons averred: "There exists in the breast of every Jew an unconquerable desire to inhabit the land which was given to their Fathers. . . . Destroy, then, the Ottoman Empire, and nothing but a miracle would prevent their immediate return from the four winds of heaven." And as Jewish settlement of Jerusalem, Safed, and Hebron increased, and international interest grew, so the unfolding prophecy became increasingly clear. By 1841, a full half-century before the First Zionist Congress, the Mormon leader Orson Hyde could declare: "The idea of the Jews being restored to Palestine is gaining ground. . . . The great wheel is unquestionably in motion, and the word of the Almighty has declared that it shall roll."[18]

Just in case it did not, some were ready to push the wheel along. In 1844, Warder Cresson became the American consul in Jerusalem and hoped to be able to missionize among Palestine's Jews. Instead, he helped establish a Jewish settlement in Jerusalem's Valley of Refaim, supported by a joint Jewish-Christian society in England. Half a century later, Christian Zionism had gathered considerable force. In 1891, after pogroms in Eastern Europe had led to mass Jewish emigration, the American evangelist William Eugene Blackstone was able to muster the support of over four hundred prominent Americans—including John D. Rockefeller, J. P. Morgan, and leading congressmen, jurists, and newspaper editors—for a petition to President Benjamin Harrison to work for the reinstatement of the Jewish people in their land. "For over seventeen centuries they have patiently waited for such a privileged opportunity," wrote Blackstone. "Let us now restore to them the land of which they were so cruelly despoiled."[19] So committed was Blackstone to the idea of the return of the Jews to their land that when the possibility of a Jewish national home in Africa was being discussed, he sent Herzl a copy of the Old Testament—with the prophetic references to the Jewish return to the Land of Israel clearly marked.

The rise of Christian activism coincided with the emergence of an entirely secular phenomenon in the non-Jewish world: a growing scientific interest in studying the biblical heritage. Throughout the nineteenth century the novel techniques of archaeology, philology, and cryptology were applied successfully in Mesopotamia and elsewhere in the Middle East. But the land of the Bible beckoned like no other object of study. Were the biblical accounts historical fact or fiction? Did the places mentioned in the text really exist? Where precisely were they located? What could be discovered by excavating them?

The scientific effort to answer these questions was international in scope. It involved ingenious pioneers, each expanding on his predecessor's findings: the American Edward Robinson (surveying in 1837–38 and again in 1845–47), the German Titus Tobler (1845–46), the Frenchman H. V. Guerin (1852–75), and the Englishman Claude Conder (1872–77). The American archaeologist Frederick Jones Bliss, who excavated in Palestine in the 1890s, summed up the pivotal contributions of these pioneers:

> The work of these four men shows a logical progression. Robinson established the correct principles of research. Tobler applied these more minutely, but over a limited geographical range. Guerin endeavored with the same minuteness to cover

the whole field—Judea, Samaria, Galilee*—but was subjected to
the limitations of an explorer travelling singly and with strait-
ened resources. Conder, heading a survey expedition ade-
quately manned and splendidly equipped, was enabled to fill in
the numerous topographical lacunae left by his predecessors.[20]

Their ranks were joined by Sir Charles Wilson and Sir Charles
Warren (who made important contributions to the archaeology of
Jerusalem), Charles Clermont-Ganneau (who identified the biblical city of Gezer), and Flinders Petrie (who systematized the study
of pottery as a means of archaeological dating).

Several European governments encouraged such surveys by
their nationals, for under a scientific cover the potential military
and political benefits of the land might also be explored. No government seized on biblical exploration with greater alacrity than
Great Britain. On June 22, 1865, under the auspices of Queen Vic-
toria, a distinguished array of British statesmen, scholars, and clergymen established the Palestine Exploration Fund (PEF), which
was to have a decisive impact on the attitude toward Palestine
evolving in Britain and elsewhere. It was the PEF that later commissioned many of the above explorers, but undoubtedly its most
influential project was to dispatch Conder to carry out his monu-
mental survey of western Palestine. Assisted by an able team that

---

*Writing near the turn of the century, Bliss and all of his contemporaries used the ancient
names of Judea and Samaria for the central mountain ridge in the land, and not "West
Bank," which had not yet been invented. The term *West Bank* was forced onto the international lexicon only after Jordan conquered the territory in 1948. Jordanian king Abdullah
called Judea the "West Bank" in order to obliterate the historic and ongoing Jewish connection to the land—much as the Romans two thousand years earlier had sought to
achieve the same goal by changing Judea to Palestine. In using the term *West Bank,* he
sought to associate this territory with his kingdom, which lay on the east bank of the Jordan River.

The same routine and entirely apolitical usage of the names Judea and Samaria to describe the West Bank can be found over and over again in quotes from before 1948 by such
travelers as Mark Twain (on pages 42–43 of this book) and the cartographer Arthur Penrhyn
Stanley (page 44); and the name *Judea* is used interchangeably with Palestine by statesmen
such as President John Adams (page 15) and Lord Robert Cecil (page 49).

The idea that, by using the historical terms Judea and Samaria, it is Israel that is politi-
cizing the geographical nomenclature rather than the Arabs, who obliterated these names
with the politically loaded name West Bank, is one of those characteristic reversals of truth
that are the mainstay of the Arab campaign against Israel.

included the twenty-five-year-old Lieutenant Horatio Herbert Kitchener (later Lord Kitchener, of Khartoum and World War I fame), Conder produced the first modern map of the country—from the Jordan River to the Mediterranean, from the consigned Lebanon to the Sinai.

The scientific exploration of the land had the important effect of demystifying its place in the international psyche. For if Palestine had hitherto been confined to the realm of biblical imagination, now it was made concrete and real again. Jerusalem was not in heaven but very much on earth. So were Bethlehem, Nazareth, Hebron, and Jaffa. These places may have become impoverished and pitifully underpopulated, but they did not have to remain that way. Studying the land, its climate, and the history of its deterioration, many of the researchers concluded that it could be restored to its ancient prosperity—provided that the Jews were permitted to return to it. Thus, in 1875 the archaeologist and explorer Sir Charles Warren published *The Land of Promise*, in which he proposed British colonization of Palestine, "with the avowed intention of gradually introducing the Jew." To Warren it was obvious that the land could support the Jews. Therefore, he believed:

> Israel are to return to their own land. . . . That which is yet to be looked for is the public recognition of the fact, together with the restoration, in whole or in part, of Jewish national life, under the protection of some one or more of the Great Powers.[21]

To Claude Conder as well, it was clear that no other people would have the enthusiasm and energy for such a restoration;[22] and it was equally clear that once applied, such energy would bring the land back to life. Thus, for Jew and non-Jew alike, scientific exploration made the promise of Zionism tangible and realizable.

This scientific enthusiasm produced practical plans of settlement, such as Sir Laurence Oliphant's 1879 proposal to settle Jews in Gilead on the East Bank of the Jordan, a project that received the support of the British prime minister, the British and French foreign ministers, and the Prince of Wales. In 1898, after a century of religious and scientific attention focused on the land, Edwin Sherwin Wallace, the U.S. consul in Palestine, captured the growing international mood:

> Israel needs a home, a land he can call his own, a city where he can work out his salvation. He has none of these now. His present home is among strangers. . . . the lands in which he lives are not his own. . . . Israel's hope of a homeland is possible of realization, but it will be realized only in Palestine.

He concluded:

> My own belief is that the time is not far distant when Palestine will be in the hands of a people who will restore it to its former condition of productiveness. The land is waiting, the people are ready to come, and will come as soon as protection of life and property is assured.[23]

The writings, philanthropic activities, exhortations, and explorations of non-Jewish Zionists, British and American, secular and religious, directly influenced the thinking of such pivotal statesmen as David Lloyd George, Arthur Balfour, and Woodrow Wilson at the beginning of the century. These were all broadly educated men, and they were intimately familiar with the decline of Palestine and the agonized history of the Jews. "My anxiety," wrote Balfour, "is simply to find some means by which the present dreadful state of so large a proportion of the Jewish race . . . may be brought to an end."[24] Thus, it was the non-Jewish Zionism of Western statesmen that aided Jewish Zionism in achieving the rebirth of Israel.

But still another factor was even more important than biblical heritage, the scientific rediscovery of the land, and the awareness of Jewish suffering in persuading these leaders of the justice of

Zionism. The men of Versailles were first and foremost *political* thinkers, and it was primarily from prevailing political conceptions of national rights and the question of self-determination that they addressed the problem of the Jewish restoration, just as they approached the problem of other national claims within this framework. It was in these terms that the Jewish Zionists were able to appeal to them successfully.

Indeed, the leaders of Zionism from Herzl onward formed a ready partnership with the leading statesmen of the day. (That partnership in some cases developed out of earlier ties; well before becoming prime minister of the British Empire, Lloyd George had served as Herzl's lawyer, representing the Zionist movement in Britain, and he had drawn up its proposal to build a British protectorate.)[25] Herzl, Nordau, and their followers understood that if Zionism were to succeed in its extraordinary task of ingathering a nation scattered in a hundred lands to a dusty corner at the edge of Asia, it had to have broad international support, and it had to muster and deepen the widely held conviction of the historical justice and the political necessity of this remarkable undertaking. The Jews, the Zionists said, must have a state of their own in Palestine, and the world's leaders agreed, even though they knew that such attempted re-creation of a state was unprecedented. Furthermore, they knew the effort might come into conflict with the possible interests of the local population, which might make a political claim to that same land. Yet at the beginning of the century, public opinion unhesitatingly adjudicated in favor of the Jews.

Why was this so? The Arabs now assert that at the time of Versailles, the Jews had no political rights over the land, that these developed upon the Arabs then inhabiting it—and that therefore the original sin in favor of Zionism was committed by the international community not in 1948 (the year of Israel's founding) or in 1967 (the year Israel gained control over Judea, Samaria, and Gaza) but in 1917, when the British government endorsed the

Balfour Declaration promising the Jews a national home in Palestine.

Yet clearly the leaders of the international community of the day viewed things differently. They believed the Jewish people enjoyed a unique historical and political right to the land, one that took precedence over any potential claim by the local residents in that small backwater of the recently defunct Ottoman Empire.

What were the sources of the widespread recognition of the Jewish people's historical rights to the Holy Land? To answer this question, we must first examine the nature of such historical rights generally.

There are those who believe that a theoretical discussion of the rights of nations is meaningless, and that in practice the configuration of states is a product of many competing forces that ultimately settle themselves by means of a simple rule: The more powerful prevails. This may be true if the question is raised in purely empirical and not in moral terms. If might makes right, then the last conqueror is always right. Israel, by this definition, is therefore the rightful and undisputed sovereign in the land. But this is clearly not the criterion with which to address the Jewish national restoration. If, as Winston Churchill said in 1922, "The Jews are in Palestine by right, not sufferance,"[26] then it is crucial to understand the moral basis of the Jewish state.

In the case of the Jewish national claim, the central issue is this: Does a people that has lost its land many centuries ago retain the right to reclaim that land after many generations have passed? And can this right be retained if during the intervening years a new people has come to occupy the land? Advocates of the Arab case commonly present these questions, and they answer both of them in the negative. Further, they add, if the Jews have a historical "quarrel" with anyone, it is not with the Arabs but with the Romans, who expelled them from their land in the first place. By the time the Arabs came, the Jews were gone.

These arguments, forcefully and clearly presented by the Arab side, are seldom challenged by the Jews and their supporters, but they deserve to be addressed. Most people have some familiarity with the first millennium of Jewish history, the period described in the Bible: how the Hebrew slaves of Egypt were transformed into a nation by their flight to freedom and their adoption of the Law of Moses, and how they returned under Joshua to build their national home in the land of their fathers. Fused into a unified state by David in 1000 B.C.E.,* they subsequently pursued their unique quest for political and religious independence against a succession of empires. The biblical historical account ends shortly after the restoration of Jewish autonomy under the Persian king Cyrus ("the Persian Balfour") in 538 B.C.E. Alexander the Great, who took over the land from the Persians, did not grant the Jews sovereignty, but in 167 B.C.E., under the Hasmoneans, they successfully revolted against his successors, only to lose their independence once more to Rome in 63 B.C.E.[27] Yet while the Jews were subjugated for considerable parts of this first millennium and a half of their history and even experienced exile (the deportation of the northern ten tribes by the Assyrians in the eighth century B.C.E., and the Babylonian Exile in the sixth), they responded by driving their national roots deeper into the soil.

How, then, were the Jews finally forced off the land? The most prevalent assumption is that the Jewish people's state of homelessness was owed solely to the Romans. It is generally believed that the Romans, who had conquered Palestine and destroyed Jewish sovereignty, then took away the country from the Jews and tossed them into an exile that lasted until our own century. However common this view, it is inaccurate. It is true that the Roman destruction of Jerusalem in 70 C.E. was a highly important factor in the ultimate decline of Jewish power and presence in Palestine. But it was not the exclusive factor; nor did it depopulate the country of its Jewish inhabitants. Therefore, the common refrain about "two thousand years of exile," uncritically repeated by many Jews

---

*The terms B.C.E. (Before the Common Era) and C.E. are the nondenominational equivalents of the Christian designations B.C. and A.D., respectively.

and non-Jews alike, is misleading. The Diaspora did not begin with the Roman destruction of Jerusalem—vibrant Jewish communities in Alexandria, Babylon, and elsewhere had antedated the Roman conquest by centuries. Nor did the Romans end Jewish national life in Palestine. That did not come until many centuries later. Thus in 135 C.E., sixty-five years after the razing of Jerusalem, the Jews under Bar Kochba revolted once more against Rome, "until the whole earth seemed to have been stirred up over the matter," according to the third-century Greek historian Dio Cassius.[28]

Although this three-year Jewish revolt against Rome was also brutally crushed, the country remained primarily Jewish, and shortly thereafter the Jews were granted a considerable measure of autonomous power, an authority that was recognized by Rome and later by Byzantium. In 212 C.E., when the Roman emperor Caracalla bestowed Roman citizenship on most subjects of the empire, he denied that privilege to those who lacked a country of their own. The Jews were granted Roman citizenship, because they were recognized as a people with their own country.[29] This is not to say that they did not continue to rebel, attempting to expel Rome yet again in 351. And it should be noted, too, that the great Jewish legal works of the Mishna and the Jerusalem Talmud were composed in Palestine during the centuries of Roman and Byzantine domination, reflecting the dynamic Jewish intellectual life that persisted there even in the face of occupation. In 614 the Jews were, incredibly, still fighting for independence, raising an army that joined the Persians in seizing Jerusalem and ousting the Byzantines from Palestine. The size and vitality of the Jewish population at the beginning of the seventh century may be judged by the fact that in the siege of Tyre alone, the Jews contributed more than twenty thousand fighters.[30]

But in 636, after a brief return of the Byzantines under Heraclius, the Arabs burst into the land—after having destroyed the large and prosperous Jewish populations of the Arabian Peninsula root and branch. The rule of the Byzantines had been harsh for the Jews, but it was under the Arabs that the Jews were finally reduced to an insignificant minority and ceased to be a national force of any consequence in their own land. The Jews initially vested their hopes in the "Ishmaelite conquerors" as they called them in contemporary sources, but within a few years these hopes were dashed as Arab policy became clear. Unlike previous conquerors, the Arabs poured in a steady stream of colonists, often composed of military battalions and their families, with the intention of permanently Arabizing the land. In order to execute this policy of armed settlement, the Arabs relied on the regular expropriation of land, houses, and Jewish labor. In combination with the turmoil introduced into the land by the Arab conquest, these policies finally succeeded in doing what the might of Rome had not achieved: the uprooting of the Jewish farmer from his soil.[31] *Thus it was not the Jews who usurped the land from the Arabs, but the Arabs who usurped the land from the Jews.*

Why is this important? After all, more than twelve hundred years have passed since this change occurred. Nations come and go, and history moves on. Even if it was the Arabs who finished off the Jewish presence in Palestine, what of it? They conquered the land, and it has become theirs.

In many ways the argument between Jews and Arabs over their respective historic rights to a national home resembles an argument over the rights of an individual owner to his house. If the original owner is tossed out of his home but never relinquishes his right to return and reoccupy the premises, he may press his claim. But suppose a new occupant has fixed up the place and made a home of it while the original claimant is still around but prevented from pressing his claim? In such a case, even if the new occupant has resided there for a considerable period of time and improved the premises, his claim to the place is considered inferior to that of the original owner. Yet if in the meantime *no one* has set up house and the place has become a shambles, there can be no rival claim, and the original owner is clearly entitled to have his property returned to him.

The two crucial questions to ask about the conflicting Jewish and Arab historical claims to the land are therefore these: First, did the Jews sustain their claim to the land over the centuries? Second, did the Arabs create a unique national claim to the land after the Jews departed?

Clearly, conquest alone does not endow a conqueror with national rights to a particular land. It is the emergence of a separate, distinct people with continuous ties to a defined territory that is at the heart of all national territorial claims. This is the basis of the Jewish claim. And this is why the Arabs, in their efforts to overturn it, are now careful to assert that centuries ago a separate and distinct Arab nation was created in Palestine—the "Palestinians."

Unlike civil disputes over property rights between individuals, the passage of time alone does not necessarily resolve claims to the ownership of a national home, as we are seeing in the current resurfacing in Eastern Europe of national conflicts going back hundreds of years. Consider the case of the Arabs' subjugation of Spain in their great expansion. The Arabs conquered Spain in the year 711 and held most of it for centuries. The Spaniards retained only a tiny patch of the mountains in the north, and the entire composition of the country was transformed. The Christians became a minority, the Moslems a majority. By the time the Spaniards began their slow and painful reconquest, Spain had become a different country socially and politically. Seville and Cordova were recovered by the Spaniards after five centuries of Arab rule; the Kingdom of Granada after eight. Yet despite the enormous span of time between the Arab conquest and the restoration of Spanish sovereignty, Spain never ceased to be the Spaniards' homeland—notwithstanding Moorish Arab attachment to the land and the creation of an impressive Arab civilization there. This is an important reason why no one seriously suggests that the

Spaniards who rolled back the Arab tide that had swept over their land committed a "historic wrong."

What the Spaniards achieved after eight centuries, the Jews achieved after twelve—but the principle is identical. More important are the differences in the manner and circumstances in which the two national restorations were accomplished. The Spaniards reconquered their land with fire and blood; the Jews embarked on a peaceful resettlement, resorting to arms only in self-defense. The Spaniards battled against a Moorish nation that had built one of the great intellectual and cultural centers of mankind there, and they regained a land that had largely been cultivated. What the Jews found when they returned to Palestine was a ruined land, largely unpopulated.

What is common in the cases of Spain and Israel is *the continued existence of the people whose country had been conquered, and the persistent aspirations of that people to be reestablished in its national home.* The Spaniards, to be sure, retained a corner of their country from which they could begin their restoration, but this merely facilitated the task; it did not create their basic right of recovery.

Against the accepted reasons for Jewish restoration such as these, some sympathizers of the Arabs tried to invent arguments to weaken the Jewish case. The British historian Arnold Toynbee, for example, who resented the Jewish people for not behaving according to his iron laws of history ("fossils," he believed, do not come back to life), argued that a statute of limitations should be imposed on national claims, just as in civil disputes. If the Arabs were to recover Palestine from the Jews within, say, fifty years of Israel's establishment, that would be a legitimate reconquest. But if the Jews had taken the land from the Arabs after a longer period, that could not be considered legitimate. While applicable in certain civil cases, statutes of limitations are woefully unsuited for these kinds of national claims. Toynbee's toying with numbers aside, the mere passage of time cannot render a national claim obsolete. If the claim is historically laid, it disappears only with the disappearance of the claimant.*[32]

Here, indeed, is where the case of the Jews differs from that of all other nations. Dispersed for more than a thousand years, they refused to disappear. History is replete with examples of nations that have succumbed to forced dispersion. But in all other cases of exile, the displaced peoples were assimilated over time into other nations, or occupied a new land for themselves that then became their national home. The Jews refused to do either. As individuals, some Jews have assimilated (a process much in evidence in the West today). But as a collective body, the Jews rejected this course. They also rejected the notion of establishing an independent Jewish polity anywhere other than in their historical home. When this idea was offered to them in modern times, they refused Birobidzhan, Argentina, Uganda, even Manchuria as possible alternatives to a permanent Jewish homeland, and insisted on returning to the Land of Israel. In 1903, in the wake of the Kishinev pogrom in Russia, the Zionist movement faced a schism over the question of whether to consider even a temporary home in British East Africa in order to save the lives of Eastern Europe's Jews. The controversial "Uganda Plan" was later abandoned when the Eastern European Jewish leadership refused even to consider the option, insisting on the Land of Israel as the only possible Jewish home. Perhaps in retrospect one can appreciate Herzl's rationalist

---

*The other criterion Toynbee offered to adjudicate competing claims was that the question of who should be granted sovereignty should be determined by comparing the suffering caused to each side by being *denied* sovereignty. This definitely works in favor of the Jews. Certainly the suffering experienced by the Jews for being stateless has far exceeded any suffering that may have been caused to the Arabs by the Jewish national restoration. This point is so obvious that it defies rebuttal. Nevertheless the Arabs, aided by European anti-Semites, are trying to rebut it by making the incredible claim that the Holocaust did not happen, or by attempting to equate the suffering experienced by the Palestinian Arabs to the murder of six million Jews. As if the ovens of Auschwitz could be compared to an Israeli administration that from 1967 until the establishment of the Palestinian Authority in 1993 built five universities for the Palestinian Arab population, placed severe restraints on its own soldiers and court-martialed offenders, and enabled the Arabs to appeal to the Israeli Supreme Court to reverse the decisions of the army. (The fact that this preposterously asymmetrical "symmetry" found currency in cartoons and editorials of serious newspapers in the West shows that Goebbels was right in arguing that a lie spreads in proportion to its size.)

view that a haven, any haven, was needed to save millions of European Jews. But the Jewish people's attachment to the Jewish land was more powerful, and only its force could ultimately harness the Jewish masses to concerted political action. Herzl tried in vain to explain that he viewed Uganda as a mere way station, not as the final destination for the Jewish people, which could only be the Land of Israel. When Vladimir Jabotinsky voted against Uganda, he admitted that he did not know why. It was "one of those 'simple' things which counterbalance thousands of arguments."[33]

My own grandfather, Rabbi Nathan Mileikowsky, was more explicit in explaining why as a young man he resolutely opposed and finally helped defeat the Uganda Plan at the Zionist Congress of 1905. Twenty-five years later, after the relationship between Britain and Zionism had soured, my father asked him if the opposition to Uganda had derived from the belief that the project was impractical and that the British would not see it through. He clearly remembers my grandfather's reply:

> On the contrary. We believed that the British would be faithful to their word. In those days England enjoyed a great reputation among the Jews. But it was precisely because we believed that the project *could* be carried out that we were all the more opposed to it. For so many centuries the Jewish people had made so many sacrifices for this land, had shed their blood for it, had prayed for a thousand years to return to it, had tied their most intimate hopes to its revival—we considered it inconceivable that we would now betray the generations of Jews who had fought and died for this end. It would have been a terrible moral and emotional collapse. It would have rendered the whole of Jewish history meaningless. We *had* to oppose it.

Indeed, throughout the centuries, the Jews kept alive the hope of Return to their old homeland. This desire was no mere sentimental impulse, soon to be discarded. Indeed, rather than diminishing with the passage of time, it got stronger. It contained the essence of Jewish peoplehood, the memory of the Jews' unique history and struggle, and their desire to rebuild their national and spiritual life in their ancient land now occupied by foreign conquerors—not merely because it was the land of their forefathers but because it was the irreplaceable crucible in which their identity and faith had been forged and could be reforged anew after centuries of formless, helpless wandering.

It is impossible to exaggerate the importance of the idea of the Return in Jewish history and its centrality to the rise of Israel. Yet the fashionable ahistoricism prevalent today assumes that the Holocaust was the main force that propelled Jewish statehood. Undeniably, the Holocaust was a pivotal event not only in Jewish history but in all history. Undeniably, too, it moved many to sympathize with the suffering of the Jews. But it was the ultimate act of destruction, wiping out the millions of Jews whose hearts had been set on Zion, almost obliterating the human basis for a durable Jewish state. It was the culmination of the tragic—and to the founding Zionists, predictable—trajectory of ever-growing calamities of pogrom and expulsion that had afflicted the Jews of England in the 1290s, the Jews of France in the 1390s, the Jews of Spain in the 1490s, the Jews of the Ukraine in the 1640s, the Jews of Russia in the 1880s.

Without the idea of the Return, the Holocaust could have elicited a horrified sympathy but not much more. The addition of millions of Jewish corpses could have spelled only the final death blow to the Jewish people. Had this destruction not been preceded by a millennial yearning for Return and restoration, by a century of Zionist activists, and by the Jews' tremendous efforts to rebuild and revive a desolate land, the State of Israel would never have come into being. The Jewish remnants would have been scattered even farther afield, and denied a vital center, the Jewish people would have declined into irrelevance and oblivion.

The idea of the Return is therefore an integral part of the se-

cret of Jewish longevity. It was the driving force in the rebirth of Israel, and it is the key to Israel's future. This dream was preserved
intact from antiquity into modern times through the unique nature of Judaism itself. Westerners often assume that Judaism, like
Christianity, is only a faith and is therefore lacking in national consciousness. But from its genesis, Judaism comprised both nation
and religion, and while it readily accepted converts, such converts
not only joined the faith but became "naturalized citizens" of the
Jewish nation as well. (As Ruth, one of the most famous converts,
tells Naomi: "Your people will be my people.")

In the Jews' dispersion, the dual nature of Judaism assumed
vital importance. Stripped of their homeland, their government,
and their language and dispersed into myriad communities, the
Jewish religion became the primary vehicle by which the Jews
maintained their national identity and aspirations. Into this vessel
they poured their dreams of Return and ingathering in the Land of
Israel. The Jewish religion—with its cycle of bitter fast days
mourning the destruction of Jerusalem, its thrice-daily supplica-
tions to "gather up the exiles from the four corners of the earth,"
and its smashing of the glass at every joyous occasion "lest I forget
thee, O Jerusalem" became the repository for their memory of
an inspiring past and a hope for a better future in their ancestral
home.[34]

This concrete attachment of a particular people to a particular
place distinguishes Judaism from all other religions. Catholics, for
example, do not pray, "Next year in the Vatican." In other religions,
pilgrimages are periodic journeys to holy sites where the faithful
can achieve a heightened sense of communion with God. But
when in a hundred different lands, century after century, Jews
prayed, "Next year in Jerusalem," they meant something entirely
different: not merely an individual's desire to return to a holy site
for prayer, but the wish of an entire people to return and rebuild
its life in its own national home, of which Jerusalem was the
heart.[35] This powerful longing was so unique that it was sometimes dismissed as the pitiful gasp of a dying race. It was nothing

of the kind. The persistent yearning to return was an expression of the very life force of the Jewish people, the idea that held it together, a distilled defiance of its historical fate.

The final undermining of the Jewish presence in the Land of Israel was followed by an unbroken centuries-long tradition of intellectual and popular longing for restoration of Jewish sovereignty, most frequently evoked in religious themes. Pick a century at random, and you will find not only wide expression of this Jewish yearning among the common people but moving poetic and philosophic longings penned by virtually every leading man of genius. Thus in the tenth century, the Jewish philosopher Saadia Gaon:

> May it be your will, O Lord our God, that this era may mark the end of the dispersion for your people the House of Israel, and the time for the termination of our exile and our mourning.[36]

In the twelfth century, the great Jewish poet Yehuda Halevi, writing of Jerusalem, in Hebrew, from Spain:

> O great King's city, mountain blessed!
> My soul is yearning unto thee
> From the furthest West.
> And who shall grant me, on the wings of eagles,
> To rise and seek you through the years,
> Until I mingle with your dust beloved
> The waters of my tears?[37]

Later in the same century, the philosopher Moses Maimonides declared that the return to Israel was the only hope of an end to Jewish suffering at the hands of the Arabs, of whom he writes that "Never did a nation molest, degrade, debase, and hate us as much as they." But he promises,

The future redeemer of our people will . . . gather our nation, assemble our exiles, [and] redeem us from our degradation.[38]

In the thirteenth century, the scholar Nahmanides went further, ruling that the return to live in the Land of Israel was an obligation morally binding on every Jew[39]—a stricture he would dutifully fulfill by coming to the land and helping to rebuild the Jewish community there that had been nearly annihilated during the Crusades.

By the sixteenth century, the idea of a Christian-Jewish alliance taking the land back from the Moslems elicited enthusiasm from many Jews in Italy and some of the Marranos (Christians of Jewish descent) of Portugal.[40] Jewish exiles from Spain rebuilt the Jewish quarter in Hebron, and the Portuguese Jew Don Joseph Nasi rebuilt the city of Tiberias with the permission of the sultan. This wave of return also sparked an unprecedented intellectual and cultural revival in the Galilee city of Safed, which drew between ten thousand and twenty thousand Jewish immigrants by the end of the century. The renowned Rabbi Yehuda Leowe of Prague, known as the Maharal, was no less clear that full-scale Return would have to come:

Exile is a change and departure from the natural order, whereby the Lord situated every nation in the place best suited it. . . . The place [the Jews] deserved according to the order of existence was to be independent in the Land of Israel.[41]

In the seventeenth century among the Jews of Poland, large-scale preparations for the Return began (and a few years later abruptly ended) with the rise and fall of the would-be Jewish "messiah" Shabtai Zevi. Despite this disappointment, the Gaon of Vilna and the Ba'al Shem Tov, the foremost leaders of eighteenth-century European Jewry, both inspired their students to organize groups to come and settle in the land. One of the Gaon of Vilna's

students described the great sage's insistence that his pupils personally take up the responsibility of realizing the Return:

> Who is greater among us in all the recent generations than our
> teacher, the Gaon of Vilna, who with his impassioned words
> urged his students to go up to the Land of Israel and to work to
> ingather the exiles, and who frequently exhorted his students to
> speed the end of the exile, [and] to bring the redemption closer
> by means of settling the Land of Israel. Almost every day he
> would tell us with trembling emotion, that "in Zion and
> Jerusalem the remnants will see salvation," and that we should
> not miss it. Who can describe in words the concern of our
> teacher when he told us these things in his exalted spirit and
> with tears in his eyes. . . .[42]

Indeed, when the Zionist pioneers began arriving in the Land
toward the end of the nineteenth century, they found the small
communities, built by the disciples of these great religious figures
and by other Jews already on the Land, in Jerusalem comprising
the majority of the city's inhabitants.

Thus, in spurts and trickles, sometimes even in streams, Jews
went back to their land throughout the centuries. Some walked
the plains of Russia and, after pausing in Damascus or Beirut, entered Palestine from the north. Others sailed a pirate-infested
Mediterranean and landed in Jaffa. Once there, they joined the
Jews of Hebron, Safed, or Jerusalem who down the ages had kept
an uninterrupted vigil over a ruined land. As a consequence, there
was no period during which the land was devoid of Jews. (In the
villages of Peki'in and Shefar'am in the Galilee, Jews have lived
continuously from ancient times until the present.)[43]

But a truly large-scale return was not possible until the emergence of modern Zionism in the second half of the nineteenth
century, when the traditional longing for Zion on the part of the
Jewish multitudes and the scholars of the exile first found practical political expression. Such works as Moses Hess's *Rome and*

Jerusalem (1862) and Leo Pinsker's *Auto-Emancipation* (1882) were able to build on ancient feelings to contribute to a belief in the possibility of contemporary action. In the wake of the great anti-Jewish pogroms in Russia in 1881, these longings were quickly translated into an emotional proto-Zionist movement for the settlement of Palestine called Hovevei Zion, the "Lovers of Zion," which in turn fostered the first large-scale immigration to Palestine.

It was these towering ideas, emotions, and traditions that set the stage for the appearance of political Zionism a hundred years ago, when the next to last of the series of empires that had occupied the land began collapsing of its own weight. It was then that men of vision like Theodor Herzl and Max Nordau emerged, foreseeing the historic opportunity presented by the Ottoman Empire's decline. In addition to offering a concrete political solution—namely, the founding of a Jewish state—Herzl also established the institutions, such as the World Zionist Organization and the successive Zionist Congresses, beginning in 1897, that were to put his plan into action.

What Herzl was able to do was to translate a native, emotional Zionism that beat in millions of Jewish hearts into a political movement that took account of the modern world. He understood the forces of politics and power, of personality and persuasion; above all, Herzl was animated by a profound understanding of history and by a vision of the impending tragedy of European Jewry and of the triumphant possibility of revived Jewish statehood. He therefore pressed the Zionist claim with all the urgency he could muster.

While his disciples in many countries propelled the ideas of political Zionism toward the concrete goal of the founding of the state, Zionist pioneers undertook the massive effort of settling a land that had been allowed to fall into disuse by absentee Arab landlords living the good life in Beirut and Damascus. The Jews turned barren scenery, alternating between rock and swamp, into productive farmland, dotted first with villages, then towns, then cities. This effort was assisted by a few wealthy Jews, most notably Moses Montefiore and Baron Rothschild, who put up the funds for many of the pivotal early projects. The first such enterprise was appropriately titled Rishon Le-Zion ("The First of Zion"), an agricultural settlement founded in 1882 by Russian Jewish settlers who soon received Rothschild's assistance.

When Abraham Markus, my maternal great-grandfather, arrived at Rishon Le-Zion several years later, in 1896, it was still a cluster of red-tiled whitewashed houses springing up in the middle of a sandy wilderness. (Today it is prime real estate, minutes away from Tel Aviv on the coastal highway.) One of the "Lovers of Zion," Abraham wanted to be a scholar-farmer, planting almond trees by day and studying the Talmud at night. By the time my mother was born in nearby Petah Tikva ("Gate of Hope") in 1912, the family was living, amid orchards they had planted, in a fine house with a promenade of palm trees leading up to it.

But these luxuries were enjoyed only by the few "established" families; newcomers had to face much tougher conditions. When my paternal grandfather Nathan arrived in Palestine in 1920, there were hardly any paved roads and virtually no modern transport. The family disembarked from the ship in rowboats, as there were no mooring facilities in the port of Jaffa at the time. After spending some time in Tel Aviv, the new Jewish suburb of Jaffa, they traveled for two days on a dirt road to Tzemah on the southern shore of the Sea of Galilee. There my grandfather and my father boarded a boat to take the luggage to Tiberias five miles away, while the rest of the family continued by carriage. It was late afternoon, and the sudden violent gales so typical of the lake nearly smashed the vessel in two. They stayed overnight in Tiberias, then made their way by horse-drawn carriage up the steep slopes to Safed, changing horses in Rosh Pina, another point of Jewish settlement in the barren wilderness that was otherwise relieved only by sparse Bedouin encampments. As late as 1920, the trip from Jaffa to Safed took more than three days. Today it can be done comfortably in three hours.

Beginning with the first wave of Zionist immigration in 1880 and continuing through successive waves before and after World War I, the country was rapidly transformed. The Jews built roads, towns, farms, hospitals, factories, and schools. And as Jewish immigration increased their numbers, it also caused a rapid increase in the Arab population. Many of the Arabs immigrated into the land in response to the job opportunities and the better life afforded by the growing economy the Jews had created—so much so that in 1939 President Franklin D. Roosevelt was moved to observe that "Arab immigration into Palestine since 1921 has vastly exceeded the total Jewish immigration during this whole period."[44]

The improved economic conditions that the influx of Jewish industry and commerce created fueled a steep rise in income and industrialization among the Arabs of Palestine that had no parallel in any neighboring Arab country. Thus by 1947, the wages of the Arab worker in Haifa were twice what his counterpart was receiving in Nablus, where there was no Jewish presence.[45] Similarly, the number of factories owned by Arabs increased 400 percent between 1931 and 1942, while the number of their employees increased tenfold between 1931 and 1946.[46]

The most dramatic increase in Arab immigration was to the areas of Jewish habitation. Between 1922, the advent of the Mandate, and 1947, the Arab population in the Jewish cities grew by 290 percent in Haifa, 158 percent in Jaffa, and 131 percent in Jerusalem, as compared with 64 percent in Hebron, 56 percent in Nablus, and 37 percent in Bethlehem, where there were few or no Jews.[47] But the fact that Arabs migrated into what would eventually be a domain of millions of Jews hardly altered the prevailing international conception that this was to be a Jewish land, albeit one with an Arab minority. Thus, the unceasing Jewish claim to the land has been backed up in the last hundred years by unrelenting Jewish efforts to settle it and bring its open wastes back to life.

*   *   *

However valid the Jewish claim has been, its relevance would have been mitigated if the Arabs had been able to show an equally persistent claim to the land over the prior centuries. The Arab side makes precisely this claim today—that in recognizing the Jewish historical claim, the men of Versailles disregarded the presence of a nation that had come into being in the intervening period and that had developed unique cultural and historical ties to the land that overshadowed and superseded those of the Jews. The world's leaders, the Arabs claim, erred in believing that they were "giving a people without a land a land without a people."

Lloyd George, Lord Balfour, Woodrow Wilson, and many of the other statesmen of Versailles were men of education, intelligence, and vision. But were they really so fired up with the passions of biblical restoration and humanist ideals that they were simply blinded to the basic demographic and national facts on the ground?

In fact, they were not. They acted from a reasonable assessment of the well-known and well-documented situation in Palestine in their day—anchoring their policies in facts that have since grown increasingly unfamiliar to many people.

The basic Arab claim is that the Jews seized Palestine from an Arab people who had lived there for ages and was its rightful owner. At his speech at the United Nations in 1974, Yasser Arafat declared:

> The Jewish invasion began in 1881. . . . Palestine was then a verdant area, inhabited mainly by an Arab people in the course of building its life and dynamically enriching its indigenous culture.[48]

Arafat and Arab lore thus date the beginning of the Zionist invasion at 1881, when the first wave of the modern Zionist immigration began. (By then, Jews had outnumbered Arabs in Jerusalem for sixty years.)[49]

By now, the idea that the Zionists stole the land from its age-old native inhabitants has been so deeply implanted by Arab spokesmen that in many circles in the West it is almost impossible to dislodge. But it is not supported by history. The description offered by Arafat and others of Palestine before the return of the Jews as a verdant area teeming with people is flatly contradicted by the hundreds of eyewitness accounts of European and American visitors to the Holy Land in the eighteenth and nineteenth centuries, including the reports of the great archaeological explorers from Robinson onward.

In recent centuries, as the interest in biblical scholarship and archaeology grew in Europe and America, diplomats, writers, scholars, soldiers, and surveyors toured the Holy Land in increasing numbers. They produced detailed records of what they saw, most often in the form of books, travelogues, and articles published in various periodicals. Without exception, they give an account of the demographic and physical condition of the country that is completely different from the one the Arabs offer today. As early as 1697, Henry Maundrell wrote that Nazareth was "an inconsiderable village," that Nablus consisted of two streets, that Jericho had become a "poor nasty village," that the fortress city of Acre was "nothing here but a vast and spacious ruin."[50] In 1738, English archaeologist Thomas Shaw wrote of a land of "barrenness and scarcity . . . from the want of inhabitants."[51] In 1785, Constantine François Volney described the "ruined" and "desolate" state of the country:

> [W]e with difficulty recognize Jerusalem. . . . [The population] is supposed to amount to twelve to fourteen thousand. . . . The second place deserving notice is Bait-el-labm, or Bethlehem. . . . [A]s is the case everywhere else, cultivation is wanting. They reckon about six hundred men in this village capable of bearing arms. . . . The third and last place of note is Habroun, or Hebron, the most powerful village in all this quarter, and . . . able to arm eight or nine hundred men.[52]

Yet in 1843, Alexander Keith wrote that "in his [Volney's] day, the land had not fully reached its last prophetic degree of desolation and depopulation."[53]

In 1816, J. S. Buckingham had described Jaffa as "a poor village," and Ramleh as a place "where, as throughout the greater portion of Palestine, the ruined portion seemed more extensive than that which was inhabited."[54] By 1835, the French poet Alphonse de Lamartine gave this description:

> Outside the gates of Jerusalem, we saw indeed no living object, heard no living sound. We found the same void, the same silence as we should have found before the entombed gates of Pompeii or Herculaneum. . . . a complete, eternal silence reigns in the town, in the highways, in the country . . . The tomb of a whole people.[55]

And in 1857, the British consul in Palestine, James Finn, reported back to England, "The country is in a considerable degree empty of inhabitants and therefore its greatest need is that of a body of population."[56]

Perhaps the most famous traveler to the Holy Land was Mark Twain, who visited Palestine in 1867 and wrote of his experiences in *The Innocents Abroad*:

> Stirring senses . . . occur in this [Jezreel] valley no more. There is not a solitary village throughout its whole extent—not for thirty miles in either direction. There are two or three small clusters of Bedouin tents, but not a single permanent habitation. One may ride ten miles, hereabouts, and not see ten human beings.

For dreary solitude, Twain recommended the Galilee:

> These unpeopled deserts, these rusty mounds of barrenness, that never, never, never do shake the glare from their harsh out-

lines . . . ; that melancholy ruin of Capernaum: this stupid village of Tiberias, slumbering under six funereal palms. . . . A desolation is here that not even imagination can grace with the pomp of life and action. . . . We reached [Mount] Tabor safely. . . . We never saw a human being on the whole route.

In "the barren mountains of Judea," as he called them, he found more of the same:

Jericho the accursed lies a moldering ruin today, even as Joshua's miracle left it more than three thousand years ago. . . . [Bethlehem,] the hallowed spot where the shepherds watched their flocks by night, and where the angels sang, "Peace on earth, good will to men," is untenanted by any living creature.

And around Jerusalem:

The further we went . . . the more rocky and bare, repulsive and dreary the landscape became. There could not have been more fragments of stone . . . if every ten square feet of the land had been occupied by a separate and distinct stone-cutter's establishment for an age. There was hardly a tree or a shrub anywhere. Even the olive and the cactus, those fast friends of a worthless soil, had almost deserted the country. . . . Renowned Jerusalem itself, the stateliest name in history, has lost all its ancient grandeur, and become a pauper village.

And for the country as a whole, he gave this bereaved lamentation:

Palestine sits in sackcloth and ashes. Over it broods the spell of a curse that has withered its fields and fettered its energies. . . . Palestine is desolate and unlovely. . . . It is a hopeless, dreary, heartbroken land.[57]

Twain's observations were echoed fourteen years later in the report of the eminent English cartographer Arthur Penrhyn Stanley on Judea: "In Judea it is hardly an exaggeration to say that for miles and miles there was no appearance of life or habitation."[58]

Stanley wrote these words in 1881—the very year that Arafat designates as the beginning of the Zionist "invasion" and the "displacement" of the dynamic local population. That Arafat is caught in another lie is by itself unimportant. What is important is that this lie, endlessly repeated, refined, and elaborated, has displaced what every civilized and educated person knew at the close of the nineteenth century: that the land was indeed largely empty and could afford room to the millions of Jews who were living in intolerable and increasingly dangerous conditions in the ghettos of Europe and who were yearning to return to the land and bring it back to life.

It is true, of course, that there were Arabs living in Palestine, and that in the middle of the nineteenth century they outnumbered its Jewish population. But by the third quarter of the century the total population of the entire country, Arabs and Jews, was still only 400,000—less than four percent of today's figure.[59] By the end of World War I, that number had reached 900,000 on both banks of the Jordan, and roughly 600,000 in western Palestine (the present state of Israel), although these are still insignificant numbers when compared with the overall potential of settlement and habitation.[60] As the German Kaiser, who visited Palestine in 1898, said to Herzl, whom he met there, "The settlements I have seen, the German as well as those of your own people, may serve as samples of what may be done with the country. There is room here for everyone."[61]

When intelligent and humanitarian men such as Woodrow Wilson and Lloyd George considered this wasteland of Palestine, they understood that its minuscule Arab presence, making use of virtually none of the available land for the people's own meager needs, could hardly be considered a serious counter to the claim of millions of Jews the world over to a state of their own—especially when the vast reaches of Arabdom (which extends over five hundred times the area of today's Israel and the administered territories combined)* would be considered a homeland for the Arabs. As Zionist leader Vladimir Jabotinsky put it a few years later, in his testimony before the Peel Commission:

> I do not deny that [in building the Jewish state] . . . the Arabs of Palestine will necessarily become a minority in the country of Palestine. What I do deny is that *that* is a hardship. It is not a hardship on any race, any nation, possessing so many National States now and so many more National States in the future. One fraction, one branch of that race, and not a big one, will have to live in someone else's State. . . . I fully understand that any minority would prefer to be a majority, it is quite understandable that the Arabs of Palestine would also prefer Palestine to be the Arab State No. 4, No. 5, No. 6. [Today there are twenty-one Arab states] . . . but when the Arab claim is confronted with our Jewish claim to be saved, it is like the claims of appetite versus the claims of starvation.[62]

In trying to shore up their historical claim to Palestine, the Arabs have not merely distorted the demographic and physical conditions of the country in the nineteenth century. They have tried to persuade the world that the Arabs of Palestine had forged a distinct and unique national identity over the centuries; otherwise, they knew, they would not qualify for self-determination. Thus, they claimed that when the Jews "invaded," they took over what had been an independent country, "Palestine," inhabited by a distinct nation, "the Palestinians."

But this claim, too, makes a farce out of history. As Bernard Lewis states, after the Arab conquest there was no such thing as Palestine: "From the end of the Jewish state in antiquity to the be-

---

*The land mass of the Arab states today is 5,414,000 square miles, as compared with 8,290 for pre-1967 Israel, and 2,130 for Judea, Samaria, and Gaza (together 10,420 square miles). This is a ratio of 540 to one.

ginning of British rule, the area now designated by the name Palestine was not a country and had no frontiers, only administrative boundaries; it was a group of provincial subdivisions, by no means always the same, within a larger entity."[63] The Turks parceled the land out among four distinct administrative districts, or *sanjaks*. The Jerusalem District included the Sinai and stretched into Africa, while Samaria, Galilee, and Transjordanian Palestine were three additional, separate districts. A succession of rulers had carved up the country's territory and distributed the parts among the various districts of their empires, so that there was never an Arab state of Palestine, or even an Arab province of Palestine. Even the very name Palestine fell into disuse among the Arabs, only to be revived by the British—and appropriated from them by the Arabs in this century.

Who were the champions of the presumed Palestinian nation under the two centuries of Mamluk dominion or under the four centuries of Turkish rule? In what political organizations, social institutions, literature, art, religion, or private correspondence were expressed the ties of this phantom nation to that carved-up land? *None can be cited.* Throughout this long period the Arab inhabitants of Palestine never showed a hint of a desire for independent nationhood, or what is called today self-determination. There were Arabs who lived in Palestine, as elsewhere, but there was no such people as Palestinians, with a national consciousness, or a national identity, or a conception of national interests. Just as there was no Palestinian state, so too there was no Palestinian nation or culture. Such was the conclusion of the 1937 British Royal Commission, which attempted to determine what should be the disposition of the land:

> In the twelve centuries or more that have passed since the Arab conquest, Palestine has virtually dropped out of history. . . . In economics as in politics, Palestine lay outside the main stream of the world's life. In the realm of thought, in science or in letters, it made no contribution to modern civilization.[64]

Some may argue that by the 1930s the issue had already become politicized and therefore that the historical truth cannot be ascertained from pronouncements from that decade. But no such objection can possibly apply to eyewitness accounts of visitors to the Holy Land from a century earlier. Here, for example, is the conclusion of Swiss scholar Felix Bovet, who visited Palestine in 1858 and reported on the state of civilization he found there:

> The Christians who conquered the Holy Land never knew how to keep it, and it was never anything to them other than a battlefield and a graveyard. The Saracens [i.e., Arabs] who took it from them left it as well and it was captured by the Ottoman Turks. The latter . . . turned it into a wasteland in which they seldom dare to tread without fear. The Arabs themselves, who are its inhabitants, cannot be considered but temporary residents. They pitched their tents in its grazing fields or built their places of refuge in its ruined cities. They created nothing in it. Since they were strangers to the land, they never became its masters. The desert wind that brought them hither could one day carry them away without their leaving behind them any sign of their passage through it.[65]

When Edward Robinson, Claude Conder, and the other archaeologists first toured the land, they could identify the ancient Jewish sites with relative ease because the Arabs usually had not bothered to give them new Arabic names, leaving the original Hebrew names in place (albeit slightly modified to be more easily pronounced in Arabic). The Hebrew names the explorers found virtually intact included: Jeremiah's birthplace of Anatoth (Antha), the Maccabee battlefields at Lebonah (Luban) and Beth Horon (Beth Ur), the site of Bar Kochba's last battle at Betar (Batir), the site of the tabernacle at Shiloh (Seilun), Arad (Tel Urad), Ashkelon (Asqalan), Beersheba (Bir es Saba), Benei Brak (Ibn Ibreiq), Beth Shean (Beisan), Beth Shemesh ('Ain Shams), Adoraim (Dura), Eshtamoa (Es-Samu), and hundreds of others.[66] In fact, in the twelve centuries of the Arab presence in Palestine before the return of the Jews in modern times, *the Arabs built only a single new town*—Ramleh.[67] These obvious facts moved Sir George Adam Smith, author of *The Historical Geography of the Holy Land*, to write in 1891, "Nor is there any indigenous civilization in Palestine that could take the place of the Turkish except that of the Jews who . . . have given to Palestine anything it ever had of value to the world."[68]

Hence, when the world leaders at Versailles weighed the question of competing Jewish and Arab claims, they were justifiably not concerned with any "Palestinian" national claim. No Arab leader at Versailles (or in Palestine, for that matter) came forward to present such a claim. Headed by Feisal, son of the Sherif of Mecca and later to become King Feisal of Iraq, the Arab delegation was preoccupied with securing independence for an Arab state that they envisioned would include present-day Syria, Iraq, and the Arabian Peninsula. In fact, they saw the Zionists as potentially useful allies. In January 1919, a month before the opening of the Versailles Conference, Feisal signed an agreement with Chaim Weizmann calling for "the closest possible collaboration" between the Jewish and Arab peoples "in the development of the Arab State and Palestine," and stating that the constitution of Palestine should "afford the fullest guarantees for carrying into effect the British Government's [Balfour] Declaration of 2nd November, 1917," and that "all necessary measures shall be taken to encourage and stimulate immigration of Jews into Palestine on a large scale." In return, the Zionist Organization agreed to "use its best efforts to assist the Arab State in providing the means for developing the natural resources and economic possibilities thereof." The Arab and Jewish peoples also undertook to "act in complete accord . . . before the Peace Congress." In March, Feisal wrote to Felix Frankfurter, who was then a member of the American delegation: "Our deputation here in Paris is fully acquainted with the proposals submitted yesterday by the Zionist Organization to the Peace Conference, and we regard them as moderate and proper. . . . We will wish the Jews a hearty welcome home." (These documents are reproduced in full in Appendixes A and B.)

It should be noted—again, contrary to present claims—that both the British and the League of Nations knew full well that some of the local Palestinian Arabs were resisting the arrangement whereby a small part of the Middle East was to be excluded from Arab sovereignty for the purpose of creating a Jewish home. Full civil rights had been guaranteed to them, and since Palestine contained not much more than 5 percent of the millions of Arabs whom Britain had just liberated from the Ottoman Empire, Lord Balfour insisted that a compromise such as Feisal's was perfectly fair. To Balfour, Zionism was "rooted in age-old traditions, in present needs, in future hopes, of far profounder import than the desires and prejudices of the 700,000 Arabs who now inhabit that ancient land."[69] The Versailles signatories concurred, granting the Mandate over Palestine to Britain at the San Remo Conference in April 1920—*after* agitators from Damascus inspired violent outbreaks in Jerusalem, in which six Jews were beaten to death and hundreds more were wounded. Significantly, the Palestinian Arab rioters demanded the incorporation of Palestine into an independent Syria.[70]

British policy clearly expressed the consensus that there were two peoples, Arab and Jewish, and that both would receive their due. In December 1917, immediately after the signing of the Balfour Declaration, Assistant Foreign Secretary Lord Robert Cecil had proclaimed his country's policy simply: "Our wish is that Arabian countries shall be for the Arabs, Armenia for the Armenians, Judea for the Jews."[71]

Looking back on the results of Versailles years later, Lloyd George was outraged by the claim that the Arabs had somehow been treated unfairly in Palestine and elsewhere:

No race has done better out of the fidelity with which the Allies re-deemed their promises to the oppressed races than the Arabs. Owing to the tremendous sacrifices of the Allied Nations, and more particularly of Britain and her Empire, the Arabs have already won independence in Iraq, Arabia, Syria, and Trans-Jordania, al-though most of the Arab races fought throughout the War for the Turkish oppressors. . . . [In particular] the Palestinian Arabs fought for Turkish rule.[72]

Similarly, the South African Jan Smuts, a member of the British War Cabinet who was actively involved in the discussions behind the Balfour Declaration and the Versailles Treaty, recalled the views of the British Cabinet in deciding to favor a Jewish home-land in Palestine:

It was naturally assumed that large-scale immigration of Jews into their historic homeland could not and would not be looked upon as a hostile gesture to the highly favoured Arab people . . . [who,] largely as a result of British action, came better out of the Great War than any other people.[73]

It therefore came as no surprise that Balfour formally wrote down these sentiments on November 2, 1917, in his letter to the British Zionist Federation via Lord Rothschild: Britain favorably viewed Jewish aspirations for a Jewish National Home in Palestine, aspirations that were commonly known to include the establish-ment of a Jewish majority there and the ultimate administration of the country by the Jew. This letter became known as the Balfour Declaration:

His Majesty's Government view with favour the establishment in Palestine of a national home for the Jewish people, and will use their best endeavors to facilitate the achievement of this object, it being clearly understood that nothing shall be done which may prejudice the civil and religious rights of existing non-Jew-

ish communities in Palestine, or the rights and political status
enjoyed by Jews in any other country.

As for the Arab inhabitants, the Balfour Declaration specifically
stipulated that they should enjoy "civil and religious rights" in
Palestine. It was believed that there was nothing wrong with an
Arab minority living among the Jews so long as their individual
rights were guaranteed, which is precisely what the declaration required.

When the League of Nations charged Britain with the Mandate
for Palestine at the San Remo Conference in 1920, it did so based
on Britain's pro-Zionist Balfour Declaration of 1917, which it incorporated into the language of the Mandate. Thus, the Mandate
dictated, "The Mandatory shall be responsible for placing the
country under such political, administrative and economic conditions as will secure the establishment of the Jewish national
home." It also called for facilitating Jewish immigration and "close
settlement by Jews on the land." (The full text of the Mandate can
be found in Appendix C.)

Britain felt justified in making such an arrangement because it
had just liberated the Arabs from four centuries of Turkish
rule and had given them immense lands for their national self-
expression. It also felt that the Jews deserved special recognition
for their loyalty and service in World War I. Many Jews had fought
in the Allied armies and thus had contributed to the liberation
from Ottoman rule of Arab and Jew alike. But the Arabs had done
practically nothing to shake off the Turks (most Arabs and, as
Lloyd George noted, Palestinian Arabs in particular, had supported the Moslem Turks), with the exception of a few forays
against the Hejaz railroad line made by irregular bands led by T. E.
Lawrence, who later did much to promote and inflate their (and
especially his) contribution to the war effort. In addition to the
hundreds of thousands of Jews who had served in the Allied
armies,[74] the special Jewish Battalions formed by the Zionist leadership and led by Colonel John Henry Patterson made a tangible

contribution to the British campaigns against the Turks in Samaria, Galilee, and Transjordan.[*]

Thus, both as a reward for services rendered and as a recognition of historical Jewish national rights, British policy was clearly committed to the historical Jewish claim to Palestine. It was British statesmen who introduced this Jewish right into the wording of the Mandate at the League of Nations—not a difficult task, since this right was then widely recognized. In fact, the wording of the League of Nations Mandate did not *give* the Jews the right to the land, but *recognized* a right understood to already exist, stating that "recognition has thereby been given to the historical connection of the Jewish people with Palestine and to the grounds for reconstituting their national home in that country." It was possible to extend such recognition only because educated men believed that the Jewish right to the land had been granted to the Jewish people by history and by the unceasing yearning of the Jews to be restored to their national life.

The recognition of this right was most eloquently championed in 1921 by Lloyd George's one-time protégé, Winston Churchill:

> It is manifestly right that the scattered Jews should have a national centre and a national home to be re-united, and where else but in Palestine, with which for three thousand years they have been intimately and profoundly associated? We think it will be good for the world, good for the Jews, good for the British

[*]Patterson was a remarkable non-Jewish Zionist. A British officer, he commanded the first Jewish fighting units in centuries—the Zion Mule Corps, founded by Joseph Trumpeldor— which participated in the Gallipoli campaign. (Trumpeldor was a Jewish former officer in the Russian army who had lost his arm in the Russo-Japanese War and died a hero's death in 1920 defending the Galilee community of Tel Hai against Arab marauders. He was the kind of Jewish fighter that Patterson hoped to see emerge in this century.) Patterson went on to command the Jewish Legion, founded by Jabotinsky. Soldier and intellectual, he collaborated with my father in America at the outbreak of World War II, when my father came to the United States as a member of Jabotinsky's delegation to campaign for the establishment of a Jewish state. Such was the friendship between them that my parents decided to call their first-born son Jonathan, the "Jon" in honor of Patterson and the "Nathan" in honor of my grandfather. Now and then, on special occasions, my family brings out a silver cup with the inscription: "To my darling godson, Jonathan, from your godfather, John Henry Patterson."

Empire, but also good for the Arabs who dwell in Palestine
. . . they shall share in the benefits and progress of Zionism.

Churchill was a firm believer that the Jews could build their
home in Palestine while benefiting the Arab residents. He told
Arabs who petitioned him to keep the Jews from buying land in
Palestine and settling there, "No one has harmed you. . . . The
Jews have a far more difficult task than you. You only have to enjoy
your own possession; but they have to create out of the wilder-
ness, out of the barren places, a livelihood for the people they
bring in." Attacked in the House of Commons for granting the
Jews concessions for hydroelectric projects on the Jordan River,
Churchill said:

> I am told the Arabs would have done it for themselves. Who is
> going to believe that? Left to themselves, the Arabs of Palestine
> would not in a thousand years have taken effective steps toward
> the irrigation and electrification of Palestine. They would have
> been quite content to dwell—a handful of philosophic people—
> in the wasted sun-scorched plains, letting the waters of the Jor-
> dan continue to flow unbridled and unharnessed into the Dead
> Sea.[75]

As noted, these sympathetic attitudes toward Zionism were
widely shared on both sides of the Atlantic. It therefore came as
no surprise that the United States soon recognized the Balfour
Declaration. It was accepted in June 1922 by both Houses of Congress, then in September by President Warren G. Harding, who
signed a bill endorsing it.

So it was that in 1922, after decades of political activism, Zionism had reached a peak of international appeal. Its cause was
widely viewed as just, its leaders were admired and respected, and
its basic goal of establishing a Jewish homeland on both sides of
the Jordan River was increasingly accepted worldwide. True, the
home for the Jews was to be of modest proportions, much of it

covered by swamp and sand and all of it exposed to an unforgiving sun. But it was empty and roomy enough, and it would do.
Had not their ancestors tilled the soil of Gilead east of the Jordan,
built terraced vineyards in Judea in the west, fished in the Sea of
Galilee to the north, and set off to sea from Jaffa on the coast?
Their descendants would do all that and more. As Herzl had en-
visaged it in his novel *Altneuland* ("Old-New Land"), the Jewish
state would revive ancient traditions alongside its thriving science
and technology, creating, precisely as George Eliot had foretold, a
republic "carrying the culture and sympathy of every great nation
in its bosom" and bringing "the brightness of Western freedom
amid the despotism of the East." In 1922, despite the ominous
clouds gathering over the Jewish community of Europe, the creation of a safe haven and a home seemed imminent. The Jewish
future had not seemed brighter for two millennia.

2

THE BETRAYAL

But it was not to be. Even before Britain was granted the Mandate to build a Jewish National Home at the San Remo Conference in 1920, forces within the British imperial establishment had started working to dissolve Britain's commitment to the promise of Versailles. By the time the council of the League of Nations confirmed the Mandate in 1922, the will of British policymakers to actually implement the Balfour Declaration had begun to evaporate.

Under its changed policy, Britain turned its back on the promises it had undertaken in the Balfour Declaration. What had been regarded as obvious moral truths and obligations before the British had formally received the Mandate were now quickly discarded as policies unsuited to the moment. Britain tore off Transjordan from the Jewish National Home in 1922: With one stroke of the pen, it lopped off nearly 80 percent of the land promised the Jewish people, closing this area to Jews for the remainder of the century (see Map 4). It sanctioned the entry into Palestine of Abdullah, the Hashemite chieftain from Mecca, titled him emir, and created a new country called Transjordan (now Jordan), which to this day suffers from the artificiality of its birth. At the end of the

1920s, claiming that the settlement of Jews had "provoked" anti-Jewish rioting, Britain issued a White Paper that severely restricted Jewish immigration and the purchase of land by Jews. By the eve of World War II, after successive White Papers, the British had choked off Jewish immigration almost entirely and had limited Jewish land purchase to a tiny fraction of the country, prompting President Franklin Roosevelt to declare to Secretary of State Cordell Hull: "I was at Versailles, and I know that the British made no secret of the fact they promised Palestine to the Jews. Why are they now reneging on their promise?"[1]

Why, indeed? Where had this shift come from? What political forces were able to drive the most powerful nation on earth to unilaterally abandon the commitment it had made to a national home for the Jewish people—leaving the Jews homeless and helpless just as Hitler's machine of destruction was rolling across Europe?

The government of Lloyd George had adopted the Balfour Declaration and pursued it at Versailles for two reasons not dissimilar to those that many Americans have used for supporting Israel today. Lloyd George believed that British support for the Jewish National Home was morally correct because of the justice of the Jewish cause. But he had also advocated supporting Zionism for a second reason, no less important: that Zionism was in Britain's own interest. Lloyd George believed (as had the Kaiser before him) that the Jews were a power in the world to be reckoned with, and that an alliance with a Jewish nation in Palestine, situated by the crucial Suez Canal and straddling the land route to India, would be a lasting asset to Britain.[2] He was therefore convinced that strengthening the Jewish people in Palestine would in fact strengthen the British people and ultimately the Western values of which he believed Britain was the guardian.

The shift to an anti-Zionist Britain over the course of the next few years entailed a dual change in British governmental opinion. British policymakers came to believe, first, that an alliance with the Arabs, rather than with the Jews, was in Britain's interest. Sec-

ond, since many Arab leaders rejected Feisal's diplomacy and opposed the settlement of Jews in Palestine, British officials came to
believe that it would be unjust to override local Arab opinion and
support Zionism. Fixed during the interwar period, these British
positions on both interest and justice have retained their vitality
well into the second half of the century. Laying the foundations for
a remarkable readiness to accept even the most exaggerated
claims of later Arab propaganda as truth, they have had immense
influence in determining Western, and most recently American,
policy toward Israel up to our own time. It is therefore necessary
to understand the genesis of these beliefs and to gauge how well
the policies based on them actually served the causes of justice
and interest.

Clearly, the rejection of the Jewish National Home was not the
policy of either Balfour or Lloyd George. Rather, it came from the
imperial calculations of the officials of the British War Office and
Foreign Office, who grabbed much of the Arab world from the Ottomans during World War I. The idealism of Wilson and Balfour
was fine for wartime propaganda, but once Palestine, Syria, Iraq,
and Arabia were actually in British hands, someone had to govern
them—and that someone was a small army of rather clannish For
eign Office "Arabists," who had spent their lives learning to speak
Arabic, moving about places such as Cairo and Khartoum, and becoming intoxicated with the romance of the "noble" Bedouin.
Dreaming of a vast pro-British Arab federation from the Sudan to
Iraq (creating a continuous overland empire from South Africa to
India), these men had spent the war fighting zealously for the
"liberation" of the Arabs. They had schemed tirelessly to manufacture Arab "leaders" who could bring the scattered and chroni-
cally divided Arab tribes of the Ottoman Empire into an alliance
with Britain—and with one another. Strangely, these Arabists
seem to have been untroubled by the fact that hundreds of thousands of Arabs were fighting and dying for the Moslem Ottomans
and that only the most lavish "subsidies" and the most exorbitant
promises of future independent Arab kingdoms could pry a few

thousand disunited Bedouin raiders away to side with the Western Allies.

To the Arabists, the small, relatively backward Arab population of Palestine was of little interest. But Palestine itself, as the land bridge between Cairo on the one hand and Damascus and Baghdad on the other, was an indispensable link in their chain. Restless to win the affections of their new Arab subjects, they were more than eager to co-opt the Arab antagonism toward Zionism into their policies in Palestine, which they at first believed might be incorporated into a British-dominated Syria.

As early as the British conquest of Jerusalem on December 11, 1917, one month after the Balfour Declaration, resistance to Zionism was manifest among the imperial administrators, who saw their job not in terms of serving justice or even keeping British promises but in winning over the Arabs. Thus, General Sir Edmund Allenby's chief political officer, Brigadier-General Gilbert Clayton, worried that the declaration had been a mistake: "We have . . . to consider whether the situation demands out and out support for Zionism at the risk of alienating the Arabs at a critical moment."[3] His argument to the pro-Zionist Sir Mark Sykes foreshadows the argumentation of generations of Arabists:

> I must point out that, by pushing [for] them [i.e., the Zionists]
> as hard as we appear to be doing, we are risking the possibility
> of Arab unity becoming something like an accomplished fact
> and being ranged against us.[4]

In this Clayton was backed by the high commissioner in Egypt, Sir Reginald Wingate, who warned Allenby that "Mark Sykes is a bit carried away with 'the exuberance of his own verbosity' in regard to Zionism and unless he goes a bit slower he may quite unintentionally upset the applecart."[5]

The new military governor of Jerusalem, Ronald Storrs, also

worked to cool British enthusiasm for Zionist plans and declarations. He urged sympathy for the point of view of the local Arabs and demanded that any changes come about only "gradually," so as not to leave "an abiding rancour."[6]

For his part, General Allenby refused even to allow the publication of the Balfour Declaration in Palestine. Instead, the military government issued a declaration of its intentions of "encouraging and assisting the establishment of indigenous government and administrations in Syria and Mesopotamia," which the local Arab notables assumed to apply to them since they understood Palestine to be part of Syria (and since the British went to the trouble of sending them copies). Jabotinsky summed up the approach of the administration as being "to apologize to the Arabs for a slip of the tongue by Mr. Balfour."[7]

Soon, reports of this resistance to official policy began to alarm the Foreign Office in London, which was still under Lord Balfour. On August 4, 1918, the British administration in Palestine received a cable explicitly ordering it to consider the Balfour Declaration to be British policy.[8]

But to no effect. The British administration's contempt for the Jewish National Home policy and for the Jews themselves only grew more open. General Arthur Money, Allenby's successor as head of the military administration who complained about Lloyd George's "hook-nosed friends,"[9] ordered that government forms should be printed in English and Arabic only[10] and refused to stand for the playing of "Hatikva," the Jewish national anthem.[11] The military governor of Jaffa, Lieutenant-Colonel J. E. Hubbard, organized and funded the first political organizations among the Arabs with the intention of relying on the opinions of these "representatives" to undermine Zionism.[12] Hubbard was reputed to have announced that if the Arabs wished to riot against the Jews, he would not stop them.[13] As for allowing Jews to actually come and live in the land, British Intelligence feared the effects of this bold step as well, and it urged the Foreign Office to deny immigration applications to Jews until the military situation could be resolved.[14] Jabotinsky, who had been an ardent advocate of cooperation with the British, was now forced to conclude ruefully that the British administration had been swept up in "an unprecedented epidemic of anti-Semitism." He wrote: "Not in Russia, nor in Poland had there been such an intense and widespread atmosphere of hatred as prevailed in the British army in Palestine in 1919 and 1920."[15]

But the British establishment continued to boast a handful of genuine Zionists, who waged a tireless (and ultimately futile) battle to implement the policies of Lloyd George and Balfour. These few believed the exact opposite of what the proponents of Arab appeasement were advocating. They thought that Britain ultimately could not rely on the Arabs, and that even those Arabs who were in league with Britain were weak and unstable. They believed that it was in the interest of Britain to help the Jews build a solid Western base in the heart of the Middle East—which paradoxically would help stabilize the Arab domains around it.

No one argued this more forcefully than Colonel Richard Meinertzhagen, the British chief of intelligence in the Middle East who had used brilliant deception techniques to help drive the Turks out of Palestine in 1917. Although himself a onetime anti-Semite, Meinertzhagen's opinion of Jews and Zionism had changed after he started using Jewish and Arab agents in the Middle East. By the time he was appointed chief political officer in Palestine in 1919, Meinertzhagen had become one of the greatest non-Jewish Zionists in history, a commitment that eventually culminated in his meeting with Hitler to try to rescue Jews from Germany and bring them to safety in Palestine. Meinertzhagen was a thoroughly independent-minded British patriot, and his approach to Zionism was fashioned first and foremost by its coherence with British interests. The remarkable character of this man is revealed in his first meeting with Hitler. The Führer marched up to Meinertzhagen, extended his arm, and said, "Heil Hitler!" Not missing a beat, Meinertzhagen responded: "Heil Meinertzhagen!"[16]

As the representative of Balfour's foreign office in Palestine,

Meinertzhagen found himself "alone out there among gentiles, in upholding Zionism."[17] Nevertheless, he argued that support for the Jewish National Home was unassailably in Britain's interest:

> The force of nationalism will challenge our position. We cannot befriend both Arab and Jew. My proposal is based on befriending the people who are more likely to be loyal friends—the Jews. . . . Though we have done much for the Arabs, they do not know the meaning of gratitude; moreover they would be a liability; the Jew would be an asset. . . . The Jews have moreover proved their fighting qualities since the Roman occupation of Jerusalem. The Arab is a poor fighter, though an adept at looting, sabotage and murder. . . . [Mine] is a proposal to make our position in the Middle East more secure.[18]

Three decades before Israel's independence, Meinertzhagen was convinced that the alliance with the pro-Western Jews would ultimately be the only way to defend Britain's position in the Middle East:

> We [will] cease to control the Suez Canal in 1966; by that time we shall have been pushed out of Egypt[,] who can then close the Canal against our shipping. . . .
> I have always regarded Palestine as the key to Middle East Defence. I therefore approached Weizmann last week with a view to ascertaining whether, when and if Palestine becomes a Jewish Sovereign State, Great Britain would be granted air, naval and military bases in Palestine in perpetuity. Moreover the Jews can be relied on to keep agreements, the Arabs can never be relied on. . . . With British Bases in Palestine our position in the Middle East is secure forever.[19]

The struggle between Meinertzhagen and the British anti-Zionists over the future direction of the Mandate finally boiled over in March 1920 with the installation of Feisal, the candidate of the British Arabists, as king of all Syria—including Palestine. The British administration in Palestine, unable to officially recognize his kingship over Palestine,[20] orchestrated violent demonstrations demanding the end of the Jewish National Home policy and the incorporation of Palestine into Syria. In coordination with Feisal, Storrs, the governor of Jerusalem, and his chief of staff, Richard Waters-Taylor, had cultivated a coterie of Pan-Arabist radicals led by Haj Amin al-Husseini, who they believed could be counted on to support the incorporation of Palestine into a British-controlled Syria under Feisal's family, the Hashemites. According to Meinertzhagen (who had been forced to plant agents to monitor the anti-Zionist activities of his own government), Waters-Taylor approached these Arabs in early 1920 with the idea of organizing "anti-Jew riots to impress on the Administration the unpopularity of the Zionist policy." Both Storrs and Feisal were informed of this effort.[21]

Waters-Taylor met with Husseini to emphasize the importance of the riots, as Meinertzhagen later related:

> Waters-Taylor saw Haj al Amin on the Wednesday before Easter and told him that he had a great opportunity at Easter to show the world that the Arabs of Palestine would not tolerate Jewish domination in Palestine; that Zionism was unpopular not only with the Palestine Administration but with Whitehall; and if disturbances of sufficient violence occurred in Jerusalem at Easter, both General Bols and General Allenby would advocate the abandonment of the Jewish National Home.[22]

On the day of the rioting Jerusalem was covered with posters reading: "The Government is with us, Allenby is with us, kill the Jews; there is no punishment for killing Jews."[23] Arab inciters shouted, "Long live our King—King Feisal! In the name of our King we urge you to fight the Jews!"[24] Jewish police officers had been taken off duty, and the security forces were nowhere to be found (except for some of the Arab policemen who took part in the rioting), as the Arab mob beat, raped, and looted for three days. Most of those whom the British detained were released again before the violence had ended and simply went back to rioting.[25] Six Jews were killed and 211 wounded. When order was finally "restored," the British had arrested two Arabs for raping Jewish women and twenty Jewish men (including Jabotinsky) for having organized a Jewish self-defense unit. Husseini, who had orchestrated the mayhem, slipped out of the country. At a meeting of Moslem notables immediately following the riots, a leading agitator, Aref el-Aref, said: "Fortunately, the British Administration is on our side and we shall not be hurt. My advice, then, is to continue the assault on the Jews."[26]

In the aftermath of the rioting, it looked at first as though Meinertzhagen's views might prevail. His protests to the still-sympathetic Foreign Office and his subsequent testimony before the commission of inquiry so shocked the government in London that it determined to dismantle the military government. General Sir Louis Bols and Waters-Taylor were dismissed, and in July 1920 Palestine was turned over to a high commissioner, Lord Herbert Samuel, who was a professed Zionist. Jabotinsky and his men were amnestied for their activities during the riots. Meanwhile, the French invaded Damascus and deposed the British-installed Hashemite government, staking their own claim to Syria and ruining forever the Arabist scheme of incorporating Palestine into a British Syria.

But within months it became clear that the battle for Britain's fulfillment of its commitments would be protracted and bitter. "Bols went," wrote Colonel Patterson, "but the system he implanted remained. The anti-Semitic officials that he brought with him into the country remained."[27] The well-meaning Lord Samuel proved inadequate to the task of resisting his subordinates, and the situation rapidly deteriorated. These underlings harangued ceaselessly about the hatred that was growing against Britain because of the Jews, and they saw to it that key non-British positions were filled by Arabs, even in the security services.[28] They prevailed upon Lord Samuel to pardon Husseini as a "gesture" and allow the instigator of the riots to return to Jerusalem, where he immediately resumed orchestrating more of them.

Worried about being "led into a clash with our Arab friends,"[29] Samuel, after some initial opposition, finally acquiesced in the scheme to detach Transjordan from the rest of Palestine. When the post of Mufti (Moslem religious leader) of Jerusalem became vacant, Husseini grew determined to use the prestige and financial muscle of the post against the Jews, and he ran for the position. Although he lost the election, coming in fourth, the anti-Zionists in Samuel's administration deposed the actual winner and duped Samuel into believing that Haj Amin alone represented Palestinian Arabs. Samuel appointed Haj Amin al-Husseini to the newly manufactured post of "Grand Mufti," Mufti for life— in one fateful stroke legitimizing the most violent and radical element among the Palestinian Arabs to a position of preeminent leadership and establishing a pattern that was to continue through the rest of the century. "He hates both Jews and British," wrote Meinertzhagen. "His appointment is sheer madness."[30] "Samuel is rather weak," Lloyd George concluded glumly.[31]

By 1921, hostility to Zionism was quickly making inroads in London as well. In that year, the authority over Palestine was transferred from the Foreign Office to the new Middle East Department at the Colonial Office, made up of old empire-building hands from colonies such as Kenya, Sierra Leone, the Gold Coast, and southern Rhodesia.[32] The new department was headed by Sir John Evelyn Shuckburgh; a man "saturated with anti-Semitism, [he] loathes Zionism and the Jews."[33] Shuckburgh was among the leaders of the effort to convince the government that it could maintain Britain's hold on the Middle East by opposing Zionism and thereby earn the gratitude and loyalty of its new Arab subjects in Egypt, Iraq, and the Gulf. Although they were captivated by the mystique of the Arab, the British Arabists had another, much less romantic interest in backing the Arabs. In a peculiar combination of patronizing sympathy and subconscious contempt, they believed that the Arabs were a backward people who could be more easily controlled than the Jews and indefinitely manipulated to postpone demands for independence—as long as their disdain for Jews did not rile them into opposition to British domination. Shuckburgh was joined in the Colonial Office by veterans of relations with the Arabs during the war, including T. E. Lawrence. "Lawrence of Arabia" had been made famous in Britain and America by a widely exaggerated stage-show about the war effort against the Ottomans which had depicted him and his minuscule band of Arab raiders as the heroes of the war. In order to substantiate this undeserved reputation, Lawrence worked doggedly to promote the impression that Britain owed a great deal to the Arabs in general and to Feisal and the Hashemites of Mecca in particular.[34] Seasoned subordinates like Shuckburgh and Lawrence were able to play on the inexperience of the new minister above them (as had happened to Lord Samuel and countless other top officials over the course of this century) and convert him to their policies: In this case, the man in charge was the mercurial colonial secretary, Winston Churchill.

Churchill took office as a man of outspoken sympathy for Zionism. In February 1920, he sent chills down the spines of government Arabists by telling the *Sunday Herald* that he envisioned "a Jewish State by the banks of the Jordan ... which might comprise three or four million Jews."[35] In this he was heir to the tradition of Versailles, which had clearly supported the idea that, as in biblical times, the Jewish nation was to be reinstated on *both* banks of the Jordan River. On this matter Lord Balfour had written to Lloyd George that Palestine's eastern border had to be well east of Jordan "for the development of Zionist agriculture."[36] Lord Samuel had concurred that

> ... you cannot have numbers without area and territory. Every expert knows that for a prosperous Palestine an adequate territory beyond the Jordan [River] is indispensable.[37]

The *Times,* too, had argued that Palestine needed a "good military frontier . . . as near as may be to the edge of the desert." According to the *Times,* the Jordan River

> . . . will not do as Palestine's eastern boundary. Our duty as Mandatory is to make Jewish Palestine not a struggling State but one that is capable of a vigorous and independent national life.[38]

Lord Arnold, the Undersecretary for the Colonies, retrospectively summed up the position of official Britain during the war for Parliament a few years later:

> During the war we recognized Arab independence, within certain border limits. . . . There were discussions as to what territories these borders should take in. But there was no dispute as to Trans-Jordan. There is no doubt about the fact that Trans-Jordan is within the boundaries to which the [Balfour] Declaration during the War refers.[39]

Even Abdullah, the emir of the new entity of Transjordan, recognized that Transjordan had been intended by the British to be part of the Jewish National Home:

> [God] granted me success in creating the Government of Transjordan by having it separated from the Balfour Declaration[,] which had included it since the Sykes-Picot Agreement [in 1916] assigned it to the British zone of influence.[40]

Like his brother Feisal, Abdullah was apparently convinced of the value of Jewish immigration to building Transjordan's economic base, and at various points between 1924 and 1935 he attempted to arrange the sale and lease of land in Transjordan to Jews from western Palestine. These efforts were eventually aborted by the British government in western Palestine.[41]

With such strong currents in favor of Jewish settlement east of the Jordan, it was clear that Churchill, if left to his own devices, might well act out his idea of "a Jewish State by the banks of the Jordan"—and the functionaries of the new Middle East Department moved quickly to ensure that he did not. It was Shuckburgh, Lawrence, and their associates who led Churchill to believe that Transjordan had been promised to Feisal and the Hashemites of Mecca during the war. They thereby triggered the installation of Feisal's brother Abdullah and his army of two hundred Bedouins as rulers of Jordan—despite the objection by High Commissioner for Palestine Sir Herbert Samuel and others that Jordan was part of Palestine. Lloyd George, too, insisted that even if there were no choice but to make Transjordan Arab, it had to be considered an "Arab province [of] or adjunct to Palestine."[42]

But Churchill's subordinates were convinced that by throwing such favors to the Arabs, they would earn the Arabs' loyalty. They told Churchill that making such a gift would really not harm the Jews—a line which Churchill, like so many other Western leaders after him, did not know enough to refute. Meinertzhagen, who had been assigned to the Middle East Department in London, once again found himself alone in attempting to maintain the commitment that Britain had made to the Jews:

> The atmosphere in the Colonial Office is definitely hebraphobe [i.e., anti-Semitic], the worst offender being Shuckburgh who is head of the Middle East Department. . . .
>
> I exploded on hearing that Churchill had severed Transjordan from Palestine. . . . Abdullah was placated at the expense of the Jewish National Home which embraces the whole of Biblical Palestine. Lawrence was of course with Churchill and influenced him. . . . This reduces the Jewish National Home to one-third of Biblical Palestine. The Colonial Office and the Palestine Administration have now declared that the articles for the mandate relating to the Jewish Home are not applicable to Transjordan. . . . This discovery was not made until it became necessary to appease an Arab Emir.

Outraged, Meinertzhagen insisted on seeing Churchill:

> . . . I went foaming at the mouth with anger and indignation[.]
> Churchill heard me out; I told him it was grossly unfair to the
> Jews, that it was yet another promise broken and that it was a
> most dishonest act, that the Balfour Declaration was being torn
> up by degrees and that the official policy of His Majesty's Gov-
> ernment to establish a Home for the Jews in Biblical Palestine
> was being sabotaged; that I found the Middle East Department
> whose business was to implement the Mandate, almost one
> hundred percent hebraphobe. . . . Churchill listened and said he
> saw the force of my argument and would consider the question.
> He thought it was too late to alter[,] but a time limit to Abdul-
> lah's Emirate in Transjordan might work.
>
> I'm thoroughly disgusted.[43]

To Churchill's credit, he rejected effort after effort to persuade
him not to implement the Balfour Declaration *west* of the Jordan
River. But his rejections were not enough to discourage the Arabs,
who correctly recognized that Britain was caving in under the
pressure of their violence. Less than two months after Churchill's
decision, in March 1921, to establish Abdullah in Transjordan, Arab
mobs, somehow not appeased, again went on the rampage. A
British judge in the Mandatory government named Horace
Samuel (no relation to Lord Herbert Samuel), who was involved in
the subsequent trials, recorded the events in Jaffa:

> The Arabs of Jaffa . . . started to murder, wound, and loot the
> Jews under the official protection and assistance of a substantial
> number of Jaffa police. . . . A mob of Arabs . . . began to attack
> [the Zionist Commission immigration depot] with stones and
> sticks, but were at first successfully kept at bay by the immi-
> grants. Finally, reinforcements for the attackers were supplied by
> certain Arab policemen, well equipped with rifles, bombs, and
> ammunition. The door was forced by the police, and under their

leadership and escort the mob burst into the building. Thirteen of the immigrants were murdered.

Faced with the murder of Jews, the British instantly knew what to do. As Judge Samuel explained:

> The riots of the 1st of May and the massacre of the Jews at the Immigration Hostel were a pretty broad hint that the Jaffa Arabs resented any further Jewish immigration into the country. Under these circumstances the High Commissioner [Lord Samuel], preferring a policy of tact to one of drastic repression, within forty-eight hours of the massacre telephoned Mr. Miller, the Assistant Governor of Jaffa, instructing him to announce to the Arabs that in accordance with their request, immigration had been suspended.[44]

Still unappeased, Arab mobs spent the following week attacking Jewish communities all over the country. British soldiers were under orders not to shoot.[45] In the end, thirty-five Jews were left dead and hundreds more wounded. According to Judge Samuel, Storrs argued for a policy of "throwing the Arabs as many sops as they could swallow, in the hope of thereby getting them to desist from open revolt."[46] His view prevailed, and a general freeze on Jewish immigration was imposed for the first time. And while the freeze lasted only two months, it set a precedent of sacrificing Jewish rights to Arab blackmail, which was soon to replace the Balfour Declaration as London's policy.

But by this time, many of the Arabists did not see the Arab threats as blackmail at all. On the contrary, the Arabists found themselves in sympathy with Arab revulsion against this "nowhere very popular people," as Storrs called them.[47] With astonishing hypocrisy, these avowed imperialists and colonialists began to argue that "foreign" Jewish control of Palestine was an injustice to the indigenous Arabs. Thus in 1920 the new foreign minister, Lord Curzon, a staunch colonialist, argued that the Mandate, which "reeks of Judaism in every paragraph," was inherently unfair to the local Arabs.[48] He was joined in his opinion in 1921 by the new commander of the British Army in Palestine, General W. N. Congreve, who circulated a memorandum to his troops decreeing that while the army of course was not supposed to have political opinions, it could not ignore the injustice being done to the Arabs by allowing the Jews to settle in Palestine.[49] The effect of this new moralizing on the part of the British imperial establishment had an almost immediate effect on the execution of British policy. It propelled Lord Samuel's adviser on the Arabs, Ernest Richmond, to conclude that the Zionist policy was "inspired by a spirit which I can only regard as evil"[50]—and to engineer the appointment of Haj Amin al-Husseini to the post of Grand Mufti as a curative.

In London the increasing distaste for Zionism and fear of Arab threats hobbled support for constructing a strong, pro-Western Jewish Palestine, and British policy became mired in equivocation. The trend in matters of Jewish immigration and settlement affected strategic issues as well, as Meinertzhagen found out in 1923, when he tried to arrange an agreement for future Jewish-British military cooperation in Palestine:

> [Churchill] did not wish me to bring it up to the forthcoming Committee on Palestine as it would have a hostile reception. I asked if the government still stood by the Balfour Declaration; he said it did but that things must go slow for the moment as the Cabinet would never agree to a policy which would antagonize the Arabs. Appeasement again.
>
> We are backing the wrong horse and, my God, we shall suffer for it if and when another war is sprung on us.[51]

Devotion to the Balfour Declaration flickered on in the form of a handful of British parliamentarians such as Lord Josiah Wedgwood, Wyndham Deedes, and Leopold Amery, but within a few years their influence had almost entirely waned.

In August 1929, on the Jewish fast day of Tish'ah beAv, which marks the destruction of Jerusalem by the Romans, Arab mobs attacked Jews in Hebron, Jerusalem, Safed, and elsewhere. They rampaged for eight days, killing 113 Jews, wounding hundreds more, and destroying six Jewish settlements entirely, including the ancient Jewish community of Hebron. The British once again withheld fire but worked to confiscate any "illegal" arms they found among the Jews. In despair, the Hebrew daily *Davar* asked, "Is there a law which compels our men to deliver their lives and the lives of their children to massacre, their daughters to rape, their property to plunder? What theory and what kind of regime is it that demands such things of men?"[52]

Despite the fact that Jewish immigration to Palestine had declined sharply over the preceding two years, the Colonial Office under Lord Passfield (Sidney Webb, the noted Fabian Socialist) again concluded that Jewish immigration had been one of the causes of the bloodshed. Once again capitulating in the face of Arab demands, Lord Passfield announced the severe curtailment of the land available for Jewish settlement, called for strict controls on Jewish immigration, and urged the Zionists to make concessions on the idea of a Jewish National Home.[53] The Arabs also demanded that Jabotinsky be banned from Palestine because he advocated a Jewish state, and in this, too, the British administration obliged.[54]

For anyone with sober vision, it was suddenly and completely clear that Britain was prepared to betray the idea of the Jewish National Home. But incredibly, many Jews did not see this. They were frustrated by Britain's policies, but after each rebuff they were mollified by the government's public declarations of its friendliness and irrevocable commitment to the Jewish people. Having been stateless for so many centuries, the Jews now suffered from an acute political myopia and refused to recognize the true motives of British policies and the catastrophic consequences of failing to forcefully challenge them—much as Jews in Europe did not recognize where Nazism was leading a few years later.

The handful like Jabotinsky who did understand had to overcome the tendency of the majority not to *want* to understand, for this would necessarily involve a confrontation with Great Britain, then the preeminent world power. For the majority of Jews, schooled in centuries of submission to the powers that be, such a confrontation with Britain was unthinkable. As a result, the Jewish people remained largely docile during the period between the two world wars, as their patrimony and national rights were progressively whittled away and as millions of their fellow Jews were being imperiled.

True, there was some reaction in public opinion to the anti-Zionist measures that the Colonial Office took in 1930. For example, the League of Nations Mandates Commission stripped the British of their moral standing in the dispute by announcing in 1930 that Britain had caused the Arab riots in Palestine by failing to provide sufficient police protection.[55] But what influence the League still had evaporated when it gaped helplessly while the Japanese violated the Kellogg-Briand Pact and invaded Manchuria in 1931 and while Mussolini conquered Ethiopia in 1935. The idea that the new world order would honor the commitments that the great powers had made to the smaller nations was on its last legs. And in the case of Britain this was just the dress rehearsal for its final abandonment of Zionism, which was to come a few years later.

In 1933 Hitler came to power in Germany. Within three years, the Jewish population of Palestine had almost doubled. Anti-Zionists, British and Arab alike, understood that the promise that Palestine would be a safe haven for Jews who were fleeing for their lives was being acted out before their eyes. If action were not taken immediately, a Jewish majority would materialize in Palestine within a few years, and then a Jewish state. The dream of a continuous Arab realm under the control of the British Empire was in serious trouble.

On April 19, 1936, an Arab general strike was declared that was intended to cripple the country and bring it to its knees if Jewish immigration were not suspended. The British collaborated by permitting the strike. Gangs in the pay of the Mufti, numbering several thousand, imposed a reign of terror on the country. For three years they maintained the "revolt" by torturing and murdering Arab dissenters, while seeking out Jewish victims when and where they could get them. Through much of the uprising the British Army withheld fire, continuing its policy of disarming the Jews while allowing weapons and Arab volunteers from neighboring countries to pour across the border into the Mufti's hands. In all, more than five hundred Jews were killed out of a total Jewish population of a few hundred thousand. Surveying the carnage, Meinertzhagen sensed what was coming: "God, how we have let the Jews down. And if we are not careful we shall lose the Eastern Mediterranean, Iraq, and everything which counts in the Middle East."[56]

Even at this late date, there were still a precious few within the British administration who argued that the Arab violence proved that only the Jews could be relied upon to protect the interests of Britain in the area. Most important among them was Captain Orde Wingate, who largely on his own initiative recruited and trained Jewish antiterror units known as the Special Night Squads, which were used to take offensive action against the Arab insurgents. Wingate explained the need for Jewish troops:

> The military, in spite of their superior armament, training and discipline, are in comparison with the guerilla warrior at a disadvantage as far as knowledge of the ground and local conditions are concerned; it is advisable to create mixed groups of [British] soldiers and faithful local inhabitants. The Jews are the only local inhabitants who can be relied upon. They know the terrain well and can speak the languages fluently. Moreover, they grasp tactical training quickly and are well disciplined and courageous in combat.[57]

In 1939 Wingate was summarily removed from Palestine with the specific order not to return. He later died in Burma. In the face of continual upheaval in Palestine, the inclination of most people in the British government was to capitulate to Arab demands. They believed that it was Jewish immigration that was driving the Arabs to oppose the British and support the Nazis, threatening everything they had worked so hard to create. As Evelyn Shuckburgh, attaché in the British embassy in Cairo, wrote to his Arabist father, John, in 1937, succinctly capturing the essence of Western Arabism for the rest of the century, "How can we risk prejudicing our whole position in the Arab world for the sake of Palestine?"[58]

London agreed. In July 1937, the Royal (Peel) Commission gave explicit sanction to Arabist policy. The Mandate for a Jewish National Home in Palestine, it concluded, simply could not be filled in the face of Arab sensibilities. Instead, it recommended that Palestine be partitioned: The Jews would receive their "state," which was to consist of parts of the coastal strip and the Galilee (roughly 5 percent of the original homeland granted the Jews by the Palestine Mandate), the British would retain Jerusalem and Haifa, and an Arab state (to be merged with Transjordan) would receive everything else—more than 90 percent of Palestine. Yet the Arabs, recognizing a complete loss of nerve when they saw one, rejected the plan unequivocally and demanded everything. In September 1937, Arab terrorists assassinated the new British district commissioner for Galilee, whom they believed to be working to implement partition. The uprising resumed with the same demands: a complete end to all Jewish immigration and a complete renunciation of the Jewish National Home.

In the end the British complied. Early in 1939, Prime Minister Neville Chamberlain concocted the formula that was to bring "peace in our time" to the Middle East. His solution to the Arabs' unhappiness with the Balfour Declaration was to abrogate the declaration once and for all. The Chamberlain White Paper of May 1939 was issued four months before the outbreak of World War II and the final countdown to the Holocaust. It decreed that Jewish immigration was to be finally terminated after the entry of another seventy-five thousand Jews, and that Britain would now work to create a "bi-national" Arab-Jewish state. Anyone who could read and count understood that this meant that Chamberlain had finally dealt a death blow to the idea of a Jewish state. A mere six months after he betrayed the Czechs at Munich, Chamberlain went on to betray the Jews. The League of Nations Mandates Commission rejected the British action as not in accord with the Mandate, but the League's opinion was no longer of interest to anyone.[59]

The extent of the British betrayal of the Jews can be understood only in the context of what was happening in Europe in the 1930s and thereafter. Responding to pressure from the Arabs, the British restriction of Jewish immigration (there was no analogous restriction on *Arab* immigration) cut off the routes of escape for Jews trying to flee a burning Europe. Thus, while the Gestapo was conniving to send boatloads of German Jews out onto the high seas to prove that no country wanted them any more than Germany did, the British dutifully turned back every leaking barge that reached Palestine, even firing on several.[60] To some, such as Meinertzhagen, the meaning of these events was all too clear:

> The Nazis mean to eradicate Judaism from Germany and they will succeed. Nobody loves the Jews, nobody wants them and yet we are pledged to give them a home in Palestine. Instead we slam the door in their faces just at the moment when it should be wide open. We even whittle down their home at a moment when we should enlarge it. The action of His Majesty's Government in Palestine is very near to that of Hitler in Germany. They may be more subtle, they are certainly more hypocritical, but the result [for the Jews] is similar—insecurity, misery, exasperation and murder.[61]

For over ten years the British shut the doors of the Jewish National Home to Jews fleeing their deaths. In so doing they not only worked to destroy the Jewish National Home, which no one believed could survive without immigrants, but made themselves accomplices in the destruction of European Jewry.

Of the ideals that had led Britain to promise the Jews a national home, Foreign Minister Lord Halifax (who imposed the restrictions) averred: "There are times when considerations of abstract justice must give way to those of administrative expediency."[62] When news of the destruction of Europe's Jews reached the Colonial Office during the war, pleas to open the gates and allow some to be saved were dismissed by John Shuckburgh as "unscrupulous Zionist sobstuff."[63] He explained: "There are days in which we are brought up against realities, and we cannot be deterred [from our policies] by the kind of perverse, pre-war humanitarianism that prevailed in 1939."[64]

Indeed, the British adhered to their policy of opposing "perverse humanitarianism" with a vengeance. During all the years of World War II, as European Jewry was being fed into Hitler's ovens, Britain regularly turned away Jewish refugees seeking to reach the safe shores of Palestine. Some managed to "illegally" run the blockade, and they and their children now live in Israel. Most were unsuccessful and were forced to return to Europe, sent by the British to their deaths. No other country would have them, and the only place that would was cruelly blocked.

By war's end in 1945, the pro-British Chaim Weizmann was forced to give up the leadership of the Zionist movement (although he was later to receive the ceremonial post of first President of the State of Israel). In his last address as chairman of the Zionist Organization, he bitterly surveyed the end result of a quarter of a century of unflagging faith in British goodwill:

Sometimes we were told that our exclusion from Palestine was necessary in order to do justice to a[n Arab] nation already endowed with seven independent territories covering a million

square miles; at other times we were told that the admission of
our refugees might endanger military security through the
war. . . . It was easier to doom the Jews of Europe to a certain
death than to evolve a technique for overcoming such difficulties.[65]

Astonishingly, not even the confirmation of the destruction of
most of Europe's Jews and the photographs from the death camps
could melt the stone hearts of British policymakers, who had determined that no Jewish state would be allowed to come into existence at any price, and who were prepared to make sure that
every last survivor of the Holocaust stayed in Europe.[66] Britain
continued to fight tooth and nail after 1945 to prevent the entry
of the survivors into Palestine, resorting to deportations to
Cyprus, Africa, and the Indian Ocean. Earlier, in the middle of
World War II in 1942, they refused passage to Palestine to the ship
Stuma, which subsequently sank taking down with it 768 refugees
from the Holocaust. There was only one survivor. The pathetic
number of Jews permitted to enter Palestine fell even lower than
it had been during the war.[67] As if this were not enough, the British
equipped the Arab armies preparing to wipe out the Jewish communities in Palestine. In April 1948, with Arab irregulars already
pouring over the borders, the dying British administration used its
last breath to keep out the Jews.[68]

Yet for all this, the British anti-Zionist policy was an abysmal
failure. The British lost their influence with the Arabs—not, of
course, because of the Jews, but because of the overall decline of
British power in the world. This was coupled with the antipathy of
the Arabs toward *any* Western and Christian power—a resentment that had been suppressed only by the overwhelming force
of British troops and the overwhelming enticement of British subsidies. The Arabs' unrelenting antipathy to the West was such that
neither their liberation from the oppressive Ottomans, nor the
consistent British hostility to Zionism, nor the return of boatloads
of Jews to the European inferno succeeded in winning their affections. As Meinertzhagen had predicted, when the first big test of

Arab loyalty to Britain came during the darkest days of the British battle for survival during World War II, the Arabs repaid the British as they saw fit: In Iraq, in Egypt, and in Syria they openly allied themselves with the Nazis, flocking to Berlin to enlist in the war effort and lobby Hitler for favors. They even formed an Arab Legion in Berlin that eventually became part of the SS.[69]

A popular song at the time caught the spirit of the Arab masses as they enthusiastically waited to rid themselves of the detested British and French who were working so hard to win their affection:

> No more Monsieur, no more Mister
> In heaven Allah, on earth Hitler.[70]

Later, when he was asked about this Arab abandonment of the Allies to whom they owed their independence, the Palestinian Arab leader Jamal al-Husseini replied, "I have read somewhere that it was a Jewish war anyway."[71]

The Jews of Palestine, on the other hand, formed a Jewish Brigade that fought with distinction under the British command, again confirming Meinertzhagen's prognosis. After the war, at a point when the fate of a hundred thousand Jews in the displaced persons camps hung in the balance, David Niles, one of President Harry Truman's closest advisers, used the fact of Palestinian Jewish support for the Allies as an argument to advocate Jewish immigration to Palestine:

> I am also inclined to think that 100,000 [more] Jews would be of great assistance to us in that area, as the Jews of Palestine were during the second World War, which is generally admitted by everybody who is familiar with the situation. The Allies got no help from the Arabs at all, but considerable help from the Jews in Palestine.[72]

Bartley Crum, a member of the committee investigating the situation of the refugees, echoed this sentiment:

[I]t should never be forgotten how the entire Jewish community of Palestine set aside its differences with Britain and gave its complete support to the defeat of the Nazis. . . . They wrote a glorious chapter which is yet to be told in full. In contrast the Arab community was largely indifferent to the war.[73]

But British Arabist policy drew no such lessons and never wavered from its course. Within a few years, every inch of the British Middle Eastern empire was lost, as the lands they had so carefully contrived to control had spun out of their grasp forever. Britain's policy of catering to Arab "sensibilities" had led to the loss of every toehold, every garrison, and every privilege it had had among the Arabs. All that remains of its presence today is a nostalgic attachment to British habits in Jordan and Oman.

Britain's policy of appeasing the Arabs at the expense of the Jews, which it pursued for three decades, gained it nothing and cost the Jews a great deal. But it had yet another pernicious result whose effects are very much alive today: the transmission of British policy preferences to almost every foreign ministry and foreign policy establishment in the world. Britain, after all, was the dominant international power between the two world wars, its diplomats venerated, its policies everywhere emulated.

Thus, the Arabist thinking of Richard Waters-Taylor and John Shuckburgh spread from the British Colonial and Foreign offices to the American State Department—especially after American companies developed huge petroleum reserves in Arabia in the 1930s. Reserves of oil in the Persian Gulf were being systematically uncovered during the first four decades of this century: in Iran (1908), Iraq (1923), Bahrain (1932), Saudi Arabia (1937), Kuwait (1938), and Qatar (1940). Although the cost of finding and developing this oil was substantial, the enormous size of the reserves and the high yield for each well drilled more than made up for the investment. The oil industry underwent a tremendous expansion during World War II and in its aftermath, as rapid industrialization in the West and elsewhere increased the worldwide demand for oil. By the early 1960s, Arab oil amounted to 60 percent of the world's proven oil reserves.

When the Arab oil-producing states imposed an oil embargo on the West in 1973, some people thought that the Arabs could control the world's energy supply forever, raising prices higher and higher. But it soon became clear that this was not the case when other, previously uncompetitive producers such as Norway and Britain came onto the market with the development of North Sea oil, as did suppliers of alternative energy such as natural gas. Further, the Western economies retooled their industries to become more energy efficient and produced vehicles that consumed considerably less fuel. As a result, by 1981, the real price of oil had fallen dramatically. To the surprise of many, it turned out that the oil market was just that—a market—and that not even the Arabs could corner it.

But back in the 1930s, none of this was known. (Even a half-century later, when it did become known, the psychological hold of Arab oil producers on the Western political psyche remained significant.) It is thus hardly surprising that the excitement of the first petroleum discoveries in Arabia led many American officials to be particularly considerate of Arab demands, including the demand to curtail Zionism. Indeed, the State Department quietly but consistently supported the Chamberlain White Paper and then the closing of Palestine to immigration during World War II,[74] and it continued to oppose the immigration of Jews to Palestine throughout the postwar period and up to the creation of the State of Israel. When President Harry Truman, against the opposition of virtually his entire administration, decided to support the Partition Plan creating a Jewish state, George Kennan, the head of the State Department planning staff, wrote that "U.S. prestige in the Muslim world has suffered a severe blow, and U.S. strategic interests in the Mediterranean and the Near East have been seriously prejudiced."[75] Truman later wrote that during the entire period, "the State Department continued to be more concerned about the Arab reaction than about the suffering of the Jews."[76]

This concern was promoted most forcefully by a coterie of Arabists who had entrenched themselves in the 1930s in the Near East and Asian Affairs Bureau of the State Department. Thus, while public opinion in the United States has traditionally supported the Jews and later Israel and is often unsympathetic or downright antagonistic to the Arabs (even after years of negative portrayal of Israel in the media), the American foreign policy elite often exhibited exactly the opposite attitude. In the corridors of the State Department, where plans are daily laid for the new world order that is heir to Britain's, the Arabist belief that wresting concessions from the Jews or forcing them to relinquish valuable assets will somehow win the favor and loyalty of the Arabs endures among many to this very day. And it is as shortsighted today as it was in the 1930s.

Nor has the influence of British Arabism in the United States and elsewhere been limited to the professional diplomats. In every capital there is a foreign policy establishment consisting of academics, politicians, and journalists who specialize in foreign affairs. Long before the gush of Arab oil wealth in the 1970s and the rapid expansion of Arab influence in the West that followed, most of these foreign policy establishments were already following their present pro-Arab courses. Half a century after the Jewish state was created, the notion still endures among Arabists that somehow Israel was conceived in geopolitical sin—that sin being, in Arabist eyes, that its very existence deprived the West of cherished Arab support.

It is hard to understand how tenaciously a very small but influential circle of diplomats still clings to this notion. They seldom voice it in public, and some may not even admit it to themselves, but a great many of them believe it nonetheless. This was brought home to me one afternoon in New York, on my last day as Israel's ambassador to the United Nations, when I was saying good-bye to several Western diplomats. One of them, an American with whom I had a cordial relationship, invited me for a drink. After several vodkas, he turned to me and said, "It's all a mistake." Knowing he was critical of many of Israel's policies, I asked which policy he was referring to. "No," he said, "not a policy. I'm saying the whole damned country is a mistake. We should have prevented it in the first place and saved everyone the trouble."

But after the Holocaust, not even the powerful Arabist establishments were able to prevent the reemergence of the popular sentiment that justice must be done with the Jews—that they must finally, after their incomparable suffering, be enabled to have a state of their own. By then, Arab pressure and Western complicity had reduced the territory originally promised to the Jews to a pittance, but to a brutalized people barely hanging on to life, even a pittance was better than nothing.

The Jews could wait no longer. At the end of World War II, the Jewish underground movements redoubled their campaign to break open the gates of Palestine to the survivors of the Holocaust and to oust the British administration. The campaign lasted several years, gathering momentum through concerted military actions of escalating boldness against the British Army in Palestine. These actions—led most prominently by Menachem Begin's Irgun (National Military Organization) and the Lehi (Fighters for the Freedom of Israel, of which Yitzhak Shamir was operations officer), and joined for a time by the Hagana (Defense Organization) under David Ben-Gurion—eroded and eventually broke the will of the British government to retain its hold on the country. The majority of these attacks were launched against the installations used by the British authorities to control the country. The targets included bridges (in one night in 1946, a Hagana-led operation blew up twelve critical bridges), railway lines, police stations, army bases, officers' clubs, military headquarters, and prisons in which jailed underground members were being held—including the Irgun-led breakout in 1947 of 251 inmates from the Acre prison fortress, previously thought to have been impregnable.* A few months later, when the British intended to hang a number of captured Irgun members, the Irgun warned that this would lead to the hanging of two captured British sergeants. Tragically, both acts took place. The unfolding of these events shocked public opinion in Britain and strengthened the hand of Churchill, who was by then in opposition, in demanding that Britain depart from Palestine.

The effect of the Jewish campaign on British rule in Palestine was decisive. The British Empire, tottering and drained of energy at the end of World War II, could not afford to keep an army of a hundred thousand men there. British public opinion demanded that the troops be brought home. In 1947, Britain finally declared its intention to evacuate, and it unceremoniously handed the decision as to what to do with the country to the United Nations.

Thus was born UN Partition Resolution 181 of November 29, 1947. Although it granted the Jews a mere 10 percent of Mandatory Palestine, with the rest going to the Arabs (see Map 5), this resolution at least reinstated the principle that the Jews must have an independent state. Not that it would amount to much, many of the professional Arabists believed. The consensus in the govern-

---

*These Jewish actions against British military targets were quickly branded by Britain as "terrorism." The Arabs have been only too happy in more recent times to try to taint the Jewish resistance with this same term, to justify by means of a supposed symmetry their own ruthless violence against Israel and others.

This effort at symmetry readily reduces the Jewish resistance to the false cliché that "one man's terrorist is another man's freedom fighter." But terrorism can be reasonably defined. It is the *deliberate and systematic* assault on civilians, on innocent noncombatants outside the sphere of legitimate warfare. One could argue that in the case of the Jewish underground organizations a few isolated incidents could possibly qualify under the definition of terrorism, but there can be no question that the many hundreds of operations carried out by these organizations were indeed concentrated on military rather than civilian targets (including the British military headquarters, then housed in the King David Hotel).

This is a far cry from the flood of unprovoked peacetime attacks on civilians that has characterized Arab terrorism over the past decades. In *thousands* of remorseless attacks, Arab terror organizations have deliberately and systematically sought out civilians as targets, attacking them in markets, airports, schools, universities, bus stops—even at the Olympic games, which had been declared off-limits to violence since ancient times. For a detailed discussion of the nature of terrorism, see Benjamin Netanyahu, ed., *International Terrorism: Challenge and Response* (New Brunswick: Transaction Books, 1980) and *Terrorism: How the West Can Win* (New York: Farrar, Straus and Giroux, 1986).

ing circles of the West, friendly and unfriendly alike, was that the pinhead-size state would instantly be overrun by the Arabs, and Western military strategists concurred. The international community could clear its conscience by according the Jews a gerrymandered state that was smaller in area than the Bahamas, and the combined might of the Arab armies would do the rest.

Nevertheless, the Jews of Palestine accepted the Partition Resolution. The Arab world unanimously and unequivocally rejected it and called for war. Arab irregulars began pouring into Palestine immediately after the UN vote, seeking to prevent the Jewish state from coming into existence, and they were followed within months by the regular armies of Egypt, Syria, Jordan, Iraq, and Lebanon. By the time the Jewish state was officially declared on May 14, 1948, upon the departure of the British, the War of Independence against the invading Arabs was already under way. The common belief was that it was only a matter of time before the Jewish state, hardly in its infancy, would be terminated.

Israel was coming into its War of Independence with severe handicaps imposed on it by the British. The British had reduced almost to nothing the territory accorded to the Jews and the number of Jews who were allowed to immigrate into it, then proceeded mercilessly to prevent the Jews from arming themselves while allowing progressively more substantial armament of the Arabs in Palestine (reinforced by troops crossing the border from neighboring Arab lands, whom the British seemed not to notice). The result was that Israel's ragtag forces were overwhelmingly outnumbered and outgunned, possessing virtually no tanks, no artillery, and no planes. As the Arab armies invaded, Israel's life hung in the balance. In those twenty horrible months of fighting, the carnage consumed six thousand Israelis, quite a few of them recent survivors of the Nazi death camps. (This is out of a population of 600,000 and is the proportional equivalent of 2.5 million Americans dying today.) By June, the Jews had come close to a state of complete exhaustion. Yet even on the brink of disaster, they somehow held on. Not fully realizing how weak Israel was, the Arabs agreed to a cease-fire. Israel used it to rearm and mustered its forces to roll back the Arab onslaught (see Map 6). The Jewish state was now a fact. It had come into the world after an agonizing labor. It would have no happy childhood, either, with frequent cross-border attacks by Arab marauders and daily promises from Egypt's President Nasser and other similarly disposed neighbors that Israel would shortly be "exterminated."

Yet, Arab bellicosity aside, the young state enjoyed a relatively hospitable international clime during its early years. In the first two decades of its life, the influence of professional Arabist hostility was tempered by the worldwide moral identification with Israel in the aftermath of the Holocaust and in the wake of the courage and tenacity shown by the Jews in their War of Independence. During this time, before Arab propaganda organized its later campaign and before the Arabists themselves could regroup, this innate sympathy produced enthusiastic support for the fledgling nation across Western Europe and North America. In Holland, France, Denmark, Italy, Britain, and above all in the United States, acclaim for Israel was acclaim for the good guy. As at Versailles, there was on this point not confusion but perfect clarity. But as the Holocaust and the miracle of Israel's birth receded from memory, so did the influence of this sympathy. (It resurged most forcefully in the days of siege before the Six Day War, then steadily declined in the aftermath of Israel's stunning victory, only to be rekindled during the Iraqi Scud attacks during the Gulf War, which briefly reminded the world who was the victim and who the aggressor.)

In the first half of this century, political anti-Zionism had been led by British imperial interest and aided by the Arabs. The second half of the century saw these roles reversed: The initiative now passed on to the Arabs themselves, who were aided by Western Arabists. The newly independent Arab states found themselves in control of modern presses, radio, and later television, as well as embassies and diplomatic services—and the enormous wealth to make use of all this. At first they showed little recognition of the power of these resources as international political weapons. Early

Arab propaganda against Israel was largely directed *inward,* with the aim of convincing the Arab populations themselves, rather than outward, toward Westerners. The newly installed Arab regimes had not yet mastered the art of propaganda; only later were they to begin couching their antagonism in more moderate and palatable phraseology. Thus, the bulk of Arab pronouncements came out sounding like King Saud of Saudi Arabia in this statement from 1954:

> Israel to the Arab world is like a cancer to the human body, and the only way of remedy is to uproot it just like a cancer. . . . Israel is a serious wound in the Arab world body, and we cannot endure the pain of this wound forever. We don't have the patience to see Israel occupying part of Palestine for long.
>
> We Arabs total about fifty million. Why don't we sacrifice 10 million of our number and live in pride and self respect?[77]

In this way, the Arab regimes were able to satisfy the need they felt to fire the passions of their own people and troops. Quite apart from their animus, Israel was a useful scapegoat on which they could pin all their failings and shortcomings. Still, these early efforts did little to rejuvenate the flagging forces of international anti-Zionism, since few people in the West could accept such stark language and the purposes evident behind it.

Thus, the respite in international public opinion that Israel enjoyed between 1948 and 1967 resulted from the combined effect of a basic Western sympathy for the Jewish state and Arab apathy toward Western audiences. The Arabists were still calling the tune in Washington, urging Eisenhower, for example, that Israel should trade the Negev (the southern half of the country) in exchange for peace.[78] But during those years there was little public sympathy for officials who had treated the Holocaust as "Zionist sobstuff."

This grace period came to an end after the Six Day War in 1967. As opposed to Western governments, Western public opinion has tended to support whomever it perceives as the underdog. For some Westerners, the Israeli victory in the Six Day War instantly transformed Israel from underdog to superdog in the space of the few days it took to win the war—a perception reinforced by the cockiness of some Israelis, who believed that single brilliant victory would end Israel's ongoing struggle to survive against a hostile Arab world of immense size and wealth. The Arabs soon exploited this reversal in public opinion, portraying Israel as a frightening power that preyed on its weaker Arab neighbors. Further, the fact that in the ensuing years Israel was militarily administering territories from which it had been attacked was soon stripped of that wartime context, and the unprovoked nature of the Arab attack was forgotten. The only thing that remained clearly fixed in public opinion was the fact that Israel was governing territories on which a substantial Arab population lived—or, as the parlance would soon have it, it was "occupying Arab land"—thereby removing the mantle of culpability from the shoulders of the Arabs and placing it on the Jewish state.

The Arabs exploited these propaganda benefits, but the results of the Six Day War nonetheless presented them with a difficult military obstacle to their designs on Israel. The Israeli victory pushed the border from the outskirts of Tel Aviv to the Jordan River, a few dozen miles to the east over a range of mountains, cliffs, and wadis. It became clear to the Arabs that Israel could no longer be crushed with one swift blow. If they were to excise Israel from their midst, they now realized, Israel would first have to be territorially reduced—to the starting conditions of the Six Day War.

The Arabs came to perceive that they could not achieve this goal militarily—that they could attain it only if the West, especially the United States, applied overwhelming political pressure on Israel. But in the wake of Israel's astounding victory in the Six Day War, a powerful sentiment was developing in the United States to form a political and military alliance with Israel as the new preeminent regional power. This sentiment was translated into a liberal infusion of military aid to Israel's army, making the Arabs' job of overcoming Israel still more difficult. The shrewder political minds among the Arabs, however, slowly parted from the view of America as irreversibly committed to supporting Israel and came to see the usefulness of cultivating the old Arabist lines of argumentation, albeit suitably adapted to a more contemporary Western audience. Moreover, they grew to appreciate the decisive role that Western public opinion played in making and maintaining policy—a public opinion that had been none too keen on the Arab cause up until then. Hence the principal effort of the ongoing Arab war against Israel since 1967 has been to defeat Israel on the battlefields of public opinion: in the media, in university lecture halls, and in the citadels of government.

In order to capture the sympathy of the Western public, its beliefs concerning the history, causes, and nature of the Arab-Israeli conflict had to be revised. No Westerner was interested in hearing that the Jewish state was a "cancer" that had to be "uprooted." A new history had to posit plausible explanations for the relentless Arab campaign against Israel, along with reasons for the West to abandon its support for the Jewish state. The core of the new history had to be the critique of the birth of Israel itself in moral terms comprehensible to Westerners. For if the very creation of the Jewish state could be presented as a moral error, a vehicle not of justice but injustice, as the British Arabists had claimed it was, then the West could become sympathetic to efforts to redress the "injustice" that had been committed.

In this, the Arabs found that all the foundations had already been laid. The British Arabists had already spent decades injecting the West with the idea that Jewish immigration to Palestine was based upon a moral mistake; that such immigration had "caused" Arab violence against the Jews (rather than the Arabs causing it themselves); and that the presence of the Jewish home in the Middle East would compel the Arabs to unite against the West, gravely harming Western interests. After 1967, the Arabs gave new life to all these arguments, parading them before the West to explain international Arab terrorism, Arab fulminations at the UN, and the

Arab oil embargo of 1973. By the early 1970s, all eyes (and cameras) were turned to the Arab governments, as they rehearsed for a world audience the themes that the British colonialists had invented in the 1920s.

In the court of public opinion, as in any court, the question of who attacked whom—who initiated an assault and who acted in self-defense—is central to the verdict. The Arab states embarked on an unprecedented campaign to persuade the West that it was not they, the Arabs, who had attacked Israel, but Israel that had attacked them. Thus, the *results* of their own aggression against Israel—the bloodshed, the refugees, the capture of Arab-controlled land—were instead presented as its *causes*. These were now deemed unprovoked evils that had been perpetrated by the Jews, grievances that the Arabs were now merely and innocently trying to redress. It was not the Arabs who were the guilty party, but Israel that had fended off their attacks. (See Chapter 4, "Reversal of Causality.")

Still, the task of the Arabs was far more difficult than that of their Arabist predecessors had been. The British Arabists had had only to convert the Colonial and Foreign offices to their views in order to bring the absolute authority of the Mandatory government and the British Army to bear against Zionism. But to create American opposition to an independent State of Israel that had many friends and admirers in Washington would require a much more sweeping, much more comprehensive campaign of disinformation than had ever been conceived by the British anti-Zionists. It would entail the fabrication of ancient historical rights to nullify those of the Jews; the obliteration from memory of Versailles, the League of Nations, and the Balfour Declaration; and a complete revision and rewriting of the Arab wars against the Jews following the establishment of Israel.

Before a lie of such incredible proportions could hope to make any headway against the common sense of the common man in the west or of his government, the ground would have to be prepared by means of a direct assault on Zionism itself as a moral movement, as a movement seeking justice. The Arabs aimed to render the rest of their arguments plausible by building their house of canards on the bedrock of Israel's *inherent* immorality: The post-Holocaust-era view of the Zionist as the good guy had to be forcibly brought to an end.

For this ambitious undertaking, the Arabs attacked Israel through every channel, at every gathering, from every platform. But none of these forums proved to be as effective as the most powerful of instruments available to the Arabs, an instrument of universal reach and appeal that at the time enjoyed not only respectability but reverence, and that therefore was trusted by many around the world—the United Nations.

And at the UN, as elsewhere, the Arabs also found a new ally. The British Empire had capsized, but a new empire had arisen that quickly replaced the British as the patron of Pan-Arab aspirations. Cultivating Gamal Abdel Nasser's Egypt and a string of other despotisms, the Soviet Union, much like the British Arabists before it, came to see Israel as a challenge to its imperialist ambitions in the Middle East and in the eastern Mediterranean. The Soviets were accomplished masters of propaganda, who had taught expressions such as "peace-loving" and "self-determination" to every anti-Western terror organization in the world. And it was the Soviets who hit upon the precise formulation that the Arabs needed to stab at the heart of Israel's moral standing in the West.

In Mexico City in 1975, the Soviet and Arab blocs took over a United Nations Conference on Women and forced it to adopt one of the great slanders of all time. They then brought this resolution to an obedient UN General Assembly, which confirmed it. They achieved this aim by means of political and economic intimidation. At the time, the Arab oil blackmail was at its height, and it seemed that nothing could stand in its way. Many countries that should have known better, that *did* know better, nevertheless succumbed.

Thus in November 1975, a mere eight years after their great defeat in the Six Day War, the Arabs achieved their greatest victory on the field of propaganda: The General Assembly of the United Nations, by a vote of 72 to 35, with 32 abstentions, resolved that Zionism, the national movement of the Jewish people, constituted "racism."

Such an achievement had eluded even the great anti-Semitic propagandists of our millennium like Torquemada and Joseph Goebbels. For what they and their disciples had failed to do in the Inquisition and in the Holocaust had at long last been achieved by the General Assembly of the United Nations. Never before had anti-Semitism acquired a tool of such *universal* dissemination as the UN. Never before had any of the slander of the Jewish people, of which there had been so many, been promulgated and applauded by an organization that purported to represent humankind.

The Arabs knew that Israel's strength was not rooted in its numbers, its size, or its resources. In all these areas the Arabs were far stronger. Israel's greatest shield, they understood, was its moral stature. They therefore sought to tarnish that shield, to crack it, and ultimately to crush it. Their weapon was an extraordinary vilification of a movement that had inspired millions. For Zionism is a unique moral phenomenon that has won the support of many people of goodwill around the world. The Jewish people had suffered degradation, humiliation, oppression, and mutilation like no other. But the Jewish legacy is one of the principal founts of Western civilization, contributing above all to advancing the concepts of freedom and justice. The Zionist movement had come into being to seek for its own people freedom and justice. After two millennia of bondage, the Jewish people was entitled to its own liberation as an independent nation.

This is the true and only meaning of Zionism. At the close of World War I, and again after World War II, it had been so understood not only by the Jewish people but by virtually the entire world. Many nations and peoples had admired the tenacity, courage, and moral strength of the Zionist movement. They had marveled at Israel's achievement in rebuilding a modern state on the ruins of an ancient homeland. They had applauded the ingathering of the exiles from a hundred lands and the seemingly miraculous revival of an ancient tongue. And they had thrilled at Israel's ability to maintain its democratic and human ethic in the face of one of the most remorseless campaigns of hatred in history. All this had been appreciated by people not only in Europe and America but in Africa and elsewhere in the developing world, where Israel and Zionism had served as a shining example of the independence and progress that so many other nations, coming out from under the heel of empire, hoped to achieve.

These realities were not lost on the Arab regimes or on the Soviets. Indeed, their attack on Israel was not driven by political interest alone. Deep down, they experienced an unforgiving resentment. For nothing so effectively unmasks dictators and despots who hide behind the rhetoric of "liberation" and "self-determination" as a genuine movement of national liberation. Israel and Zionism, by their very existence, exposed the claims of the tyrants and totalitarians for the sham that they are.

But the sham was particularly preposterous in labeling so completely color-blind a movement racist. Theodor Herzl, the founder of modern Zionism, had himself declared the plight of blacks to be a cause of fundamental concern to him, like that of the Jews:

> There is still one problem of racial misfortune unresolved. The depths of that problem, in all their horror, only a Jew can fathom. . . . I mean the Negro problem. Think of the hair-raising horrors of the slave trade. Human beings, because their skins are black, are stolen, carried off, and sold. . . . Now that I have lived to see the restoration of the Jews, I should like to pave the way for the restoration of the Negroes.[79]

Almost a century later, Israel's rescue of Ethiopia's Jews showed Zionism to be the only movement in history to transport blacks out of Africa not to enslave them but to liberate them.

In 1985, on the tenth anniversary of the adoption of the resolution defaming Zionism, I organized a symposium on the United Nations premises to attack this infamy. The Arab states and the PLO were especially irked by this affront (how dared we convene a conference on "their" ground?), and they tried unsuccessfully to block it. But what irritated them even more was that one of the speakers, Rahamin Elazar, was an Ethiopian Jew. He described in moving terms his own personal salvation in coming to Israel. Since then, tens of thousands of members of his community have followed in their great exodus from Ethiopia. An accusation of racism against the Zionists by the Arab world—whose contemporary customs include the keeping of indentured black servants in the Gulf states and a prolific history of trading along the slave coast of Africa, as well as the repeated massacres of blacks by the Sudanese Arabs—should have been received like a witless joke.

It wasn't. The combined power of the Arab and Soviet blocs gave them complete control of the UN, its microphones, and its printing presses. To be sure, even without the campaign against Israel, one would have been hard pressed to consider the UN General Assembly a pure arbiter of moral truth. Indeed, what can be said of an institution that failed to curb in even the slightest way the Soviet aggression in Afghanistan, a war that claimed a million lives and turned five million people into refugees; that for seven years did not lift a finger to stop the sickening carnage of the Iran-Iraq War, in which another million perished; that did not even address, much less remedy, such outrages as the genocide in Cambodia, the horrific slaughter of the Ibo in Biafra, and the massacre of hundreds of thousands of civilians in Uganda under Idi Amin, all in flagrant violation of the UN's own Universal Declaration of Human Rights?[80]

Yet despite all these and other enormous affronts to conscience, nothing injected such calumny into the arteries of international opinion as the Zionism-racism resolution did against Israel. It may be tempting to dismiss this resolution as a meaningless absurdity, especially after its belated renunciation in December 1991.[81] But that would be a mistake. We must remember that the Arabs had a full sixteen years to drive home their racism message, and that even after its formal renunciation, this defamation lives on in the minds of many nations and their leaders. I stress again that, for the first time in history, a world body had given its stamp of approval to the libeling of an entire people. In the very century of the Holocaust, one must not forget the insidious power of uninhibited libel. Without the torrents of slander poured on the Jews by the Nazis, the Holocaust would never have been possible. Had the Nazis not succeeded in brainwashing Germans and non-Germans alike into believing that the Jews were reprehensible, subhuman, and in fact a different species, they would not have secured the collaboration of thousands upon thousands of ordinary people in moving the machinery of genocide.

We know that in the two or three European countries where such collaboration did not take place the majority of Jews were saved. Well known is the example of Denmark, in which the king himself declared that if any of his subjects wore the yellow badge, then he too would wear it; Denmark's Jews were successfully smuggled to safety in Sweden. Less well known but equally dramatic is the case of Bulgaria, where the entire educated elite of the country opposed the implementation of official anti-Semitism. Thus, the Union of Bulgarian Lawyers and the Union of Writers respectively denounced the German-imposed anti-Jewish legislation as "socially damaging" and "very harmful." The head of the Bulgarian Orthodox Church described the directives as "thunder from a clear sky." A German report attributed Bulgarian disobedience of these laws to the "inactivity of the police and the complete indifference of the majority of the Bulgarian people." Particularly telling is the explanation that the German ambassador in Sofia offered to his superiors in Berlin: He told them that the "Bulgarian public lacks the understanding of the Jewish question in historical terms." This failure of understanding was in fact directly due to the stubborn refusal of the country's leadership—writers, clergy, teachers, politicians—to spread the Nazi slander, as a consequence of which Bulgarian Jewry was saved.[82]

In other words, libel is the prelude to murder. It is a license to kill. The libeling of an entire people separates that people from the rest of humanity, making the lives of its members dispensable, its oppressors and murderers immune to blame.

Appearances notwithstanding, the libel of "Zionism equals racism" is the very same libel that was preached by the Nazis. It is the same anti-Semitism dressed up in trendy terminology. For the bitter truth is that the horrors of the Holocaust did not make anti-Semitism unfashionable; they only made some of the old terminology embarrassing. *Zionism* and *Zionist* now serve as euphemisms for *Judaism* and *Jew*. And since there is no worse epithet in today's lexicon than *racist*, it is the term that is used to replace the whole range of old-fashioned invective. It is the contemporary equivalent of *Christ-killer, traitor, usurer, international conspirator*. All this has stolen into vogue under the sham disclaimer of "I'm not anti-Semitic, I'm just anti-Zionist"—the equivalent of "I'm not anti-American, I just think the United States shouldn't exist."

Building on the Zionism-racism resolution, the Arab propaganda machine has now been at work for a quarter of a century, ever since the Six Day War, spinning a web of falsehoods that have permeated every issue and colored every opinion on the subject of Israel. Even now, with the resolution overturned, the spires of untruth that it erected and buttressed remain standing, having taken on a terrible life of their own. So successful has been the demonization of the Jewish state that many people are willing to overlook the most heinous crimes, to pardon virtually any excess on the part of the Arabs, since, after all, one has to take into account their "plight" and "all they have suffered." Just as they had planned, the Arabs have succeeded in foisting their historical fabrications into the media and from there onto the world public and its representatives everywhere. With this, the Arabs have achieved an astonishing transformation, making themselves over into the aggrieved party demanding justice, and Israel into an "entity"—unnatural, alien, immoral—capable of virtually no right because its very existence is itself an irredeemable wrong.

Thus it is that Zionism, once considered a noble and legitimate national movement worthy of broad international support during the establishment of the new world order at the opening of the twentieth century, is itself the odd man out at the initiation of the new world order at the close of the century. Israel is the only nation on the face of the globe that important sections of opinion consider to be *guilty* for being a nation—wrong for claiming its homeland as its own, culpable for building its homes, schools, and factories on this land, and unjust for trying to defend itself against enemies who wish its destruction. This is the view that the British colonialists fashioned for their own purposes, but today it has been accepted as truth by many who have no conception of where these ideas came from—or where they might lead.

Of course, there are many people who argue that they have not given up on the basic promise that was made at Versailles to the Jews. After all, they say, we have no desire to see Israel destroyed—we are only looking for balance between Israel and the Arabs. But this position obscures what is in fact an astonishing disregard for the most basic demands of Israel's survival. Hence many in the United States, which measures its strategic depth in terms of *thousands* of miles, chastise Israel for its insistence on having a few *tens* of miles of strategic depth. Hence while Western leaders constantly blare warnings that Israel must seek peace, they allow their arms dealers to sell the Arab states almost *twenty times* the weaponry they sell Israel, including the pick of the most advanced systems in their arsenals. Hence some European countries provide the means to produce even *nuclear* weapons clearly aimed at Israel's destruction to the most fanatical of its enemies, then condemn Israel for acting against the menace. Hence important political figures, knowing full well that without immigration Israel's position is precarious at best, are cynically willing to impede or endanger the movement of Jewish refugees to Israel, for the dubious end of ingratiating themselves with the Arabs.

True, the betrayal of Zionism by the West cannot today be found in explicit calls for an end to the Jewish state. Rather, the betrayal is found in the nonchalance with which virtually the entire Western world demands that Israeli governments accept risks that no elected official in any Western state would ever willingly accept for his own country. It is found in the insistence, backed up by increasingly militant political and economic coercion, that Israel is an aggressor when it behaves like any other nation, and is righteous only when it passively sits by and waits for the next blow to land. This creeping annulment of Israel's right to self-defense constitutes a continual erosion of the promise of Versailles. For once a nation no longer has the *means* to freely defend its existence, its very *right* to exist is put into question. A right that cannot be defended is eventually rendered meaningless.

As we have seen, the extraordinary constriction of the support for Zionism's geographic and demographic needs has largely been the result of a systematic campaign, originating with Western anti-Zionists in the first half of the century and led by the Arab world in the second half, aimed at undermining belief in the justice of Israel's cause. This campaign could not have achieved such dramatic results without synchronizing its message with an appeal to Western self-interest. The argument that wringing concessions from Israel is in the West's interests, and particularly America's, is identical to that which was presented to the British during the 1920s and 1930s—and that led them to try to prevent the development of the Jewish state by force of arms. It took a mere twenty years for Britain to be transformed from the sincere protector of the Jews and the guarantor of their national restoration to one of the principal opponents of the restoration, abandoning the Jewish nation at the brink of annihilation. The engine for this transformation was the idea that it was in the interest of Britain to concede to the demands of the Arabs in their hatred of the Jewish nation. Like the British, who were told that they would earn the gratitude of the Arabs if only they would prevent the immigration of the Jews to Palestine, America is now told that it will earn that same gratitude if only it will force Israel to give up the West Bank and curb immigration—steps that would purportedly cure all the problems of the Middle East, thereby stabilizing world peace and assuring the flow of oil. In the next chapter I will examine how this exceptionally implausible claim has been rendered plausible.

3

THE THEORY OF PALESTINIAN CENTRALITY

The first casualties of the 1991 Persian Gulf War were not people but cows. For years, opponents of Israel had tended and nurtured a herd of sacred cows, unchallengeable axioms that had come to constitute the basis for a false and misleading—but very widely held—conception of the nature of the Middle East and Israel's role in it. Only the harsh reality of Iraqi armor grinding over a defenseless Arab state was finally able to drive some of these creatures from the field of rational discourse.

First among the sacred cows to be crippled in the Iraqi onslaught was the belief that all the turbulence in the Middle East was somehow the consequence of what had come to be known as the "Palestinian Problem." Before Iraq invaded Kuwait, this untouchable assumption had been the linchpin of nearly all analyses of the region's problems, as well as of proposals for resolving them. For years, not a day had passed without a spokesman for some Arab nation or organization declaring that the "core" or "root" or "heart" or "underlying cause" of the Middle East conflict was the Palestinian Problem. Those who made such pronouncements were always careful to refer to "*the* conflict"—in the singular—as though life in the Middle East would have been idyllic were it not for this solitary, frustrating sticking point. Consequently, the impression relentlessly presented to the media and the world was that all one had to do was to solve that Palestinian Problem, and there would be peace in the Middle East.

The proponents of this account of the endless turmoil in the region were by no means only the representatives of the Arab regimes. The choir chanting the monotonous tones of the Theory of Palestinian Centrality included numerous Third World governments, in addition to the leadership of the then-still-vibrant Soviet bloc. With the help of the United Nations, this theory was ceaselessly proclaimed and endlessly elaborated.

Nor did it take long for Westerners to join the chorus. At nearly all the diplomatic functions I can remember, from the day I first came to Washington as deputy chief of the Israeli mission in 1982 right up to the day of the invasion of Kuwait, Western diplomats of all ranks and extractions would solemnly point out that peace would not be achieved in the Middle East as long as the Palestinian Problem was not resolved. And each one of them was utterly convinced that this was so "because, after all, it is the core of the conflict in the region." Thus, what had started out two decades earlier as a transparent slogan of Arab propaganda had assumed, through constant embellishment, a patina of self-evident truth—and had been accepted as such by many of the men and women responsible for the safety and governance of our world.

Then, in August 1990, came Iraq's invasion of Kuwait. It is difficult to appreciate the astonishment with which the international community received this unexpected event. For here was one Arab country (Iraq) invading a second Arab country (Kuwait) and threatening still other Arab countries (Saudi Arabia and the Gulf states)—all with no discernible connection to the Palestinian Problem, nor to anything else that was directly or indirectly attributable to Israel. Worse, a few months later, Saddam Hussein began to launch daily Scud missile attacks on Israel, even though he knew full well that some of the Scuds might undershoot Israel's cities and instead hit the Palestinian areas in the territories (which some of them actually did). When Saddam was asked how he could possibly justify such callous disregard for the very people whose champion he was supposed to be, he replied that he did not concern himself "with sorting beans."

The true nature of Saddam Hussein and his regime came as a genuine shock to countless well-meaning officials the world over, including many who count themselves friends of Israel. After all, during the preceding decade, Saddam had been regarded not merely as unthreatening but as a *friend* of the West and the Gulf states, and he had been wined, dined, and fed extraordinary quantities of assistance and armaments based on this premise. During the Iran-Iraq War, numerous op-ed pieces in the American press by so-called experts on the Middle East advocated a "tilt toward Iraq" as serving the best interests of the United States. So when Western leaders finally realized that Saddam hadn't been named the Butcher of Baghdad by his own people for nothing, it came not as an insight but as a revelation.

Still, one cannot help but feel amazed at the amazement that then prevailed in political circles in the West. After all, one did not have to wait for the destruction of Kuwait to realize that the Middle East is rife with wars that are utterly unconnected to the Palestinian Arabs. Barely a year before the invasion of Kuwait, Iraq itself had emerged from a nine-year crusade against neighboring Iran, a devastating conflict that had claimed well over a million lives and demolished vast sections of both countries. And even the most cursory survey of the region would have readily revealed that such bellicosity had never been confined solely to Iraq. Ever since independent Arab states emerged in the first half of this century, virtually every one of them had been involved in wars, attempts at subversion and assassination, and unending intrigue against one or more of its Arab neighbors—and against its non-Arab neighbors, too.

In North Africa, for example, Libya has clashed with Tunisia and bombed the Sudan, and in 1977 it narrowly avoided a war over the penetration of Libyan tanks into Egyptian territory.

(These are all countries that Qaddafi has wished to persuade to "merge" with his.) Declaring its support for various "liberation movements" as part of Muammar Qaddafi's "Third Universal Theory," Libya has financed numerous efforts to topple other Arab regimes or assassinate their leaders, including those of Egypt, Iraq, Morocco, Sudan, Tunisia, and Somalia. It has also announced a campaign to liquidate Libyan exiles in the West. Similarly, Egypt under Nasser tried to assassinate the leaders of Jordan, Lebanon, and Iraq. In 1958 Egypt attempted to impose its regime on Syria, and in 1962 it began a brutal occupation of the nation of Yemen that sputtered on in various forms for half a decade. In the meantime, for years Algeria coveted the Colomb-Bechar and Tindouf regions claimed by Morocco. It clashed with Moroccan troops along the border and finally went to war with that country in 1963. Since 1975, Algeria has channeled its antagonism toward Morocco into a relentless war in the Western Sahara, which it pursued through its Polisario proxies.[1]

No more pacific has been life on the Arabian Peninsula, where until recently South Yemen regularly launched subversive forces into the Dhofar in an attempt to tear this region away from Oman. North Yemen and South Yemen have each viewed the other as an integral part of its own territory, actively promoting subversion and intrigue against each other. Hostilities erupted into border incursions and armed conflict in 1972 and again in 1979, after the President of North Yemen was killed by an envoy from South Yemen carrying a booby-trapped briefcase.[2] In 1991, a union of the two was once again attempted, and it remains an uneasy one. When they had not been fighting with each other, both Yemens lived in constant fear of Saudi Arabia, which under its founder Ibn Saud raided not only the territory of Yemen but those of Oman, Kuwait, and the other Gulf emirates, as well as Iraq and Jordan.[3] More recently, Yemen had to contend with absorbing the hundreds of thousands of former Yemenis who had been forcibly expelled by the Saudi regime, which in turn feared Yemeni subversion during the Gulf War.[4]

The fact that Kuwait had fretted for years over Saudi encroachment on its territory, even though it was Iraq that had actually invaded the country in 1973, is especially worth contemplating. Only the *second* Iraqi invasion of 1990 seems to have stilled Kuwait's fear of Saudi Arabia, at least for the moment. But Iraq itself had racked up an impressive record of aggression long before it attacked Kuwait. For years, it had carried out an energetic campaign of subversion and terrorism against a number of Arab states, including its traditional enemy, Syria, and its western neighbor, Jordan. Hostilities with Syria reached a peak in 1976, when Iraq closed an oil pipeline through Syria, leading Syria to completely seal its border with Iraq for two years. Iraqi efforts to depose the Syrian government continued throughout the Iran-Iraq War because of Syrian support for the Ayatollah Khomeini.[5]

Syria, too, qualifies as a predator of considerable standing. It has repeatedly threatened Jordan, murdered its diplomats, set off bombs in Amman, and even invaded Jordanian territory. It has vilified its fellow Ba'thists in Iraq and openly and tirelessly worked to overthrow the regime in Baghdad, its main rival for control of the Euphrates River basin and therefore of crucial parts of "Greater Syria." Similarly, the reason for Syria's ongoing and brutal occupation of almost all of Lebanon is neither to topple a regime that has already been vassalized, nor to change a border that it treats as meaningless, but to swallow the country whole. These designs go at least as far back as 1946, when both countries gained independence; even at the time, Syria refused to accept the existence of a separate state in Lebanon or extend it diplomatic recognition, a policy that has endured to this day. Since the early 1970s, Syria has declared Lebanon to be part of its "strategic defense sphere," and it has flooded the country with its troops. In pursuit of a thorough Syrianization of Lebanon, the Assad regime, with impeccable impartiality, has slaughtered any Lebanese who thought to oppose it—whether Christians, Moslems, or Druze. To justify this conquest, Syria has always maintained that its forces in Lebanon are a "peace-keeping" force mandated by the Arab league (and "invited" into the country in 1976 by a desperate Lebanese government), and that only an all-Arab directive could terminate its mission.[6] Finally, in 1991, with all eyes on the crisis in the Persian Gulf, Syria did to Lebanon what Iraq had failed to do to Kuwait. It devoured its neighbor outright, then asserted legitimacy for its action with a fake Syrian-Lebanese amicability treaty.

Just as Syrian regimes have always claimed Lebanon to be an integral part of Syria, so too have they always asserted that Palestine is part of Syria. Anyone who has any doubts as to what kind of relationship would exist between Syria and a Palestinian Arab state, should one ever come into existence, ought to consider what Syrian president Hafez Assad once told PLO leader Yasser Arafat:

> You do not represent Palestine as much as we do. Never forget this one point: There is no such thing as a Palestinian people, there is no Palestinian entity, there is only Syria. You are an integral part of the Syrian people, Palestine is an integral part of Syria. Therefore it is we, the Syrian authorities, who are the true representatives of the Palestinian people.[7]

Indeed, Syria savaged Arafat's PLO in Lebanon in 1976, and in 1983 it backed a successful military effort by pro-Syrian Palestinians to expel the PLO from Tripoli in northern Lebanon.

With such a record of chronic aggression against their brothers, it can hardly come as a surprise that Arab regimes have also created problems for their non-Arab neighbors. Libya, for example, conquered a large part of the country of Chad, sent a suitcase full of explosives to its cabinet, and even succeeded in installing a puppet regime in the capital, until it was pushed out of Chad following the American raid on Tripoli in 1986. Qaddafi has trained special units to bring down black African governments and has been implicated in plots as far afield as Senegal.[8] As the Egyptian government has testified, he has been engaged in conspiracy on a global scale, commissioning the assassination not only of fellow

Arab rulers in Saudi Arabia, Kuwait, and the United Arab Emirates but also of such non-Arab leaders as Margaret Thatcher, François Mitterand, Helmut Kohl, and Zia al-Haq of Pakistan.

Like that of Libya, Syria's appetite does not limit itself to Arab prey. Syria claims for its own, for example, the region and city of Alexandretta in Turkey. The dispute was supposedly settled in 1939, but official Syrian maps continue to include Alexandretta within Syrian territory, and the government has on occasion assured the press that it fully intends to regain this land.[9] The Syrians have supported both Kurdish and Armenian rebel groups in Turkey, providing them with training and money and helping them infiltrate the country.

The Gulf War made Iraq the Arab regime best known for its aggressiveness. Yet a full decade before the Gulf War, Saddam had sought to move on Kuwait. He amassed troops on its borders, rekindled Iraq's alleged historical claims to the country, and proceeded to fabricate border provocations in preparation for an invasion. But then Saddam's attention was suddenly drawn to what he thought were better pickings: postrevolutionary Iran, which he perceived as weak and ripe for plunder after the collapse of the Shah. Saddam swiftly renounced the border agreement he had signed five years earlier with the Shah and seized the disputed Shatt al-Arab waterway, which abuts Iran's oil-rich provinces. The result was the Iran-Iraq War, which raged nearly a decade during which chemical weapons and poison gas were used and civilian populations were targeted, exacting a toll in lives horrific even by the standards of this century's bloody wars.[10]

Nor is the violence in the Middle East limited to aggression *across* borders. Many Arab regimes are also ready practitioners of violence against the citizens of their own countries, relying on force and the threat of even greater brutality in order to stay in power. This habitual willingness to resort to violence against their own citizens is a feature of most governments throughout the Arab world. Not surprisingly, many of them are military dictatorships. Thus, Libya is ruled by a colonel and a small clique of officers, as Algeria was for many years. In Saudi Arabia, not one but *two* armies (they watch each other) protect the princes from their own subjects. In Syria, an officer corps dominated by the minority Alawite sect suppresses dissent with the assistance of no fewer than five independent intelligence organizations (which also watch one another). To such a regime, not even the slaughter of a significant part of the population of an entire Syrian city is too great a price to pay for staying in power—as Assad demonstrated in 1982, when his tanks ringed the city of Hama, thought to be sympathetic to the Moslem Brotherhood, and leveled the city center, killing an estimated 10,000 to 20,000 civilians.[11]

It is little consolation that most of the movements for "democracy" in the Arab world, such as in Algeria and Jordan, are dominated by Moslem fundamentalists seeking not to break down and distribute the government's absolute monopoly of power but to transfer that power—to themselves. With opponents such as these, it is difficult to judge which is more oppressive, the people's current rulers or their would-be liberators. The difficulty is greatest in Lebanon, where a kaleidoscope of armed gangs of various persuasions have for two decades competed for the right to brutalize the country. This nightmare out of Hobbes has finally been ended only through the imposition of an even more ruthless Pax Syriana—a "peace" extorted through the application of limitless fear. Remove the Syrian boot, and the internecine violence will be unleashed again.

Like Arab aggression across borders, domestic violence within the Arab states is also applied to non-Arabs. A powerful Arab nationalism regards the area from Morocco to the Persian Gulf as belonging exclusively to Arabs, despite the presence of numerous other peoples and religious minorities throughout the area—Berbers, Kurds, Copts and other Christian denominations, Druze, Jews, Circassians, Assyrians, blacks, and others—constituting a substantial proportion of the overall population. And while the presence of these non-Arab or non-Moslem peoples is usually tolerated by Arab governments, they are accepted only in a state of subjugation, never as equals. Those who have refused to agree to this arrangement have been suppressed, often mercilessly.

In 1933, the Iraqi authorities massacred the ancient Assyrian Christian community and incited the Arab population to murder and plunder the survivors. Thousands fled the country.[12] On December 15, 1945, the Kurds of Iraq declared an independent republic that was immediately aborted by the Iraqi army.[13] The Kurdish quest for independence began anew in 1961 and was savagely suppressed. Tens of thousands of Kurds were killed and 200,000 were left homeless, but this was not the end of Kurdish suffering. In the 1970s, Saddam drove another 200,000 Kurdish refugees into Iran.[14] Hundreds of thousands more have been forcibly resettled in barren regions outside their homeland, a method perfected by Saddam's precursor and hero Nebuchadnezzar as a means of destroying peoples. (Saddam likes to have his bust juxtaposed with that of the famous Babylonian conqueror.) The Kurds were promised at Versailles that they would at least be granted autonomy, but Kurdistan was subsequently incorporated into Arab Iraq because of Britain's desire to maintain control over the oil of the Kurdish region of Mosul. The continued absence of any international interest in keeping the Versailles promise has given Saddam free rein in his efforts to "Arabize" the Kurdish areas. Still, Kurdish attempts to achieve independence continue to this day. One recent attempt was crushed by Iraq after it lost the Gulf War.

Other minorities have not fared much better. Syria massacred its Christian community in the 1920s and drove tens of thousands of Armenians out of Syria after World War II. Under the Syro-French agreement of 1936 the Druze were promised autonomy in the Jebel Druze (Mount Druze) region of Syria, where they constitute a majority, but their efforts to assert this autonomy have likewise been ruthlessly crushed.[15] Nasser's Egypt expelled its Greek Christian community in the 1950s and continued to encourage public violence against the Coptic Christian community for years thereafter. Even more tragic has been the fate of the

Christian blacks in the southern part of the Sudan. Sudan's Arab government has waged a series of campaigns of forced conversion, starvation, and chattel enslavement against them since 1956. Conservative estimates put the number killed during the height of this campaign in the 1970s at 500,000, but other sources say the toll is actually in the millions. Hundreds of thousands have fled to neighboring countries, despite efforts by the Arabs to trap them in the Sudan.

Thus, the penchant for violence of many Arab rulers has led to the continual prosecution of wars against Arabs and non-Arabs abroad, and the continual persecution of Arabs and non-Arabs at home. With such a record, it is hardly a surprise that these rulers have been paid back with a fusillade of assassination efforts, a considerable number of them successful. Listed chronologically, this gallery of victims is a who's who of leaders in the Arab world, as one can see from the table below.

Partial Chronology of Arab Violence Against Arab Rulers

1949   President Zaim of Syria is executed by a military court after being overthrown by a pro-Hashemite coup.

1951   King Abdullah of Jordan is assassinated by agents of the Mufti for holding secret talks with Israel.

1958   King Feisal of Iraq is murdered, along with the regent, Nuri Said, during the revolution that ends the monarchy in Iraq.

1960   Prime Minister Majali of Jordan is killed by Egyptian agents in an attempt on the life of King Hussein.

1963   President Qassem of Iraq is murdered by the cabal of Ba'th activists and nationalist officers that topples his regime.

1964   President Shishakli of Syria is assassinated by a Druze in revenge for the bombing of Jebel Druze during his rule.

1967   President Boumedienne of Algeria barely survives an attempt by military officers to overthrow his regime.

1971   Prime Minister Wasfi al-Tal of Jordan is assassinated in Cairo in November 1971 by the PLO in revenge for the massacre of Palestinian Arabs in Jordan a year earlier.

1972   King Hassan of Morocco escapes the aerial bombing of his royal palace by renegade fighter planes of the Moroccan Air Force.

1975   King Feisal of Saudi Arabia is assassinated by his nephew, who is then executed for the murder.

1977   President Hamdi of North Yemen is assassinated, probably by a pro-Saudi group.

1978   President Ghashmi of North Yemen is killed by an envoy from South Yemen carrying a booby-trapped briefcase.

1981   President Sadat of Egypt is murdered by Islamic fundamentalists during a parade marking the anniversary of the Yom Kippur War.

1982   President Bashir Gemayel of Lebanon is killed in the bombing of the Christian Phalanges headquarters in Beirut.

1984   Colonel Qaddafi of Libya is attacked in his residence in Tripoli by the National Front for the Salvation of Libya.

1985   President Numeiri of the Sudan manages to escape with his life from the coup that ousts him from power.

1987   Prime Minister Rashid Karameh of Lebanon dies when his helicopter is blown up in mid-air.

1989   President Renee Mouwad of Lebanon is killed by a car bomb just a few days after taking office.

1992   President Boudiaf of Algeria is assassinated by an Islamic extremist, four months after his imposition of martial law to prevent an Islamic takeover of the country.

1995   Egyptian President Hosni Mubarak's motorcade is attacked shortly after his arrival in the Ethiopian capital, Addis Ababa. Mubarak escapes unharmed.

1995   Crown Prince Hamad bin Khlifa Al Thani of Qatar ousts
         his father, Emir Khalifa bin Hamad Al Thani, in a
         bloodless coup and assumes power.
1996   Iraqi president Saddam Hussein's son Uday is wounded
         in a drive-by shooting by unknown assailants.
1998   Colonel Qaddafi of Libya is reportedly injured in an
         assassination attempt near Benghasi.

For the sake of brevity, I have omitted the countless assassinations and attempted assassinations of lesser ministers, opposition leaders, intellectuals, journalists, diplomats, and minor officials. Nor have I focused in detail on the smaller Arab countries, which unhappily have not escaped this phenomenon. One scholar examined political life in the string of tiny despotisms that make up the United Arab Emirates on the Persian Gulf and published his findings in 1977:

> Sheikh Zayid of Abu Dhabi had overthrown his brother
> Shakhbut in 1966; Rashid of Dubai had deposed his uncles in
> 1932; Ahmed of Umm-al-Qaywayn had shot an uncle who had
> just murdered his father; Saqr of Ras-al-Khayma had expelled his
> uncle in 1948; and, in a more recent coup, 1972, Sheikh Sultan
> of Sharja assumed power after his brother Khalid had been shot
> by his cousin and the former ruler, Saqr ibn Sultan. In Abu
> Dhabi, the core state of the federation, 8 of the 15 emirs of the
> Al bu Falah dynasty of the Bani Yas tribe, which had ruled unin-
> terruptedly since the 1760s, have been assassinated.[16]

While it may be true that the frequency of such assassinations in the Arab world has declined in the last decade, this is primarily because the regimes have consolidated their domination over their populations (as in Syria and Iraq) and have drastically improved their capacity to wipe away all traces of internal opposition.

A disturbing aspect of the continual bloodletting in Arab political conflicts is that many of its practitioners accept no limits to their violence, either in the means they choose to pursue it or in the victims they select as its targets. At least three of the exceedingly rare uses of gas warfare since World War I have been by Arab states. Nasser used gas in Yemen in the early 1960s; more recently, Saddam repeatedly gassed both the Iranian army in Baghdad's war against Teheran and the Kurdish civilians in his own country. (In the only gas attack against the Kurds for which figures are available, two thousand people died.)[17] During the Iran-Iraq War, both sides incessantly bombed the neutral shipping of many countries. And in the Gulf War, Saddam's flooding of the seas with crude oil and his positioning of military matériel at archaeological sites served notice that not even nature and history were out of bounds.[18]

But against the West, the use of such brazen violence has been the exception, not the rule. The radical Arab regimes have understood that the West is simply too powerful, and that frontal assaults on Western interests or nationals may therefore be too dangerous. As a result, these regimes have resorted to the much safer technique of terrorism. Terrorist warfare has allowed Arab regimes to attack Western targets while denying any responsibility for these attacks. Sovereign Arab states such as Syria, Iraq, and Libya have provided arms, embassies, intelligence services, and money to various terror organizations operating against the West and other objects of their animosity, thereby transforming terrorism that had been a local peculiarity of Middle Eastern politics into an international malignancy. For international terrorism is the quintessential Middle Eastern export, and its techniques everywhere are those of the Arab regimes and organizations that invented it. The hijacking and bombing of aircraft, the bombing of embassies, the murder of diplomats, and the taking of hostages by Arab terrorists have since been adopted by non-Arab terror organizations the world over. Indeed, before a determined policy under the leadership of the United States curtailed its operations, Arab terrorism's sphere of operations had grown to include the entire world outside the Communist bloc. Its victims, both Arab and non-Arab, were as likely to be attacked on the streets of London and Paris, of Bangkok and Karachi.

Its attacks on the West notwithstanding, Arab terrorism has also exacted a terrible toll on the Arabs themselves. It has probably killed more people in Lebanon alone than in the entire non-Arab world combined. In 1984, Muhsen Muhammad, editor of the Egyptian daily *Al-Gumhuria,* lamented the penchant of Arab terrorists for choosing Arab targets:

> The number of terrorist organizations in the Arab and Moslem world has grown. These are organizations which kill Arabs and Moslems everywhere. . . . some of these were created by governments [specifically for the purpose of] killing [Arab] opponents, adversaries, emigres, and refugees in all countries of the world.[19]

True, not every Arab state is Syria or Libya. Although some Arab regimes are truly predatory, others are more often prey. Still, this does not alter the picture before us, a picture that is unpleasant to contemplate, but that must be understood if one is to form any reasonable opinion about the politics of the Middle East. Violence is ubiquitous in the political life of nearly all the Arab countries. It is the primary method of dealing with opponents, both foreign and domestic, both Arab and non-Arab.

So far, I have not mentioned the Arab-Israeli dispute. There is a simple reason for this: Virtually none of the above conflicts and none of the violence they have produced has anything to do with Israel. Yet it is undeniable that almost every discussion on the subject of "achieving peace in the Middle East" begins and ends with Israel and the Palestinians, as a consequence of a deliberate campaign to divert attention from the true sources of perennial turmoil in the Middle East. As we have seen, this is achieved by implanting belief in a false center of this maelstrom: the Palestinian Problem.

Nowhere have the efforts to bury the true character of the Middle East been more intense than in the United States. When I first came there as Israel's ambassador in late 1984, I discovered that every year the UN devotes not one but *two* full sessions of the General Assembly, each lasting close to a week, to promoting the Theory of Palestinian Centrality. In the first session, called "The Question of Palestine," country after country, Arab and non-Arab, lines up to excoriate Israel for its various alleged crimes against the Palestinians and demands that Israel comply with its ideas of a just solution to the Palestinian Problem. These ideas often range from Israel's gradual dismemberment to its immediate dissolution.

The second session is entitled "The Situation in the Middle East." To my chagrin, I discovered that this consisted of the *same* harangues against Israel, almost word for word, that were delivered during the first session. When I rose to speak during such a session in 1985, I asked about the purpose of having two separate debates; after all, if the same claims and arguments are to be made twice, the UN could save everyone the time, the trouble, and the money and have just one discussion. The only possible justification for this second debate, I suggested, could be to discuss the subject of the session's name, *the situation in the Middle East.* I proceeded to distribute to the delegates a compendium of Middle Eastern violence for 1985, compiled by the impartial American Foreign Broadcasting Information Service, which regularly monitors news reports from the Middle East. I had excluded reports of incidents relating to Israel. "Those," I said, "were discussed in the 'Question of Palestine' debate, in the UN's Second Committee, in a host of Special Committees, reports, letters and other documents." (After four years at the UN, I had to wonder if there was a forum in which this subject was *not* discussed.)

Given that 1985 was widely considered an "uneventful" year in the Middle East, this was a remarkable compilation. It was a catalogue of bombings, kidnappings, assassinations, executions, coups, hijackings, and border incursions, alongside the outright war raging at the time between Iran and Iraq. The targets were diplomats, journalists, embassies, and airline offices. The victims were Iraqis, Moroccans, Sudanese, and Libyans, bearing almost every passport in the Arab world, as well as Americans, British, French, Italians, Swiss, Dutch, Soviets, Japanese, and many others.

Calendar of Middle East Violence, April 1985

1 April   Egypt uncovers Libyan plot

1 April   Amal hijacks Lebanese plane

1 April   Dutch priest killed in the Bekaa Valley, Lebanon

2 April   Saharan People's Liberation Army claims it killed 120 Moroccans

3 April   Sidon, Lebanon, fighting kills 54

3 April   Iraq bombs Teheran

4 April   Jordanian plane attacked in Athens by group calling itself "Black September"

4 April   Iraq downs Iranian plane

4 April   Jordanian embassy in Rome attacked by Syria

6 April   Coup in Sudan

12 April   Islamic Jihad group bombs restaurant in Madrid, killing 20

13 April   Assassination attempt on Lebanese imam

16 April   United Arab Emirates oil minister escapes assassination attempt

16 April   Iraq downs Iranian plane

17 April   Amal surrounds refugee camps in Lebanon

18 April   Murabitoun headquarters destroyed in Tripoli

23 April   Iraq shoots down three Iranian planes

30 April   Iraqi terrorist plots against Libyan and Syrian embassies uncovered

SOURCE: U.S. Foreign Broadcasting Information Service

Such a list—a single *month* of which is reproduced in the table above—could hardly have been obtained from any other region in the world, because the Middle East has for decades consistently been the most violent area on the globe. Yet virtually none of the conflicts enumerated has anything to do with the Arab-Israeli conflict. Needless to say, none of the violence listed was found suitable for discussion in the General Assembly. The Arab delegates were quite peeved to be handed this compendium. By what right, they wanted to know, does the Israeli representative meddle in the "internal affairs" of the Arab world? These are all disputes within "the Arab family" and do not belong under the UN's purview of international matters. (I was hearing this last rejoinder at a time when both Iran and Iraq were declaring that the road to liberate Jerusalem went through each other's capital. On this, the Iranians at least had geography on their side.)

In the UN, as in the media and diplomacy generally, the Arabs were adept at sweeping all inter-Arab and inter-Moslem violence under the rug. Yet there is something uncanny about the world's capacity to focus on the Arab-Israeli dispute (with total casualties estimated at 70,000 dead over five decades) in the face of the carnage of the *other* Middle Eastern conflicts, such as the Egyptian invasion of Yemen (250,000 dead), the Algerian civil war (1,000,000 dead), the Lebanese civil war (150,000 dead), the Libyan incursion into Chad (100,000 dead), the Sudanese civil war (at least 500,000 dead), and the Iran-Iraq War (over 1,000,000 dead). Even the least of these conflicts far outstrips the entire half-century of Arab-Israeli tension on any devisable scale of casualties or misery. But especially after the Gulf War (at least 100,000 dead, and possibly many more), no fair-minded person can accept the pretense that the turbulent conflicts raging everywhere in the Middle East can be forced into the Palestinian straitjacket.

If the Palestinian Problem is not the core of the Middle East conflict, then what is? Where can we look for the political, social, or psychological roots of phenomena so powerful that they have reduced to habitual strife the entire Arab nation 150 million strong, a people that once hosted impressive centers of scholarship and culture that influenced all of civilization? To answer this question, we must consider three forces that have largely been obscured in the view of the Arab world that is commonly held in the West: the crisis of legitimacy, the yearning for a unified Arab domain, and resentment against the West. Each of these forces feeds upon the others in a circle of unending instability and violence.

Ever since the end of Ottoman rule after World War I, the absence of any popular consensus as to what constitutes a legitimate Arab government has ensured that even the most towering political structures in the Arab world have rested on foundations of quicksand. The demise of the empire that had subjugated the Arabs for centuries left the Arab world in the hands of a patchwork of British and French colonial administrations. Their interests were primarily material, and when it proved unfeasible for them to maintain direct control over the vast reaches of the Arab lands, they sought to grant independence to the newly fashioned Arab "states" in a manner that would least interfere with the functioning of their economic empires, particularly with the supply of oil to their industries. They carved the region into numerous states (today there are twenty-one members of the Arab League), each of them far too small to become a world power in its own right, and they granted sole proprietorship of these new entities to friendly Arab clans who were considered likely to be favorable to maintaining relations with their European benefactors. Thus was born a collection of monarchies from Morocco to Iraq.[20]

The Middle East, of course, had no tradition resembling that of the Western nation-state, which is predicated on the existence of separate nations. The French are sharply aware and even genuinely proud of those elements of character and culture that distinguish them from the Spanish, the English, and the Germans, and the feeling is at least mutual. The special institution of the European nation-state, like that of the Greek and Italian city-states before it, could catch on among the people in Europe precisely because the French, for example, naturally consider themselves to be loyal to and bound to obey the government of France, whatever government that might be, and no other. But as many Arabs are quick to point out, this is not the case among Arabs, who consider themselves loyal principally to their family or clan,[21] and beyond that to the Arab people as a whole. The intermediate state-unit was generally taken to be an arbitrary, unnatural, and undesirable division imposed on the Arab people—much as Americans would probably feel if outsiders were to make each of the fifty states into an independent country. Thus a tension between subjects and rulers was introduced into the Arab states from the very start, with the European-appointed "king" demanding a loyalty that his subjects were at best ambivalent about granting. Often the monarch was therefore not so much a national leader expressing the general will of his people as the scion of a particular fief-holding family, interested in the state apparatus mostly as a means of assuring himself and his relations a lush life, usually with ample help from interested foreigners. As Amir Shakib-Arslan, a Lebanese who was one of the most popular writers in the Arab world between the wars, put it:

> Moslems offer help to these foreigners betraying their own brethren, and enthusiastically assist them with advice against their own nation and faithfully cooperate with these foreigners from greed and perfidy. But for the assistance obtained by the foreigners through the treachery of one section of the Moslems and the zeal with which the latter rendered them help . . . these foreigners would have neither usurped their sovereignty . . . [nor] contravene[d] and supersede[d] their religious laws . . . , nor would they have dragged down the Moslems into the valley of the shadow of death and led them to a disgraceful death.[22]

The readiness of the Arabs to reject their own monarchs, their own states, and the borders that divide them is thus a consequence of a general crisis of political legitimacy. Since they ac-

cepted the governments and boundaries that the Europeans devised only superficially, if at all, there was nothing other than force
that could silence the cacophony of claims to legitimate rulership
(because of superior pedigree or ideology) over any particular
parcel of land. And since every one of these claims has been
backed by the threat of insurrection or coup, the result has been
terminal instability. Most of the Arab regimes have by now mastered the suppressive techniques of "crowd control" and have
thus gained a measure of apparent solidity, but the underlying
problem remains the absence of any notion of legitimacy for either the various governments or the borders that separate their
countries.

This explains the preoccupation of Arab leaders not only with
their fears of coup and assassination but with "mergers" of one
sort or another—each merger (like many corporate mergers)
thinly masking one government's effort to delegitimize and dissolve the other government. Thus Nasser attempted to fuse Egypt,
Syria, and Iraq; Iraq tried to merge with Jordan and absorb Kuwait;
Qaddafi has attempted marriages with Tunisia, Sudan, and even
Morocco; and Syria has absorbed Lebanon as an interim step in its
effort to build a Greater Syria. All these unions failed for lack of
any real willingness by any Arab leader to cede any power (except
for Lebanon's absorption into Syria in 1991, which was pulled off
at gunpoint), fulfilling Lawrence's prophecy that "it will be generations before any two Arab states join voluntarily." It is the Arabs'
frustration over their inability to unite and stabilize their domain
that explains why Saddam's conquest of Kuwait inspired jubilation
throughout the metaphorical "Arab street" that runs from Morocco to Mesopotamia—notwithstanding the fears of some Arab
rulers that they might be Saddam's next victims. For the majority
of ordinary Arab people, the arbitrary divisions that Europeans
scrawled all over the Arab map were an injustice far worse than
any cruelty that Saddam might inflict on the Kuwaitis. They
cheered for an Arab Bismarck who would erase the borders and
unify the Arab realm, earning their respect through the ruthless

application of force and thereby creating for himself, out of the ruins of Kuwait, legitimacy.

This feeling was particularly evident among Palestinian Arabs, both in Israel and in Jordan, who backed the destruction of Kuwait with a unanimous enthusiasm that was incomprehensible to most Westerners. For Palestinian Arabs, Kuwait symbolized the kind of colonial intrusion into Arabdom that they associate with Israel and Lebanon. The dismantling of the Western-leaning principality of Kuwait seemed to be a step toward the dismantling of Israel. Thus an opinion poll in August 1990, following Iraq's invasion, suggested that 80 percent of Palestinian Arabs supported Saddam.[23] When *The New York Times* interviewed Palestinian Arabs, it came away with opinions such as: "Saddam is our leader, and I'd go fight for him to remove the Americans." And: "This is an Arab problem. America has no right to be here. . . . Saddam is . . . the second Saladin." And. "If Saddam succeeds in getting the oil weapon, he will show the world there is another power, an Arab power, and he will use the weapon for us." Meanwhile, the Mufti of Jerusalem, during the Gulf War, called upon Saddam to "abolish the filth of the American Army and their collaborators from the holy lands." In the following days, the *Times* reported that the Arabs of the West Bank were holding mass demonstrations at which they chanted, "Saddam, we are with you until victory."[24]

These dreams of recapturing lost Arab glory and the popular resentment against the artificial colonial borders serve as the backdrop for Pan-Arab nationalism, which by the end of World War II had become the most powerful movement in the Arab world. Pan-Arab nationalism demands the rectification of all wrongs committed against the Arab people through the immediate dismantling of these borders and the unification of the Arab people into a single Arab superpower "from the Atlantic Ocean to the Persian Gulf." In practice, this first means the eradication of the monarchies, which are considered to be a continuation of the humiliation and exploitation of the Arab people at the hands of the West. One by one, military coups inspired by Pan-Arabism have replaced the kings with leaders like Nasser, Qaddafi, and Saddam—each of whom has contributed his own efforts to pulling more monarchical governments down. By now, only a handful of the monarchies remain (in Jordan, the Gulf states, and Morocco), and their grip on power is continuously challenged by radicals, precisely because they are viewed as the last vestiges of an era that will soon pass.

Because the explicit rallying point of Pan-Arabism is its desire to overcome borders, any government that is Pan-Arabist is convinced that the entire Middle East, or at least a significant part of it, belongs to it—and it alone. This explains Nasser's 1962 invasion of Yemen (which had been a crucial toehold on the Arabian Peninsula for the Pan-Arabists before it came to serve the same function for the Communists), and Saddam's wars to liberate the "Arab lands" in Iran and later in Kuwait. It likewise explains Syria's "friendship treaty" with Lebanon of May 1991, which effectively grants control of all of Lebanon to Syria. The most famous Syrian attempt to overrun Jordan was that of September 1970. When Israel issued a warning to Syria that it would intervene on Jordan's behalf, it saved Jordan's existence as an independent state.

Yet despite its passionate rejection of all current political divisions, the most obvious failing of Pan-Arab nationalism has been its inability to overcome the very Western-defined borders that its adherents believe have shackled and shamed the Arab nation. As though consciously acting out Lawrence's prediction, Pan-Arab nationalism has never been able to offer a method for determining the ruler of the proposed unified Arab state. There is no lack of claimants to the throne. The official national map of Libya, for example, shows Qaddafi with outstretched arms embracing the entire Arab world. Pan-Arabists in Egypt, Syria, and Iraq have each always sought to make the future Arab superpower *theirs*. Ironically, the divisions among the Pan-Arab nationalist governments of the various states have proven to be one of the greatest obstacles to unification. Thus it is that the bile spilled between Assad of Syria and Saddam of Iraq has been among the most bitter in the Arab world, for their fight was over which of these two potential centers of the new empire—to which *both* were committed—will consume the other.

In the last two decades, full-blown Pan-Arabism in the style of Nasser has been somewhat on the wane and is being replaced with the more limited aspirations of rulers to dominate first a single region of the Arab world, such as North Africa, the Gulf, or the Fertile Crescent. Since no leader has emerged to succeed Nasser as the clear champion of the Arab masses, and since the various contenders to the title have only managed to stalemate one another, enthusiasm for Pan-Arab nationalism has been dampened. But should a leader again arise with enough power to dangle a promise of unity before the Arab world, Pan-Arab nationalism would be instantly rekindled—as is evident from the heady response of Arabs across the Middle East in the first days after Saddam's conquest of Kuwait.

The thirst for Arab unity amid disunity remains unquenched. If Pan-Arab nationalism is not up to satisfying it, another force awaits in the wings. For the weakening of Pan-Arabism in recent years has been countervailed (not accidentally, I believe) by an almost universal resurgence of Islamic fundamentalism. Nothing could stir the caldron more. Sometimes working together with Pan-Arabism (as in Libya) but more often at odds with it (as in Iran, Egypt, and Syria), Islamic fundamentalism is a force somewhat more familiar in the West than Pan-Arabism, thanks to the attention-riveting activities of the Islamic revolution in Iran, especially after its disciples held hostage the entire American embassy in Teheran. Perhaps because images of this extraordinary event were broadcast directly into American living rooms every night for over a year, Westerners seem to be more willing to understand that fundamentalist Islam is unreasonable, dangerous, and odious. Westerners take its claim that it aims to consume Israel and the West seriously, whereas they dismissed the similar claims of Pan-Arab nationalists as "posturing" or "saber rattling." This difference also explains Western readiness to regard the Hamas (the Palestinian

Islamic fundamentalist movement) as a genuine menace to Israel and an obstacle to peace, whereas the Palestinian Authority, which systematically violates its commitments, continues to be treated as a force for genteel moderation and is seldom if ever even lightly reprimanded for excesses against human rights and peace.

The celebrated goal of Islamic fundamentalism is to secure the worldwide victory of Islam by defeating the non-Moslem infidels through *jihad,* or holy war. But in practice the immediate targets of the contemporary jihad are not the non-Moslem governments, which are usually too powerful to be attacked in the first instance, but Moslem ones. Fundamentalists thus seek the overthrow of all "heretic" governments in some forty Moslem states and the elimination of these states altogether in favor of a unified Islamic dominion. (The sequence of these two projected developments varies depending on whether it is a practical or a utopian fundamentalist who is speaking.) Its immediate targets are therefore the secularizing rulers of the Arab states, including the soldiers controlling the Pan-Arab nationalist regimes. These regimes have proven to be particularly hostile to Islamic fundamentalism, arresting, torturing, and murdering Islamic activists in the tens of thousands. Ten years in Nasser's jails drove the leading Islamic theoretician, Sayyid Qutb, to reject Pan-Arab nationalism. Before his execution in 1966 he wrote:

> [Jihad] is solely geared to protect the religion of Allah and his Law and to save the Realm of Islam and no other territory. . . . Any land that combats the faith, hampers Moslems from practicing their religion, or does not apply Islamic Law, becomes ipso facto part of the Realm of War. It should be combated even if one's own kith and kin, national group, capital and commerce are to be found there.[25]

The same idea was expounded by 'Ab al-Salam Faraj, the ideologue of the Islamic group that murdered Anwar Sadat in 1981 (Faraj, too, was executed):

There are some who say that the jihad effort should concentrate nowadays upon the liberation of Jerusalem. It is true that the liberation of the Holy Land is a legal precept binding on every Moslem. . . . but let us emphasize that the fight against the enemy nearest to you has precedence over the enemy farther away. All the more so since the former is not only corrupted but a lackey of imperialism as well. . . . In all Moslem countries the enemy has the reins of power. The enemy is the present rulers. It is hence a most imperative obligation to fight these rulers.[26]

Although the goal of Islamic fundamentalism to subjugate the entire world to Islam may appear to be rather distant, when the call for it is joined with traditionalism and the promise of heaven, it makes for a combination of remarkable potency. The startling appeals of the most radical Islamic fundamentalists for "greater democracy in the Arab world" indicate how confident they are of being able to carry the great mass of the Arab population with them in an election. In some cases, they are clearly correct. The Algerian military's 1992 imposition of martial law preempted election results that would have granted Islamic fundamentalists control of Algeria.

Here, too, ideology is the key to making sense of events. Iran's war with Iraq, while defensive at first, was later prosecuted as a war to liberate "the holy places," which are located in Saudi Arabia and Israel, both occupied by the infidel. (Saudi Arabia's cruel, literal enforcement of Koranic punishments ought to qualify it as an Islamic fundamentalist state, but the ruling Wahabi sect nevertheless is perceived as heretical in the eyes of many other Moslems who consider its practices to be a rejection of received Islamic law.) This strain in Arab thought also explains Qaddafi's incessant meddling in the black countries of Africa, as well as his undying enmity toward America, which is regarded less as a Christian nemesis than as a "Great Satan" (to use Khomeini's phrase) that seeks to tempt the people of the world away from the path of God with promiscuity and VCRs. The removal of this "cancerous" influence from the Middle East was the purpose of overthrowing the pro-Western Shah, as well as countless acts of fundamentalist violence. Fear of Islamic revolution caused the Saudi massacre of four hundred fundamentalist pilgrims in Mecca in 1987, and the Syrian destruction of the rebellious city of Hama in 1982.

The competition between Islamic fundamentalism and Pan-Arab nationalism, as well as the influence of each movement on the other, has had tragic consequences not only for Arabs and Moslems. The refusal to accept anything less than a unitary Arab state and a unified Islamic domain has meant the rejection of all claims for political and religious independence by non-Arabs and non-Moslems. The various splinters in the Arab world may not be able to decide who will rule the unified realm, but they are nonetheless absolutely united in their uncompromising conviction that it will be an *Arab* and *Moslem* realm. This belief derives in no small measure from the Islamic division of the world into Islamic and infidel domains (the "Realm of Islam" versus the "realm of War") locked in eternal struggle.[27] Within the lands of the Islamic domain, the Koran enjoins the nonnegotiable inferiority of all non-Moslems. The Arabs have seen themselves as the stewards and rulers of all Islam ever since the earliest Islamic conquests, and there is little indication that they are ready to give this up now. But as we have seen, the vast region from the Atlantic Ocean to the Persian Gulf that the Arabs designate as exclusively theirs contains people of many other ethnic groups and faiths who do not necessarily or readily accept the supremacy of Moslem Arabs. These groups, numbering in the tens of millions, form an important part of what is commonly referred to as "the Arab world." No matter—they will all be *made* to accept Moslem Arab hegemony in a unified Arab state.

It is in these terms that we may grasp the special opposition of the Arab world to Israel. For centuries, the Jews suffered degradation, persecution, and periodic massacre at the hands of the Arabs,[28] as did other minority peoples. But of all of the minority peoples strewn across the vast reaches of the Arab realm, the Jewish people is the *only* one to have successfully defied subjugation and secured its independence. Worse, the Jews were able to establish an "alien" sovereignty smack in the center of the realm, splitting the Arab world in two and dividing its eastern from its western part. Still worse, the people who succeeded in this ultimate act of defiance are *both* non-Moslem and non-Arab. Thus, the specific Arab enmity currently directed toward Israel is rooted in older, more generic antagonisms that would have existed even if Israel had never come into being.

The durability of the twin fanaticisms of Pan-Arab nationalism and Islamic fundamentalism—their militarism, xenophobia, irredentism, and irreducible hatred of the existing order—is the true core of conflict in the Middle East, and of much of the violence that emanates from that region to the rest of the world. While many Arabs and Moslems in the Middle East have no desire to follow the hellish courses that these ideologies offer, fear of their disciples effectively prevents the emergence of a leadership willing to speak out against them. The absence of any democratic tradition in the Arab world stifles any such voices, just as it prevents the peaceful adjudication of the ongoing rivalries and claims in accordance with rights legally respected under the rule of law. Yet the absence of such Western political ideas in the Arab world is no accident. The rejection of democracy is but a part of the Arab world's abiding resentment of the West and is so deeply ingrained that it must be considered the third core component of Middle Eastern strife. The least understood of the forces at work beneath Arab political turbulence, this burning resentment of the West may perhaps be the most important for understanding the international aspects of the conflicts in the Middle East. Again, to make any sense of the Arab obsession with the West, one must look at history.

Just as surely as individuals, nations undergo traumatic experiences in parts of their history that continue to shape their behavior and attitudes. All Americans, for example, bear the formative imprint of their Civil War, the Depression, and Vietnam, even if they themselves were not around to witness these events personally. For the Jewish people, an older nation, the two most indelible traumas in the last two millennia were the razing of Jerusalem by the Romans in 70 C.E., which marked the collapse of Jewish sovereignty until our own time, and the Holocaust in this century, which destroyed European Jewry. Both experiences overshadow countless other disasters, however awful, that took place during the intervening centuries. The result of these two historical traumas is the present tenacity with which Jews strive to recreate and sustain sovereign Jewish power, especially the power to defend themselves. The destruction of the Temple at the hands of the Romans while Jewish factions in besieged Jerusalem were literally knifing each other to death also gave rise to the emphasis now placed on Jewish unity and the taboo on political killings among Jews, which has resulted in the virtual absence of civil war among Jews for two thousand years. With remarkably few exceptions, Jews do not kill Jews over politics.[29] This is why the assassination of Yitzhak Rabin was so shocking to Israel and the entire Jewish people.

I relate these examples because many people in the West, and especially in the relatively young United States, tend to underestimate the influence of pivotal historical experiences on the Arabs (or on anyone else). Yet it is precisely such national traumas that have molded the Arab attitude toward the West. The Arabs burst onto the world scene in the seventh century, after Mohammed had forged a new religion, Islam. In a remarkably short time they conquered the entire Middle East and North Africa and plunged deep into Europe. To Arab eyes, these lightning victories were clear evidence of provident design and signified the supremacy of Arabdom and Islam over Christianity and the West. They were regarded as the prelude to the world dominion promised by Mohammed. The glory that was to belong to Arab Islam is described by Amir Shakib-Arslan in 1944 in *Our Decline and Its Causes*:

[Islam] gathered together and consolidated the scattered races and tribes of Arabia. . . . Renovated and inspired by this dynamic force they made themselves masters of half the world in the short span of half a century. But for the internecine strife . . . no power on earth could have prevented them from conquering the whole world.[30]

But it was not to be. Almost as rapidly as the expansion took place, the Arab world empire began to contract. In 732, Charles Martel turned the Arabs back at Poitiers, 180 miles from Paris, signaling the beginning of the centuries-long Christian reclamation of lost ground. In some parts of Europe, this *reconquista* took longer than in others, it took 250 years to regain Sicily, but a full eight hundred years in the case of Spain. The durability and success of Western Christendom's opposition to the dreams of grandeur marked Western civilization as *the* enemy for subsequent generations of Arabs. Furthermore, the humiliation of the West's early victories over Islam was repeated in 1099, when the numerically inferior but highly organized Christian Crusaders captured Jerusalem. Although the Moslem leader Saladin finally expelled the Western interlopers from Jerusalem in 1260, his victory was short-lived because the Arabs were soon themselves conquered by the Mamluks, then subjugated by the Turks for four hundred years. (The Islamic Turks proved no less intent on conquering Christendom than the Islamic Arabs had been, and they succeeded in extending Turkish rule deep into Europe. But the Moslem bid for dominance of Europe was finally lost in 1683, when the Ottoman armies were defeated outside Vienna.)

The Arab world's next pivotal encounter with the West came with Napoleon's invasion of Egypt in 1798. By now, it was a different West. It had undergone the Renaissance and the Enlightenment and had produced a modern, technologically superior civilization. Napoleon's conquest of Egypt with only a few thousand men could not have been more shocking to the Arabs. The historical enemy, whom they had always looked down upon with scorn, had left them far behind. Even Napoleon's withdrawal from Egypt was the result of pressure not from the Arabs but from Europe.

Nor did the Europeans stay away for long. By the 1830s, the French and British had set up permanent bases in Algeria and on the coast of the Arabian Peninsula respectively, setting the stage for their assault on the heart of the Arab world. The British conquered Egypt in 1882, and those parts of the Arab world that British, French, and Italian expansion had not already taken before World War I fell into European hands after it, with the overthrow of Ottoman control. The entire Arab world remained under European rule up to the middle of the twentieth century. To Arab sensibilities, this was the ultimate humiliation, the complete turning of the tables. The Europe that they had once nearly made their own was now everywhere supreme in the Arab world, the descendants of Charles Martel lodged in Damascus and Algiers, and the descendants of Richard the Lion Heart flying the cross over Cairo and Baghdad.

This ultimate defeat at the hands of the arch-nemesis produced a crisis of confidence and identity that permeates the outlook of the Arab world to this day, even after the achievement of Arab independence. Particularly prominent among Arabs is the sense of frustration and alienation, the constant fear of discovering and rediscovering Arab inferiority, which was described by the Moroccan nationalist Abdallah Laroui:

> In February 1952 [the influential Egyptian author] Salama Musa entitled one of his articles, "Why Are They Powerful?" The "they" has no need to be defined; "they," "them" are the others who are always present beside us, in us. To think is, first of all, to think of the other. This proposition . . . is true at every instant of our life as a collectivity. . . . For a long time the "other" was called Christianity and Europe; today it bears [the] name . . . of the West.[31]

Yet despite this pervasive fear, the power of the West is precisely what the Arab finds all around him. According to Amir
Shakib-Arslan:

> It may be said without exaggeration about the Moslems that
> their condition, spiritual as well as material, is deplorably unsat-
> isfactory. With very few exceptions, in all countries where
> Moslems and non-Moslems live side by side, the Moslems lag far
> behind in almost everything. . . . [Moslems cannot] come any-
> where near the nations of Europe, America, or Japan.[32]

Even more significant, the West has penetrated Arab and Islamic society, infesting it with the philosophy, science, law, and
ideology of the victors, thereby making defeat total and final. This
pervasive shame and alienation was expressed by the Egyptian intellectual Muhammad Nuwayhi:

> In truth, anyone who reflects on the present state of the Islamic
> nation finds it in great calamity. Practically, changing circum-
> stances have forced it to adopt new laws taken directly from for-
> eign codes, . . . to arrest its ancient [religious] legislation. . . .
> The nation is tormented and resentful, plagued by inner contra-
> dictions and fragmentation, its reality is contrary to its ideals and
> its comportment goes against its creed. What a horrible state for
> a nation to live in.[33]

The despair over the dominance of Western ideas was given
grim voice by Salah al-Din al-Bitar, the disfavored founding father
of the Ba'th party, a few months before he was assassinated in
1980: "The Arabs," he said, "have not created an original idea for
the last two hundred years, instead devoting themselves entirely
to copying others."[34]

Nor has political independence allayed Arab resentment and
frustration; rather, it has provided a more effective means for expressing both—in the form of Pan-Arab nationalist and Islamic

fundamentalist governments claiming to be reviving the Arab people and returning it to the justly deserved glory of which the West has deprived it. Anti-Westernism and Arab power were therefore at the heart of the nationalist socialism of Nasser, whose regime hung banners in the streets telling Egyptians: "Lift your head, brother, the days of humiliation are over."[35] Indeed, the theme of settling the score with the West was the cornerstone and raison d'être of Nasser's politics. In 1954, he declared, "I assure you that we have been getting ready, ever since the beginning of the revolution, to fight the great battle against colonialism and imperialism until we achieve the dignity the people feel is due to Egypt."[36]

Much the same is true of the Ba'th Pan-Arab nationalism of Hafez Assad and Saddam Hussein, as expressed by Ba'th founding father Michel Aflaq: "Europe today, as in the past, fears Islam, but it knows that the force of Islam . . . has revived and appears in a new form which is Arab nationalism. For this reason Europe turns all its weapons against this new force."[37] Likewise, the strength of Muammar Qaddafi's fundamentalist Islamic version of Nasserism is built on a foundation of anti-Western sentiment. Qaddafi's manifesto *The Third Way* declares:

> We were prey, but now . . . the prey is standing on its own two feet and desires to resist its predators. . . . The Arabs, deformed by colonialism, were beginning to doubt themselves. It was becoming impossible for them to believe that the foundations of contemporary civilization were laid by Arabs and Moslems . . . that the Arabs or the Moslems created the science[s] of astronomy . . . chemistry, accounting, algebra, medicine. . . . The time has come to manifest the truth of Islam as a force to move mankind, to make progress, and to change the course of history as we changed it formerly. . . . [T]he truths about which we speak were present before the formation of American society.[38]

Arab anti-Westernism does not stop at words. It has manifested itself in the pro-Soviet orientation of the leading Arab states up to the collapse of the Soviet Union as a superpower, in the anti-Western agitation of the Arabs among the "nonaligned states" and at the UN, in the terrorism launched from the Arab world at Western targets, and in the particular glee that the Arab rulers showed at the height of the oil embargo, imposed in 1973, when they throttled the Western economies. In many Arab eyes, this last was a vindication that history was finally coming full circle, and that a renascent Arab nation was delivering the West its due, as American congressmen rode bicycles to work and chief executives in New York, London, and Paris waited in line for gasoline.

The friendliness of a few Arab rulers toward the United States deludes some Westerners into believing that this reflects the real sentiments of the Arab masses. But such rulers frequently represent only a thin crust lying over a volatile Arab and Islamic society. It is instructive to recall that "moderate" and "pro-Western" states like Iraq and Libya were transformed overnight into centers of anti-Western fanaticism after the toppling of King Feisal and King Idris. (The same phenomenon was in evidence in non-Arab but Moslem Iran, with the toppling of the Shah.) Any Western reliance on a friendly Arab regime is basically a reliance on individuals, not on peoples. These individuals may disappear in a flash, often swiftly replaced by elements pandering to the deep-rooted attitudes of the population.

Only against the background of this intense animus toward the West can the Arab rejection of Israel be truly grasped. In the theology of Arab resentment, Israel, a state founded by European Jews and built on the model of the liberal states of the West, is understood as a tool or weapon by which the Western governments can inflict further defeats and humiliations upon the Arab nation. As early as the 1930s, Emil Ghouri, architect of the slaughter of Arab "collaborators" in Palestine, declared that the 1929 massacre of the Jewish residents of Hebron was an assault on "Western conquest, the [British] Mandate, and the Zionists"—in that order.[39] This worldview was directly incorporated into Nasserist Pan-Arab nationalism, as expressed in Nasser's Egyptian National Charter:

Imperialist intrigue went to the extent of seizing a part of the Arab territory of Palestine, in the heart of the Arab Motherland, and usurping it without any justification of right or law, the aim being to establish a military fascist regime, which cannot live except by military threats. The real anger is the tool of imperialism.[40]

It was this imagery of Western usurpation that Nasser invoked on May 29, 1967, to whip the Arabs into a fury one week before the Six Day War:

We are confronting Israel and the West as well—the West, which created Israel and despised us Arabs and which ignored us before and since 1948. They had no regard whatsoever for our feelings, our hopes in life, or our rights. . . . If the Western powers disavow our rights and ridicule and despise us, we Arabs must teach them to respect us and take us seriously.[41]

This spirit was the animating force of the Ba'th nationalist rejection of Israel on the eve of the Six Day War, when the Syrian chief of staff announced his reason for warring against Israel:

I believe that Israel is not a state, but serves as a military base for the Imperialist camp. . . . He who liberates Palestine will be the one to lead the Arab nation forward to comprehensive unity . . . [and] can throw all the reactionary regimes into the sea.[42]

Similar beliefs were expressed by Saddam Hussein when he said: "Imperialism uses Zionism as a strategic arm against Arab unity, progress and development. This is a well-known fact."[43]

Nasser, the archetypal Pan-Arabist dictator, was instrumental in establishing the PLO in Cairo in 1964, and he suffused it from the start with his fervent Pan-Arab approach. His legacy can be seen in the anti-Western venom of the various PLO factions, each of which adhered to its own Pan-Arab ideological basis for the rejection of Israel as an outgrowth of the imperialist West. Thus, PLO executive member Mubari Jamal Tsurani said in 1986: "Nothing that is called peace is likely to come about. What is possible is a state of cease-fire. As long as imperialism exists, and as long as Israel is there, peace will not be possible."[44]

In our age, when history is often either unknown or disregarded, it is easy for Arabs to plant the view in the West that if only Israel had not come into being, the Arab relationship with the West would be harmonious. But in fact, the Arab world's antagonism for the West raged for a thousand years before Israel was added to its list of enemies. *The Arabs do not hate the West because of Israel; they hate Israel because of the West.*

From day one, the Arab world saw Zionism as an expression and representation of Western civilization, an alien implantation that split the Arab world down the middle. Indeed, a common Arab refrain has it that the Zionists are nothing more than neo-Crusaders; it is only a question of time before the Arabs succeed in uniting themselves under a latter-day Saladin who will expel this modern "Crusader state" into the sea. That, in this larger anti-Western context, the Arab world perceives Israel as a mere tool of the West to be used against the Arabs can be seen in the constant references made by Saddam, Assad, and Arafat to Saladin. As Arafat is fond of saying, "The PLO offers not the peace of the weak, but the peace of Saladin."[45] What is not stated but what Arab audiences understand well in its historical context is that Saladin's peace treaty with the Crusaders was merely a tactical ruse that was followed by Moslem attacks, which wiped out the Christian presence in the Holy Land.

Perhaps this is why Syria's Hafez Assad displays in his office a large painting of the triumphant Saladin expelling the last Crusader.[46] The powerful appeal of the idea of reenacting Saladin's victories in modern times has stimulated Arab leaders to make not only repeated attacks on Israel but repeated subversions aimed at toppling pro-Western Arab rulers and continual attempts to drive the Western presence out of the Middle East—as Iraq tried to do in Kuwait in 1991, and as Syria has by now more or less succeeded in doing in Lebanon. The fact that, in the wake of the Soviet collapse, regimes such as Syria's are forced to make a tactical peace with the West should not be allowed to obscure the contempt and antagonism for the West that lurks just beneath the surface, and that could resurface instantly at any sign of Western weakness or with the emergence of powerful new forces on the world scene.

We can now appreciate what has prevented a resolution of the Arab-Israeli dispute year after year. The Arabs' wars against Israel and their smoldering hostility in between those wars stem from three mutually reinforcing factors that together constitute the true core of the many conflicts in the Middle East: the Pan-Arab nationalist rejection of any non-Arab sovereignty in the Middle East; the Islamic fundamentalist drive to cleanse the region of non-Islamic influences; and the particularly bitter historic resentment of the West. In all three, it is clear that Arab antagonism directed at Israel in its origins is in no way specific to the Jewish state. Rather, Arab enmity toward Israel and the Jews is merely a particular instance of far more generalized antipathies that would have existed even had Israel never been established.

It is also clear that the grievances the Arabs present as grounds for attacking Israel are mere pretexts. For Arabs were already attacking Jews, killing any they could without mercy, thirty years *before* there was a Jewish state—which is to say thirty years before there was a single refugee who could qualify as a "Palestinian Problem." The three causes I have described explain why Arabs were committing pogrom after pogrom against Jews *outside* Palestine, both before and after the founding of Israel, even though the Jews of Arab lands presumably had nothing to do with any "Palestinian Problem." They explain why the Arabs went to war with Israel repeatedly *before* there was a single Jewish settlement or a single Israeli soldier in the Golan Heights, Judea, or Samaria. After all, the wars of 1948 and 1967 were both waged against a truncated Israel, *without* the disputed territories. What is more, the years between those wars saw thousands of terrorist raids and arbitrary assaults by Arab armies against Israeli civilians—in which hundreds of Jews died. Sniper fire across the border was an everyday occurrence, not only against Jewish farmers working the fields of the Galilee but even across divided Jerusalem.[47]

The Arab campaign against Israel is hence rooted not in a negotiable grievance but in a basic opposition to the very existence of Jewish sovereignty. To hope for the abandonment of such a deeply entrenched animosity while Pan-Arab nationalism and Islamic fundamentalism—both of which thrive by fueling this fire—wrestle for control of the Arab psyche is to hope for too much, too quickly. This is not to say that peace is impossible between Arabs and Israelis, or between Arabs and Arabs, for that matter. But it does point to the special nature that peace must have in the Middle East and the special requirements that must be satisfied if it is to endure. (I will discuss these issues in Chapter 6.)

There flickers in the West a tendency to see the end of the Cold War as the "end of history," the end of the threat of major upheaval and violence. Within this context, it is thought that since the conflict between the superpowers had ended in peace, it must be a matter of only a little bit of pressure and a little bit of compromise, and peace will come to the Middle East as well. But while the end of the Cold War has thankfully deprived the Arabs of their Soviet patron, it unfortunately has little to do with terminating Middle Eastern bloodshed, a perpetual-motion machine that requires no outside assistance to maintain itself or to threaten the peace and stability of other regions. Long after fears of Soviet expansionism have become blurry memories, Israel and the West, and quite a few Arabs, will still be contending with radical Arab regimes, immersed in their culture of violence, mesmerized by their successes, and bent on furthering their ambitions of conquest and domination.

It is easy for Westerners to dismiss the threat that any Arab state poses as exaggerated. After all, the populations of the Arab states (except for Egypt's) are rather small, their military capacities are still questionable, and they are far away. But to dismiss the threat would be a terrible mistake. When even a minor regime like Libya, which rules over only four million people, used the machinery of a sovereign state to act out its ruler's twisted fantasies, the result was a campaign of global terrorism. When a more substantial and more powerful country like Iraq (seventeen million people) armed itself feverishly, the threat exceeded that of Libyan terrorism a thousand times. Indeed, Saddam's Iraq was, and still is, a menace of the sort that has previously been the stuff only of suspense novels: a terrorist state with a leader seeking to graduate from car bombs to nuclear bombs. If Saddam's continuing quest for a nuclear capability were ever to succeed, it would be the first time in history that a nuclear weapon could be launched on the decision of a single individual, without the moderating and restraining influence of any scientific, political, or military echelons who were actually willing or able to voice disapproval. The threat to world peace would be unprecedented—as would also be the case if nuclear weapons fell into the hands of Syria or Iran.

During the 1980s, instead of heeding Israeli warnings that the threat posed by Iraq was imminent, foreign governments fell into the trap that Arab propaganda had set for them and accepted the assertion that endemic instability in the region either did not exist or was rooted somehow in the Arab-Israeli conflict and the Palestinian Problem and could be mitigated or eliminated altogether with Israeli concessions. Such was the power of the Theory of Palestinian Centrality that it entirely obscured Iraq's feverish building of its arsenal for an entire decade, between 1980 and 1990, and it even served as a cover for Western supplies to that burgeoning arsenal. Israel's protestations fell on deaf ears.

In 1981, when Israel destroyed Saddam's nuclear reactor, which was primed to produce nuclear bombs, the entire international community, including the United States, condemned it. No nation has yet apologized to Israel or even withdrawn its condemnation to this day. It goes without saying that there have been no expressions of gratitude. (Although there was some *unofficial* jubilation: Over the years, Iraq's representatives at the UN had referred to Israel as "the Zionist entity." I am told that when news of the Israeli raid on the Osiraq reactor reached the Pentagon situation room, a triumphant cry was heard: "Hurray, the entity strikes back!") Even after the Gulf War, it is tragically clear that the world has simply failed to perceive what was clear to T. E. Lawrence in 1928: that many Arab regimes are "tyrannies cemented with blood"; that whatever the nonradical Arab governments may wish in private, they are ultimately under the thumb of the more extreme positions in the Arab world; and that only external force will curb Arab dictators and terrorists who, in possession of a modern state apparatus, will use it again and again to pursue their Pan-Arabist or Islamic fundamentalist visions.

Western perception of this has been successfully obscured by an Arab world steadily spouting the Palestinian Problem, caused by Israel, as the explanation for all strife in the Middle East. By 1990, a quarter-century after the Six Day War, this axiomatic truth had spread to every corner of the earth. The sacred cow of Palestinian Centrality appeared inviolable.

Until the Iraqi conquest of Kuwait. For Saddam's invasion forced many Arab leaders to make some quick calculations. As much as the Arab states resent the world's discovery of the true face of inter-Arab conflict and its peering into what they traditionally call their "internal disputes," they also understand that they cannot afford to neglect the dangers that Saddam poses to them.

When Saddam himself realized that he would face a coalition that included Arab states, he sought to emphasize his Pan-Arab appeal by transforming the invasion of Kuwait into an Arab-Israeli dispute, a transformation that was to be achieved by invoking the apparently irrelevant Palestinian Problem. The invasion of Kuwait, he claimed, was a blow to the West and its Arab lackeys; it was the necessary first step toward building an Arab state that would be strong enough to liberate Jerusalem. He backed up this claim by demanding that any concessions he made in Kuwait be preceded by Israeli withdrawals from Palestinian land.

At that point the Arab countries poised against Saddam found themselves in the incredible position of having to refute the central tenet that they themselves had worked so laboriously to plant in Arab and non-Arab minds. No, said Syrian, Egyptian, and Saudi spokesmen, the invasion of Kuwait has nothing to do with the Palestinian Problem. Egyptian president Hosni Mubarak admitted, "If we say we want to link the two issues, this means we do not want to solve anything at all."[48] Likewise, according to the Kuwaiti ambassador in Washington:

> [W]e see no linkage whatsoever between these crises. . . . [I]f anyone thinks that Saddam Hussein is caring for the interests of the Palestinian people or the Lebanese by invading and killing their brothers in Kuwait [he] is completely mistaken.[49]

This forced admission of the truth, even if it was brought to the surface for only a few weeks, did much to damage the Arabs' most basic success: their creation of a false idea of a Palestinian core to all Middle Eastern conflicts. For the first time in decades, many in the West (and in the East) were exposed to the complex inter-Arab turbulence as they had never been before. After the Gulf War it was difficult, at least temporarily, to completely disregard the intensity and influence of inter-Arab and inter-Moslem hostilities.

But the sacred cow of Palestinian Centrality is by no means dead. It is still limping along, patched up by convoluted attempts to explain that one way or another Israel drives or exacerbates all conflict in the region. And with the passage of time, the Kuwait invasion slips from memory and the idea of Palestinian Centrality is allowed to rise once more, again obscuring the real picture of the Middle East. To understand the consequences of this obfuscation, we need only think back to the period immediately preceding the Gulf War.

On a visit to the United States in May 1990, I was besieged by some of Israel's staunchest Jewish-American allies who were concerned about an altercation that had occurred near St. John's Hospice in East Jerusalem. A yeshiva had rented, with Israeli government aid, a building adjacent to a Christian monastery and turned it into a dormitory for its students. The furor that arose when the church objected to this arrangement gave much comfort to Israel's enemies and much discomfort to its friends. Some of these friends, members of the Presidents of Major American Jewish Organizations, were now pressing me on how Israel's government, which was then led by the Likud party, could allow such a "fiasco" to take place.

"You're right. It's a big problem for us now," I said. "But it will blow over in a week. There's a much bigger problem that won't go away."

"What's that?" they asked.

"Saddam," I answered. "Saddam Hussein is the Middle East's, and Israel's, number one problem."

The response to that was as dismissive as it was scornful: "Come on," I was told in exasperation. "That's just a Likud diversion."

Few incidents illustrate the distortion of Middle Eastern reality that is rendered by the Theory of Palestinian Centrality as well as this exchange, three months before Saddam's invasion of Kuwait. Israel's friends and foes alike falsely believed the "Palestinian Problem" to be synonymous with the "Middle East Problem." This perversion of truth is a monument to the success of the Arab propaganda machine, and it certainly has done great damage to Israel. But a still more far-reaching effect has been its capacity to cloud Western perceptions of the real nature of the Middle East and the dangers that loom inside its fabric of fanaticism for the security and well-being of the world.

4

THE REVERSAL OF CAUSALITY

No less successful than the Arab campaign for the Theory of Palestinian Centrality was the campaign for the Reversal of Causality. If in the first instance, the Arabs said that all the problems in the Middle East were telescoped into the Palestinian Problem, they now proceeded to explain exactly what that problem was: not a by-product of wars in which the Arab states attacked Israel, but in fact the *cause* of those attacks in the first place.

With each year's harvest of propaganda, the reality of the Arab world's war against Israel began to recede in the popular mind, leaving only the image of Israel against the Palestinian Arabs. (Saddam's missile attacks on Israel during the Gulf War were a rude but brief reminder of this larger context.) The Arab Goliath was turned into the Palestinian David, and the Israeli David was turned into the Zionist Goliath. Not only were size and power reversed, so was the sequence of events. In the Reversal of Causality, it is not the Arabs who attacked Israel, but Israel that attacked the Arabs—

or more specifically, since the Arab states deliberately substituted "Palestinians" for "Arabs," it was Israel that attacked the Palestinians. In a nutshell, the new chain of reasoning went like this: All the problems in the Middle East are rooted in the Palestinian Problem; that problem itself is rooted in Israel's occupation of Palestinian lands. Ergo, end that occupation and you end the problem.

This elegant construct, nonexistent before Israel's victory in the Six Day War, came into being with amazing speed. By the 1970s, it had made its way from Arab to Western capitals. I recall a conversation with a British diplomat, perhaps the foremost Arabist of the British Foreign Office, in which I pointed out that Israel's reluctance to cede the administered territories to the Arabs was based in no small measure on its fear of being attacked from these territories again. His reaction startled me. "Come now," he sniffed, "you don't seriously expect us to believe that. After all, it was you who started the Six Day War."

What are the facts? After their attempt to destroy the newborn Jewish state in 1948 failed ignominiously, the Arab regimes resorted in the 1950s to a relentless campaign of cross-border terrorism. Attacks were leveled against Israel from all sides, especially from terrorist bases that had been established for this purpose in the Gaza Strip, which was then under Egyptian control. Ending these deadly raids was the primary aim of Israel's foray into Sinai in 1956. The Sinai campaign eliminated the Arab terrorist bases and temporarily brought the Sinai under Israeli control. It was returned to Egypt a few months later under Soviet-American pressure, despite the absence of any indication by Nasser that he would renounce his oft-stated intention of destroying Israel. (The Americans were especially irked that, unknown to them, Israel had coordinated its military action with Britain and France, which had landed paratroops in the Suez Canal zone in an attempt to roll back Nasser's takeover of the international waterway.)

After a short respite, the Arab terror campaign began gathering steam again in the early 1960s. Attacks on Israelis from the Syrian-controlled Golan Heights became a commonplace, and by

1966 the recently established PLO was launching escalating terrorist attacks from the Jordanian-controlled West Bank as well. In November 1966, Israel launched a retaliatory raid on the village of Es-Samu (the biblical Eshtamoa), wiping out the terrorist bases there. Tension increased. In April 1967 the Israeli air force downed six Syrian MiGs over a Syrian attempt to divert the headwaters of the Jordan River—the source of much of Israel's water. The Egyptian military had by then fully recovered from its earlier defeat. Emboldened by the acquisition of the latest weaponry from the Soviet Union (and from Britain, in Jordan's case), Syria, Jordan, and Egypt prepared to attack Israel in May 1967. Arab states farther afield also readied their military forces to be sent to what many of them confidently assumed would be the final assault on the Jewish state. Arab leaders were not reticent in proclaiming their aims. "The problem before the Arab countries," declared Nasser in May 25, ". . . [is] how totally to exterminate the State of Israel for all time."[1] "Our goal is clear: to wipe Israel off the map," declared President Aref of Iraq on May 31.[2] "The Arab struggle must lead to the liquidation of Israel," explained Algerian president Boumédienne on June 4.[3] And on June 5, the day the war broke out, Radio Damascus exhorted simply: "Throw them into the sea."[4]

Six days earlier, on May 30, King Hussein of Jordan had gone to Cairo to sign a mutual defense pact with Egypt, effectively fusing his army into a joint military command with Egypt and Syria and tightening the noose around Israel's neck.[5] Egypt had already escalated the crisis into an outright state of war by cutting off Israel's southern shipping through the Gulf of Aqaba. Israel asked the Jordanians to stay out of any Arab assault, but on June 5, when the fighting began, King Hussein joined in as well, shelling the entire Israeli frontier, including Jerusalem, Tel Aviv, and Israel's international airport at Lod. On June 7, Hussein broadcast this to his army: "Kill the Jews wherever you find them. Kill them with your arms, with your hands, with your nails and teeth."[6]

What had led the Arabs to adopt this heady approach was a

combination of Soviet deception (the Soviets falsely told the Arabs that Israel was amassing troops along the Syrian border) and the Arabs' own belief that, having licked their wounds from their previous defeats and having stockpiled an enormous arsenal in the interim, they could easily finish the job of overrunning the outnumbered and outgunned Israeli army. (The ratio of artillery was five to one in the Arabs' favor, planes 2.4 to one, and tanks 2.3 to one.)[7]

The promise of victory was especially beckoning, since all the Arabs had to do was slice Israel into two at its narrowest point, between the Jordanian border and the Mediterranean, where it was only ten miles wide. In a combined attack, with Egypt in the south and Syria in the north, even a mediocre Jordanian tank commander could hope to cross that minuscule distance swiftly and reach the sea. In fact, since the Jordanians probably had the best of the Arab commanders, the temptation for Hussein to join the attack turned out to be irresistible. Moreover, Jordan had the full strategic backing of Iraq. As in 1948, approximately one third of the Iraqi army crossed Jordan and by June 5 was approaching the Israeli border. Furthermore, after Egypt flooded the Sinai with 100,000 troops in May (in flagrant violation of the armistice agreements of 1956, following the Sinai campaign, which stipulated that the Sinai would be demilitarized), Nasser felt that from the old Egyptian-Israeli border he was in easy striking distance of the densely populated Israeli coastal plain. Tel Aviv, after all, is only about forty miles from the Gaza district, which was then under Egyptian control, and the Israeli city of Ashkelon is less than five miles away. Finally, Syria, poised on top of the Golan Heights, from which it had tormented the Israeli settlements in the valley below for nineteen years, could launch a quick assault from its superior high ground, penetrate the Israeli Galilee, and reach the vital coastal plain from the north.

In hindsight, it is easy, as some do now, to dismiss the Arab military's belief that with such promising starting conditions they could overrun Israel. Indeed, the Arabs were encouraged in this belief by political developments. Israel's pleas to the United States, Western Europe, and the United Nations to help break the siege that the Arab states had thrown up fell on deaf ears. Three weeks before the war, when Nasser closed the Straits of Tiran, Israel's vital sea outlet to the south, Israel turned to the United States and asked that it live up to its commitment to keep that channel of water open (a promise that the United States and the European countries had given to Israel in exchange for Israel's withdrawal from the Sinai in 1956). In Washington, no friendlier American administration could have been imagined. The president was the sympathetic Lyndon Johnson, the undersecretary of state was the supportive Eugene Rostow, the UN ambassador was the lifelong Zionist Arthur Goldberg. Yet when Israel asked that the written commitment that the Americans had given be honored, this friendliest of all possible administrations hemmed and hawed and said it could not find a copy of the commitment.[8]

The noose was tightening, and although public opinion was squarely behind Israel, the world's governments did nothing. Israel stood alone.

The mood of the country was somber. War was not new, and the threat of war still less so. But the last time Israel had experienced a full-scale military conflict was eleven years earlier, during the battle over Sinai. Although I had been born and raised in Israel, my own experience with that war was sharp but not traumatic. I remember as a seven-year-old taping the windows and pulling the blinds in case the Arabs attacked Jerusalem. My clearest recollection from that war is of the father of the boy next door, wearing dusty fatigues, sweeping into the neighborhood, splotches of sand still covering the floor of his army jeep. "Here," he said with an outstretched hand, "this is for you." He gave the children of the neighborhood Egyptian chocolate that he had brought from El Arish, a town in the northern Sinai that had just fallen to Israel. "I *bought* them," he added with extra emphasis, to make it clear to us that he hadn't just taken them.

The Arabs didn't attack our cities—that time. But now, eleven years later, as war rushed toward us, the windows were taped again. This time it proved necessary. On the morning of June 5, I was awakened by a deafening noise outside the apartment. I ran to the roof and watched in fascination as Jordanian shells exploded yards away from my building in the heart of Jerusalem. Most of the shells fell in open spaces, but a number slammed into residences, killing twenty civilians and wounding hundreds. The parliament building of the Knesset and the Israel Museum, housing the ancient Dead Sea Scrolls, were also targeted but were not hit.

This was a new sight for me. I was eighteen years old, and I had spent the last three years in an American high school in Philadelphia, where my father was doing historical research. In the latter part of May, as the Arab intention to go to war became clearer, I had taken my exams early and set off for Israel. My parents did not try to stop me. They merely asked, "Are you sure there will be a war?"

"Positive," I answered. "The Arabs will go through with it. Besides, I want to see Yoni before the war starts." Yoni was the Hebrew nickname by which we called my older brother, Jonathan. This sealed the argument.

When I landed in Lod Airport near Tel Aviv on the evening of June 1, the airfield was enveloped in utter darkness, including the runways. After staying overnight in an equally darkened Jerusalem, I set out to find my brother. At twenty-one, he had been released a few months earlier from service as an officer in the paratroops. In the last week of May he had been mobilized again (Israel's army in wartime consists of virtually all of the able-bodied men in the country called up for reserve duty). The problem was where to find him. "Look in the orchards around Ramleh," I was told through the unofficial grapevine that instantly and mysteriously spreads classified information to people who need to know in Israel, and to them alone. "That's where you'll find Brigade Eighty." The trouble was, there are an awful lot of orchards around Ramleh. The reserve paratroop brigade was bivouacked under its leafy shade, the better to hide it from possible aerial reconnaissance. I walked into one of the groves along the road leading from Ramleh to Gedera. Several reservists were preparing coffee on a makeshift stove. They were in their early thirties at most, but to me they looked far too old for this. They should have been home with their families, I thought.

"Yoni?" One of them scratched his head. "Oh yeah, the young guy. Look in the next grove."

I wandered through the next cluster of citrus trees, but I didn't find him. Then, at the other end of a long row of trees, I saw him staring at me in utter disbelief "What are you doing here?" he asked, and broke into his broad grin as we ran toward each other.

Over a cup of "military coffee" (a sickeningly sweet blend of coffee and residues of tea with which I was to become intimately familiar over the next five years of my own army service), I asked him what he thought was going to happen. "We'll win," he said simply. "We have no other choice."

The next time I saw him was ten days later, in a hospital bed in Safed. His unit had landed in helicopters at Um Katef, behind the lines of the Egyptian forces poised to choke the Negev, smashing their fortification and paving the way for the sweep of Israeli armor into the Sinai. From there they were taken up to the foothills of the Golan, where they fought their way up the steep incline nine hundred feet to the plateau above, on which the Syrian guns were still trained downward on the Israeli villages that lay spread like a map beneath them.

Three hours before the end of the war, Yoni led a three-man advance squad to reconnoiter the storming of Jelabina, a Syrian outpost. A sudden burst of machine-gun fire tore open the neck of the soldier next to him. As Yoni leaned forward to grab the stricken man, his own elbow was shattered by a Syrian bullet, leaving the nerve exposed and causing horrific pain. He later said that as he crawled back to safety on that scorched field, bullets whizzing past him, he felt for the first and only time in his life that he was going to die. When he reached Israeli lines, he stood up on his feet.

"Can you make it on foot to the field hospital?" he was asked. "No problem," he answered, and promptly collapsed.

Now in Safed, with the war ended just a day earlier, I entered the long orthopedic ward. His was the last bed on the left. His arm was in a heavy cast. He was the only patient in the ward who was not an amputee.

"You see," he said with quiet sadness, "I told you we'd win."

Seven hundred and seventy-seven Israeli soldiers died in the Six Day War. In less than a week they and their comrades had purchased a brilliant military victory against those who sought to snuff out Israel's life. King Hussein lost control of all the territories his grandfather's troops had forcibly seized in 1948—Judea, Samaria, and eastern Jerusalem. Syria lost the Golan Heights; Egypt lost the Sinai and Gaza. Israel, which before the war had been a tiny country, now became a small country (see Map 7). The border, which had previously been ten miles from the sea, was pushed back to the Jordan River forty miles away. The Sinai provided a large buffer against Egypt, as well as supplying most of Israel's oil needs. And on the Golan Heights the tables were turned, with the Israelis gazing down at the Syrians for the first time.

Whatever it was that had made the Arabs drop all caution in word and deed on the eve of the Six Day War, this was the last time they would unreservedly expose before the entire world their undisguised goal of annihilating Israel. They did not anticipate Israel's preemptive air strike during the first three hours of the war, which destroyed the entirety of Egypt's air force, the backbone of Arab air power. Later in the day, after Syria and Jordan attacked, Israel destroyed their air forces as well. (This gave Israel's armored divisions complete freedom to maneuver on the ground with total Israeli air supremacy in the skies above, a devastating combination in desert warfare that was to disappear by the time the next war came around.)

Israel did not fire a shot on the Syrian and Jordanian fronts until it was attacked from these lines. On June 5, hours before the Israeli operation began, the Syrians bombed the Israeli air force base at Megiddo, as well as targets in Haifa and Tiberias, and spewed fire at Israeli positions from the Golan. The war on the Jordanian front began when Jordan opened up a full-scale bombardment on Israeli targets.[9]

Thus my Arabist colleague may have been right in saying Israel fired the first shot in 1967—but only against Egypt, which in any case had already committed an act of war by closing the Straits of Tiran. Faced with the choice of either eliminating the escalating threats to its life or being driven into the sea, Israel chose to live. It took decisive and unforeseen action to avoid the fate that the Arabs had planned for it. This mood is captured in a story told among the Israeli troops during the tense days before the outbreak of the war, which Yoni related in a letter he wrote from the orchards of Ramleh on May 27, 1967, a week before the war:

> We sit and wait. What are we waiting for? Well, it's like this: An Englishman, an American and an Israeli were caught by a tribe of cannibals. When they were already in the pot, each of them was allowed a last wish. The Englishman asked for a whiskey and a pipe, and got them. The American asked for a steak, and got it. The Israeli asked the chief of the tribe to give him a good kick in the backside. At first the chief refused, but after a lot of arguments, he finally did it. At once the Israeli pulled out a gun and shot all the cannibals. The American and the Englishman asked him: "If you had a gun the whole time, why didn't you kill them sooner?" "Are you crazy?" answered the Israeli. "And have the U.N. brand me an aggressor?"[10]

But that is exactly what the UN (and most of the world) proceeded to do. It would soon condemn Israel for refusing to be stewed in the pot that Nasser and the Arabs had prepared for it. This did not happen right away. The resolutions adopted by the Security Council, written under threat of veto by the United

States, were initially "evenhanded," calling for restraint and negotiations toward peace on all sides. But not the resolutions of the
General Assembly. There, all the shame the Arabs felt over their
defeat exploded into tantrums of impotent rage, which the Soviets and their servants joined for reasons of their own. Having
"invaded Africa" (according to a prevalent Third World interpretation) by capturing the Sinai, Israel was not only the aggressor but
a neocolonialist regime—not merely the tool of imperialism but
an oppressor empire in its own right. All over the East bloc and
the Third World, states severed diplomatic relations and condemned their newly discovered aggressor foe. China declared of
Israel's act of self-defense: "This is another towering crime against
the Arab people committed by U.S. imperialism and its tool Israel,
as well as a grave provocation against the people of Asia, Africa and
the rest of the world."[11] Pakistan asserted that it was "[n]efarious
and naked aggression . . . against the territorial integrity of the
United Arab Republic and the adjoining Arab States. . . . Israel is an
illegitimate child born of fraud and force."[12] In Bulgaria, it was felt
that "[t]he adventures and aggressive actions of Israel arouse disgust and anxiety among world public opinion."[13] And Moscow,
which had helped to trigger the war by feeding the Arabs false intelligence, piously informed the world that "in view of the continued Israeli aggression against Arab States and its gross violation of
the Security Council resolutions, the Soviet government has decided to sever diplomatic relations with Israel."[14]

That all this could occur because Israel had succeeded in defending itself was no ordinary propaganda victory. Still, the Arabs
understood that such condemnations, coming from the Soviet
bloc, China, and the Third World, would not suffice. The shock of
their defeat in the Six Day War led them to a fundamental reeval-
uation of their tactics. Having lost areas strategically vital to waging war against Israel, especially the commanding heights of Judea
and Samaria, the Arabs realized that no easy military solution
would be forthcoming until they first forced Israel to retreat to the
vulnerable pre-1967 lines. This would require the exertion of

enormous political pressure, and such pressure could be effective only if it came from one place: the West. Israel, after all, was a Western country dependent on Western, and especially American, support. The Arab states would therefore have to win over public opinion in the West by means of a lengthy, sophisticated, and comprehensive campaign. They would have to change the terms of the conflict so as to obscure its real nature and present it in a manner that would be plausible, even persuasive, to audiences outside the Middle East.

For one thing, the kind of open declaration of intent that they had made so freely up to the eve of the Six Day War would have to be muted or even dispensed with. Obviously, it would not do to speak again of driving the Jews into the sea. To much of the world, this was simply unacceptable.

New arguments would have to be marshaled to justify continued hostility against Israel. And what better proof of Israel's innate aggressiveness could there be than the incontestable fact that it had come out of the war a bigger country than when it entered it? All the territories that the Arabs had lost in 1967, territories that had been used by Arab leaders as staging areas for a war that they themselves had brought on, were now held up as examples of unbridled Israeli expansionism. The consequences of Arab aggression were thereby presented as its causes.

The Arab leaders now demanded that these same territories be handed over to them. That they have managed to persuade many people of the justice of their demand is, to say the least, curious. They present, after all, an entirely new theory in international relations. Never before have states that lost territory in wars of aggression assumed so easily the mantle of the aggrieved party. Germany after World War II certainly did not. Neither did the other aggressor states from that same war. In fact, there is hardly a case in history in which a repelled aggressor was permitted to demand anything, much less the territory from which his aggression was initiated.

The wide acceptance of the idea of Israel's relinquishing Judea and Samaria has much to do with the notion, promulgated in the UN Charter, that the acquisition of land by force should be considered illegitimate.[15] The advocates of this position like to remind us—frequently—that taking land by force is like stealing the property of an individual. But there is no small amount of hypocrisy in the fact that this principle is today so piously preached by states that only a few years ago were themselves ardently pursuing international empires spanning the globe—with force the preferred method of acquisition. When it comes to their own interests, these states, including Western ones, have no real regrets over past uses of force, and they continue to use it to keep what they have captured whenever they see fit.

Yet Israeli "acquisitions" of territories by force stand in marked contrast to most examples that one could adduce, including American actions against the Indians and against Mexico, by means of which the continental United States came into being. For Israel has at no point set out to conquer anything. It has been repeatedly forced into wars of self-defense against Arab regimes ideologically committed to its destruction.

Of paramount importance is the fact that the lands in question—the mountain ranges of Golan, Samaria, and Judea—were all used as springboards by the Arab armies to attack Israel during the Six Day War and as staging areas for terrorism during the years before the war. Syria, as we have seen, used the Golan to threaten Israel's water supply as well. In such a case, the argument over the use of force to acquire territory is like the argument over whether you may use force to take a gun away from someone who has already fired two shots at you and is about to fire a third time. Countries that have been the object of aggression have a legitimate interest in protecting themselves against potential attacks, a principle that has been recognized repeatedly in international relations, even in cases in which the threats were considerably less than those facing Israel.

Thus, for three decades after World War II, the United States kept Okinawa (eight thousand miles from California) as a hedge against the possible resurgence of Japanese aggression, while East Germany, Poland, Czechoslovakia, Bulgaria, and Romania were kept under Soviet control (with American acquiescence) as a hedge against renewed German aggression. The actual possibility that a "next war" would be launched from either of these utterly ruined, disarmed, and subjugated opponents was almost nonexistent, but neither the Americans nor the Soviets were willing to take even the slightest risk where their national security was concerned. Compare this to Israel's case: The West Bank—the Judean heartland of the Jewish people—is only a few miles from the outer perimeter of Tel Aviv, and the Arab regimes surrounding Israel continue to arm themselves feverishly, rarely bothering to disguise their plans to use the territory against Israel once more should Israel vacate it.

But what is even more amazing is the fact that the Arab-inspired myth of "Israeli expansionism" persists, even though in 1979 Israel, in pursuit of peace at Camp David, willingly agreed to give up *91 percent* of the territory it had won in a war of self-defense, land containing billions of dollars of investments and the oil fields that it had developed and that met most of its energy needs. Further, Israel ceded additional territories to Palestinian control under the Oslo Accords. No victor in recorded history has behaved similarly. What other nation would give up its oil supply and become dependent on imported oil for the sake of peace?

Clearly, however indignant some Arab leaders may be over the loss of territory in 1967, this loss cannot have been the cause of a conflict that began much earlier. If not the loss of territory, are the Palestinian Arab refugees the cause of the conflict? Prior to 1967, in fact, it was "the refugee problem" that was the constant refrain of the Arab chorus in explaining the Arab enmity toward Israel. But there was no such thing as the refugee problem when the Arabs embarked upon their first full-scale war against the fledgling Israel in 1948. On the day five Arab armies invaded the new State of Israel, Azzam Pasha, secretary general of the Arab League, declared: "This will be a war of extermination and a momentous massacre which will be spoken of like the Mongolian massacres and the Crusades."[16]

In several cases—as in Haifa, Tiberias, and in other well-known examples documented by the British authorities and Western correspondents on the scene at the time—the Jews pleaded with their Palestinian Arab neighbors to stay. This was in sharp contrast to the directives the Palestinian Arabs were receiving from Arab governments, exhorting them to leave in order to clear the way for the invading armies. No matter: The idea that Israel expelled the refugees, repeated ad nauseam, has caught hold over the decades since. But in the years immediately after the conflict, there were many moments of candor. For example, the Jordanian newspaper *Filastin* wrote in February 1949, "The Arab States encouraged the Palestine Arabs to leave their homes temporarily in order to be out of the way of the Arab invasion armies."[17] And in the New York Lebanese daily *Al-Hoda* in June 1951:

> The Secretary General of the Arab League, Azzam Pasha, assured the Arab peoples that the occupation of Palestine and of Tel Aviv would be as simple as a military promenade. . . . Brotherly advice was given to the Arabs of Palestine to leave their land, homes, and property and to stay temporarily in neighboring fraternal states, lest the guns of the invading Arab armies mow them down.[18]

In 1954 the Jordanian daily *Al-Difaa* quoted this telling comment from one of the refugees: "The Arab governments told us: Get out so that we can get in. So we got out, but they did not get in."[19] As late as 1963, the Cairo *Akhbar al-Yom* was still able to write: "May 15th arrived. . . . [O]n that very day the Mufti of Jerusalem appealed to the Arabs of Palestine to leave the country, because the Arab armies were about to enter and fight in their stead."[20]

Not only have the Arab leaders chosen to forget this history, they have created a new one, at once absolving themselves of any responsibility for the refugees and pinning the blame on Israel. Again, as with the territories lost in 1967, the consequence of the 1948 war—Arab refugees—was presented as its cause.

But to make this scheme work, the refugees had to be maintained as refugees, permanently wretched, perpetually unsettled. Most people unfamiliar with the Middle East are shocked to learn that the PLO actually has acted to prevent Palestinians from leaving the refugee camps, as have various Arab states. For the PLO, these camps served as a propaganda bonanza and fertile soil for the recruitment of new "fighters," and it was willing to resort to violence to keep them intact. For some reason, the Western press seems to have had little interest in reporting on this sordid bit of manipulation.

The consistent refusal of Arab leaders to solve this problem is particularly tragic because it would have been so easy to do. After all, since World War II there have been well over fifty million refugees from many countries, and almost all have been successfully resettled.[21] The truth of this assertion is driven home by the fact that in 1948 Israel, with a population of 650,000 Jews and a crushing defense burden, successfully absorbed 800,000 Jewish refugees from the same war that produced the Arab refugees. Israel, of course, did not incarcerate its refugees in special camps as the Arabs did, but quickly integrated them into Israeli society. That the fifty million Arabs in 1948 could not absorb 650,000 Arab refugees—and have not finished the job even after half a century, and even after the fantastic multiplication of their oil wealth—is an indication of the merciless cynicism with which the Arabs have manipulated the refugee issue to create reasons for world censure of Israel. As Dr. Elfan Rees, the adviser on refugees to the World Council of Churches, noted: "The Arab refugee problem is by far the easiest post-war refugee problem. By faith, by language, by race, and by social organization, they are indistinguishable from their fellows of the host countries."[22]

Indeed, after 1948 foreigners seeking to resolve the refugee problem were singularly impressed by the desirability of the refugees' absorption into the Arab states. Thus, a U.S. congressional study mission sent to investigate the situation of the refugees in 1953 reported: "The status of the refugees as a special group of people who are wards of the United Nations should be terminated as soon as possible. The objective should be for refugees to become citizens of the Arab states."[23] And a Chatham House study in 1949 concluded that, given international financial support, the great majority of the Arab refugees could be absorbed by Iraq and Syria, both of which boasted millions of acres of undeveloped land suitable for agriculture.[24] Similarly, a 1951 study by the International Development Advisory Board found that the entire Arab refugee population could be absorbed by Iraq alone.[25]

Still, despite the deliberate Arab policy to keep the problem alive, the reality that Dr. Rees noted has proved even stronger than Arab intent. For over the years, nearly all of the refugees *have* been absorbed into the economies and societies of the countries of their residence. Indeed, most Palestinian Arabs have homes. Many of them, in fact, live as full citizens in eastern Palestine— today called the Hashemite Kingdom of Jordan. Similarly, most of the Arabs of Judea-Samaria are not homeless refugees; they live in the same homes they occupied before the establishment of Israel. The number of actual refugees is close to nil. Some live on the West Bank, but most live in Gaza (although most of Gaza's residents are *not* refugees). Israel's attempts to dismantle the remaining camps and rehabilitate their residents were continuously obstructed by the PLO and the Arab world. Now that the Palestinian population lives entirely under Palestinian rule, it is the job of the Palestinians themselves to dismantle the remaining camps.

A serious case of *genuine* Palestinian homelessness was created in the wake of the Gulf War, when Kuwait embarked on a campaign of vengeance against its own large Palestinian population, which had collaborated with Saddam in conquering and occupying the country. More than three hundred thousand Kuwaitis of Palestinian origin were driven from the country (the largest forcible transfer of Palestinian Arabs in history). Almost all of them fled to Jordan, which accepted them all as citizens. If a comparable number of Palestinian Arabs in Judea-Samaria and Gaza remained unintegrated, until recently it was because political pressure from the Arab world and PLO terror have prevented their rehabilitation. Yet the theme of "homelessness" persists, having been repeated endlessly—not without success—as a powerful weapon in the Arab political arsenal against Israel.

As the years passed, however, Arab propagandists discovered that their claims about "usurped territories" and "homeless refugees" could not withstand critical examination. Before knowledgeable audiences, the embarrassments of chronology and causality could not be waved away.

They were compelled to resort, therefore, to a third and final argument. Brandishing the ever-popular slogan of "self-determination," they asserted that the "Palestinian people" have been denied their "legitimate rights," and that one of the rights that has been denied, they claimed, is the right to a "homeland." Significantly, the slogans of "Palestinian self-determination" and "legitimate rights" were introduced into common currency only after the failure of the Arab attempt to destroy Israel in 1967,

For it is an uncontested fact that during the nineteen years of Jordanian rule over Judea-Samaria, the Arab leaders, the Arab media, and Arab propaganda said virtually nothing about a "homeland" or "legitimate rights" for the Palestinian Arabs living in Judea-Samaria. When "Palestinian rights" *were* spoken of, it was always in reference to Israel behind its 1967 lines, to Haifa, Jaffa, and Acre, and the message was crystal clear: Israel was to be destroyed in order for the Arabs to obtain those rights.

It is noteworthy that under the British Mandate, it was the Jews of the country who called themselves Palestinians. The *Palestine Post* and the Palestine Philharmonic were Jewish. Likewise the Jewish soldiers who made up the Jewish Brigade of the British

Army were called by the British "Palestinians," a term that at the time referred mainly to Jews. There were thus Palestinian Jews and Palestinian Arabs, although in those days the Arabs did not stress a distinct Palestinian nationhood but always emphasized that they were part of the larger Arab nation.

This deep-rooted identification with the Arab nation did not diminish over the years. Yasser Arafat, head of the PLO, has said, "The question of borders does not interest us. Palestine is only a small drop in the great Arab ocean. Our nation is the great Arab nation extending from the Atlantic to the Red Sea and beyond."[26] And Zuhair Mohsin, a member of the PLO executive, put it this way: "There are no differences between Jordanians, Palestinians, Syrians and Lebanese. We are one people."[27] Yet soon after 1967, the Arab world began speaking with one voice about the newly occupied "Palestinian people," as though a distinct Palestinian nation had somehow come into being out of thin air.

The process of forming a separate nation is a complex one. The development of a unique "peoplehood" is always a long historical process, and its culmination is expressed by the emergence of several shared attributes, most often a distinct language, culture, religion, and history. But let us grant that through a miraculous telescoping of history, what took other peoples centuries was achieved by the Palestinian Arabs almost overnight, by dint of declaration, and that they are entitled to a national home. But who are the Palestinian Arabs, and where is their homeland? Let us hear what the Arab leaders themselves say.

The PLO, supposedly committed to "Palestinian self-determination," asserted from its inception in 1964 that its design encompasses the entirety of Palestine, both its western and eastern parts, *both* Israel and Jordan. This was underscored time and again, as in the Palestine National Council's Eighth Conference, in February–March 1971:

> In raising the slogan of the liberation of Palestine . . . it was not
> the intention of the Palestine revolution to separate the east of

the river from the west, nor did it believe that the struggle of the
Palestinian people can be separate from the struggle of the
masses in Jordan.[28]

Given the embrace between the PLO and Jordan after the Oslo
Accords, PLO leaders were naturally reluctant to publicize this
long-standing claim. But their candid statements in the past are
revealing. For example, Chafiq el Hout, a PLO official, said in 1967,
"Jordan is an integral part of Palestine, just like Israel."[29] And Arafat
made this same point in his speech before the United Nations in
1974: "Jordan is ours, Palestine is ours, and we shall build our national entity on the whole of this land."[30]

Some would expect the Jordanians to contest this claim. But
until some years ago they did not. In 1970, Crown Prince Hassan,
addressing the Jordanian National Assembly, said, "Palestine is Jordan, and Jordan is Palestine. There is one people and one land,
with one history and one destiny."[31] King Hussein (also—significantly—before an Arab audience) said on Egyptian television in
1977, "The two peoples are actually one. This is a fact."[32] In an interview with an Arab newspaper in Paris in 1981, Hussein said,
"The truth is that Jordan is Palestine and Palestine is Jordan."[33] And
in 1984, he told the Kuwaiti paper *Al-Anba* that "Jordan is Palestine. . . . Jordanians and Palestinians must . . . realize that their fate
is the same," and that "Jordan in itself is Palestine."[34] In 1988 the
PLO leader Abu Iyad reemphasized precisely the same point: "We
also insist on confederation with Jordan because we are one and
the same people."[35]

In recent years, to ward off the inevitable conflict between
them over who will control eastern Palestine (Jordan), Hussein
and the PLO had somewhat amended such pronouncements. But
whether whispered or spoken out loud, these declarations of the
Arabs themselves confirm what both history and logic tell us: The
area of Palestine is indeed the territory of Mandatory Palestine, as
decreed by the League of Nations, and comprises the present-day
states of Israel and Jordan. It is absurd to pretend that an Arab in

eastern Palestine who shares the language, culture, and religion with another Arab some ten miles away in western Palestine, an Arab who is often his close relative if not literally his own brother, is a member of a different people. Indeed, the PLO's officials and Jordan's rulers have been the first to admit this.

We must therefore wonder: How *many* Palestinian Arab peoples are there? Is there a "West Palestinian Arab people" on the West Bank, and just across the border an "East Palestinian Arab people" in Jordan? How many Arab states in Palestine does Palestinian Arab self-determination require?

Clearly, in eastern and western Palestine, there are only two peoples, the Arabs and the Jews. Just as clearly, there are only two states in that area, Jordan and Israel. The Arab state of Jordan, containing over four million Arabs, for a long time did not allow a single Jew to live there—it expelled those Jews who came under its control in 1948. Jordan also contains four-fifths of the territory originally allocated by the League of Nations for the Jewish National Home. The other state, Israel, has a population of five million, of which one-sixth is Arab. It contains less than one-fifth of the territory originally allocated to the Jews under the Mandate. In the territory disputed between these two states (Judea, Samaria, and East Jerusalem) live another 1,150,000 Arabs and 300,000 Jews (another million or so Arabs live in Gaza).

The claim that none of the Palestinians have been granted "self-determination," then, is misleading. For the inhabitants of Jordan—which Hussein's grandfather Abdullah originally wanted to call the Hashemite Kingdom of Palestine—are all Palestinian Arabs (Arabs from Palestine), and within that population western Palestinian Arabs—those whose families came from the part of Palestine west of the Jordan River—are the decided majority. It cannot be said, therefore, that the Arabs of Palestine are lacking a state of their own, the ultimate expression of self-determination. The demand for a second Palestinian Arab state in western Palestine, and a twenty-second Arab state in the world, is merely the latest attempt to push Israel back to the hopelessly vulnerable armistice lines of 1949.

No one interested in the future of Mideast peace would challenge the legitimacy of the Hashemite Kingdom of Jordan. I certainly do not. Regardless of the tortuous history of eastern Palestine, and the broken promises of the League of Nations to the Jewish people, the modern state of Jordan is a fact. By integrating its Palestinian population into all levels of Jordanian society, the modern state of Jordan has assumed a respectable legitimacy that all who are committed to peace should acknowledge. Equally, the Jewish people, while attached historically to the Gilad and Moab regions of Jordan, must recognize that the Jewish historical claim to these lands has no practical consequence at the close of the twentieth century. Moreover, it is in Israel's best interest to see Jordan stable, secure, and prosperous. This is why, as opposition leader in 1995, I led the vote of the Likud party in the Knesset approving the peace treaty between Israel and Jordan, thereby helping to seal the peace between Jordan and all parts of Israeli society.

I believe that a permanent agreement of peace can be reached between Israel and the Palestinian Arabs of Judea, Samaria, and Gaza. I have been advocating such a peace settlement because I believe it is in the best interest of Israel and the Palestinians alike. This final peace would achieve a balance between the Palestinians' understandable desire to run their own lives and Israel's need to preserve vital national interests, foremost of which is security. In fact, arrangements that would give the Palestinians of the West Bank and Gaza effective control over their lives have been in great part implemented by now, since the Palestinian Authority after the Oslo Accords directly controls over 98 percent of the Palestinian population. A final peace settlement between Israel and the Palestinians would resolve primarily the outstanding questions of any additional territory (virtually empty of Palestinians) that might be handed over to the Palestinians, and the all-important question of who controls crucial powers such as *external* security. If peace is to prevail, Israel must retain these powers.

The civil enfranchisement of the Palestinians is by now a moot issue, since they have their own flag, their own passports, and, most importantly, their governing institutions and the ability, however one may criticize it from a Western democratic perspective, to vote for their representatives and leadership. What I am stressing here is that the issue at the core of the Palestinian conflict with Israel is not lack of Palestinian self-determination as such, but the Palestinian demand for *unlimited* self-determination, beyond their current integration in Jordan and the arrangement for self-governance in a final peace settlement with Israel. That Palestinian demand for unbridled self-determination is not in itself a demand for greater freedom to insure Palestinian liberties, but a demand for the freedom to extinguish the liberty and life of the Jewish state. For unbridled Palestinian self-determination would mean a Palestinian state armed to the teeth, in league with such regimes as Iraq (whose leader, Saddam Hussein, has been repeatedly adulated by the Palestinians), and with powerful elements like Hamas and Islamic Jihad, inspired by Iran, all openly calling for Israel's destruction. Such a radical state, strategically poised on the hills above Tel Aviv, would make Israel's existence a precarious one at best.

If the Palestinians' wish is merely to control and better their lives, that wish could have been accommodated many times during the twentieth century. It certainly can be fulfilled in a final peace agreement with Israel. But if the Palestinians continue to harbor a desire not to run their own affairs but to free themselves of Israel's very existence, that wish will bury any chances for a true and lasting peace. It is my fervent hope that the mainstream elements of Palestinian society will rid themselves of this poisonous ambition, so that a genuine and enduring peace may finally be established between our peoples.

The Arab-Israeli conflict, therefore, is not rooted in the territories that changed hands in 1967, nor in the refugees that resulted from the Arab attack on Israel in 1948, nor in any claimed lack of self-determination for the Arabs of Palestine. The real root of the conflict is the persistent Arab refusal to recognize Israel within *any* boundaries.

These devices of Arab propaganda, especially the most recent one of self-determination, have been directed solely against Israel and therefore have received the credulous support of many governments. These governments will soon have to reexamine just how tenaciously they wish to support this claim. For the Arab campaign against Israel has developed what I call the Palestinian Principle, which dictates that any minority that does not want to be a minority does not have to be one. The Arabs, I should emphasize, were not demanding *civil* rights for the Palestinian population in the West Bank and Gaza. If that were the demand, Israel could have satisfied it by annexing the territories and making all the Arabs citizens of Israel or offering them full individual rights under Israeli law as resident foreign nationals who would retain their present Jordanian citizenship.

The Arab governments and the PLO summarily rejected such options. They refused to consider the Arabs of the territories living under an Israeli state in *any* condition, even as equal citizens. They were not interested in *civil* rights. Instead, they demand *national* rights over the territories—which means the creation of still another Arab state, another Arab regime, another Arab army. It is not enough that the Palestinians enjoy full integration in Jordan, a country with a solid Palestinian majority encompassing the majority of the territory of Palestine. It is not enough that members of the same people living across the border from Jordan in the West Bank and Gaza should enjoy equal civil rights and self-governance in any political settlement. On the contrary, we are told that the Palestinian Arabs of Judea-Samaria, a tiny area sixty miles long by thirty miles wide, should be given a state of their own, as demanded by the Palestinian Principle. That is, the Palestinians demand unlimited self-determination, with no limitation of potentially destructive sovereign powers.

What will this Palestinian Principle do to the post-Communist world? I described in the opening of this book how the international community is going back to Versailles to seek organizing principles for according sovereignties to various national groups. While Wilson at Versailles strove for a world in which each distinct nation has its own distinct state (a demand that the subsequent conferences could not universally fulfill), neither he nor his disciples ever said that each *minority* should have its own state—that is, in addition to a homeland in which the co-nationals of that minority constitute a majority. The issue here is not whether the Lithuanians are entitled to have a state of their own, independent from Russia. The issue, rather, is whether the *Russian minority* in Lithuania is entitled to have its independence from Lithuania despite the existence of an independent Russia. Similarly, the issue is not whether the Czechs and the Slovaks should have retained their union or formed independent states, but rather whether the Hungarian minority *within* Slovakia can legitimately agitate for independence *despite the existence of an independent Hungary.* Eastern Europe is replete with examples of minorities of one national population overlapping into the national territory of another people. So is Western Europe, for that matter. So are all the republics of the former Soviet Union. So is Africa. So are vast parts of Asia. Will each and every one of these minorities have its own state?

The United States is not exempt from this potential nightmare. In a decade or two the southwestern region of America is likely to be predominantly Hispanic, mainly as a result of continuous emigration from Mexico. It is not inconceivable that in this community champions of the Palestinian Principle could emerge. These would demand not merely equality before the law, or naturalization, or even Spanish as a first language. Instead, they would say that since they form a local majority in the territory (which was forcibly taken from Mexico in the war of 1848), they deserve a state of their own. "But you already have a state—it's called Mexico," would come the response. "You have every right to demand civil rights in the United States, but you have no right to demand a second Mexico." This hypothetical exchange may sound far-fetched today. But it will not necessarily appear that way tomorrow, especially if the Palestinian Principle is allowed to continue to spread, which it surely will if a new Palestinian state comes into being.

Ironically, the inevitable effect of the Palestinian Principle is to *diminish* respect for minority rights internationally. For if every minority can be considered a serious threat to the long-term integrity and viability of any state, then governments will find themselves seeking ways to suppress and ultimately eliminate all recognizable minority groupings within their borders. What this means could be seen recently in Bosnia-Herzegovina, where Serbian nationals were engaged in a campaign of "ethnic cleansing" against a Moslem minority that constituted a local majority. The mentality behind the horrifying efforts to drive the Moslems from their homes is not unrelated to the Palestinian Principle. For if every minority has the right of secession, it is not surprising that some wrongly conclude that they had better expel the minority and avoid the trouble altogether.

What I am arguing is that the Palestinian Principle has potentially divisive and destabilizing consequences in the search for a new world order. It is a political fragmentation bomb that will explode the civil and national peace of many lands, not only because the Arabs have promoted the incendiary idea that no minority must remain a minority, but also because the PLO until very recently demonstrated grisly *methods* to pursue its realization: terror, blackmail, extortion, and the co-option of the entire world stage without moral inhibitions or limits. Up until the collapse of Communism, it was possible for many governments to subscribe to the Palestinian Principle without thinking too carefully about its consequences for themselves. The Cold War not only froze the national conflicts within the vast territories controlled by the Soviet empire; it put a cap on the amount of leeway that contending sides in national disputes had outside the direct Soviet dominion. The United States and the Soviet Union may have supported competing sides in Latin America or Asia or Africa, but they made sure that things would not get out of hand. Now that the superpower rivalry has abated, the paradoxical result is *less* order and less security in national conflicts, not more. New champions of unlimited self-determination proclaiming their "national rights" can crop up in the most surprising of places, and if the feverish attempts of the arming of Iraq, Iran, and other countries with weapons of mass destruction is any indication, their capacity to acquire formidable weapons to exercise their perverted versions of "self-determination" is expanding, not shrinking.

This, then, is the new threat posed by a new Palestinian state in the Middle East. It is not merely the obvious physical threat to Israel, which I will discuss in detail in Chapter 7. It is not even the danger to peace and stability in the Middle East as a whole, which will surely be threatened by the emergence of such an independent state capable of purveying terror and other dangers. Even more than these, it is the impact that the creation of such a state will have on the problem of limiting the demands of minorities for sovereignty the world over.

At present, the chief contribution of the Palestinian Principle has been to obstruct the achievement of a negotiated settlement to the Arab-Israeli dispute. For it is important to make one point clear: No matter how the borders are drawn, any durable settlement would leave a significant number of Arabs living side by side with their Jewish neighbors under Israeli sovereignty. (Twenty percent of Israel's citizens are Arabs.) It has long been recognized that being a minority is not necessarily a tragedy. All nations have their minorities. The tragedy is to be *everywhere* a minority. This was precisely the situation of the Jews before the creation of the State of Israel. But the Arab rejectionists employ the reverse logic: For them, it is a tragedy that Arabs should be a minority *anywhere* in the Middle East. They find it intolerable that some Arabs should live as a minority in Israel, even as non-Arab peoples live as minorities in *their* midst—and this despite the fact that the Arab citizens of Israel enjoy the civil liberties and rule of law that are denied to many non-Arab peoples living under Arab regimes.

The Palestinian Principle is not a standard that the Jewish state can apply to its Arab minority, and it is not a standard the Jewish people has ever applied to itself. The Jews who constituted significant minorities in many lands for centuries before the Holocaust (for example, 10 percent of Poland's population) never demanded a state of their own in the areas in which they formed a local majority. Nor did the Jews, once they had attained statehood, possess twenty-one states and ask for more, as the Arabs today demand for themselves.

The Palestinian Principle has been, of course, enthusiastically accepted by Moslems all over the world, who see it as the logical extension of the idea of a Realm of Islam. The American writer Charles Krauthammer was able to point out that the intifada (the mass violence of Palestinian Arabs against Israel) is not restricted to the Arab-Israeli dispute—it is a worldwide enterprise directed at many non-Moslem governments by radical Moslem minorities demanding secession: in Azerbaijan and Tajikistan from the Soviet Union before their independence; in Kashmir from India; in Kosovo from Yugoslavia; in Xin Jian from China; and so on. The Palestinian Principle seems to mean that if there is ever a significant Moslem majority in any section of Britain or France, there will eventually be a demand for secession there as well.

If the Palestinian Principle is transparently false and obviously dangerous, how is it that it has been accepted by so many people around the world? The first reason is that the Arabs took pains to invent a new Palestinian identity in the West Bank, in effect creating a "West Bankian" people presenting the demands of an entirely new "nation." If the issue had been presented in irredentist terms—that is, that the Arabs in Samaria and Judea wished to be reunited with Jordan—the conflict would have been reduced to a squabble over where the border should be drawn and the whole issue would have lost its hold on Western imaginations so captivated by the idea of self-determination.

The second reason for the virtually unchallenged spread of the Palestinian Principle is Arab oil. One cannot overlook the power and influence of the Arab League and OPEC, which in the 1970s transformed themselves into mighty propaganda machines for the cause of self-determination of the Arabs of Palestine. The Palestinian cause was critical for the oil sheikhs of the Persian Gulf, who were able to get away with subsidizing the PLO and anti-Zionist propaganda instead of actually shelling out the funds necessary to build homes for the refugees. Thus the participation of the oil states became a decisive factor in focusing attention on the Palestinian Arabs. It is quite likely that if there were 150 million Basques in twenty-one Basque countries controlling 60 percent of the world's oil supply, incessantly agitating and fulminating for a quarter of a century about the need for self-determination for the Basques of Spain (all the while threatening oil cutoffs and aircraft hijackings if this self-determination were not granted), many would believe today that the main obstacle to peace in Europe, possibly in the world, is the "Basque Problem."

In this regard the Arab world's campaign against Israel is not the first time that totalitarian regimes have used a perversion of the concept of self-determination in concert with threats of force as a weapon against a small democracy. The most striking precedent for this strategy in this century is Nazi Germany's campaign against Czechoslovakia. This campaign deserves a reexamination because so many of its particulars are being eerily reenacted today against Israel.

Czechoslovakia was strategically placed in the heart of Europe, and its conquest was central to Hitler's plans for overrunning Europe. Though small, Czechoslovakia could field over 800,000 men (one of the strongest armies in Europe), and it had a highly efficient arms industry. To complicate matters from Hitler's point of view, it possessed a formidable physical barrier to his designs in the shape of the Sudeten mountains, which bordered Germany and guarded the access to the Czech heartland and the capital city of Prague only miles away. A system of fortifications and fortresses had been built in the mountains over many years, making passage by force a very costly proposition, perhaps even impossible. We now know from the Nuremberg trials and other sources that Hitler's generals were utterly opposed to an assault on the Czech fortifications. After the war, numerous German generals stressed the point, including Field Marshal Wilhelm Keitel, chief of the German high command:

> We were extraordinarily happy that it had not come to a military operation because . . . we had always been of the opinion that our means of attack against the frontier fortifications of Czechoslovakia were insufficient. From a purely military point of view we lacked the means for an attack which involved the piercing of the frontier fortifications.[36]

Worse, from Hitler's point of view, the Western powers had promised at Versailles to guarantee the Czech border against any aggressive attack. France, which in 1938 could field one hundred divisions (an army 50 percent larger than Germany's), had agreed in writing to come to the Czechs' defense, and Britain and Russia were committed to joining in if France did so.

Since an outright military victory seemed impossible, Hitler embarked on an unprecedented campaign to *politically* force the Czechs to give up the land, and with it any hope of being able to defend their capital or their country. The inhabitants of the Sudetenland, he said, were predominantly German, and these three million Sudeten Germans deserved—what else?—the right of self-determination and a destiny separate from the other seven million inhabitants of Czechoslovakia; this despite the fact that the country was a democracy and that the Sudeten Germans enjoyed economic prosperity and full civil rights. To buttress his claim, Hitler organized and funded the creation of a new Sudeten political leadership that would do his bidding, which was, in the words of the Sudeten leader Konrad Henlein, to "demand so much that we can never be satisfied."[37] Henlein was instructed to deny that he was receiving instructions from Germany. As William Shirer, who was a reporter in Europe at the time, succinctly summarizes it:

> Thus the plight of the German minority in Czechoslovakia was merely a pretext . . . for cooking up a stew in a land he coveted, undermining it, confusing and misleading its friends and concealing his real purpose . . . to destroy the Czechoslovak state and grab its territories. . . . The leaders of France and Great Britain did not grasp this. All through the spring and summer, indeed almost to the end, Prime Minister Chamberlain and Premier Daladier apparently sincerely believed, along with most of the rest of the world, that all Hitler wanted was justice for his kinsfolk in Czechoslovakia.[38]

In addition, Hitler backed the establishment of a Sudeten liberation movement called the Sudeten Free Corps, and he instigated a series of well-planned and violent uprisings that the Czechs were compelled to quell by force.[39] Further, he secretly summoned Henlein to Berlin and briefed him, instructing him in great detail precisely how he should agitate for the so-called Sudeten independence. (Occasionally, Hitler would replace his principal demand for Sudeten independence with his second demand for reunification with Germany, literally mixing self-determination with German irredentism.)

Most important of all, Hitler's propaganda chief Goebbels orchestrated a fearful propaganda campaign of fabricated "Czech terror" and oppression of the Sudeten Germans. The Czech refusal to allow the Sudeten territories to return to their rightful German owners, Hitler prattled, was proof that the Czechs were the intransigent obstacle to peace. For what choice would Germany have but to come to the assistance of its oppressed brethren living under intolerable Czech occupation? Rejecting plans for Sudeten autonomy, he insisted on nothing less than "self-determination."[40] Moreover, the Germans reversed causality, claiming that the Czechs were trying to precipitate a European crisis in order to prevent the breakup of their state, that the choice between war and peace in Europe was in Czech hands, and even that "this petty segment of Europe is harassing the human race."[41] But there was a simple way to simultaneously avoid war and achieve justice, Hitler said. The Western powers—meaning Britain and France—could force the Czechs to do what was necessary for the sake of peace: Czechoslovakia had to relinquish the occupied territories.

And it worked. With astonishing speed, the governments and opinion-makers of the West adopted Hitler's point of view. Throughout 1937 and 1938, mounting pressure was exerted on Czechoslovakia by the leading Western powers "to go to the utmost limit" to meet Sudeten demands.[42] Czech leader Edvard Beneš was reviled as intransigent. The Western press published articles lamenting Czech shortsightedness and its total disregard for the cause of peace in Europe, as well as the injustice of not allowing the Sudetenland to be "returned" to Germany (despite the fact that it had never been part of Germany). The British envoy who was dispatched to investigate the situation even went so far as to demand that Czechoslovakia "so remodel her foreign relations as to give assurance to her neighbors that she will in no circumstances attack them or enter into any aggressive action against them."[43]

On September 18, 1938, under the gun of Hitler's September 28 deadline, a meeting was held between the British Cabinet and the French prime minister and foreign minister, in which it was determined that democratic Czechoslovakia must accede to Hitler's demands. Despite the fact that the West had promised in writing at Versailles to go to war to defend Czechoslovakia's borders, it agreed that the Czechs must give up the Sudetenland for "the maintenance of peace and the safety of Czechoslovakia's vital interests." In return, the Czechs would receive from Britain and France "an international guarantee of the new boundaries . . . against unprovoked aggression."[44] If the Czechs did not accept the plan and thereby save the peace of Europe, they were informed by the leaders of the free world, they would be left to fight Hitler alone. In Neville Chamberlain's immortal words: "It is up to the Czechs now."[45]

But in fact it was not even left to the Czechs. Chamberlain realized that if the Czechs were to fight, France and Britain might be forced to fight too. As the Czechs and the Germans mobilized, Chamberlain became increasingly hysterical about averting war by buying off Hitler with the Czech defensive wall. He shuttled repeatedly to Germany to try to arrange the payoff. Finally, minutes before his September 28 deadline, Hitler "agreed" to Chamberlain's proposal for an international peace conference to bring peace to Central Europe. At Munich, Britain and France pleaded with Hitler for eleven and a half hours to "compromise" and take the Sudetenland peacefully. In the end Hitler agreed.

Having grasped the fact that his supposed democratic allies had allowed themselves to become tools in Hitler's hand, Prime Minister Beneš announced Czechoslovakia's capitulation to the demands of the totalitarians. "We have been basely betrayed," he said.[46]

The Western leaders returned in triumph to London and Paris. In government, in parliament, in the press, Chamberlain and Daladier were praised, cheered, thanked for having traded land for peace. "My friends," said Chamberlain, "I believe it is peace in our time."

On September 30, the Czech army began its withdrawal from the Sudetenland, from the strategic passes, the mountain fortresses, the major industrial facilities that would have been the backbone of Czechoslovakia's effort to defend itself. But this was only phase one of Hitler's plan. The German annexation of the Sudetenland was followed by a renewed list of demands on the Czechs. The Nazis continued to invent incidents of violence and oppression against the ethnic German minority in what was left of the Czech state. Less than six months later, on March 15, 1939, the Nazi war machine rolled through the rest of Czechoslovakia. Shorn of their defenses in the Sudeten mountains, the Czechs were now powerless to resist. Phase two had been implemented. "It was clear to me from the first moment," said Hitler, "that I could not be satisfied with the Sudeten-German territory. That was only a partial solution."[47]

The Western powers again did nothing. Once more, all their assurances proved worthless.

Unfortunately, the parallels to today's effort to gouge the remainder of Judea and Samaria out of Israel are all too easy to see. Like Czechoslovakia, Israel is a small democracy with a powerful army much aided by defensive terrain. Like the Sudeten district, the West Bank is mountainous territory, a formidable military barrier that guards the slender and densely populated Israeli shoreline and Israel's capital city. Like the Germans, the Arabs understand that as long as Israel controls these mountains, it will not be overrun. They understand too that a military campaign to seize these mountains is at present unthinkable, and that Israel's removal from them can be achieved only by the application of irresistible political pressure by the West on Israel to withdraw.

The Arab regimes have therefore embarked on a campaign to persuade the West that the Arab inhabitants of these mountains (like the Sudeten Germans, comprising roughly a third of the total population) are a separate people that deserves the right of self-determination—and that unless such self-determination is granted, the Arab states will have no choice but to resort to war to secure it. As in the case of Czechoslovakia, Israel's insistence on not parting with territories strategically vital for its defenses is presented as the obstacle to peace. Echoing Munich, the Arabs repeatedly advocate "active" American (and European) involvement, in the hope that an American Chamberlain can be found to force "the intransigent party" to capitulate where it is otherwise unwilling to compromise its own security.

That the Arabs have borrowed directly from the Nazis in this, as in so many of their other devices against Israel, is not surprising. What is surprising, or at least disappointing, is the speed and readiness with which this transparent ruse has been received, digested, and internalized by the elite of the Western world. Not a day passes without some somber editorial or political comment from august quarters in America or Europe asking Israel to voluntarily accept the same decree that Czechoslovakia was asked to accept. Israel is told that it should divest itself of its large Arab minority, making itself ethnically more homogenous for the sake of securing internal security and demographic bliss. The London *Times,* the leading newspaper of the world in 1938, published a celebrated editorial that summed it all up:

> It might be worthwhile for the Czechoslovak government to consider whether they should exclude altogether . . . making Czechoslovakia a more homogenous state by the secession of that fringe of alien populations who are contiguous to the nation with which they are united by race. . . . The advantages to Czechoslovakia of becoming a homogenous state might conceivably outweigh the obvious disadvantages of losing the Sudeten German district.[48]

Substitute *Israel* for *Czechoslovakia,* and *Palestinian Arab* for *Sudeten German,* and you could insert this same editorial into the leading newspapers of the West today without so much as raising an eyebrow. Israel, still the object of genocidal designs by some of the Arab world, has become in the view of many Western opinion-leaders the intransigent party, the obstacle to peace; Arabs who seek Israel's destruction and say so openly within the Arab world are often presented as reasoned and moderate.

We now know that the propaganda weapon of "self-determination" is aimed at the Achilles' heel of the West. Westerners, and in particular Americans with their tradition of inalienable rights and sympathies for national freedom, find it easy to identify with the exaggerated national aspirations of the Palestinians today, just as others found themselves moved by the plight of the German ethnic nationals in Czechoslovakia in the time of Hitler. Thus the argument of self-determination has been able to succeed where earlier Arab efforts to portray the conflict as one over refugees or Israeli territorial aggression had largely failed. As soon as the Arabs recognized the susceptibility of the West to the image of an "oppressed people struggling to be free," the entire Arab propaganda machine was retooled to churn out arguments on this basis. The Arabs were suddenly capable of persuading Western opinionmakers of what they had been saying since 1967: that Israel's presence in the territories was based on an inherently immoral act, and that any effort to strengthen the Jewish state was therefore fundamentally wrong as long as it hung on to these territories.

Two things greatly assisted in driving home these ideas to the West: the outbreak of the Palestinian intifada, and the ongoing controversy over the Jewish settlements in the territories. In recent years these issues have served as lightning rods in the campaign against Israel, focusing all the anti-Israeli energy in the international scene and directing it to reverse the great injustices that Israel has allegedly committed against the Palestinian Arabs.

The intifada came as a godsend to a PLO that had been losing ground in the Arab world and internationally ever since 1982, when the Israeli army had entered Lebanon, destroying the PLO bases that had been built up there for over a decade, and depriving the PLO of the staging area it needed to launch attacks against Israel. An indication of how low the PLO's fortunes had sunk came in 1987, when an Israeli bus was bombed by PLO terrorists in Jerusalem, prompting (again, for the first time in anyone's memory) Palestinian Arab leaders in the territories to condemn this act of terror and those responsible for it. Such a brazen act of repudiation against their own "sole legitimate representative" was what the PLO had most feared for years, and with good reason.

Meanwhile, although it was far from paradise, life in the territories had been steadily improving for years. The West Bank that Israel had found in 1967 had been only lightly touched by the twentieth century. There was scarcely any industry, medical treatment was primitive, and higher education did not exist. The vast majority of the residents lived in homes without electricity or running water, and most of the women were illiterate.

Soon after the Six Day War, Israel adopted a liberal policy aimed at radically improving the lives of the Arabs. Universal education was instituted, universities were opened, hospitals were built, and modern roads were cut into the hills. By 1985, the number of telephone subscribers had grown by 400 percent, ownership of automobiles had risen by 500 percent, and the annual rate of construction in Judea and Samaria had risen by 1,000 percent. By 1986, 91 percent of Arab homes in Judea and Samaria had electricity (as opposed to 23 percent under Jordan), 74 percent of homes had refrigerators (as opposed to 5 percent), and 83 percent of homes were equipped with stoves (as opposed to 5 percent). By 1987, these Palestinian Arabs had become the most educated segment in the Arab world, infant mortality had dropped drastically, and the economy had grown by an amazing 40 percent.[49] The improvement in Gaza was even more dramatic. Ironically, the Palestinian Arabs were also enjoying rights denied to other Arabs in the Middle East, with a press consisting of newspapers representing various factions (some openly sympathetic to the PLO), and the right to appeal all government decisions directly to the democratic Israeli court system. Furthermore, Israel kept the Allenby Bridge to Jordan open, affording every Palestinian Arab the right to visit other Arab countries and see whether living conditions were better elsewhere. Most of them decided they were better off in the West Bank.

This is not to say that the Arabs in the territories had suddenly become Zionists or acquiesced in Israeli control. That is never the case with a population living under military government, especially if that government must contend with the constant threat of terrorism. Palestinian Arabs have thus had to go through such trying experiences as roadblocks, identity checks, curfews, closings of workplaces and schools, and searches of their homes. And there has been no option for speedily bringing this state of affairs to an end. During the twenty years after the Six Day War the territories' political future was kept in limbo, first by the unwillingness of Israeli governments immediately after 1967 to annex or bargain away the territories, and then after the Camp David Accords of 1978, when the Arab side refused to follow through on the agreed-upon negotiations for determining the future of the territories. As a result, the Palestinian Arabs inhabiting these territories lived for over two decades under military administration, without knowing what the future disposition of the territories would be. Such uncertainty produces inevitable political tensions that a final political settlement would otherwise reduce. For example, the Arabs of the Galilee lived uneasily under an Israeli military administration during the 1950s and became full-fledged citizens of Israel once that administration was removed. The decades that have passed since then may not have been idyllic, but the fact that Israel's Arab citizens can take part in Israeli society, and that they have a mechanism for political expression (including representation in the Knesset), has produced a relatively quiet coexistence for Israel's Arab and Jewish citizens that has defied the earlier prognostications of many.

But no such definitive political settlement or mechanism for political expression was to be found in the territories. Virtually the entire Arab world rejected the Camp David Accords, refusing to rescind its totalist and immediate demand for a Palestinian state in the territories, thereby making it impossible to make progress along the path of negotiations with Israel. Thus, by 1987, two decades after the Six Day War, a new generation of Arabs had grown up in Judea, Samaria, and Gaza that was at once uncertain about the future of these areas and continuously subjected to virulent PLO agitation that filled the political void. Inevitably, this generation adopted ever more extreme and implacable positions.

But here too the PLO could not deliver on its own incitements, and increasingly the rage of the younger Palestinian Arabs was directed not only against Israel but against the leadership of the PLO itself, which was seen as living the good life in villas along the Côte d'Azur or on the languorous beaches of Tunisia, on the other side of the Mediterranean. Like their troubled counterparts elsewhere in the Arab world who are seduced by the facile promises of religious fanaticism, more and more of these youngsters were turning to the Islamic fundamentalist Hamas movement as a vehicle to vent their rage. Fundamentalism spreads most rapidly in poverty-stricken areas and is therefore at least in part a by-product of the Arab world's investment in weapons as a substitute for refugee rehabilitation.

This was the background for the outbreak of the "intifada," which unleashed these frustrations into widespread violence. The intifada began on December 8, 1987, when an Israeli truck accidentally ran down four Palestinian Arabs in Jebalya, near Gaza. Within hours the rumor spread that this was a deliberate act of murder, touching off weeks of mass rioting. Sensing a chance to regain its standing, the PLO joined in fanning the flames. On the day after the accident, *Al-Fajr*, a pro-PLO newspaper in Jerusalem, described it as "maliciously perpetrated."[50] In Baghdad, Arafat used the frenzy of the rioting as an excuse to promise that Israel was about to be annihilated:

> O heroic sons of the Gaza Strip, O proud sons of the [West] Bank, O heroic sons of the Galilee, O steadfast sons of the Negev: the fires of revolution against the Zionist invaders will not fade out . . . until our land—all our land—has been liberated from these usurping invaders.[51]

Arafat sometimes has let his guard down. Here he was summoning Arabs to rise up and liberate "all our land," in which he specifically includes not only the West Bank but the Galilee and the Negev—that is, Israel in its pre-1967 boundaries. And when Bethlehem's moderate Christian mayor Elias Freij suggested a temporary halt to the violence, Arafat responded: "Whoever thinks of stopping the intifada before it achieves its goals, I will give him ten bullets in the chest."[52]

Within a few weeks this violence was being organized and funded by the PLO, gathering Arab youths into "intifada committees" that really believed what Arafat told them: that victory was at hand. They attacked Israeli civilian traffic with rocks and gasoline grenades and enforced repeated strikes by setting up roadblocks to prevent Arabs from going to work, firebombing Arab stores, and threatening Arab merchants who tried to keep their shops open. Raiding the schools during class time and forcing the children into the street, the activists made their riots look more popular and simultaneously increased the tragic toll of children among the intifada's casualties. Afraid of being outdone, the fundamentalist Hamas movement organized rival committees, and for the next four years the two networks of violence competed in trying to push the Palestinian population to bloodshed.

In all this the Israeli army did precisely what is required of it by the Fourth Geneva Convention: It tried to defend the Arab and Jewish civilian populations by patrolling the highways, dismantling the roadblocks, and arresting the instigators of the violence.* The intifada "committees" responded by attacking the soldiers with axes, bricks, and gasoline grenades—gaining glory for themselves and media coverage for the PLO. The PLO sent out an order not

---

*Israel does not view itself as an "occupying power" in Judea, Samaria, and Gaza, territories that were recognized as part of the Jewish National Home by the League of Nations in 1922. Consequently, Israel has never recognized the Fourth Geneva Convention, which deals with occupation, as applying to its administration of these areas. However, Israel has unilaterally committed itself to observing the humanitarian provisions of this convention in militarily governing the Arab population until a final settlement is achieved.

Article 64 of the Fourth Geneva Convention (1950) empowers an "occupying power" to "subject the population of the occupied territory to provisions which are essential to enabling the Occupying Power to fulfil its obligations under the present Convention, to maintain orderly government of the territory, and to ensure the security of the Occupying Power, of the members and property of the occupying forces and administration, and likewise of the establishments and lines of communication used by them."

The Convention does not require that the inhabitants of an occupied territory be granted the right to appeal to the Supreme Court (a right that Israel provides the residents of the West Bank and Gaza); nor does it prohibit the application of the death penalty (which Israel has refused to apply even in cases of terrorist massacres).

Israel was often castigated for expelling inciters and practitioners of violence from the territories on the grounds that the Fourth Geneva Convention forbids "deportations." Indeed it does (in Article 49), but that prohibition was inserted into the Convention, written just after World War II, in order to prevent the uprooting of *entire populations* such as the Nazis had practiced. It was not meant to address the removal from a territory of a selected few who threaten the well-being of the inhabitants and the security forces alike.

to use guns, lest they spoil the underdog image of the uprising and provoke the army to take serious action.

The West may have imagined that the young Arab hotheads in Nablus wished for nothing more than the liberation of their backyard, but the "committees" saw it otherwise. Their goals were just as Arafat and the Hamas had dictated them: to drive the Jews from every inch of Israel. They published widely circulated Arabic-language communiqués explaining this goal to those they expected to follow them. A leaflet circulated by Arafat's Fatah faction, dated January 21, 1991, said that Jews were "descendants of monkeys and pigs," the inference being to treat them accordingly. The Hamas, in a typical counterleaflet, declared, "There will be no negotiations with the enemy. There will be no concession on even one centimeter of the land of Palestine. The way to liberation is through jihad." As for their Jewish neighbors in Judea and Samaria, the leaders of the intifada called upon their followers to "burn the ground out from under their feet."[53]

On rare occasions, the Western press actually bothered to send a translator along and interview some of the intifada leaders about what they wanted. When Bob Simon of CBS News tried this novel approach, he received a straightforward answer from the leader of a group of seven masked intifada activists he interviewed: "I want all of Palestine, all of it entirely. . . . Palestine is indivisible. Haifa, Acre, Jaffa, Galilee, Nazareth—all of these are parts of Palestine."[54] None of these "parts of Palestine" is on the West Bank. These are pre-1967 areas of Israel, the regions of densest Jewish population, which the intifada's leaders believed would eventually fall into their hands.

But after a few months, all but the most extreme grew tired of pursuing this chimera, and the intifada began to lose its glitter. The interminable strike destroyed the booming economy that had been painstakingly built up since 1967, ruining businesses and impoverishing many. Law enforcement was transferred into the hands of competing gangs of local toughs funded and directed by competing PLO factions,* who used their power to abuse anyone they considered to be "collaborators": the well-to-do, the educated, political rivals, and so on. Indeed, the great majority of intifada violence ended up turning inward: against rival factions and anyone else considered undesirable. In 1990, the third year of the intifada, the total number of people killed in this grisly inter-Arab strife in the territories was one hundred, as compared to a total of fifty killed in confrontations with the Israel Defense Forces (IDF), a ratio of two to one.[55] The bodies of scores of Arabs were discovered covered with burns, swollen from beatings, disemboweled, dismembered, decapitated. Wives of "collaborators" were raped, and their children molested and beaten as warnings. The intifada was literally devouring its children.

Little publicized has been the virulently anti-Christian dimension of the intifada. In Christian towns such as Bethlehem, a campaign of violence, firebombings, and blackmail has been directed against Christians, with the intention of forcing them to sell their holdings to Moslems and leave the Holy Land. In an article in the Catholic journal *Terra Santa*, Father Georges Abou-Khazen wrote that Arab states have been pouring money into the effort to "Islamicize" the country, and that he feared the complete eradication of the Christian presence in the Holy Land. According to Father Abou-Khazen, Christians have been too terrified to speak out, fearing for their lives.[56]

Not that any of these horrors reached most of the programs of the international television networks covering the intifada. As in the mass expulsions of Palestinian Arabs from Kuwait, no one seemed to care when Palestinian Arabs were being harmed unless Israel was doing the harming. Ignoring the Arab reign of terror in the Palestinian streets, the media created for themselves nightly

---

*One of the leaders of the "Black Panthers," the intifada gang directly under the control of Yasser Arafat's Fatah faction, described the PLO's control over the killings in this way:
"We [the masked youths] don't kill just anyone. . . . [W]e consult with the Black Panthers' central committee, which is in direct contact with the Fatah military command abroad. . . . I only take my orders from the military command of Fatah. . . ."[57]

installments of a popular romance-drama: heroic underdog in search of self-determination taking on a terrifying Israel tyrant. This drama was not too difficult to create since democratic peoples do not like violence, and they do not like soldiers. They are especially revolted by the sight of a soldier beating a nonsoldier or glaring at a child. Since viewers were being told that this was an "army of occupation"—that is, it had no right to be there in the first place—the media managed to transform even the most necessary aspects of maintaining law and order into unforgivable crimes.

Utterly lost from the images on the screen was the organized nature of the rioting, the internecine violence, and the terrorized lives of the innocent Arabs (and Jews) who were ground under the intifada's heel. Similarly lost were the restrictive firing orders that stayed the hand of every Israeli soldier, and the swift trials of the 208 Israelis who in any way disobeyed these orders[58]—as against the tens of thousands of Israeli soldiers and reservists who followed the regulations with impeccable restraint.

The bashing that Israel received in the media was particularly instructive, given that next to nothing was said, either now or at the time, about the way the *Arab* governments of Jordan and Egypt had put down their intifadas in these very territories before 1967. We can, for instance, compare the actions taken by the Israeli military to that of the Jordanian Legion during the period when Jordan was the occupying power in the West Bank (which it had invaded in 1948 and illegally annexed in 1950). In October 1954, Beirut radio reported the outbreak of riots and demonstrations in Jenin, Nablus, Ramallah, and Jordanian-held Jerusalem. The army was called in, and a state of emergency was declared. The official Jordanian announcement said that fourteen were killed and 117 injured. Unofficial media reports claimed that ninety were killed.[59] In April 1957, riots in Jerusalem and Ramallah led King Hussein to resort to emergency measures: A curfew was imposed on Jerusalem and Ramallah, newspapers were closed, municipal councils were dismissed in Bethlehem, Nablus,

Tulkarm, and Jenin, and there were widespread arrests, including 169 UN teachers.[60] In April 1963 in Jerusalem, eleven were killed, 150 wounded (including seventeen schoolgirls); in Ramallah one person was killed and thirty-five were wounded; in Jenin and Irbid dozens more were wounded; 120 politicians were arrested.[61] On November 19, 1966, riots broke out in Nablus and Hebron and police opened fire into the crowds. The next day tanks were brought in and opened fire. Fifty were killed or wounded in Nablus alone. More were killed at the funerals.[62]

Similar treatment was accorded the residents of Gaza by the Egyptian army. In fairness, it should be noted that Jordan had at least given most of the Palestinian Arabs Jordanian citizenship. But Egypt refused them even this elementary amenity, deliberately keeping the entire population of Gaza in a humiliating condition of statelessness, almost half of them as passportless refugees.

With such summary treatment, it is not surprising that none of these intifadas lasted very long or amounted to very much. For the Jordanians and the Egyptians were willing to resort to means of "restoring order" in the territories that Israel would never dream of using—the Israeli army did not roll tanks in front of crowds and fire away. But the Jordanian Legion was free from such restraint: Its soldiers used not rubber bullets but lead ones. Nor were they under orders to fire only when their lives were in danger. If Israel had used the Jordanian methods, casualties would have climbed to twenty-five or fifty *per day* rather than the much smaller rate that did result from mass encounters with the IDF. In all likelihood, Israel's intifada would have died the same quick and bloody death as did its precursors under Arab regimes. But Israel, of course, was unprepared to adopt such methods, knowingly prolonging the intifada and taking upon itself punishing political costs (including claims about the inhumanity and depravity of Israeli methods) in order to avoid the use of uninhibited force.

When such a comparison is raised, Western diplomats and journalists commonly respond by claiming that Israel must be

held to a higher standard than the Arab dictatorships. True
enough. Undoubtedly a democracy should be judged by the standards of democracies. Indeed, during the years of the intifada several violent outbreaks occurred in democratic countries, the most
noteworthy in Venezuela and India. In Venezuela, in two days of
rioting in 1987, the government put down the violence with a toll
of 119 dead and 800 wounded, while in India during the ten-day
siege of the Golden Temple, 133 people died in clashes between
secessionist Sikhs and the government.[63] (These were greater
than the number killed in a full *year* of intifada confrontations
with the IDF.) When violent looting, the stoning of vehicles, or the
firebombing of shops occurs in a democracy, it must take forceful
action, since the first obligation of government—of any government—is to keep the peace. When such rioting occurred in America's major cities in the mid-1960s, the death toll in eruptions of
rioting lasting only a few days was thirty-four in Los Angeles,
twenty-six in Newark, forty-three in Detroit, and scores of others
elsewhere. Tens of thousands were arrested. When renewed rioting in 1968 hit 125 cities, the American government had no choice
but to apply massive force: 55,000 soldiers and policemen were
brought in to quell the disturbances. In all, forty-six were killed
and over 21,000 arrested.[64] Lest anyone believe that these explo-
sions were a thing of the past, rioting in Los Angeles in May 1992
left fifty-one dead in three days—and resulted in widespread criticism of the Los Angeles police for not having responded with
enough force.

Not only rioting but stone-throwing has its parallels in other
countries. In 1991, two Maryland teenagers were caught hurling
rocks at passing cars, sending a fifteen-year-old girl who was a pas-
senger in one car into a coma. (In the territories several Jewish
passengers have lost their lives and others have been crippled for
life by rocks hurled through the windshields of their vehicles.) Although the average person in the West is not accustomed to thinking in such terms, a rock the size of a baseball hurled into a car
traveling at sixty miles per hour is a weapon at least as deadly as a

knife or an ax. The offenders in Maryland were charged with ninety counts, including "assault with intent to murder, assault with intent to maim, assault with intent to disable, assault and battery, and malicious destruction of property." They were sentenced to five hundred years in prison, assuring that they will spend the rest of their adult lives behind bars.[65] The "harsh" military administration in Judea and Samaria naturally insists on similar penalties, though it should be pointed out that the penalty for those rock throwers who do *not* succeed in inflicting substantial damage is a modest fine.

That Israel was not judged according to these international norms indicates that there is not a double standard at work, but a *triple* one—one standard for the Arab dictatorships, a second for the democracies, and still a third—separate and special—for Israel. This third standard rests on the oft-repeated assumption that Israel is morally wrong *to be in the territories at all,* and that its every act there is therefore a derivative wrong. Based on this premise, the Israeli army is held to be wrong in its every use of force, no matter how restrained or proportional, no matter how necessary. It is a standard against which no country can possibly be judged favorably, and as such it has been used with consummate skill by Arab propagandists to demonize Israel during the intifada riots, obliterating for many both the history and causality of the Arab-Israeli conflict. For like the Arab campaign of international terrorism before it, the intifada's purpose soon evolved to serve as a stage in the PLO's media war against Israel. After the first weeks of spontaneous rioting, the intifada's "main events" were increasingly calculated purely from manipulating public opinion: the use of crowds of children in confrontations, the staging of riots for the press, the orders against the use of firearms, the prominent display of English-speaking Palestinian advocates of "civil disobedience," the silencing of dissent which might harm the image of "unity"—all combined with the PLO's pronouncements that no one had the power to stop the intifada, and that only a Palestinian state (under its rule) could end the violence by giving the Palestinian people in the "Israeli-occupied West Bank" their just deserts, i.e., self-determination. (Some correspondents obligingly explained that the "Palestinian people" had been "occupied for centuries" by the Byzantines, the Turks, the British, and the Israelis and were now "finally" prepared to seize their destiny and their independence.)

Despite the decline in the widespread rioting that characterized the beginning of the intifada, the years of bombardment by the carefully crafted Arab media blitz took their toll, and in the minds of many in the West the Reversal of Causality is now an established fact. For them, it is clear that the Israelis have dispossessed and oppressed the Palestinian people. After all, they saw them doing it on television.

But no matter how potent the intifada has been as a stage for political and journalistic attacks against Israel, it had a limited media-life and therefore limited political usefulness. The campaign against Israel's "usurpation" of Palestinian self-determination therefore focused on another controversy between Israel and the Arabs: the settlements. These, at least, had the benefit of not going away. They could be brought up again and again as proof of Israel's continuing efforts to "steal" the land away from its rightful owners, the Palestinians. And they had the added benefit of being opposed by a faction within Israel itself that agitated for a curtailment of settlement activity.

The right of Jews to live in Hebron, Nablus, and East Jerusalem (that is, the "West Bank") was recognized by the nations of the world at the same time as the right of Jews to live in Haifa, Tel Aviv, and West Jerusalem—in the Balfour Declaration, the Treaty of Versailles, and the League of Nations Mandate. At the time there was no such thing as the West Bank, and no one had ever suggested that Samaria and Judea could somehow be distinguished from the rest of Palestine, certainly not from western Palestine. On the contrary, Judea and Samaria were the very heart of the land, in which virtually every event of importance in pre-exilic Jewish history took place: Elon Moreh, where Abraham was promised the land, and Hebron, where he buried Sarah; Beth El, where Jacob dreamed of the ladder to heaven, and Bethlehem, where he buried Rachel; Jericho, where Joshua entered the land, and Shechem (Nablus), where he read the people the law and buried Joseph; Shiloh, which housed the tabernacle and served as the center of the Jewish people for four centuries before Jerusalem; Beth Horon, where the Maccabees defeated the Seleucids; and Bctar, where the second great Jewish revolt against Rome was finally crushed. Above all, there was the Old City of Jerusalem (today, "East Jerusalem"), the physical Zion of the Jews, the heart and breath of the Jewish people since the time of David and the prophets, and the center of its spiritual and political aspirations. At Versailles, when the Zionists claimed Palestine and when Wilson, Lloyd George, and Clemenceau recognized the claim, it was places such as these of which they thought above all others.

Hence it comes as no surprise that Jewish immigrants chose to come to these places during the period of the British Mandate. In Jerusalem and Hebron there were already large Jewish communities that were joined by new immigrants, and the immigrants founded new ones as well; Kalia and Beit Ha'arava in the Jordan River Valley; Atarot and Neve Ya'akov in Samaria; Ein Tzurim, Revadim, Massuot Yitzhak, Kfar Etzion, and Ramat Rachel in Judea; and Kfar Darom in Gaza. All of these "West Bank settlements" were founded before there was such a thing as a "West Bank," and no one knew that they were different from any of the other Jewish villages and towns sprouting all over western Palestine. No one questioned the right of Jews to live in any of these places—except for those who rejected the right of Jews to live anywhere in the land at all.

Any fair-minded observer must be moved to ask: If the right of Jews to live in Judea and Samaria was recognized by the League of Nations and was undisputed by most of the international community when Jewish communities were being founded there before the establishment of Israel, just when did Jews *lose* the right to live in these places?

In fact, they never did lose that right—only the practical ability to exercise it. The disappearance of that capacity can be dated to Israel's War of Independence in 1948. The Jordanian Legion of King Abdullah crossed the Jordan River unprovoked and uninvited and seized Judea, Samaria, and the eastern reaches of Jerusalem (including the Old City, with its ancient Jewish community). Everywhere the Jordanians came, they destroyed what they could of the Jewish presence. In East Jerusalem, the Jewish quarter was almost completely leveled by the invading Jordanians. Thousands of Jews were expelled from their homes, synagogues destroyed, and Jewish cemeteries desecrated.* The Jewish settlers of Kfar Etzion were not so lucky. Their attempts to raise a white flag and surrender were ignored, and the Jordanians kept firing until they had killed 240 people. The communities themselves were destroyed and abandoned.

In 1950, Abdullah formally annexed what he now called the "West Bank" to Jordan. This was so obviously the spoils of an illegal and aggressive war that only two countries, Britain and Pakistan, ever recognized the annexation. In 1954, a year after Hussein succeeded to the throne, Jordan formally promulgated the law prohibiting Jews from living there—a law which is on the books to this day. And while the 1949 armistice agreement with Israel stipulated that Jews should be allowed into Jordanian-held Jerusalem to visit their holy sites, the agreement was systematically violated to prevent Jews from entering the kingdom.

When Jordan seized the West Bank in 1948, it captured land

---

*After the Six Day War Israelis were shocked to discover that tombstones in the Mount of Olives cemetery, the Jewish people's most revered burial site overlooking King David's city, had been torn down and used as pavement stones for roads and slabs for latrines. Most of this state-sponsored desecration was carried out on the bottom third of the mountain, where the Jordanians built a highway right through the cemetery, and at the very top, where they built the Intercontinental Hotel. Soon after the Six Day War, my family set out with considerable trepidation to find out whether my grandfather's grave, which the Jordanians had not allowed us (like other Israelis) to visit for nineteen years, had been desecrated. Fortunately we found it intact, and my grandmother was later buried beside him.

that was almost entirely empty. Outside of the small urban centers such as Shechem (Nablus), Hebron, Ramallah, and Bethlehem, there was a scattering of villages along the crude roads connecting them, and an occasional Bedouin farther afield. The Jordanian government took direct control of most of the open space and for the nineteen years of Jordanian control made virtually no effort to develop it. Hussein's policy was to develop the East Bank alone, and he in fact was successful in moving what little industry there had been on the West Bank before 1948 across to the other side of the Jordan River.

In 1967 Jordan again attacked Israel. This time it lost all the land it had won in 1948. The Israeli army reentered the Old City of Jerusalem, Hebron, and Shechem, and Israel reasserted the right of Jews to live in these cities and towns, which the discriminatory Jordanian law had obstructed for nineteen years. The ruined Jewish communities in the Old City, Hebron, and Gush Etzion were rebuilt, in some cases by the children of those who had been driven from their homes by the Arabs in 1948. Over time, close to 300,000 Israelis have chosen to exercise their right to return to these communities and the new ones built next to them. This figure includes 150,000 Jewish residents of Judea and Samaria, 10,000 on the Golan, 3,000 in Gaza, and another 150,000 in the Old City and the sprawling suburbs of East Jerusalem (On occasion, the U.S. explains that it considers any Jewish real estate purchases, construction, and habitation in the Old City and eastern Jerusalem to be West Bank settlement. At other times, it stresses that Jerusalem will not be divided again.)[66] But as is evident from the historical and political facts, these communities, whether called "settlements" or "suburbs" or anything else, represent no new Jewish claim and no new Jewish right. They are firmly founded on the same right that was recognized by the international community at Versailles *and freely exercised by the Jews up until the Jordanians forcibly suppressed that free exercise in 1948.*

Nevertheless, many Western leaders have grown increasingly

strident about Jewish "settlement activity"—despite the fact that their own governments were signatories at Versailles and party to the decision to grant the Mandate recognizing the right to Jewish settlement. "Never mind that," they say. "You have no right to be tossing Arabs off their land."

This remarkable example of diplomatic and historical forgetfulness might conceivably be justified if Jews *were* taking land away from Arabs. Careful manipulation of the media by the Arabs has left many Westerners with the indelible impression that Arab paupers are being kicked out of their hovels in droves to make way for Jewish suburbs in the "densely populated West Bank." Yet the West Bank is anything but densely populated. It is in fact *sparsely* populated: Its population density of 150 people per square kilometer is less than 2.5 percent (one-fortieth) of the population density of Tel Aviv (6,700 per square kilometer).[67] This density is equivalent not to that of the suburban areas outside New York, London, or Paris, but to that of *rural* regions beyond the metropolitan belts of such cities. Four Arab cities located along the crest of the mountains, together with East Jerusalem, account for the bulk of the Arab population, while taking up only a small fraction of the land. The rest remains in large part vacant.

After years of looking at television shots from refugee districts, the average viewer in the West cannot help believing that Judea and Samaria are one large, squalid, teeming cluster of shanties packed one on top of the next, all the way from Tel Aviv to Jericho. The myth is readily punctured by a one-hour outing. Driving from Tel Aviv due east toward the Jordan River, one sees mountain after mountain after mountain covered with—nothing. No Arabs, no Jews, no trees, *nothing*. When here and there one finally comes to an Arab village or two, or a Jewish village or two, they are followed by yet more nothing. To the unaided eye, it is instantly obvious that entire cities can be built here without taking anything away from anyone.

This is not only a physical fact but a legal one as well. In 1967 the Israeli government took direct possession of the roughly 50 percent of the land that had been owned by the Jordanian government,[68] the vast majority of it land on which no Arabs were living and over which Arab individuals had no legal claim. In fact, Israeli courts admit Jordanian land law as the decisive factor in determining legal title to West Bank land (except for those provisions in Jordanian law that prohibited Jews from owning land at all), and while there have been cases in which West Bank Arabs have taken the government to court and won land to which they had legal title, the simple fact is that most of it was not taken from anyone. It was simply empty public land.

It is to this land, virtually as barren and lifeless as it was when Mark Twain and Arthur Penrhyn Stanley visited it over a century ago, that Israel is now bringing life. The Jewish West Bank town of Ariel, for example, now has fifteen thousand residents, a shopping mall, a hotel, a college, an orchestra, and an avenue named after George Bush for his role in the war against Saddam. The town is planned for more than a hundred thousand people, and from the car window you can see why: There's nothing in the way. Ariel was built on an empty hill, and there is plenty more where that came from in every direction you look. And the same is true for Ma'aleh Adumin, Immanuel, Elkana, Oranit, Givat Ze'ev, Efrat, Betar, and other major urban settlements.

Not surprisingly, the reassertion of the right of Jews to build their homes and their lives in East Jerusalem, Judea, and Samaria after an absence of nineteen years has raised howls of protest from the Arabs, and particularly from the PLO. It is this decision to grant Jews the right to live where Arabs do not want them that has sired the entire international campaign castigating Israelis for their "settlement activity"—which is to say, for moving into the neighborhood.

In this campaign, the sour logic of the Reversal of Causality is at its most pernicious. For what is manifestly occurring is that the West, which so sharply condemned anti-black apartheid in South Africa, is being used by the Arabs as an enforcer of the anti-Jewish apartheid that pertains in the Arabs' own countries. The Arab states generally prefer not to have Jewish residents (Morocco being the only real exception), but some are more devoted to this than others. Most zealous are some of the other "moderate" monarchies. Saudi Arabia will not honor any passport if it indicates that the bearer has ever been to Israel. In Jordan, the sale of land to a Jew was punishable by death. Yet rather than criticizing the patently anti-Semitic laws in force in Jordan and Saudi Arabia or asking these governments to alter these laws (much less imposing a UN resolution or economic sanctions to prompt them to do so), the United States and the other democracies issued statement after statement in *favor* of the application of apartheid to Judea and Samaria, demanding that Jews submit to Arab anti-Jewish strictures and stay out of territory that the Arabs wished closed to them. More incredible, the West regularly demands Israeli government intervention to *prevent* Jews from going to live where only Arabs supposedly should live. And this from people who would recoil in disgust if they heard that Jews were being told they had no right to move into any neighborhood or any suburb in any other part of the world.

The absurdity of this approach is most pronounced in the international tumult that erupts every time a Jew attempts to buy or rent a house in Silwan, a neighborhood not far from the center of municipal Jerusalem. Silwan had Jewish residents until 1948, when it ended up on the Jordanian side of the cease-fire line (by a few hundred yards) and the Jews were thrown out. Today Jews buying homes there are challenged not only on the basis of individual property claims, which can be settled in court, but by an additional principle that Jews are forbidden to live there even if their individual property rights are unassailable. Silwan is the Arabization of the Hebrew name Shiloach, given to the spring and pool that supplied water to Jerusalem in ancient times. It was around this waterworks, described in the Bible in detail and very much intact today, that King David first built and fortified the capital of the Jewish people. Silwan, in fact, *is* the City of David. It is this place, two hundred yards from the Western Wall, that Jewish "settlers" are told to stay out of.

Usually the demand to stay out of such neighborhoods and the 150 Jewish cities and towns in the territories is not presented in terms of dismantling them but in terms of a "freeze" on Jewish construction (no one ever speaks of a freeze on Arab construction). This term became even more familiar under Israeli's Labor government between 1992 and 1996, which committed to freezing some of the settlements. But freezing these communities is condemning them to gradual and certain death, as is ultimately the case with anything alive. A freeze would prevent the natural growth and health of these communities, ensuring that there would be no new hospitals or clinics, no new schools, no new stores, libraries, or services of any kind. It could mean that children could not build homes near their parents, that struggling young communities would be doomed to keep struggling forever. Why would anyone want to live in such places, frozen in time as though in a fairy tale? The answer, of course, is that no one would, which is why a "freeze" is such a handy euphemism for people who wish to find a polite way of saying, "No Jews." This is perhaps why in practice the policy did not materialize under the Labor government. Between 1992 and 1996 the Jewish population of the Israeli settlements in Judea and Samaria grew an unprecedented 50 percent. Life has a power of its own.

But it is not only the Jewish communities of Judea and Samaria that would be devastated by a freeze. Most of the "settlers" live in what in the West is usually known as a suburb: a large-scale industrial and residential development, ringing an urban center that is crucial for the natural development of all cities—and which normally develops without any relation to politics. Thus, the great majority of the 250,000 Jews living in what are being called "settlements" are for the most part suburbanites, living in much the way that New York City commuters whose homes are in New Jersey or Long Island live, driving twenty or thirty minutes from "the heart of the West Bank" to downtown Jerusalem and Tel Aviv. With-

out its suburbs, a city would become overcrowded, living conditions would decline, and industry would be forced to relocate.
The ultimate result of constraining the development of suburban
areas is the strangulation of any metropolis and its eventual decay.
Yet Tel Aviv is only a few miles from the West Bank, and Jerusalem
is surrounded by the West Bank on three sides. (In fact, more than
half the city, "East Jerusalem," may be said to be *on* the West
Bank.) To imagine the effect on these cities if all contiguous real
estate were forbidden for development, one has to imagine what
New York City would be like today if New Yorkers had never been
allowed to "settle" New Jersey, Connecticut, or Long Island. Throttled, the city would have declined long ago.

The campaign of delegitimization that has challenged the
right of Jews to live in the heartland of Israel and in its capital is
predicated on the bizarre idea that Judea, Samaria, and East
Jerusalem are "foreign land," seized by Jewish interlopers from
those who had owned them since antiquity. To entertain this idea,
of course, requires an astonishing flight of historical amnesia. For
these were places where Jews had lived—for millennia in places
like Hebron and Jerusalem, and for decades preceding the War of
Independence in the emerging Jewish communities in Judea and
southern Samaria. When my parents were students in the Hebrew
University campus on Mount Scopus in East Jerusalem in the early
1930s, a common pastime was to go down to bathe at the Jewish
resort of Kalya on the Dead Sea and find refuge from the scorch-
ing sun in the orchards of Jericho. The destruction of the Jewish
communities in 1948 did not mean that the Jews of Israel lost their
attachment to the lands that were abruptly cut off from them.
From 1948 to 1967, when the territories were occupied by Jordan,
Israelis knew much of this "foreign terrain" by heart from their
studies of the Bible and subsequent Jewish history. Some could
look out their windows and see the hills of Samaria rising above
their homes. Others knew the land from their parents who had
lived in Judea before being driven out by the Jordanians. Most of
all, Israelis remembered the Western Wall, the hallowed rampart

of the Jewish Temple that was buried inside the Arab-controlled section of divided Jerusalem. The holiest place of Judaism was barred to them as Jews—even though it was only a few hundred yards away across a no-man's-land.

The eerie feeling of imprisonment, of being so close and yet so very far away from the cradle of Jewish history, was hauntingly captured a few weeks before the outbreak of the Six Day War by the publication of Naomi Shemer's "Jerusalem of Gold," a song that deeply moved the entire country:

> Amid the slumber of trees and stone
> Imprisoned in her dreams
> The city dwells alone
> Within her heart a wall
>
> How have the wells gone dry
> The market square forsaken
> And no one climbs the Temple Mount
> In Old Jerusalem
>
> In the caves carved in the stone
> The winds cease not to cry
> And none descend the Dead Sea road
> By way of Jericho[69]

After the walls dividing the city suddenly came down during the Six Day War, thousands of Israelis streamed through the Old City to the wall—following the steps of the soldiers to the place where, just hours earlier, secular, battle-weary paratroops had wept to a man over the privilege granted to them of sewing back together the broken heart of the Jewish people. Like the soldiers, the citizens of Israel stood before the ancient Wall, touching the massive stones in wondrous awe. From there, in the days and weeks that followed, they made their way, at times wide-eyed with a barely contained excitement, to Bethlehem, Hebron, Shechem,

Jericho, Beth El, and all the other places in whose names, land-scape, and history was cemented the identity of the Jewish people.

This exhilaration was felt by almost all Israelis, and each one experienced it in a different way. My brother Yoni, like many Israelis, would often spend his weekend leaves from the army exploring such sites:

> It seems that the cradle of world civilization is all around us, everything dating back thousands and thousands of years. A few Saturdays ago I visited the Biblical Gibeon and saw the remarkable ancient pool there. It's this pool that's mentioned in Second Samuel in connection with Avner ben Ner and Joab ben Zeruya [Saul and David's generals] who "met together by the pool at Gibeon" and let "the young men arise and play [i.e., do battle] before them." The entire country is like that.[70]

I myself remember the experience less from weekend leaves than from the training that I underwent in a reconnaissance unit. We would criss-cross the hills and mountains in exhausting marches and hikes aimed at honing our navigating skills. Inevitably, if there was a craggy peak along the route, we would climb it; a steep gorge, and we would descend into it. As the shirt on your back stiffens into a mixture of sweat and dust and the soles of your feet burn as if on fire, it is difficult to feel deeply for a country. But not impossible. I remember nights when we would come to a sudden halt at the foothills of Shiloh, the first capital of the Israelites after the exodus from Egypt; or stop midway up the steep pass of Beth Horon, where the Maccabees triumphed over the Greeks in their desperate struggle for Jewish independence; or gaze up at the fortress of Betar, where Bar Kochba's revolt met its tragic end at the hands of the Roman legions. We would stand there, a handful of youngsters barely nineteen, taking in the night air and gulping water from our canteens, saying nothing. Because what we felt did not need saying. *We had come back*—for all the generations of Jews who had suffered oppression, degradation, and humiliation while they dreamed and prayed that we would return to this land.

Moshe Dayan captured this sentiment a few weeks after the Six Day War in a ceremony on the Mount of Olives in East Jerusalem, marking the reinterment of the soldiers who had fallen in Jerusalem in the battle for the city in 1948:

> Our brothers who fell in the War of Independence: we have not abandoned your dream nor forgotten the lesson you taught us. We have returned to the [Temple] Mount, to the cradle of our nation's history, to the land of our forefathers, to the land of the Judges, and to the fortress of David's dynasty [the Old City]. We have returned to Hebron, to Sh'chem, to Bethlehem and Anatoth, to Jericho and the fords over the Jordan.[71]

For the normally uneffusive Dayan this was an uncharacteristic outpouring of feeling. Israeli culture does not encourage outward displays of profound emotion, and in the years following the Six Day War many Israelis kept their deepest sentiments about this, the heart of their land, to themselves. The ones who expressed it more openly were the religious members of the settlement movement, who spearheaded the drive to rebuild the ancient (and modern) Jewish cities in the largely barren land. Even though many Israelis who did not go to live there supported their activities, the result was that the world came to believe that the claim to the land was espoused only by a "radical fringe" of the Israeli public. This erroneous view was heightened by the emergence of a vocal movement on the left that for a variety of reasons argued that Israel should leave "the territories."

Successive Israeli governments did not bother to articulate the emotional connection that so many Israelis, including a significant number on the left, felt toward the land, choosing rather to stress the more readily explainable security arguments against relinquishing the land outright. That—and the fact that, unlike most Israelis, the Arabs had no compunction in expressing their attachment and their claims, almost always embellished with a false history that few in the international media had the knowledge to debunk—soon combined to produce a commonly accepted view that the Jews had taken an Arab patrimony to which they had no moral rights and no enduring ties. Quickly forgotten was not only the fact that it was the Arabs who had driven the Jews out in 1948 and attacked them again from these territories in 1967, but also the entire course of Jewish history, the focus of which was the great Return. Return to what? Certainly not the quaint cafés of Tel Aviv or the lush villas of its wealthy suburb Savion, both of which had been sand and swamp until a few decades earlier and which had never before existed in Jewish history or Jewish memory. When the Jewish people yearned to return to their land, when they actually did so in the course of this century, their souls were enthralled by the idea of returning to all the places that Moshe Dayan enumerated, and to many more that he did not, in the mountains of Samaria and Judea.

Yet the endless parade before the television cameras of Palestinians castigating Israeli "occupiers" was able to erase all of this from the public mind. It was asserted that Israel had taken "foreign land," and that Israel must return it to its "rightful owners"; if it did not, it would suffer the risk of war.

This was not the first time in Jewish history that the Jews reclaimed these very lands from which they had been barred. More than twenty-one hundred years ago the Maccabees had done the same after a thirty-year war of liberation. It is instructive to read today the exchange of letters between the Seleucid king Antiochus and the Jewish leader Simon, the only survivor of the five Maccabee brothers who fell leading their people in the long struggle for freedom. Antiochus, just as convinced that the land was an inextricable part of his Seleucid Greek empire as the Arabs today are convinced that it is an inextricable part of their realm, demanded:

> You hold control of Joppa and Gazara and the citadel of Jerusalem; they are cities of my kingdom. You have devastated

their territory, you have done great damage in the land, and you have taken possession of many places in my kingdom. Now then, hand over the cities which you have seized. . . . Otherwise we will come and conquer you.

Simon's reply could have been written today:

We have neither taken foreign land nor seized foreign property, but only the inheritance of our fathers, which at one time had been unjustly taken by our enemies. Now that we have the opportunity, we are firmly holding the inheritance of our fathers.[72]

This land, where every swing of a spade unearths remnants of the Jewish past and where every village carries the barely altered Hebrew names of old; this land, in which the Jews became a nation and over which they shed more tears than have been shed by any other people in history; this land, the loss of which resulted in an exile of the Jews such as has been suffered by no other people and the spilling of a sea of blood such as has been spilled by no other nation; this land, which never ceased to live as a distant but tangible home in the minds of Jewish children from Toledo in medieval Spain to the Warsaw ghetto in our own century; this land, for which the Jews fought with unsurpassed courage and tenacity in ancient as well as in modern times—this is the "foreign land" that world leaders now demand be barred to Jews and that Israel unilaterally forsake. This is an unjust demand. The Palestinian Arabs on the West Bank now live under Palestinian rule. The remaining territories are almost entirely uninhabited by Palestinians, but are replete with historical significance for Israel.

The Arab campaign to keep all the West Bank free of Jews, like the campaign of the 1930s to keep Palestine free of Jews, may have garnered international support, but it is based, now as then, not on justice but on injustice. Thus the Jewish state, which was squeezed by violations of international promises and by Arab conquest to an indefensible coast, that saw Jews forcibly expelled from the ancient Jewish cities they had come to rebuild, that was attacked by Arab forces from the surrounding mountains, is now being told by virtually the entire world that it must accept a confined and stifling existence on the narrow shoreline dominated by a hostile, *Judenrein* Palestinian state on these same mountains, the very heart of the Jewish home. If Lord Cecil had proclaimed "Judea for the Jews, Arabia for the Arabs," the world was now saying, "Arabia for the Arabs—and Judea too." The Reversal of Causality was now complete.

5

THE TROJAN HORSE

alse reductionism is the central technique of the Arab campaign against Israel. Reduce all the Middle East conflicts to the Arab-Israeli one, reduce the Arab-Israeli conflict to a Palestinian-Israeli one, and you are then ready to take the next logical step: Reduce all the various Palestinian communal groupings and points of view to a single, anti-Israel "liberation movement," the Palestine Liberation Organization. This completes the role reversal whereby Israel is transformed into the heartless villain, challenged by a united band of dedicated, popular, even romantic revolutionaries, Arafat's PLO—if not George Washington and the Minutemen, then at least the Hollywood version of Emiliano Zapata and his freedom fighters.

In no time, the PLO became the "sole legitimate representative of the Palestinian people." No matter that until the Oslo Accords its officials weren't actually elected by anyone and then, too, by dubious methods. No matter that its only claim to unchallenged support lay in the fact that it slaughtered any Palestinian opponent who dared dissent. Throughout the Arab world, it was accepted that the PLO had to be pushed front and forward when discussing Israel—so that the attention of Western public opinion would remain focused on the purported sins of Zionism against the Palestinians, rather than on, for example, the Arab states' feverish arms buildup aimed against Israel and against each other. So obvious was the utility of this strategy that even the PLO's fiercest Arab antagonists supported its claim to being the "sole" spokesman for the "sole" (or at least principal) aggrieved party of the entire Arab-Israeli dispute.

Where did this organization come from, and what was its purpose? Was its espousal of terror a result of current political frustrations, or did it have deeper roots? And was its campaign of "armed struggle" against Israel developed in response to the "Israeli occupation of Palestinian lands" after the Six Day War of 1967, as the PLO repeatedly claims, or did it have an earlier genesis?

The PLO was founded in Cairo in 1964, three full years before the outbreak of the Six Day War. It was established by Egypt's Nasser as a means of continuing his unsuccessful war against Israel, and of destabilizing Jordan.[1] Since these two states together constituted the territory of Mandatory Palestine, they both readily fell under the PLO Charter's goal of liberating "all Palestinian lands." Notice that at that time Israel, the prime target, did not have an inch of what are now termed the "occupied territories" of the West Bank and Gaza. When the PLO was set up to liberate "Palestinian lands occupied by Israel," this unambiguously meant the State of Israel, especially the coastal plain between Tel Aviv and Haifa, where three-quarters of all Israelis live. It was the coastal plain from which most of the PLO leadership had originated, and it was the coastal plain to which they intended to return.

Thus, in its founding meeting, the Palestine National Council (PNC), the "legislature" of the PLO, adopted its infamous "constitution," the PLO Charter,* which laid out the PLO's most fundamental purpose:

---

*The Charter was first approved in 1964 and amended slightly in 1968. All quotes are from the 1968 version, which is the one still in force today.

ARTICLE 19: The partitioning of Palestine [by the UN] in 1947 and the establishment of Israel is fundamentally null and void, [and remains so] whatever time has elapsed. . . .

ARTICLE 20: The claim of a historical or spiritual tie between Jews and Palestine does not tally with historical realities nor with the constituents of statehood in their true sense. . . .

ARTICLE 21: The Palestinian Arab people, in expressing itself through the armed Palestinian revolution, rejects every solution that is a substitute for a complete liberation of Palestine. . . .

ARTICLE 22: [T]he liberation of Palestine will liquidate the Zionist and imperialist presence. . . .

(For the full text, see Appendix E.) While the PLO repeatedly committed itself to amend the charter (first in the 1993 Oslo Accords, and again in the May 1994 Cairo Agreement, the September 1995 Oslo 2 Accords, and the January 1997 Hebron Accord), no changes have been made despite occasional claims to the contrary. So long as it has not formally been repealed by the Palestinian National Council, the charter stands as compelling proof that the basic Palestinian grievance against Israel remains existential and not merely territorial.

Indeed, this is a central problem with the negotiations with the Palestinians. Whenever there is a major disagreement between the two sides, the Palestinian Authority ignites violent outbursts against Israel. These are often preceded by a wave of incitement in the Palestinian media and by senior Palestinian officials, who invoke language and ideas reminiscent of the Palestinian Charter in an attempt to demonize Israel. Amending the charter, or failing to do so, thus takes on added significance. The charter's central claim is that Israel is an illegal and criminal entity: "The establishment of Israel is fundamentally null and void, whatever time has passed"—that is, regardless of the location of its borders or the size of the territory under its control. The attachment of the Jewish people to the land for thirty-five hundred years, an attachment of unparalleled duration that has left an indelible mark on humanity from the Bible to the Balfour Declaration, is expunged with a wave of the hand: "The claim of a historical or spiritual tie between Jews and Palestine does not tally with historical realities. . . ." And the charter's central purpose is that Israel be destroyed: "[The] liberation of Palestine will liquidate the Zionist and imperialist presence. . . ."

The goal of what has been termed policide—the eradication of an entire country—is such a rarity that many people have difficulty believing that it could actually be the motive of organized political activity. That nations fight wars over borders, natural resources, colonies, and even forms of government is well known. But there is hardly a case in modern history in which an antagonist has sought to completely annihilate a rival nation. Not even World War II, the most terrible of wars, resulted in such an outcome. The defeat of Hitler and the capitulation of Hirohito were nowhere understood as opportunities to eradicate Germany and Japan. Yet it is precisely this most extraordinary goal, the erasure of an entire nation and its people, that the PLO had chosen to emblazon on its banner. (For this reason I insisted on the charter's annulment as part of the Wye Accords.)

To make sense out of such a movement, it is necessary to go beyond the pretense that 1967 and the "occupation of the West Bank" are the starting point of "resistance" against the Jews. The Arab war against the Jews is in fact as old as this century, and the PLO itself dates the formative period of Palestinian consciousness and resistance to Jewish settlement back to the 1920s and 1930s, the crucial decades before the creation of the State of Israel. Throughout this period, Arab bands launched murderous raids on Jewish farms and villages, assassinated Arab moderates, and rejected Jewish peace overtures and concessions. This ferocious and relentless campaign claimed hundreds of Jewish lives over two decades, yet it cannot be traced to any of the grievances that are offered today to explain the source of Arab opposition. This campaign had nothing to do with refugees, for at the time there were none. It had nothing to do with disputed borders, for there were none of those, either. Moreover, it had nothing to do with Palestinian Arab sovereignty, for the Arabs never claimed to be fighting for it in those days, and they rejected it when it was offered to them under the UN Partition Resolution in 1947. The conflict was driven not by any of these factors but by an irreducible rejection of any Jewish presence in the area.

Those who pursued this blind obsession trampled anything that stood in their way. Their favorite targets were Arabs who refused to acknowledge the "exclusive representation" of the "Arab cause" that the extremists claimed for themselves. Above all, the extremists rejected anyone who embraced the notions of compromise and coexistence, which are anathema to fanatics everywhere.

Perhaps the most prominent leader of Arab reductionism before the establishment of Israel in 1948 was the PLO's revered forebear, Haj Amin al-Husseini, the Grand Mufti of Jerusalem. As we have seen, Husseini was the preeminent agitator of the bloodiest Arab assaults on Jews in the first half of this century. A central figure in the PLO pantheon, he was the founding father of the PLO in both spirit and practice. No other figure has had such an influence on the PLO leadership. Over time, many of the Mufti's lieutenants and henchmen have assumed near-mythic status in PLO lore, among them Emil Ghouri and Abed al-Kader al-Husseini. In fact, when he was a young radical in Cairo in the early 1950s, Arafat sought to enhance his anti-Jewish image by taking the name Yasser (his real name is Abed al-Rahman) in memory of Yasser al-Birah, a leader of the Mufti's reign of terror in the 1930s.[2] Nor did it hurt his standing that he was related to the Mufti, being a member of the Al-Qidwah branch of the Husseini clan. Arafat has referred to the Mufti as his mentor and guide. In 1985, for example, during the thirtieth commemoration of the Bandung Conference of 1955 (an international forum of "unaligned" revolutionaries), Arafat extolled the Mufti with great reverence. He said that he took "immense pride" in being able to follow in the footsteps of the Mufti, who participated in the original conference. He emphasized that "the PLO is continuing the path set by the Mufti."[3]

What is that path? And what did the Mufti represent? We can gain an important insight into the goals and methods that the PLO pursued by examining the period of emerging Arab nationalism in Palestine that shaped not only the future course of the PLO as an organization but the path of its leaders, many of whom grew up in the Mufti's movement. For as in the case of Arabist attitudes toward Zionism, the interwar period proved to be pivotal in shaping the Arab nationalists' enduring concepts regarding the Jews of Palestine.

Haj Amin al-Husseini was appointed Grand Mufti of Jerusalem by the British in 1921, less than a year after they convicted him for instigating the murderous anti-Jewish riots in the Old City of Jerusalem. The Mufti's incitement and organization of enforcement gangs to back his ideas led to even more severe anti-Jewish riots across Palestine in 1921, then to the great massacres of August 1929. But the Mufti's main targets were actually Arabs. With his henchman Emil Ghouri and with funding from the Nazis and Italian Fascists,[4] he organized the torture and murder of moderate Arab leaders, landowners willing to sell to Jews, and anyone else he believed had betrayed his virulent creed. According to one scholar:

> These poor people were not always immediately murdered; sometimes they were kidnapped and taken to the mountainous areas under rebel control. There they were thrown into pits infested with snakes and scorpions. After spending a few days there, the victims, if still alive, were brought before one of the rebel courts, or commanders, tried, and usually sentenced to death, or, as a special dispensation, to severe flogging. The terror was so strong that no one, including ulema [learned men]

and priests, dared to prepare the proper burial services. In some cases, the British Police had to perform this duty; in others, the corpses were left in the streets for several days after a shoe had been placed in the mouth of the victim as a symbol of disgrace and as a lesson to others.[5]

Entire clans of Arabs who objected to the Mufti's policy, like the Nashashibi family of Jerusalem Arabs, were either wiped out or exiled, the total number of Palestinians murdered was in the thousands, and forty thousand Arabs were driven into exile.[6] The result of this consistent reign of terror was that by the end of the 1930s, moderate Arab opinion had been completely silenced in Palestine. When the Round Table Conference of Middle Eastern leaders, convoked by Britain, met in 1939 to determine the future of Palestine, the heads of the Husseini clan could claim to be "the sole representatives of the Palestinian Arabs."[7]

But for the Mufti all of this was still small change. He sought to tie his campaign to a more powerful, global engine that could ensure the creation of a Pan-Arab empire under his command— and the systematic, final annihilation of the Jews. Such an engine he believed himself to have found in the 1930s with the rise of the Fascist movement in Europe.

The Mufti first approached the German consul in Jerusalem in 1933, the year Hitler came to power, and he soon began drawing parallels between Nazi Pan-German nationalism and Pan-Arab nationalism. This analogy caught on quickly among many Arabs. Like the Arab world, the German-speaking world prior to Prussian unification had been fragmented into scores of feuding principalities and communities, many of them under foreign rule. The German psyche, too, had been wracked by a century-long crisis of confidence summed up in the question of *Was ist Deutsch?* ("What does it mean to be German?") And the profound German resentment of the Western powers for the "dismemberment" of their empire and their state at Versailles struck a sympathetic chord in Arab ears.

The German crisis of identity finally resolved itself in an emphatic, negative definition of Pan-German nationalism: German meant *not* Jewish, *not* Bolshevik, *not* polluted by the effeteness of the West. This was a formula that many Arabs found compelling as well, as evidenced by the founding of Arab national-socialist movements, parties, and youth organizations in the 1930s, the widespread dissemination of Nazi anti-Jewish literature, and the overall sympathy for Hitler's cause among the Arabs. Thus, Hitler's annexation of Austria and the Sudetenland met with jubilation among Arabs as a demonstration of the power of the oppressed. The future King Khaled of Saudi Arabia dined with Hitler on the night of Czechoslovakia's capitulation, and he raised his glass in a toast in honor of the heroic undertaking.[8] Other Arabs sympathetic to Hitler's work included key figures such as Nasser, the founders of the Ba'th Pan-Arab nationalist socialism currently in power in Syria and Iraq, and some of the guiding lights of Islamic fundamentalism. Hasan al-Banna, the founder of the fundamentalist Moslem Brotherhood, described the benefits of fascism this way:

> The world has long been ruled by democratic systems, and man has everywhere honored the conquests of democracy. . . . But men were not slow to realize that their collective liberty had not come intact out of the chaos [caused by democracy], that their individual liberty was not safe from anarchy. . . . Thus, German Nazism and Italian Fascism rose to the fore; Mussolini and Hitler led their two peoples to unity, order, recovery, power, and glory. In record time, they ensured internal order at home, and through force, made themselves feared abroad. Their regimes gave real hope, and also gave rise to thoughts of steadfastness and perseverence and the reuniting of different, divided men.[9]

One of the early Ba'thist leaders wrote of this time:

> We were racists, admiring Nazism, reading its books. . . . We were the first to think of translating *Mein Kampf.* Whoever lived

during this period in Damascus would appreciate the inclination of the Arab people to Nazism, for Nazism was the power which could serve as its champion.[10]

In Palestine the Mufti's clan founded the Palestinian Arab party, which party leader Jamal Husseini asserted was based on the Nazi model.[11] The party youth division was even briefly called the Nazi Scouts.[12] The outbreak of World War II found the Mufti in Iraq, where he organized Arab contacts with the Axis powers and solicited support for pro-Nazi insurrections in Iraq and Syria (the latter with the help of Salah al-Din al-Bitar and Michel Aflaq, the founders of the Ba'th).[13] In 1941 a Pan-Arabist regime allied with the Mufti deposed the British-installed Hashemite monarchy of Iraq and declared war on the Allies. The British army succeeded in propping its man up again, but not in saving the six hundred Jews who were slaughtered in Baghdad before British forces reentered the city.[14]

From Baghdad, the Mufti made his way to Rome and Berlin, where he offered the services of the Arab nation to the war effort on the condition that they "recognize in principle the unity, independence, and sovereignty of an Arab state of a Fascist nature, including Iraq, Syria, Palestine, and Trans-Jordan."[15] In October 1941 the Nazi government issued a formal communiqué in Berlin promising to help in the "elimination of the Jewish National Home in Palestine."[16] The Mufti then flew to Berlin and met Hitler in person for the first time on November 28, 1941. Husseini expressed his willingness to cooperate with Germany in every way, including the recruitment of an Arab Legion to fight for the Nazis. Hitler told the Mufti that the two of them shared the common goal of the destruction of Palestinian Jewry.[17]

The Mufti proceeded to work energetically on behalf of the Nazis. He made repeated broadcasts over Nazi radio urging Moslems everywhere to rise up against the Allies, and he organized sabotage and espionage in Arab lands. A representative broadcast from 1942 points out the stark relevance of the Axis war effort to Arabs:

> If, God forbid, England should be victorious, the Jews would dominate the world. England and her allies would deny the Arabs any freedom and independence, would strike the Arab fatherland to its heart, and would tear away parts of it to form a Jewish country whose ambition would not be limited to Palestine but would extend to other Arab countries. . . .
>
> But if, on the contrary, England loses and its allies are defeated, *the Jewish question, which for us constitutes the greater danger, would be finally resolved.*[18] [emphasis added]

The Mufti also recruited Moslems from the Soviet Union and the Balkans for Arab units of the German army being organized by a fellow Palestinian Arab named Fawzi Qawukji in Berlin. The Mufti's tour of Yugoslavia won six thousand recruits, who were eventually reorganized into a Waffen SS mountain unit that served in the campaign to destroy Yugoslav Jewry. "Kill the Jews wherever you find them," he said. "This pleases God, history and religion."[19]

Basing himself in Berlin from 1942 to 1944, the Mufti worked to prevent the rescue of Jews from Hungary, Romania, Bulgaria, and Croatia, countries which, although allied with Hitler, were willing to let Jews flee to Palestine and elsewhere. He protested that not enough Nazi resources were invested in preventing the escape of Jewish refugees from the Balkans.[20] A Nazi official, Wilhelm Melchers, said in evidence taken during the Nuremberg trials on August 6, 1947: "The Mufti was making protests everywhere—in the offices of the Foreign Minister, the Secretary of State and in other S.S. Headquarters."[21] These protests had the aim of urging the Nazis to greater thoroughness in preventing the escape of Jews from Europe. For example, on May 31, 1943, the Mufti personally delivered to German foreign minister Ribbentrop a letter protesting the plan to arrange the emigration of four thousand Jewish children from Bulgaria.[22]

But the Mufti was again not satisfied. He had a larger objective in mind than merely preventing the escape of some Jews. He wanted, as Melchers pointed out in the Nuremberg trials, to see "all of them liquidated."[23] As in the case of the Balkan Jews, he worked feverishly toward this goal. Adolf Eichmann's deputy, Dieter Wisliceny, said that Husseini

> played a role in the decision to exterminate the European Jews. The importance of this role must not be disregarded . . . the Mufti repeatedly suggested to the various authorities with whom he was maintaining contact, above all to Hitler, Ribbentrop, and Himmler, the extermination of European Jewry. He considered this an appropriate solution to the Palestinian Problem.[24]

Eichmann's deputy gave eyewitness testimony about Husseini's involvement:

> The Mufti was one of the initiators of the systematic extermination of European Jewry and had been a collaborator and advisor of Eichmann and Himmler in the execution of this plan. He was one of Eichmann's best friends and had constantly incited him to accelerate the extermination measures. *I heard him say that accompanied by Eichmann he had visited incognito the gas chamber of Auschwitz.*[25] [emphasis added]

How did such a war criminal escape punishment? Throughout Europe, Nazi war criminals were exposed and brought to justice. Not so in the Arab world, where Nazis and Nazi collaborators were greeted as heroes. Hundreds of German Nazis found refuge, and employment as advisers in murder, in Arab capitals. This was especially true of Egypt, which was a fierce rival of the South American dictators in trying to attract Nazis to its service,[26] netting such prizes as SS General Oskar Dirlewanger, who murdered thousands of Jews in the Ukraine and became Nasser's bodyguard, and Dr.

Heinrich Willerman, who experimented on live human beings in Dachau. The notorious SS killer Alois Brunner spent decades in Damascus as a guest of the Syrians until his reported death there in the summer of 1992. The PLO, too, has avidly continued the Mufti's tradition, consistently collaborating with neo-Nazis (and often with paleo-Nazis, as well), who have naturally found its goals and methods appealing.*

Nazism may have been defeated in Europe, but it was very much alive in the Middle East. After the war, the many Arab soldiers and agents who had fought for Hitler were warmly received back into the Arab world.[27] The Mufti himself set up shop as a guest of the Egyptian government, and went back to work spreading his poisonous doctrines throughout the Middle East. He and his cousin, the Palestinian Arab military leader Abed al-Kader al-Husseini, organized units that sought to liquidate Israel in 1947 and 1948, led by such veterans of the Nazi war effort as Fawzi Qawukji and Mahmud Rifai, a Syrian who had fought in the German paratroops[36] and was inspired by the Mufti's famous plea: "I declare a Holy War. Murder the Jews. Murder them all!" In Sep-

*Relations between Palestinian terror groups and the German extreme right date back to 1968, the year Yasser Arafat took control of the PLO. By 1970, members of the "Adolf Hitler Free Corps" under the leadership of German neo-Nazi Udo Albrecht were in Jordan assisting in the PLO's attempt to overthrow the government of King Hussein. Albrecht and his group went on to collaborate with "Black September," the terror arm of Arafat's Fatah, which committed the Munich Olympic massacre. Albrecht was eventually arrested in West Germany with PLO identity papers, but he later escaped. In 1976, four German neo-Nazis testified that they had been recruited by Albrecht to conduct PLO terror operations, and that they had been trained by the PLO in Lebanon.[28]

Albrecht also introduced Manfred Roeder, leader of the ultra-rightist "German Action Group," to PLO terrorism. In the two years that Albrecht was in prison after 1976, Roeder repeatedly traveled to Lebanon to coordinate with Abu Jihad, Arafat's lieutenant in the Fatah.[29]

Yasser Arafat's Fatah also trained the preeminent German neo-Nazi Karl Heinz Hoffman, whose "War Sports Group" began training in international terror in 1979 in Fatah's Bir Hassan training camp near Beirut.[30] In 1986 Hoffman was arrested for planning and ordering the 1980 murders of the German-Jewish publisher Shlomo Levin and his wife. Hoffman blamed the murders on one of his disciples, Uwe Behrendt, and was not convicted, but went to jail on other charges. Behrendt himself escaped to Lebanon. Another Hoffman protégé, Michael Kuhnen, founded the now-outlawed "National Socialist Action" organization in Germany, which also received its training from the PLO in Lebanon. In between jail terms, Kuhnen has been an outspoken supporter of the PLO.[31]

Perhaps the most notorious of German neo-Nazi killers is Odfried Hepp, a leader of

tember 1948 they assembled a "Government of all Palestine" whose seat was to be in Gaza. This Palestinian "government" was supported by the Egyptians as a rival to King Abdullah's government in Transjordan—which also claimed all of Palestine.[37] Yasser Arafat's brother Gamal, who had served with Abed al-Kader al-Husseini's forces, became secretary in the Mufti's "government." Arafat himself claims to have fought alongside Husseini, and there is a report that he served as his personal aide.[38] When, after the Arab defeat, Abdullah of Jordan showed signs of a willingness to make peace with Israel, he was murdered by the Mufti's agents in 1952.[39] This was an important escalation of the earlier practices of assassination, for the targets now were not merely prominent men but the leaders of whole countries. This ultimate system for intimidating entire nations, perfected by the Mufti and his disciples, is still very much with us.

Determined to keep the Mufti's radicalism firmly in line, King Farouq of Egypt allowed his guest little room to maneuver. When the Mufti actually tried to go to Gaza to take the reins of his "gov-

___

the Nazi group "V.S.B.D.," who was also trained by the PLO in the Fatah camp near Beirut. Hepp was arrested in Paris in 1985, along with his partner, Mahmad Adban, a senior operative of Abul Abbas's PLF faction of the PLO (which carried out the *Achille Lauro* hijacking later that year). The two were convicted of perpetrating terrorist attacks against Israeli targets in Vienna, Amsterdam, and Geneva. They are also suspected of involvement in the bombing of a Jewish restaurant in Paris in 1982, which left six dead. Particularly noteworthy is the fact that after the arrest, Abul Abbas, a member of the PLO executive, publicly called for Hepp's release and tried to secure it through diplomatic channels.[32]

The PLO has also worked to cultivate ties with neo-Nazis in Britain and France. In 1977, Fatah agreed to train members of "L'Oeuvre Française," a French neo-Nazi group, which in turn agreed to carry out operations for the PLO. In 1985 the British neo-Nazi Ian Michael Davison joined with two other gunmen of Yasser Arafat's "Force 17" to murder three Israeli tourists on a yacht in Larnaca, Cyprus. He is now in jail in Nicosia.[33] In recent years the British neo-Nazi group "National Front" has also established a relationship with the PLO, which has included the founding of a British front group called the "Campaign for Palestine Rights."[34]

While downplayed in the Western media, the PLO has otherwise made virtually no effort to hide its collaboration with neo-Nazism and its admiration for Nazism generally. This affinity has been markedly expressed in such overt gestures as the adoption of Nazi nommes de guerre such as "Hitler" and "Rommel" by Palestinian leaders in every faction of the PLO, including the PFLP, the Marxist DFLP, and Yasser Arafat's Fatah. Perhaps best known is Fawzi Salem al-Mahdi, a senior commander in Arafat's personal bodyguard "Force 17," who was nicknamed "Abu Hitler."[35]

ernment," Farouq quickly had him shipped back to Egypt.[40] The Mufti eventually fled to Beirut, where he died, but he lived long enough to see his revenge. King Farouq of Egypt was overthrown in 1952 and replaced by the Arab world's first totalitarian state: the Pan-Arab nationalist regime of Gamal Abdel Nasser, which set the vast machinery of government to work inculcating the hatred of the West and the dream of vengeance. Through Nasser and his pupils, the Mufti's legacy of hate was transferred intact to the most extreme quarters of the Arab world, especially to the radical Palestinians who matured in the intense political heat of Nasserist Cairo.

Such radicals, whose families had left Israel before or during the War of Independence, were plentiful in Cairo in the 1950s and early 1960s. Some of them, like Arafat, claimed not only spiritual but genealogical kinship with the Mufti, sprinkling, so to speak, the dust of royalty on their family tree.

It did not take much or long for such men to be harnessed to the Pan-Arab cause. Nasser, a would-be Saladin, daily promised Israel's destruction, having quickly realized that leading the crusade against Israel was a sure means of securing his place at the head of the Arab world. The youths who later constituted the leadership of the PLO—including Arafat, Abu Iyad, and Abu Jihad—all received their first military training in special anti-Israel Palestinian units assembled and indoctrinated by Nasser in the early 1950s.

In 1964, Nasser invited the heads of state of the Arab world to Cairo for the first-ever Arab summit to discuss the only thing they were likely to agree on—how to eliminate Israel. Nasser's proposal was the creation of an organization of Palestinian Arabs who would agitate internationally for the eradication of the Jewish state. The Arab states responded enthusiastically, agreeing to bankroll the group and to have it led by Nasser's tool Ahmed Shukeiri. It was Nasser's original intention that the PLO be a mindless implement in the hands of his Pan-Arab nationalism, slinging Palestinian slogans but otherwise under tight control, to prevent a backlash from Israel. Nasser needed time for a military buildup, and some bluster over Palestine seemed a good way of bolstering his image after his invasion of Yemen in 1962 had ended in disaster. For this job, Shukeiri—whom the Irish diplomat and writer Conor Cruise O'Brien called "the windbag's windbag" for his earlier performances as the Saudi ambassador to the UN[41]—was ideally suited.

But the PLO soon developed other ideas. Nasser's relatively inert creation was quickly upstaged by the active terrorism of Arafat's Fatah faction (sponsored at the time by the Syrian Ba'th regime and named after an earlier Syrian Pan-Arab nationalist group), which was involved in scores of raids into Israel from Jordan. The acclaim that these largely unsuccessful raids earned forced Nasser's hand, first pushing him to allow Shukeiri a string of terrorist attacks of his own, and finally causing him to reconstitute the PLO with the Fatah as its nucleus and Arafat as its head.

Gradually, the PLO was able to cut itself loose from Nasser and pursue a far more radical strategy. Under Arafat, it hoped to be not a spearhead but a tripwire. By staging raids calculated to elicit Israeli responses against the Arab states, the PLO believed it could produce an escalating cycle of violence leading inexorably to an all-out war to wipe out Israel—whether or not the Arab states decided they were ready for it at any particular moment. Thus, for the next two decades Arafat believed that while the Arab states might be deterred from going to war because they feared defeat, the PLO could force their hand. Arafat became the Arab world's perennial advocate of war: "The war of attrition against the Zionist enemy will never cease. . . . It is in my interest to have a war in the region, because I believe that the only remedy for the ills of the Arab nation is a true war against the Zionist enemy."[42]

Accordingly, up to 1967 the PLO terror campaign was directed at penetrating Israel's borders and igniting a new Arab-Israeli war. This strategy was based on the results of the fedayeen terror raids, which were encouraged by Nasser in the early 1950s. The fedayeen were Arab marauders who periodically crossed into Israel from Egyptian-controlled Gaza and from Jordanian-controlled

Judea and Samaria, murdering civilians and bombing vehicles, then returning to their bases across the border. Israel responded with daring retaliatory raids against the terrorist bases. The escalating fedayeen attacks, combined with Nasser's move to block Israel's southern shipping lane through the Red Sea, triggered Israel's Sinai campaign against Egypt in 1956, which succeeded in wiping out the bases.

The PLO carried out its early terrorist attacks with the aim of triggering a larger war against Israel. Nasser, whose army was decimated by Israel in 1956, proved unwilling to permit the PLO the freedom to conduct these raids from Egypt. As a result, the PLO moved its staging area to Jordan, which in any case it considered to be part of Palestinian territory. King Hussein found himself unable to refuse their presence for fear of retaliation from the Pan-Arabist regimes in Egypt, Syria, and Iraq, all of which were clamoring for the presence of a "Palestinian liberation army" in Jordan. But it was also clear that these states fully intended that this Pan-Arabist Palestinian army should replace the Jordanian monarchy at the first opportunity. Nasser had already been responsible for an attempt on Hussein's life in 1960 that had left the Jordanian prime minister dead. The president of Syria had openly called for Hussein's overthrow, saying that "the liberation of Jordan means the liberation of Palestine."[43] And Shukeiri himself had pronounced Hussein to be a "hired lackey" of the West and threatened the destruction of the "Jordanian entity," which was still "under colonial control by the Hashemite family," if Hussein did not allow the PLO to establish itself in Jordan.[44]

The PLO made its forays into Israeli territory from the then Jordanian-held West Bank. These attacks prompted progressively fiercer Israeli responses against Jordan, most notably the Israeli raid on Es-Samu in late 1966. Thus PLO terror, while by no means the sole or decisive factor, contributed to the escalation of tensions that culminated in the PLO's hoped-for war of total annihilation against Israel—the Six Day War.

But obviously the war did not go as the PLO and the Arab

states had expected. Far from being destroyed, as Shukeiri had confidently predicted days before the war,[45] Israel had dealt the Arab armies a stunning defeat and was now in possession of the former PLO staging areas of Judea and Samaria (the West Bank) and Gaza. This meant that new raids had to be staged from the East Bank of the Jordan, bringing the PLO into direct conflict with Hussein's authority in Amman.

Hussein found himself too fearful to reject the presence of these gunmen on Jordanian soil. The more he acquiesced in the PLO buildup, the bolder the terrorists became, encouraged in their belief that the "liberation" of the East Bank (Jordan) would be a stepping-stone to the "liberation" of the West Bank (Israel). By 1968, the PLO had entered into an open alliance with three organizations outlawed in Jordan the pro-Nasser Arab National Movement, the Ba'th, and the Communists—with the aim of taking control of the country.[46] The great flaw in this plan was that Hussein was not particularly enamored with the idea of losing his kingdom, and clashes erupted as Jordanian troops resisted the occupation of pieces of the country by armed and uniformed PLO cadres who exacted their own taxes, conscripted civilians, and issued demands concerning the composition of the government. In the summer of 1970, Arafat's men finally went too far. In response to the jailing of a number of terrorists, they rampaged through the Jordanian capital of Amman, seizing hotels and taking hostages, murdering the American military attaché, and raping several women.[47] In September, King Hussein announced war on the PLO. In the civil war that followed, Hussein's army slaughtered ten thousand Palestinians, including many women and children in the refugee camps, and utterly eradicated the PLO in Jordan. Many Palestinian gunmen and noncombatants who survived the ordeal voted with their feet and tried to flee to the Israeli side of the Jordan River, begging to be taken prisoner by the Israeli soldiers. Some succeeded in reaching Israel, where they received food and medical attention. The rest were gunned down en route by the Jordanian army.[48]

Having failed to destroy Israel by seizing Jordan, the PLO moved on to the easier task of seizing Lebanon. (The PLO has proved remarkably flexible as to the location of the territory it seeks to liberate.) With the other Arab states all but closed to PLO operations, Lebanon appeared to be the ideal stage for its renewed assaults against Israel. Unlike the exposed terrain of the Sinai and the natural divide of the Jordan River Valley, southern Lebanon forms a geographic continuum with the north of Israel; its hilly terrain, covered with lush vegetation, affords good cover and good escape routes. As early as 1969, the Lebanese army had fought PLO units that were trying to carve out a "Fatahland" in southern Lebanon, and the conflict had spread as far north as the capital. Arafat announced that he had no wish to interfere in the internal affairs of any Arab state (a cruelly laughable pledge, given the PLO's track record in Jordan, Lebanon, and later Kuwait); the Syrians threw their weight behind the terrorists in the hope of undermining the Lebanese government; and by 1975, the PLO had established a de facto state, extending from West Beirut south to the Israeli border.

From there, PLO terrorists launched repeated missions against Israeli targets, almost none of them military. The massacres of 1974 in Kiryat Shemona, in which eighteen Israeli civilians were murdered, and Ma'alot, in which the terrorists gunned down twenty-six Israelis, most of them schoolchildren, originated in southern Lebanon. So did the Coastal Road massacre of 1978, in which a PLO hijacking of an intercity bus ended with the deaths of thirty-five Israeli hostages. So did the Nahariya slayings of 1974 and 1979. (In the latter attack, a PLO "fighter" crushed the skull of a five-year-old girl in front of her father, then murdered him as well.)

In addition, the PLO used the territory of its de facto state to shell Israeli cities and towns. For years, the entire population of the northern border towns and villages was regularly driven into underground bomb shelters by barrages of PLO-launched Katyusha missiles, the little brothers of the Scud missiles that Iraq launched against Israel in 1991. By 1982, the population levels of

Kiryat Shemona and Nahariya had fallen ominously; factories, schools, and beaches were being closed repeatedly to avoid mass casualties during the shellings; and fear of economic ruin and depopulation had spread.[49]

As in Jordan, this buildup had two consequences. The first was an internal Lebanese civil war, in which Shi'ites and Christians did battle with the PLO in an attempt to expel the Palestinian overlord from their midst. More than anyone else, they could testify to what a PLO state would be like, since they lived in one: unbridled confiscation of property, wanton murder, wholesale rape, and the forcible induction of children as young as twelve into the PLO's service. Those who sing the blessings of a PLO state would do well to refresh their memories as to how the dress rehearsal went by reading the documentary material assembled in *The PLO in Lebanon* by Raphael Israeli.[50] The tab for the imposition of this PLO dominion and the subsequent civil war came to more than a hundred thousand lives, paid for by the Lebanese.

The second consequence of the rise of the PLO in Lebanon, as it had been on the Egyptian and Jordanian borders, was an Israeli response. Israel took action to defend its northern towns and kibbutzim in the form of armed intervention in PLO-controlled Lebanon, first in the Litani Operation in 1978 and later in Operation Peace for Galilee in 1982. Much maligned at the time, this latter operation indeed lived up to its name. Since the PLO's expulsion from Beirut in 1982 and the establishment of the security zone in the south of Lebanon thereafter, there have hardly been any successful terrorist penetrations from southern Lebanon into the north of Israel. And though the Peace for Galilee Operation did result, as the PLO had long hoped, in a war with Israel by at least one Arab state, Syria, it was a limited war, waged on the soil and over the skies of Lebanon (and Lebanon alone) during June 1982. While Israel's aim was the uprooting of the PLO bases, it encountered resistance from the Syrian armed forces that were, and still are, occupying most of Lebanon. Israel destroyed Syrian missile batteries and almost one hundred Syrian fighter aircraft, while

losing only a single plane. (These successes decisively demonstrated the inferiority of the weaponry upon which the Soviet bloc
was relying for its air defenses, and foreshadowed the techniques
that were to be used by the United States in the Gulf War nine
years later.) But even though Israel was pushed to commit what in
Arab eyes was a most egregious sin, entering an Arab capital (West
Beirut was the head of the PLO octopus in Lebanon), the oft-
promised mobilization of the entire Arab world to assault Israel, or
even to save the PLO, never materialized.

Having backfired on every geographic front, the PLO strategy
seemed to have been an abysmal failure. But it was not. For alongside the "land war" that the PLO unsuccessfully waged on all Israel's borders was another war, as spectacular in its fireworks as it
was in its political success. I am referring to the campaign of international terrorism that the PLO launched at the close of the
1960s and that engulfed the entire world throughout the next two
decades.

Early on in its campaign of terror, the PLO embarked on a series of massacres inside Israel: Kiryat Shemona, Ma'alot, Beit
Shean, the Savoy Hotel in Tel Aviv. In each of these attacks, the
PLO held innocent Israelis hostage in the hope that this time Israel would capitulate to its demands—usually the release of jailed
terrorists. Israel did not. The demands of the PLO were never met,
and the terrorists themselves inevitably ended up dead. Increasingly, the PLO favored war against international air traffic going to
and from Israel, which afforded a greater chance of hitting Israelis
where the PLO imagined they could not be defended.

The air war opened with the hijacking of an El Al plane to Algeria in 1968, followed by the midair seizure of an El Al flight out
of London and a ground attack on Israeli aircraft in Zurich. When
Israel began developing methods to defend its flights, the PLO
switched to non-Israeli carriers, blowing up American airliners in
the Jordanian desert and hijacking a Belgian Sabena airliner to Israel in 1972. When the Sabena plane was hijacked, I was an officer

in the Israeli special forces. My unit was assigned to storm the plane, which we did with improvised techniques. But the rapid accumulation of terrorist incidents quickly transformed such improvisations into an effective, professional discipline.

Building on the experience it gained from the repeated terrorist attacks, Israel was soon able to make its own international airport and its national carrier, El Al, almost immune to terrorist assault. As a result, the PLO had to go farther and farther afield to inflict damage on Israeli targets. In 1976, Palestinian gunmen pulled off what they thought was the greatest of hijackings: they seized an Air France jet over Europe and forced it to fly to Entebbe, Uganda, where the government of Idi Amin afforded the hijackers a safe haven and the protection of his army. There, in the heart of Africa, the non-Jewish hostages were released, but 106 Jewish hostages were herded into an abandoned air terminal and held by Arab and German terrorists who threatened to execute them if the Israeli government did not release convicted terrorists from its prisons. In an operation unprecedented in military history, Israeli troops flew two thousand miles to this hostile country, eliminated the terrorists and the Ugandan soldiers who collaborated with them, freed the hostages, and returned them to Israel. In the Entebbe raid, three hostages lost their lives, as did my brother Jonathan, who commanded the rescue force.

Operation Jonathan, as it is now officially known, proved to be the decisive battle in the war against international terrorism. The Entebbe raid inspired a series of bold counterattacks by Western security forces. Less than a year later, Dutch marine commandos simultaneously stormed a train and a school that had been taken over by South Moluccan terrorists, freeing 160 hostages. Months after this, a German team liberated eighty-six hostages aboard a German airliner that had been hijacked by Iranian terrorists to Mogadishu airport in Somalia. And in 1980 the British Special Service successfully freed the Iranian embassy in London after terrorists had held it for a week. Thereafter, the taking of hostages and skyjacking itself passed from international terrorist fashion (with a brief reappearance in the mid-1980s), and the PLO was forced to revert to other forms of terror.

From the start, the PLO was joined by others in practicing terrorism. For the PLO was not just another terrorist organization or another "liberation movement." It was the quintessential terrorist organization of modern times. It practically invented the craft of terrorizing people internationally, pioneering the arts of hijacking aircraft, blowing them up in midair, seizing hostages, assassinating diplomats, massacring schoolchildren, athletes, and tourists, and various other outrages. These methods were emulated by a rash of terrorist groups the world over, for the success of terrorism in one part of the world breeds imitation elsewhere. But the PLO did more than serve as an example to be imitated. From the early 1970s until Israel ousted it from Lebanon in June 1982, the PLO's de facto state in Lebanon was a veritable factory of terror, providing a safe haven and a launching ground for terrorist groups the world over. Who *didn't* come to the PLO bases in Beirut and Sidon? The Italian Red Brigades, the German Baader-Meinhof gang, the IRA, the Japanese Red Army, the French Action Directe, the Turkish Liberation Army, the Armenian Asala group, the Iranian Revolutionary Guards, and terrorists from all over Latin America as well as neo-Nazis from Germany—all were there.[51] They came to Lebanon, were trained there, then set off to murder their victims elsewhere. From this unpoliced PLO playground of horrors, the virus of terror was spread throughout the Western world, often with the aid of Arab governments and, until the exposure of its complicity in terror proved too embarrassing, with the aid of the Soviet bloc as well.

But what was the impact of this campaign on Israel itself? Certainly, the PLO liked to claim great damage for each operation. (Abul Abbas, a commander of one of the PLO's smaller splinters, announced that his abortive 1990 raid on the Tel Aviv beachfront claimed five hundred Israeli dead or wounded and did over five billion dollars in damage to Israel's tourist industry.[52] In fact, no one was hurt.) But in physical terms, the damage of terrorism has actually been minor. The toll exacted in human lives was also considerably smaller than in outright war. Twenty-five years of PLO terrorism have claimed the lives of a few hundred Israelis, as compared with more than sixteen thousand killed in the wars. Every life lost to terrorism is a tragedy, but in aggregate terms the human and material costs of terrorism pale before those of all-out war.

Yet the PLO's terror succeeded where its land war failed—by inflicting significant *political* losses on Israel. Terror put the PLO on the world stage and gave credibility to its claims of desperation born of oppression. Initially, the terrorist attacks were seen not as the acts of a well-financed, well-oiled machine that enjoyed the support of a dozen states, but as the work of frustrated individuals who had nothing to lose. Every time a bomb exploded in Paris, London, or Rome, the PLO promptly explained that this violence was "due to the Palestinian problem" and would not end unless the Israeli "occupation of Palestinian lands" ended as well.

Shortly after I came to the United States for college in 1972, the PLO carried out its notorious massacre of the Israeli Olympic team in Munich. Before this outrage, the PLO had carried out such actions as blowing up two American planes in the Jordanian desert and murdering an American ambassador, but it was not yet a household name. The news from Munich reached me at the home of an Israeli professor who was teaching at Brandeis University.

"Well," said one of his guests, "at least now everyone will know just who these people are."

"Exactly," the professor responded grimly. "In a very short time, everyone will know who these people are."

He was right. Within a short time, the PLO had made its way into the living room and the consciousness of every person in the West. And as its fame spread, so did the power of its argument that "Palestine" had to be "liberated." Country after country was swayed, if not by the perverted claim of the terrorists that they were fighting for human rights (even as they were trampling human rights), then by the power of sheer intimidation and blackmail. So successful was the endless parade of ghastly slayings, maimings, and hostage cliffhangers that the PLO was literally able to bring much of the West to consider the plight of the Palestinians to be the chief injustice crying out to be remedied in the modern world. By 1976, an American president, Jimmy Carter, had come to believe that underneath the savagery was a reasonable grievance that could be redressed with a negotiated settlement, just as the homelessness of the Jews had been redressed with the creation of Israel. Carter wrote:

> There is no way to escape the realization of how intimately and intertwined are the history, the aspirations and the fate of the two long-suffering peoples, the Jews and the Palestinian Arabs. . . . The Palestinians are suffering from . . . circumstances of homelessness, scattered as they are throughout many nations, and their desire for self-determination and their own national homeland has aroused strong worldwide support.[53]

Even as its terrorism quickly bullied the West into craving an immediate solution to "the Palestinian Problem," the PLO leadership was aware that if it were to capitalize on this effect and become the beneficiary of any solution, it would have to evade or at least minimize its own responsibility for the atrocities it was committing. Terror was useful for getting attention, but it had diminishing returns when it came to garnering respectability. Hence the PLO embarked on a campaign of denial. Even as the terror plague was at its height, it practiced an elaborate campaign of diplomacy and disinformation aimed at attributing the grisly deeds to "extremists" who were beyond its control, as opposed to the PLO itself, which was "reasonable" and "moderate."

By the mid-1970s, PLO speakers were covering the globe, proclaiming the organization's commitment to peace, its abhorrence of violence and terror, and its new-found realism and pragmatism.[54] The PLO was then awash with money it had extorted from wealthy Arab regimes like those of Saudi Arabia and Kuwait.

(Kuwait put a quintessentially Moslem twist on Lenin's famous phrase by providing the rope with which literally to hang Kuwaitis, as the PLO's henchmen proceeded to do following Saddam's takeover of Kuwait in 1990.) It therefore could easily afford a network of offices around the world from which to sell its message of moderation to a world audience that was becoming exceptionally eager to buy *anything* that could be used to "solve the Middle East conflict." (By now, that "conflict" had also brought them the oil embargo.) Articulate, well dressed, and soft spoken, PLO representatives in Europe and North America, Latin America, Asia, and Australia presented their moderate wares on television, in the press, in Rotary clubs, in churches—even in synagogues.

Thus, while PLO-sponsored terror was reigning everywhere, the PLO was busy denying. Indeed, this subterfuge had already been fully operational in 1970, when Black September, the first of a swarm of ostensibly independent terrorist splinters, was manufactured in order to carry out the assassination of Jordanian prime minister Wafsi Tal, the slaying of American ambassador to Khartoum Cleo Noel and his aide Curtis Moore, the Munich Olympic massacre, and other outrages. Arafat claimed to have no connection to Black September up until 1973, when a top PLO operative fingered Abu Iyad, his second in command, as its direct commander.[55] When Arafat was finally forced to admit that Black September and the PLO were one and the same, he was able to turn even this to public relations advantage by claiming that the PLO had since grown more "moderate."

In addition to concealing its involvement in terror by renaming itself, the PLO has tried to come out of the attacks as the hero by "negotiating" the release of hostages being held by its own gunmen. This is a ruse that has even succeeded on occasion, as in 1979, when the PLO negotiated the release of hostages whom a mysterious group called the "Eagles of the Palestinian Revolution" had seized in the Egyptian embassy in Turkey. The Turkish government was so grateful for the end of the crisis that it granted the

PLO diplomatic recognition. Later, it transpired that the PLO "ne-gotiator" had masterminded the hostage crisis in the first place.[56]

The most infamous example of this technique is the 1985 mur-der of a wheelchair-bound American Jew named Leon Klinghoffer on the Mediterranean cruise ship *Achille Lauro.* Klinghoffer was shot at close range and then thrown overboard. Abul Abbas, a member of the PLO executive and an Arafat protégé, arrived in Egypt and told the press that he had come at Arafat's behest to mediate an end to the hijacking,[57] for a moment gaining the hi-jackers their freedom. But this time, the matter did not end quite as planned. Freed hostages described how the killers had hailed Arafat as they beat elderly passengers. Intercepted communica-tions revealed that the murderers were not renegades but were minions of the PLO, directly under the command of Abul Abbas himself. American fighter planes nabbed the escaping PLO killers in a spectacular midair operation. In short order, the PLO was forced to switch from denying any relationship to the terrorists to denying that they had murdered anyone and asserting that the killing was a "big lie fabricated by the intelligence services of the United States."[58] (Farouq Kaddoumi, Arafat's "foreign minister," added insult to iniquity by suggesting that it was Mrs. Klinghoffer who had pushed her husband overboard in order to collect the in-surance money.[59] Abul Abbas's version was, "Maybe he was trying to swim for it.")[60]

Despite these efforts to deflect blame from itself, the PLO was run-ning into trouble because terrorism itself was running into trou-ble. The Israeli invasion of Lebanon in 1982 had led to the dismantling of the terror empire that the PLO had built in that country for over a decade, and to the expulsion of the PLO to Tunisia, where it was stripped of much of its power to wreak havoc. By the mid-1980s, an organized political counterattack had begun to undermine the political effectiveness of terrorism by ex-posing its Arab sources and the involvement of states behind the scenes—as well as pointing out the unacceptability of terror, regardless of the identity of its perpetrators or their professed motives.* Evidence was carefully marshaled that proved that terror, far from being the work of frustrated individuals, was in fact the product of a dismal alliance between terrorists and totalitarians.

The United States led the West in fighting back against terrorism, most notably in the midair arrest of the *Achille Lauro* gunmen and in the raid on Libya in 1986, in which American and British bombers struck targets in Libya, narrowly missing Qaddafi himself. In 1987, the U.S. Congress passed the Anti-Terrorism Act, ordering all PLO offices on American soil shut down, and declared: "The PLO are a terrorist organization and a threat to the interests of the United States and its allies." After twenty years of laissez-faire terrorism, these actions finally established the principle that neither terrorists nor the terror states behind them would be allowed to get off unpunished. The greater awareness of the methods of the terrorist groups, combined with the risk of further American raids, threatened to topple the entire scaffolding of international terrorism—and the PLO's hope of gaining legitimacy along with it. The climate had suddenly turned inhospitable to international terrorism, and the PLO faced the loss of its last means

---

*I was involved with one of the earliest of such efforts to delegitimize terror, the establishment of the Jonathan Institute, named after my brother. The purpose of the institute was to educate governments and public opinion in the West about the nature of terror. The idea that terrorism had become a form of political warfare waged by dictatorial regimes against the democracies of the West, expressed at the institute's first International Conference on Terrorism in 1979, encountered stiff opposition.

Conference participants, who included the late Senator Henry Jackson and then-presidential candidate George Bush, offered revelations of the direct involvement of the Soviet Union and its European satellites in international terror—revelations at which, wrote a *Wall Street Journal* correspondent covering the event, "a considerable number in the press corps covering the conference were much annoyed."[61] After the fall of Soviet Communism, I had several conversations with officials of the former East bloc who expressed amazement at the naivete of Westerners on the subject.

The recommendations of the Jonathan Institute's second conference in 1985 included the imposition of military and economic sanctions against states that sponsor terrorism. I edited the proceedings into a book, *Terrorism: How the West Can Win*. Perhaps because *Time* magazine published a lengthy excerpt from the book (which President Reagan had read) shortly after the American raid on Libya, some in the Arab world concluded that I was to blame for the attack. The Kuwaiti newspaper *Al-Rai Al-Am* branded me "the enemy's most dangerous agent abroad." Ironically, the paper was later shut down when Saddam and the PLO took over Kuwait.

of inspiring the respect of the Arab world and its funding by Arab governments.

By early 1988, the PLO had reached one of its lowest points since the organization had been founded. From its faraway seat in Tunis, unable to act out its bravado calls for the continuation of the "armed struggle" against Israel, it was fast being consigned to political irrelevance. Indeed, at the November 1987 summit of the Arab League held in Amman, Jordan, the Palestinian issue was put on the back burner for the first time in anybody's memory. (The front burner was at long last devoted to the Iran-Iraq War, which at that point had been raging for most of the decade.)[62]

For the PLO, all this spelled the urgent need to make a radical break with the terror image it had previously evaded only with partial success, and to find other ways to demonstrate that it was still capable of "liberating Palestine." After 1986 it became clear that for the PLO to earn acceptance in the West it must not only make increasingly vehement denials of its terrorist *methods* but also try to show the United States that it had changed its basic *goal* with regard to Israel.

Thus, for example, there was a self-conscious shift toward the use of terminology that expressed the same goals but could readily be misinterpreted in the West. Consider, for example, the PLO's incessant use of the phrase *occupied territories* to denote those Arabs that it seeks to liberate, or to which it will restrict its operations. The entire PLO leadership uses this term to mean *all* of Israel ("occupied" in 1948), while being fully aware that in the West it is understood to mean only Judea, Samaria, and Gaza ("occupied" in 1967). Occasionally, however, a PLO member makes a gaffe and spills the beans. Thus, in an interview with the BBC in 1985, Abu Iyad, head of the Fatah's military department, said, "When we say occupied Palestine . . . we consider all Palestine occupied. . . . Our resistance will be everywhere inside the territory and that is not defined in terms of the West Bank and Gaza alone."[63]

Similarly, Farouq Kaddoumi, in the French daily *Quotidien de Paris* that same year.:

> When we speak of the armed struggle, whose legality is recognized by the United Nations, we are speaking of all the occupied territories of Palestine. . . . It is our right to fight the enemy that has taken over our land, whether this be in the 1967 occupation or in the previous one in 1948.[64]

But in the Western press such candor was extremely rare. Most of the time the PLO took pains to obscure its intentions. Indeed, one of the most successful devices for creating the impression of moderation in the PLO's goals has been the game of Declaration and Retraction, whereby PLO leaders have issued ambiguous statements that could be interpreted as signifying a concession, such as the recognition of Israel's right to exist, only to have them withdrawn immediately thereafter. A famous illustration of this technique is a document that Arafat purportedly signed in his besieged bunker in Beirut in 1982 in the presence of visiting American congressman Paul McCloskey. According to McCloskey, Arafat said that he was prepared to recognize Israel in the context of all UN resolutions, a statement he had actually made before and whose value was dubious even then. But McCloskey, apparently enthralled by his proximity to what he believed to be a world-changing event, promptly announced this "breakthrough" to the press, which dutifully trumpeted the news of Arafat's new openness to the world—only to have the entire event denied by the PLO a few hours later.[65]

As in each of its previous Western-oriented stratagems, the principal aim of the PLO "recognition of Israel" game has been to conceptually conquer Washington. Long before the ultimate collapse of Soviet power, it had become clear to the majority in the PLO leadership that the road to putting real pressure on Israel passed through the White House, the Congress, and the American voting public—a realization that has gradually dawned on all the

Arab world, most notably on Syria after the American victory in the Gulf War in 1991. The PLO strategy was thus built logically on Arab propaganda concepts that had already gained currency. Having reduced all Middle East turbulence to the Arab-Israeli conflict, having reduced that to the Palestinian-Jewish dispute, and having reduced the Palestinians to the PLO, the Americans and the West were now to be asked to accept the last link in the chain: The PLO was to be shown as the party of compromise and peace, Israel as the obstacle resisting peace. America would then respond by engaging the "moderate" PLO and pressuring the "intransigent" Israelis.

Getting this campaign off the ground required that the PLO overcome one major hurdle. In 1975, then–Secretary of State Henry Kissinger had signed a memorandum with Israel that obligated the United States to refrain from negotiating with the PLO as long as the organization did not recognize Israel's right to exist and rejected UN Resolution 242. The United States subsequently undertook not to deal with the PLO until it had ceased engaging in terrorism. To meet the memorandum's demands, the PLO's objective of destroying Israel had to be laundered and ironed into a form that could be worn about Washington without violating this dress code. Gaining acceptance in American eyes would therefore entail that the PLO "moderate" itself enough to meet these two demands, while still uttering nothing but readily retractable doublespeak.

The PLO achieved this late in 1988, when it finally reached an agreed-upon formula for its absolution with the Americans. Arafat, debating to the last every dotted "i" and every crossed "t," would finally utter some approximation of a position tolerable to the United States at a Palestine National Council conference in Algiers in November and, with some necessary corrections from the Americans, again at a press conference in Geneva a few days later.

Leaving aside the peculiar view that words alone suffice for the political redemption of tyrants and terrorists, a view contradicted by a long list of despots in this century who have habitually lied to achieve their ends, it must be noted that these words, which the Americans extracted from the PLO the way one pulls a tooth, did not amount to much. Here is what Arafat finally did say in Geneva about terrorism:

> [The PNC has] reaffirmed its rejection of terrorism in all its forms, including state terrorism. . . . This position is clear and free of all ambiguity. And yet, I, as chairman of the Palestine Liberation Organization, hereby once more declare that I condemn terrorism in all its forms, and at the same time salute those sitting before me in this hall who, in the days when they fought to free their countries from the yoke of colonialism, were accused of terrorism by their oppressors. . . .
>
> I also offer a reverent salute to the martyrs who have fallen at the hands of terrorism and terrorists, foremost among whom is my lifelong companion and deputy, the martyr-symbol Khalil al-Wazir [Abu Jihad], and the martyrs who fell in the massacres to which our people have been subjected in the various cities, villages and camps of the West Bank, the Gaza Strip and South Lebanon.[66]

Certainly Arafat condemned "terrorism"—but only to slip the meaning of the word out from under our feet in the very next sentence. "Terrorism," according to Arafat, is what Israel has done to the Palestinians, and *this* he is willing to condemn. As for the actions of the PLO itself, he "salutes" those who have been "accused of terrorism": the PLO, and Abu Jihad, who orchestrated the Nahariya slayings in 1974, the Coastal Road massacre in 1978, the murder of three Israeli merchant seamen in Barcelona in 1985, and more. Nowhere does he agree to alter the policies of the PLO in any way. Most important, nowhere does he renounce "the armed struggle," the term the PLO has always used universally for what the West refers to as terrorism.

Likewise, the PLO's alleged recognition of Israel's right to exist was achieved with mirrors:

More than 40 years ago, the United Nations, in its Resolution
181 [the 1947 partition plan], decided on the establishment of
two states in Palestine, one Palestinian Arab and the other Jewish. Despite the historic wrong that was done to our people, it
is our view today that the said resolution continues to meet the
requirements of international legitimacy which guarantee the
Palestinian Arab people's right to sovereignty and national independence. . . .

The PLO will seek a comprehensive settlement among the
parties concerned in the Arab-Israel conflict, including the State
of Palestine, Israel and other neighbors, within the framework of
the international conference for peace in the Middle East on the
basis of Resolutions 242 and 338 and so as to guarantee equality
and the balance of interests, especially our people's rights in
freedom, national independence, and respect the right to exist
in peace and security for all.[67]

Nowhere amid these serpentine locutions did Arafat actually
say that the PLO recognizes Israel or makes its peace with it.
Worse, the prominent position of Resolution 181—the partition
plan of 1947—ensured the meaninglessness of the entire performance, since that resolution calls for granting the Palestinians not
only the West Bank and Gaza but large sections of *pre-1967* Israel,
including major Jewish urban centers such as Jaffa, Lod, Ramleh,
Beersheba, Acre, Nahariya, Kiryat Gat, Ashdod, and Ashkelon, as
well as major portions of Galilee and the Negev—not to mention
tearing away Jerusalem and placing it under international control
(see Map 5).

This is in line with the standard PLO practice of talking of
peace with Israel "in the context of all relevant UN resolutions."
That formulation is much beloved by the Arabs, because all relevant UN resolutions—some thirty-five of them—include resolutions that tear away the Golan and Jerusalem from Israel, flood its
coastal plain with Arab refugees, slap an arms embargo and economic sanctions on it—amounting, in short, to the dismantling of

the country. Being offered peace on the basis of "all relevant UN resolutions," or Resolution 181 for that matter, is like being told that someone will be your friend if you let him yank your legs off.

Nevertheless, what Arafat said at Algiers and later at Geneva, and which was so painstakingly negotiated by American officials, had been built up by the media frenzy around it into an epoch-making event. The United States and Britain immediately used the speech as a pretext for opening negotiations with the PLO, and French president Mitterrand used it as a pretext for receiving Arafat in Paris. The world's leading press organizations heralded it as a watershed almost on a par with Camp David—*The New York Times,* for example: "American perceptions about Arab-Israeli relations are in flux. . . . Last month [Arafat] renounced terrorism and more or less recognized Israel's right to exist. He thereby transformed the playing field."[68]

In analyzing the rhetoric emanating from the PLO, it must be remembered that what counts with the PLO, as with all non-democratic movement, is not what it tells the outside world but what it says to its own people. When I was at the UN, the Soviet representative spoke many times about the fervent desire of the Soviet Union for peace in Afghanistan. Everyone knew these words meant nothing, and the Soviets routinely went on with the business of slaughtering Afghanis. But when the Soviet press started interviewing Soviet soldiers from the front in the Pangshir Valley about the need to end the war, and this was heard in the streets of Moscow and Kiev, everyone knew that a real change was afoot. (In fact, such press reports heralded the beginning of glasnost and perestroika.) The same is true of the PLO. What it says at the UN in New York, and what it whispers to diplomats in the corridors of Geneva is largely meaningless. What counts is not what it proclaims to the West in English or in French, but what it says time and time again to its own people—in Arabic. Here the PLO exposes itself unreservedly for anyone who bothers to look.

In fact, within days after Arafat's supposed renunciation of terror and recognition of Israel, the carefully crafted structure of PLO moderation began to wobble. PLO spokesmen were explaining to the *Arabic* press that Arafat's statement had been made within the framework of the PLO's long-standing policies, and that in fact nothing at all had changed. First to go was the notion that the PLO had abandoned its policy of terror. In deliberately equivocating language, Arafat first modified his stance before a Western audience on December 19, 1988—just five days before speaking in Geneva. Speaking on Austrian television, he said that he "did not mean to renounce the armed struggle"[69] (a.k.a. terrorism)—and that he and other leading figures in the PLO had stated that the armed struggle would not end.

But in the Arabic media, all pretense of defending the supposed intention of the Geneva statement rapidly vanished. A little over a week after Geneva, Salim Za'anoun, deputy PNC speaker and member of the Fatah Central Committee, said, "The armed struggle must continue everywhere against the Zionist enemy and its allies. . . . We have no alternative but to carry on our armed activity in order to vanquish the enemy and establish our state."[70] And Arafat's deputy, Abu Iyad, reiterated: "The PLO has never obligated itself to stop the armed struggle, and it will not renounce it."[71] As Hani al-Hassan, a close Arafat adviser, averred: "Palestinian armed struggle has not come to an end."[72] Nayef Hawatmeh, leader of the Democratic Front for the Liberation of Palestine (DFLP), the PLO's third largest faction, said:

> The popular revolution in Palestine is resolved to continue the struggle until the Zionist occupation is abolished, thereby liberating Palestine from the [Mediterranean] Sea to the [Jordan] River, and from the south to the north.[73]

He was followed by Abu Iyad again: "We have never interpreted [renouncing] 'terror' as meaning a suspension of military operations."[74] When Farouq Kaddoumi was asked about Arafat's renunciation, he said: "That is a misrepresentation of Chairman Arafat's statements. . . . We denounce terrorism, especially the state terrorism by Israel." When asked by the interviewer whether this did not empty the meaning from the pledge on which Secretary of State George Shulz had based America's dialogue with the PLO, Kaddoumi responded, "Shulz can go to hell. I suppose he is already on his way there."[75]

The same fate met the PLO's supposed recognition of Israel, which Abu Iyad flatly denied to Arabic-speakers everywhere. On February 11, 1989, he said: "There was no PLO recognition of Israel, neither in the PNC decisions in Algiers, nor in Arafat's address to the UN in Geneva."[76] He was supported by the leader of the Popular Front for the Liberation of Palestine (PFLP) splinter of the PLO, George Habash: "The decisions of the PNC did not mention in any manner the recognition of Israel or Israel's right to exist. We did not recognize Israel."[77] On August 8, 1989, Arafat's Fatah adopted a resolution in Tunis calling for the "intensification and escalation of armed action and all forms of struggle to eliminate the Zionist occupation of Palestine," a resolution that the entire PLO executive committee affirmed on January 31, 1990.[78] This decision underscored a joint statement that Arafat with Muammar Qaddafi made that month in Libya: "The State of Israel was an outcome of the Second World War and should disappear, as the Berlin Wall has, along with the rest of the consequences of that war."[79]

The entire performance was repeated shortly thereafter with that other famous Arafatism from the days after Geneva—the supposed renunciation by Arafat of the PLO Charter and its explicit mandate that Israel be destroyed. On the rare occasions before Geneva when Westerners had pressed Arafat on the question of the PLO Charter, he had usually changed the subject. But cornered during his visit with Mitterrand in Paris less than six months after Algiers and Geneva, it became impossible for him to evade the question of how he could recognize Israel in outright contradiction of the PLO's Charter: "As for the charter, I believe there is a French expression which says: *C'est caduc,*" he announced—using a French word variously translated as "irrelevant" or "null and void."[80]

As usual, a media circus ensued that flooded the world with reports that Arafat had renounced the PLO Charter. Also as usual, within hours the PLO and Arafat himself had explained that the word *caduc* has several meanings, that Arafat had been misinterpreted, and that he in any case did not have the authority to abrogate the charter. By mid-January in Saudi Arabia, Arafat had demurred: "[*Caduc*] was legally the most appropriate description of the current state of this fundamental document. . . . One of [my] advisers had suggested using the word 'obsolete.' I said no, 'obsolete' is not the right term."[81] Hakkam Balawi, a PLO representative in the dialogue with the United States, explained:

> Yasser Arafat's use of the French word *caduc,* which means null and void, obsolete and antiquated, when talking about the Palestinian National Charter to the French media, did not at all mean the nullification of the Charter. . . . The word has various established definitions in the dictionaries, and the West can choose whichever one it wants. . . . The Palestinian leadership has the right to stick to the definitions which it believes are correct, and which embody the meaning it wants to convey.[82]

As Abu Iyad put it, "Neither Arafat, Saleh Khalef [Abu Iyad], nor any other leader can cancel the charter, because it belongs to the PNC,"[83] which requires, incidentally, a two-thirds majority to repeal it. As for the suggestion that the PLO remove from its charter Article 19, which declares the State of Israel *caduc,* Abu Iyad responded, "We in the PLO do not accept the removal of Article 19 from our Charter."[84]

Indeed, the PLO proceeded to back up its claim with a renewed campaign of terror. In the months following Arafat's December 1988 statement, PLO factions that had participated in the PNC deliberations and that had supposedly accepted its "decision" not to engage in terrorist attacks against Israel launched dozens of infiltration attempts by terror cells across Israel's border. Most of these raids, as Israel learned by interrogating the surviving terror-

ists and by looking at the maps of kibbutzim and other civilian settlements that the gunmen were carrying with them, were intended as frontal assaults on civilians. Especially galling was the
fact that several of these raids were conducted by units of the
DFLP, one of whose top commanders was Yasser abd-Rabbo, a
member of the PLO executive and also the PLO's chief negotiator
with the Americans. Israel protested to the United States, but the
American administration chose to turn a blind eye.

The PLO, encouraged in its audacity by American reticence
(much as it had been encouraged in 1970 by Jordanian reticence),
chose to escalate its attacks. In May 1990, in a sea-borne assault on
the Jewish festival of Shavuot aimed at the beaches of Tel Aviv, the
PLO's Abul Abbas faction attempted a spectacular massacre of Israeli civilians. It launched an armada of speedboats, each of which
was equipped with a heavily armed terror squad, past the
crowded shorefront. The intended targets included not only sun-
bathers and tourists but the leading international hotels on the Tel
Aviv beach, yards away from the American embassy on Hayarkon
Street. Luckily for Israel, the Israeli army foiled this attempt at
mass murder in the nick of time. Unluckily for the PLO, this was
the final straw, and the U.S. administration finally decided it could
no longer play the fool. The American Congress had already
passed legislation, the Mack-Lieberman bill, requiring the U.S. administration to make a quarterly accounting of the PLO's compliance with the commitments it had given the United States. The
beachfront attack, and the congressional and media spotlight that
was focused on it, prompted the American administration to sever
the talks with the PLO, which were then barely a year old.

Yet the PLO had not convened the entire machinery of the PNC in
Algiers and spent long days drafting and adopting resolutions just
to mislead Western opinion. Algiers, as the PLO carefully explained in the Arabic press, had been a very real conference, in
which an all-too-real decision had been made. As Rafiq Natshe explained on January 8, 1989, just days after Geneva, "Our present

political approach is rooted in the Phased Plan."[85] In this, he was echoing a statement by Arafat's deputy Abu Iyad, who had said prior to the convening of the PNC in November 1988: "We must propose a political initiative which is not new in terms of the Phased Plan. . . . The initiative which will provide new instrument for moving the Phased Plan along."[86] Days after Algiers, Abu Iyad confirmed that this is precisely what had been done there.

> The PNC decisions . . . are a refinement of the Phased Plan adopted in Cairo fourteen years ago. As the years passed, this plan remained undeveloped and without a mechanism for implementation. The PNC session in Algiers was meant to revitalize the Phased Plan and to implement it.[87]

And herein, in the activation of the Phased Plan, under the very eyes of the West, lies the greatest feat of PLO double-talk of them all.

What is the Phased Plan? In the first years after the PLO's establishment in 1964, the organization believed that it could achieve the destruction of Israel in one fell swoop—if only, as we have seen, it could trigger a general Arab war against the Jewish state. Not even the Arab defeat in 1967, however calamitous, could convince the PLO to modify this strategy. The PLO was confident that the Arab states would rearm, regroup, and resume their attack on Israel, as Egypt and Syria indeed did in the surprise attack on Yom Kippur in 1973. But to PLO eyes, the results of this war were equally disappointing. King Hussein, whose forces had been pushed beyond the Jordan River in 1967, chose to stay out altogether in 1973. With sufficient strategic depth in the Golan and the Sinai to absorb the attacks, the Israeli army quickly took the offensive, within three weeks reaching the gates of Cairo and Damascus. The PLO's dream of conquering Haifa and Jaffa had never been further away.

A few months after the Arab failure in the Yom Kippur War, the PNC met in Cairo to consider the situation. It concluded that Israel in its post-1967 boundaries could not be destroyed by a frontal military assault. What was required was an interim phase in which Israel would be reduced to dimensions that made it more convenient for the coup de grace. Thus was born the Phased Plan, adopted by the PNC in that meeting on June 8, 1974. The Phased Plan had two important stipulations: First, create a Palestinian state on any territory vacated by Israel (Article 2); second, mobilize from that state a general Arab military assault to destroy a shrunken and indefensible Israel (Article 9). The precise language of this resolution, in cumbersome but nonetheless clear PLO jargon, can be found in Appendix I.

Although the Phased Plan was formally adopted by the PNC, it was often disputed within PLO ranks. There were those, like the PFLP's George Habash, who thought that fussing with an interim phase was an unnecessary bother, since the force of an escalating campaign of terrorism in and around Israel, and especially spectacular terrorist action worldwide, would ultimately be sufficient to achieve the PLO's aims. But Arafat and Abu Iyad clung tenaciously to the view that bombs and diplomacy were infinitely more potent than bombs alone—a view reinforced by the growing Western resolve, led by the U.S. secretary of state, George Shultz, to take concrete action against terror. After the American air strike on Libya in 1986, the powerful American message that governments and organizations would henceforth be held responsible for the terror they spawned was registered in Damascus, Teheran, and other terror capitals of the Middle East, but most especially in PLO headquarters in Tunis. The PLO quickly circumscribed its field of terror operations. By 1987, the organization was fading fast.

Then came the intifada. Though it was not started by the PLO, it gave the organization new life and purpose. Equally important, the nightly bashing of Israel on the world's television screens created enormous pressure on Israel to vacate the West Bank and Gaza, and it gave the champions of the Phased Plan within the PLO a supreme advantage over the doubters. The dispute finally ended in the PNC conference in Algiers in 1988, when Arafat and

Abu Iyad lined up all the main PLO factions behind the concept of the gradual destruction of Israel.

Abu Iyad in particular was celebrating a personal victory. More than anyone, even more than Arafat, he had tirelessly advocated this strategy. A year earlier, for example, he had explained:

> According to the Phased Plan, we will establish a Palestinian state on any part of Palestine that the enemy will retreat from. The Palestinian state will be a stage in our prolonged struggle for the liberation of Palestine on all of its territory. We cannot achieve the strategic goal of a Palestinian state in all of Palestine without first establishing a Palestinian state [on part of it].[88]

Days after the PLO's supposed recognition of Israel at Geneva, Abu Iyad spelled out PLO strategy: "At first a small state, and with the help of Allah it will be made large, and expand to the east, west, north, and south. . . . I am interested in the liberation of Palestine step by step."[89] On other occasions he was even more concise: "The Palestinian state will be the springboard from which to liberate Jaffa, Acre, and all of Palestine."[90]

As the leading ideologue of the PLO, Abu Iyad painstakingly explained that the Phased Plan in no way contradicted the PLO Charter seeking Israel's elimination. On the contrary, it was merely a tactical response to changing geopolitical circumstances and would provide the means to implement the charter. As he put it, "the Phased Plan reflects the current situation . . . and does not require the casting aside of the charter."[91] On December 6, 1988, he said:

> We swore that we would liberate even pre-'67 Palestine. We will liberate Palestine stage by stage. . . . The borders of our state as we declared it represent only part of our national aspirations. We will work to expand them in order to realize our aspirations for all the land of Palestine."[92]

Noting that a gradual approach was indispensable for world-wide acceptance of PLO moves, he basked in his victory after Arafat's statement in Geneva: "The armed struggle must be accompanied by a strong political basis which will help the world accept the results of the armed struggle. The PLO acts through the rifle and diplomacy."[93]

Terror and duplicity had won out over terror alone. This view was not limited to Abu Iyad. In the heady days after the PLO's supposed recognition of Israel, its leaders lined up to spell out exactly what it was that they were now committed to. Thus, in 1990 Yasser Arafat again gave voice to the same sentiment that all PLO leaders have continuously stressed:

> The Palestinian people's struggle will continue until the complete liberation of the Palestinian land. . . . The Palestinian people's struggle ought to be assisted *until the complete liberation of Palestine from the [Jordan] River to the Sea.*[94] [emphasis added]

Once more—in Arabic, of course—we see that Arafat did not limit the Palestinian Arabs' goal to recovering the West Bank, the territory from the Jordan River to the old Israeli border, but the territory right on through to the Mediterranean. Farouq Kaddoumi, head of the PLO's political department and in charge of its foreign affairs, had this to say: "The recovery of but a part of our soil will not cause us to forsake our land. . . . We shall pitch our tent in those places where our bullets shall reach. . . . This tent shall then serve as the base from which we shall pursue the next phase."[95] This was echoed by Sheikh Abdel adb-Hamid al-Sayah, speaker of the PNC:

> Even if the PLO succeeds in establishing a state in the West Bank and the Gaza Strip, this would not prevent a continuation of the struggle until the liberation of all of Palestine. . . . If we succeed in gaining a part of Palestine upon which we will establish a

state, we can later ask the world at large, while standing on
Palestinian soil, to act so we may obtain our right as a nation and
as a people. . . . We are working to achieve what is possible in
the present phase, and later we will demand more.[96]

And Sayah again: "The PNC has accepted an interim solution,
implying that we will accept whatever territories we can get. Then
we will demand the rest of Palestine."[97]

Every one of the PLO's recalcitrant factions lined up behind
this "moderate" policy of liquidating Israel by stages. Here is the
statement of the PFLP, the PLO's second largest faction, formerly a
stubborn opponent of the Phased Plan:

> The establishment of a Palestinian state in the West Bank and
> Gaza will be the beginning of the downfall of the Zionist enter-
> prise. We will be able to rely on this defeat in order to complete
> the struggle to realize our entire goal, which is the complete lib-
> eration of the national Palestinian soil.[98]

The PFLP's *Al-Hadaf* publication put it squarely on April 9,
1989: "We seek to establish a state that we can use in order to liberate the other part of Palestine."[99] So did Nayef Hawatmeh, head
of the DFLP, another "extreme" constituent PLO organization:
"The Palestinian struggle should now be aimed at creating a state
in the West Bank and Gaza. This will not prevent us from achieving our final aim of liberating all of Palestine."[100]

Thus with the adoption of the Phased Plan, the divisions between the "extremists" and the "moderates" in the PLO vanished.
Now, with such unprecedented harmony among the PLO's constituent parts, the ideological rift between the "one-steppers" and
the "two-steppers" shifted elsewhere: It shifted in fact to the split
between the PLO, led by Arafat's Fatah, and the Hamas, the Islamic
fundamentalist movement that was quickly gaining ground among
Palestinian Arabs. Noticing this trend, many in the West urged Israel to hurry and cut its deal with the PLO "moderates," lest the

Jewish state find itself having to deal with the religious extremists instead. The well-wishers could have been usefully tutored by Rafiq Natshe, a member of the Fatah central committee and PLO representative to Saudi Arabia, who succinctly summarized the difference between the rival movements:

> [Hamas says] all of Palestine is ours, and we want to liberate it from the river to the sea in one blow. But Fatah, which leads the PLO, feels that a Phased Plan must be pursued. Both sides agree on the final objective. The difference between them is on the way to get there.[101]

There are those who claimed that an exception to this bleak landscape of extremism could be found among those West Bank Palestinian Arabs whom the PLO first designated as its spokesmen in the Madrid Peace Conference. While it was certainly hoped that moderates will eventually assume positions of leadership among the Palestinian Arabs, these PLO media-workers regrettably do not deviate one iota from the PLO line. Among the most prominent is Feisal al-Husseini, the son of Abed al-Khader al-Husseini. Just weeks before being received by President Bush at the White House in December 1992, Husseini explicated the Phased Plan for destroying Israel at some length in a Jordanian newspaper:

> A "grand strategy" is the product of dominant interests and principles, which are unrelated to the political slogans of the movement or to any particular period. Thus Russia, for example, has had a permanent interest—which still holds true today—in attaining "warm water [ports]." In the same manner Germany has had a permanent interest in dominating Europe, for which reason it embarked on the two world wars in which it was defeated; but it has not given up on this strategic aim, and still holds fast to it.
>
> The stage in which we are living—as Palestinians, as Jorda-

nians, and as Arabs—is an historic opportunity which will not repeat itself for a long time. It is similar to what occurred after
World War I and World War II, periods when nations and countries were wiped off the map of the world. It is incumbent upon
us . . . to work with all possible diligence in the face of these
new historic circumstances to position ourselves . . . to form
new alliances which will bring us closer to [realizing] our grand
strategy. . . .

We must bear in mind that the slogan of the present phase
is not "from the [Mediterranean] Sea to the [Jordan]
River." . . . [Yet] we have not and will not give up on any of our
commitments that have existed for more than seventy years.

Therefore, we must bear in mind that we have within the
united Palestinian and Arab society the abilities to contend with
this uncompleted Israeli society. . . . Sooner or later, we must
force Israeli society to collaborate with a greater society, our
own Arab society, and later we will bring about the gradual dissolution of the Zionist entity.[102]

Thus, according to Husseini, the Arabs must not lose sight of
what is really meant by the slogan demanding "only" a West Bank
state. For just as the Russian Czars and Soviet leaders never gave
up on extending their empire to the Mediterranean, and just as
the Kaisers and the Nazis never gave up on ruling Europe, so too
the Palestinian-Jordanian-Arab people can never give up its
seventy-year-old "commitment"—"the dissolution of the Zionist
entity."

What emerges from all this is that the PLO produced not one
but *two* basic documents that guide its long-term activity. Both
were adopted in pivotal PNC meetings in Cairo—one at the PLO's
founding in 1964, the second ten years later. The first is the PLO
Charter, which set the *political goal* of destroying Israel. The second is the Phased Plan, which spelled out the *political method* of
achieving that goal. Though many people in the West are familiar
with the charter, it is only in conjunction with the less familiar

Phased Plan that the overall PLO strategy can be understood. Thus, explains Ahmed Sidki al-Dejani, a member of the fifteen-man PLO executive: "We in the PLO make a clear distinction between the charter and the political programs. The first includes the permanent political objective, and the second includes the step-by-step approach."[103] And Rafiq Natshe sums it up: "The PLO Charter is the basis of the political and military activity of the PLO. Our present political approach is rooted in the Phased Plan. . . . We must aim at harmonizing the various political decisions with the Charter and the Phased Plan."[104]

Thus, far from breaking with the virulent hatred of the Mufti, ending decades of terrorism, and giving up on its dream of an eventual war of annihilation, the PLO did precisely the opposite. Its commitment to the Phased Plan merely united the PLO's warring camps as never before, permitting even the most fanatical among them to justify partial gains from Israel as a step toward the land war they hoped to ignite in the not-too-distant future from their sovereign, if initially truncated, State of Palestine. It remains to be seen whether the leadership of the Palestinian Authority is genuinely and fully prepared to break with the past.

But the land war launched from a future West Bank state was not the only poisoned arrow being prepared for the PLO's quiver. The PLO has also maintained at the top of its list of demands what it refers to as the "right of return" of all Arabs who lived in Palestine before 1948 to the cities that they abandoned. Teaching this futile dream to the generations of children who are trapped in the refugee camps has been one of the cruelest and most cynical of schemes in the entire PLO palette. In the camps, the wretchedness inflicted by the Arab states that refuse to absorb the refugees is blamed on Israel, ensuring that the pain of 1948 is not allowed to heal. While many refugees have left the camps and been assimilated into the surrounding Arab populations, others have been forced to remain in the camps by Arab pressure. There the PLO teaches them that the only way out is to return to Haifa and Jaffa—

thereby guaranteeing itself another generation of recruits for acts of terrorism.

If there has been any effort to alleviate the refugee problem since 1967, it came not from the Arab governments but from Israel. As part of an ongoing program, Israel attempted to dismantle some of the worst camps in Gaza, spending Israeli government funds to build modern apartment buildings for eleven thousand families so far.[105] But if the refugees have apartment buildings in which to live, this means that they are no longer homeless, no longer refugees, and no longer the embittered people the PLO prefers them to be. This rehabilitation was violently opposed by the PLO. In the end, Israeli security had to be brought in to protect families that wanted to move into apartments against PLO threats.

About a year after the outbreak of the intifada, I learned firsthand of the power of this PLO stratagem when I visited the Jabaliya refugee camp in Gaza. By then, the large-scale riots had subsided and there was relative calm. I left behind my military escort and strolled with an interpreter through the alleys of Jabaliya. Next to one cement structure I found an elderly Arab, with whom I struck up a conversation.

"Where are you from?" I asked.

"Majdal," he answered, using the Arab name for the Israeli town of Ashkelon, a few miles north of Gaza.

"And where are your children from?" I asked.

"Majdal," he answered again. Since his children were probably my age, it is conceivable they had been born there. On a hunch I queried him further.

"Where are your grandchildren from?"

"Majdal," he answered.

"And will you go back to Majdal?" I asked.

"Insh'allah,"—"God willing"—he replied. "There will be peace, and we will all go back to Majdal."

"Insh'allah," I repeated. "You'll go to Majdal, and we'll go to Jabaliya."

His smile vanished. "No, we'll go back to Majdal. You'll go back to Poland."

With tens of thousands of refugees ready to repeat this Palestine liberation fantasy to any journalist or diplomat who asks, these camps have become a political weapon used to fuel a desire for a right of return that does not exist, and to fan Western opposition to Jewish immigration to Israel. After all, the Arabs often ask Westerners, how can it be that an Arab born in Jaffa cannot return there, while a Jew from Odessa who has never before set foot in Israel is welcomed with open arms? Rather, as Hani al-Hassan, an aide of Arafat's, recently explained, the return of the *Arabs* should be the world's priority:

> Americans and Soviets interested in the Middle East peace process have to understand that the problem requiring solution is not the immigration of the world's Jews to Palestine, but how to return Palestinian refugees to Palestine. . . . The Arab states will not be willing to settle the Palestinian refugees. . . . Every refugee from 1948 or 1967 must be allowed to return to Palestine.[106]

Thus, the "right of return" is intended to mimic, counteract, and annul the *Jewish* dream of return by means of a false symmetry: The Jews have returned, and now the Palestinian Arabs must return. Yet the Arab refugees of 1948 cannot be viewed without considering the *Jewish refugees* of 1948, who were expelled in roughly equal numbers from the Arab states. (Most of the Arab refugees left voluntarily, out of fear or because of the exhortations of Arab leaders to "clear the way" for the Arab armies, as noted in Chapter 4.) At a cost of $1.3 billion, the fledgling Jewish state took in Jewish refugees from Arab states from Morocco to Iraq and housed, educated, and employed them, so that today they are no longer distinct from any other Israelis.[107] For the vast, oil-glutted Arab states to now demand that tiny Israel *also* resettle all the Arab refugees is preposterously unjust. There was, in fact, an even exchange of populations between the Arab and the Jewish states as a consequence of the Arabs' war against Israel and their expulsion of the Jews from their lands. Such exchanges of population have occurred a number of other times this century: Millions of people were exchanged between Bulgaria and Greece in 1919, between Greece and Turkey in 1923, between India and Pakistan in 1947, and so on. In none of these cases has anyone ever seriously suggested reversing the exchanges, let alone reversing only *one side* of them.

That half a century later the Arab regimes say that they refuse to accept their side of an equation that they themselves formulated is particularly telling. For the Arab leaders are well aware that if Israel were to agree to such a Palestinian "right of return," the country would be demographically overwhelmed and destroyed. The "right of return" is therefore nothing but a subterfuge to undermine the Jewish state. As Qaddafi himself has said: "By then [i.e., the return of the refugees], there would be no more Israel. . . . If they accept, then Israel would be ended."[108]

Nevertheless, the demand of the "right of return" has never been renounced by the PLO, and it remains at the top of its list of preconditions for any step toward a permanent peace settlement with Israel. Arafat has made this clear: "The Palestinian uprising will in no way end until the attainment of the legitimate rights of the Palestinian people, including the right of return."[109] Likewise, the PLO's acceptance of Israel's right to exist (as required by Resolution 242) is predicated on the Palestinian "right of return," which Qaddafi says would destroy Israel. As the PLO's representative to Saudi Arabia, Rafiq Natshe, confirms: "all members of the [PLO] executive committee reject [Security Council Resolutions] 242 and 338 if the declared rights of the Palestinians are not understood to include . . . return of the refugees to their birthplace."[110] In the same vein, Arafat also sets the "right of return" as a precondition for peace in the entire Middle East. In 1991, he said:

There will be no peace and stability in the region as long as the inalienable national rights of the Palestinian people are ignored, including *the right of return, self-determination, and the establishment of its independent state* whose capital is Jerusalem.[111] [emphasis added]

This last statement is revealing in itself. If all the PLO wants is an independent state on the West Bank, why bother to include the redundant terms "self-determination" and "right of return"? After all, an independent West Bank "Palestine" ought to satisfy the supposed yearnings for self-determination of all Palestinian Arabs and absorb the remaining refugees. But in separating these terms, as it habitually does, the PLO is indicating to an Arab audience in a well-understood code that a West Bank state is merely one part of its plan to bring an end to Israel. The term *self-determination* is intended for the Arab communities *inside* Israel who, after the establishment of a Palestinian state on the West Bank, will claim the right of self-determination (that is, independence) in regions with an Arab majority in Galilee and the Negev. And if these multiple amputations are not enough to finish Israel off, the "right of return" will ensure that the Jewish remnants are asphyxiated by a flood of Arab refugees.

This trinity—West Bank State, Self-Determination, Right of Return—alongside the PLO Charter, the Phased Plan, and the Armed Struggle, form the PLO's catechism. This doctrine gives direction and guidance to its disciples as they pursue under changing circumstances the unchanging goal of a holy war, a jihad aimed at Israel's ultimate destruction. Even in the midst of peace negotiations between Israel and the Arabs, Arafat continued to extol the same holy war he has espoused since the founding of the PLO in 1964. Thus, on March 15, 1992, the chairman of the PLO exhorted:

Through the peace negotiations . . . the creative Palestinian mind has created the third side of the triangle of [which the first two are] the Palestinian struggle and jihad toward certain victory. We are involved in a political-*cum*-diplomatic battle. . . . We have to intensify the struggle and continue the sincere and honest jihad. . . . The jihad is our way and Palestine is our road.[112]

Scarcely a word about this PLO strategy reaches the newspapers and television news programs of the West, which almost never bother to report on the PLO's actions inside the Arab world or PLO statements made in Arabic. Little more reaches Western leaders. When they are asked why no attention is paid to the PLO's incessant promises to destroy Israel and its elaborate laying of plans to do so, Western political leaders and media figures, if they can be persuaded to address the issue at all, habitually shrug it all off as meaningless "posturing" or even as a kind of joke or game, certainly an irrelevance—with an implied, condescending message: "Never take anything an Arab says seriously if he's only speaking to Arabs." But this stands logic on its head. Dictatorial regimes and organizations will tell foreigners any lie that suits their ends; it is only what they say to their own followers that in any way reflects their designs. To understand this is to understand much about the PLO, which continues to peddle peace in the West while ceaselessly promising terror and the annihilation of Israel to Arab audiences in the Middle East.

How can it be that the PLO's fabrications are understood in the West to be truth, while the truth itself, no matter how often rehearsed in word and deed, is taken to be of not even the slightest consequence? In fact not even "believing" Westerners believe *everything* the PLO says to them. For instance, not even the most avid consumers of PLO lies were willing to swallow Arafat's infamous "secret map" that supposedly proved Israeli designs on the entire Middle East—which a few years ago he announced he had discovered on the back of an Israeli coin. In a specially convened press session at the United Nations in Geneva, Arafat presented to a crowded hall of journalists a map of an Israel encompassing most of the Middle East, reaching as far as the Nile and the Euphrates and into Southern Turkey. Arafat explained that this "map," appearing in rough contour, comprised the lands that the territorially expansionist Israel intended one day to claim as its own. It had been etched on Israeli coins so that every Israeli could share in the unspoken conspiracy every time he fumbled through his pockets.

As Arafat was leaving his press conference, surrounded by an army of aides (in all my years at the UN, where I encountered most of the world's leaders, I had never seen such a huge procession), I walked into the conference room he had just vacated. I produced the coin (a ten-agora piece, roughly equal to a nickel in value) and explained that the pattern imprinted on it is the impression of an ancient coin from the reign of the Jewish king Mattathias Antigonus (40–37 B.C.E.). Most modern Israeli coins include impressions of such ancient Jewish coinage. I showed a photograph of the original coin that had been used to make the impression: Arafat's "secret map" was nothing more than the outline of its corroded edges.

Although Arafat's attempt to manufacture yet another lie met with immediate failure in this case, what struck me was that so many of the PLO's other lies are just as outrageous, even if they don't lend themselves to instant visual puncturing. Yet most people in the West receive the overwhelming majority of these falsehoods as either the truth or else a reasonable approximation of it. Uncontested, this particular flight of fancy might also have become a regular part of the PLO's web of slanders and falsifications—just like the PLO's purported recognition of Israel, and its alleged willingness to be satisfied with a state on the West Bank.

It therefore seems that the ignorance of both the media and the politicians about the basics of PLO politics is not merely due to the facility with which the PLO spews forth its fabrications. It is at least as much due to a profound Western desire to believe what the PLO is saying. Westerners deeply wish to believe that everyone can be reformed and that even the worst enemies can eventually become friends. This is why, despite the termination of the American talks with the PLO on the grounds of its continuing terrorism in 1989, the view that the PLO must be engaged persisted in Washington and European capitals. Ways were constantly sought to bring the PLO back into the fold openly. Behind the scenes, feverish maneuvers took place, through PLO-approved middlemen, to get the PLO's agreement to this or that American move. The goal was ultimately to restore PLO legitimacy in the eyes of the American public and Congress and to ensure its continued participation in the political process.

Schooled in compromise, Westerners found it difficult to realize that the PLO's obsession with destroying Israel was not a passing "interest" or "tactic." In fact, this goal defined the very essence of the PLO. It is the PLO's reason for existing, the passion that has united its members and wins their loyalty. This is what distinguishes the PLO from the Arab states, even the most radical ones. While these states would clearly prefer to see Israel disappear, neither Libya nor Iraq, to take the most extreme examples, sees its own national life as *dependent* on Israel's destruction. But the PLO was different. It was constitutionally tied to the idea of Israel's liquidation. Remove that idea, and you have no PLO.

Indeed, if Western governments genuinely wanted to test whether the PLO was interested in reforming itself, they would have to ask it to take practical steps to stop *being* the organization for the "liberation of Palestine." They would have demanded that the PLO formally abrogate its charter and the Phased Plan, as well as the various other PLO resolutions calling for steps toward Israel's destruction. They would have demanded that the PLO dismantle its terror apparatus and accede to international monitoring to ensure that it has done so. They would have demanded that it cease its organized inculcation of hatred in Palestinian youngsters in refugee camps, and that it quit obstructing the rehabilitation and resettlement of the Palestinian refugees. Such elementary demands were seldom made because it is intuitively clear to even the most befuddled observer that the PLO would find it hard to accept all of them, let alone implement them. What must be asked is why. And the answer is that many of the PLO leaders are committed, sinews and flesh, tooth and nail, to the eradication of Israel by any means.

Can there be no deviation from this line? Are there no dissidents? There were, but they didn't last long. They met the fate of PLO dissidents like Issam Sartawi, who was cut down in cold blood in 1983 for calling for negotiations with Israel, or of the Moslem religious leader Imam Khossander, who was murdered in Gaza in 1979 during a spree of PLO killings of Arabs who had supported Sadat's arrival in Israel.[113] Farouq Kaddoumi, Arafat's "foreign minister," explained the rationale behind such executions in chilling terms:

> The PLO and the Palestinian people in the occupied territories and outside them know very well how to use such methods to prevent certain personalities from deviating from the revolutionary path. Our people in the interior recognize their responsibilities and are capable of taking the necessary disciplinary measure against those who try to leave the right path.[114]

Hundreds of other, lesser-known Palestinians who tried to deviate "from the revolutionary path" by advocating a genuine peace with Israel received "the necessary disciplinary measure" and were summarily cut down—a practice that the intifada death squads enthusiastically took up in murdering over seven hundred Palestinian Arabs, including nurses, teachers, and students accused of "collaborating" with Israel.[115]

I have spoken with quite a few prominent Palestinian Arabs, mostly in discreet meetings. Invariably, they said that they would seek a genuine compromise and coexistence with Israel but were afraid to say so openly for fear of PLO or Hamas terror. These people were not pro-Israel by any stretch of the imagination. But they had given up on the PLO's wild fantasies of drowning Israel with returning refugees or of conquering Haifa and Jaffa. Most of all, they would like a negotiated solution that would enable them to throw off the ideological yoke, initially imposed from the PLO base in Tunis a thousand miles away, and to take charge of their own destiny.

This is why it is so ironic to hear some people speaking in such lavish terms about the "new local spokesmen" who emerged as "Palestinian leaders" during the intifada and while accompanying the Palestinian negotiators at the Madrid Peace Conference. Seeing Western-educated West Bankers on television sporting the latest in verbal accessories has given many in the West the impression that these are Palestinian Arab leaders who have built their own independent base of power and are rising to challenge the unpolished Arafat and his coterie. Precisely the opposite is true. The intifada was a highly efficient instrument of intimidation for the PLO, and left in its wake there were virtually no Arabs in Judea and Samaria who were willing to deviate from Arafat's bidding (unless, that is, they were even more intimidated by the fundamentalist Hamas, or "protected" by it Mafia-style). As was first demonstrated at Madrid when these new spokesmen left the conference in midcourse to fly to Tunis and confer with Arafat, they were spokesmen for no one but the PLO.

That the West found this so hard to accept is a symptom of the much deeper problem underneath: No matter what the evidence, the West is entirely confounded by fanaticism if it wears a suit and tie. Equally, it cannot seem to comprehend the fact that the PLO genuinely *likes* and *admires* totalitarianism—despite its own extraordinary openness on this point. While the nations of the free world condemned China when Chinese government tanks massacred thousands of defenseless nonviolent, pro-democracy demonstrators in 1989, Arafat sent a public message of congratulations to Beijing:

> I take this opportunity to express extreme gratification that you were able to restore normal order after the recent incidents in the People's Republic of China.[116]

While Saddam Hussein devoured his Arab neighbor Kuwait, Arafat cheered him on:

> I say welcome, welcome, welcome to war. . . . Iraq and Palestine represent a common will. We will be side by side after the great battle, God willing, we will pray together in Jerusalem. . . . The Iraqi fighters and the Palestinian stone-throwers have an appointment with victory.[117]

And as the neo-Stalinist coup seemed to end democracy in the Soviet Union in August 1991 and plunge the world back into the Cold War, the PLO praised the putsch:

> The PLO has always viewed this experiment in perestroika with great skepticism, and with trepidation mingled with sadness.[118]

In midcoup, the official PLO organ, Radio Palestine, added further clarification: "What happened in the USSR proves that the [struggle against the West] is natural and inevitable, and that perestroika was the anomaly."[119] In the West, those few commentators who even noticed that the PLO was evincing such a sweet tooth for oppression insisted on lamenting that it "always seems to back losers"—just another bad roll of the dice.

But it is not luck that is responsible for the PLO's choice of friends. It is its chronic affinity for the goals and methods of tyranny, which has consistently allied it with the likes of the Nazis and the Soviets, terror organizations of almost every description, and Arab despots from Nasser to Saddam. The PLO pedigree of tyrannophilia goes all the way back to June 1940, on the occasion of the Nazi dismemberment of Czechoslovakia, Poland, and France, when the Mufti sent *his* personal congratulations to Hitler:

> [I wish] to convey to his Excellency the Great Chief and Leader my sincerest felicitations on the occasion of the great political and military triumphs which he has just achieved. . . . The Arab

nation everywhere feels the greatest joy and deepest gratifica-
tion on the occasion of these great successes. . . . The Arab people . . . will be linked to your country by a treaty of friendship
and collaboration.[120]

It is impossible to escape the perverse but utterly consistent
logic that has compelled the PLO and its progenitors to follow the
path from the Mufti's pact with Hitler to "destroy the Jewish National Home," to Shukeiri's pact with Nasser to "drive Israel into
the sea," right down to Arafat's pact with Saddam to "burn half of
the Jewish state." They may all have failed, but their legacy of hatred persists, following a straight, unbroken line.

Someday, it will be one of those famous historians' riddles
how terrorists and totalitarians who murdered Westerners for
decades were able to manipulate the Western democracies into
besieging the solitary democracy in the Middle East on their behalf. But we can solve the riddle with a myth—the myth of the Trojan horse. For the PLO is a Pan-Arab Trojan horse, a gift that the
Arabs have been trying to coax the West into accepting for over
twenty years, so that the West in turn can force Israel to let it in
the gates. The Arabs paint their gift up prettily with legitimacy,
with the pathos of its plight, with expressions of love for the cherished ideas of freedom, justice, and peace. Yet no matter how it is
dressed up to conceal the fact, the ultimate aim of this gift remains: to be allowed within Israel's defensive wall, to be parked
on the hills overlooking Tel Aviv, whence it can perform its grisly
task. Every inch of Western acceptance—the cover stories, the
banquets, the observer status, the embassies, and any territory the
PLO has ever been able to get its hands on—it uses to push it ever
closer to its goal. And while it is difficult for uninitiated Westerners to imagine the Arabs destroying Israel as the Greeks laid waste
to Troy, it is all too easy for anyone familiar with Israel's terrain to
imagine, precisely as Arafat has promised, that a PLO state implanted ten miles from the beaches of Tel Aviv would be a mortal
danger to the Jewish state.

That the West has succumbed to such a ploy is a remarkable failing, of memory and of a sense of justice. For how long ago was it that Yasser Arafat had Americans and Europeans murdered? That Israel, which knows the PLO, has not averted the increasing acceptance of this Trojan horse is also a remarkable failing: of communication, of concern for the importance of ideas, and of common sense in seeing that it must take the truth straight to the people who count—the citizens of the democratic nations. Israel has no choice but to begin, even at this late date, to explain what the Trojan peace proposed by the PLO means to Israel, and what it means for the world. And Israel must explain what kind of a peace it demands instead.

The above chapter was written (with very few amendments) one year before the Oslo Accords, in which Israel signed a preliminary peace agreement with the PLO. The basis of the Oslo agreement was that Israel first would hand over the areas populated by Palestinians in Judea, Samaria, and Gaza to the control of the Palestinian Authority headed by Arafat. The Palestinian Authority in turn would suppress in these areas anti-Israel terrorism, annul the PLO Charter, and fulfill other commitments, such as ceasing anti-Israel propaganda, thus heralding a new era of peace between the two peoples. While Israel kept its part of the bargain, the Palestinian Authority did not. While the PLO itself eventually refrained from terrorist attacks, the Palestinian Authority enabled the enormous expansion of the terrorist organizations of Hamas, Islamic Jihad, and others in the areas under its jurisdiction. Contrary to the specific promises given to Israel in the Oslo Accords (and yet again in the Hebron Accords of 1997, which I concluded with Arafat, with the United States underwriting the agreement), the Palestinian Authority did not dismantle the terrorist organizations, did not collect their illegal weapons, did not extradite terrorists to Israel, did not stop incendiary incitement to violence in the Palestinian-controlled media, and did not cooperate consistently and systematically with the Israeli security agencies to fight terrorism. In fact, on many occasions, Palestinian Authority leaders, including Arafat himself, engaged in vitriolic calls for violence, gave the green light for terrorism to the Hamas terrorists, and lionized the suicide bombers who murdered scores of Israeli civilians, calling these killers "heroes of the Palestinian nation" and naming public squares after them.

The result was an unprecedented explosion of terrorism in Israel's cities, coming on the heels of the agreement to end all terrorism. In the two and a half years after the Labor government signed the Oslo Accords to end all terror, two hundred and fifty Israelis died in these savage attacks, equivalent to ten thousand American dead. The people of Israel reached one conclusion: This is not peace. While many agreed to continue with the Oslo agreement, with all its flaws (Yitzhak Rabin described it as "being perforated with more holes than Swiss cheese" because its central framework had not been cleared in advance with Israeli's military and security chiefs), they nevertheless demanded two things: that Arafat keep his commitments under Oslo and that Israel maintain the necessary security defenses.

This is precisely the platform on which I was elected as Prime Minister in 1996 and which my government proceeded to implement thereafter. We have insisted that the Palestinians carry out their part in the agreement, most notably to fight terrorism and to annul the PLO Charter. At our demand, the Palestinian Authority annuled the passages in the PLO Charter calling for Israel's destruction. This was done in the presence of President Clinton to make backtracking difficult. Our insistence of this symbolic act was the first step on the long road of Palestinian acceptance of Israel, but many steps remain. Equally, we have been prepared to withdraw from additional territories, but not at the expense of Israel's security. These demands are consistent not only with the agreements we signed but also with common sense. They are the minimal safeguards to assure us that the PLO has abandoned the strategy of the Trojan horse, and they provide Israel with secure and defensible boundaries in case it hasn't.

6

TWO KINDS OF
PEACE

B y now, readers must be asking themselves if the attainment of peace is at all possible in this Middle Eastern morass of depravity and duplicity. If Arab politics is so predisposed to violence and strife, if non-Arabs and non-Moslems are hardly tolerated, if much of Arab society manifests an incorrigible anti-Westernism that finds its focus in anti-Zionism, is it even possible to conceive of, let alone achieve, a durable peace between Arab and Arab, and between Arab and Jew?

I answer this question with a clear affirmative. This may sound surprising in view of what I have presented thus far, but there is no need for either surprise or despair. It is possible to reach peace in the Middle East, provided that we know what kind of peace it is we are setting out to achieve.

The most important step is to recognize that there are two kinds of peace. The first is the kind we mean when we use the word *peace* in the West: open borders, commerce, tourism, mutual exchange and cooperation in areas such as science, education, culture, the environment, the curtailment of hostile propaganda, the absence of fortifications and standing armies, the elimination of military preparations and preparedness, and above all, the absolute certainty of the absence of any aspiration for armed conflict. This is the kind of peace that prevails in North America between the United States and Canada, the United States and Mexico, and for that matter between Canada and Mexico. It is the kind of peace prevailing among the countries of Western Europe, where you can literally cross the border from one state to another without noticing it until you actually have to buy something. (With the introduction of a common European currency, that too may be changing.)

This is not to say that there are no conflicts, even acute ones, among these states. Canada regularly accuses the United States of polluting its forests with acid rain that American industry produces across the border. The United States has serious problems with drug smuggling along the Mexican border, not to speak of the entry of millions of illegal immigrants from Mexico into American territory. In fact, if you scratch the surface, you will find a multitude of grievances over trade imbalances, environmental problems, border controls, and the like harbored by each of these states against each of its neighbors. In addition, there are often national jealousies and bigotries, as well as historical rivalries whose psychological dust has not yet settled and that whirl up again at any time.

Yet clearly these nations are irrevocably at peace with one another, because just as clearly they will not resort to war to settle any of these disputes. This is not because of a balance of power and the fear of the response that armed action might elicit from their neighbors. Certainly the more powerful among them would have no military difficulty in squashing their neighbors. But the reason they will not resort to force is that it is simply unthinkable—because they are immersed in a physical, psychological, and political state of peace.

There is one attribute common to all countries that are in such a state of peace: They are democracies. They share a system of values that is inherently antagonistic to the initiation of the use of force. In this century, modern democracies have shown a marked reluctance to initiate wars. This is not to say that they have not *responded* to attacks, impending or actual. But even these responses, whenever they required a full-scale war (as opposed to a limited operation of a few days' duration), have generally been undertaken only with exceeding caution. Witness, for example, the hesitation of the United States to enter World War I (joining only in the last year of the war, 1917), World War II (its fleet in Pearl Harbor had to be bombed first by the Japanese, despite the obvious threat posed by Hitler), and the Gulf War (in which the United States undertook a campaign to reverse naked aggression only after months of agonizing domestic debate). Even the Vietnam War, which many believe the United States entered too hastily, was characterized throughout by a marked ambivalence as to whether the war should be prosecuted, and ended with an American withdrawal as a consequence of growing domestic opposition. Similar examples can be drawn from the democracies of Western Europe. Indeed, in the postcolonial world it is difficult to provide examples in which democratic nations have pursued unprovoked aggression against other nations and have done so in full-scale war.

One reason for this is that democracies require the consent of the governed to go to war, and that is not easy to secure. Parents will not readily vote for a government that endangers their sons in unnecessary military adventures. But there is a second reason connected to the first that is less obvious and that relates to the inherent predisposition of democratic societies against violence. After all, within a democracy, the use of force is strictly limited and applied only against violators of the law. Within the law there is more than enough room for conflict, competition, and contest. The sharper a dispute, the more encompassing the scope of the disagreement, the more likely it is to become an issue on the agenda of national elections. In other words, such confrontations are settled by ballots, not bullets. Other, lesser conflicts are resolved in parliamentary compromises or are adjudicated in the courts. In fact, the whole idea of politics in democratic states is the *nonviolent* resolution of conflict—not harmonious agreement, not even tolerable disagreement, but the dynamic reconciliation of opposing views and conflicting interests. The point is that this dynamic reconciliation is always peaceful; otherwise, the democracy is endangered internally.

It is not surprising, therefore, that this built-in psychological inclination toward "conflict resolution" (a social science jargonism that happens to be useful in this case) is so ingrained in the minds of the citizens of democracies and their governments that they are inclined to apply it to *all* disputes. That is, *democracies tend to resolve their external disputes the way they resolve their internal ones*: by argument, even by heated argument, by cajoling, by applying various pressures, and very often by compromise—but *not* by resorting to force in the first instance, or even in the second or third. The peaceful tendencies of democratic governments are therefore a product of the practical limits that their electorates impose and of the moral constraints that the system of values shared by the entire citizenry sets upon them.

The desire for this kind of peace—*the peace of democracies*—may be common in the West, but it suffers from one main drawback: It is not necessarily common elsewhere. In fact, since modern democracies have evolved only in the last two centuries, this "internally enforced" peace, deriving from built-in reluctance of the citizenry to go to war, is rather new in the history of nations and in the history of conflict. (The warlike disposition of some of the "democractic" city-states of ancient Greece does not alter this fact, since neither their value systems nor the regimes in question were comparable to those of modern democracies.) Until very recently, we should remember, most of the world was composed not of democracies but of despotisms of one shade or another, and despots are under none of the inhibitions and constraints described above. They certainly have no upcoming elections they have to consider carefully.

Worse, they exhibit innate tendencies opposed to those found in the democracies. For dictatorships, too, tend to resolve their external disputes the way they resolve their internal ones, except that here this tendency leads them toward, and not away from, the use of force. The very definition of dictatorship is the maintenance of internal power not by popular consent but by the use of force or threats of violence, a principle that despots are naturally inclined to extend to their foreign disputes as well. This is why in the last century virtually all the major wars and most of the minor ones have been launched by dictatorships.

This issue used to be hotly contested before the fall of Communism in Russia. Many people in the West explained away the Soviet Union's aggressive politics as "defensive" in nature, as they did the aggression that the Soviet Union encouraged among its clients around the world. This is no longer a plausible argument, since even before the final collapse of the Soviet Union, Soviet leaders occasionally admitted the unprovoked nature of their military escapades, embarrassing their former apologists in the West. Similarly, the attacks of international terrorism against the democracies were initiated by a coalition of Middle Eastern and East European dictatorships, and the full scope of their involvement in terrorism is only now being revealed.

We can see the relationship between forms of government and the proclivity for war by looking at the cases of countries that changed from democracy to dictatorship and back to democracy. It is not happenstance that when such countries had military governments, they tended to initiate military action to achieve their national aspirations. The Falkland Islands, however tenaciously most Argentineans claimed them to be Argentinean territory, were physically seized when a military dictatorship ruled Argentina. Its democratic successor later agreed to enter political negotiations with Britain to resolve the dispute. Similarly, it was the regime of the colonels in Greece that sparked the Greek-Turkish war over Cyprus in 1975. The subsequent democratization of both Greece and Turkey has not ended the dispute but has diminished the prospects for a military confrontation. The armed conflict in and around Nicaragua, which seemed malignant and interminable, disappeared virtually overnight with the establishment of a democratic government in Managua.

This formulation may not be foolproof, and here and there an exception may be adduced. But few would question the powerful pattern that emerges: Democracies tend toward peace, while despotisms tend toward war. Does this mean that a world inhabited by despotisms cannot have peace? Immanuel Kant may have been the first to grapple with this question in his essay "Perpetual Peace," written in 1795, an age that saw very few democracies. Kant stressed the predominance of the first factor I described—the restraining influence of a concerned electorate—as the decisive factor for keeping the international peace:

> If, as is inevitably the case under [a democratic] constitution, the consent of the citizens is required to decide whether or not war is to be declared, it is very natural that they will have great hesitation in embarking on so dangerous an enterprise. For this would mean calling down on themselves all the miseries of war, such as doing the fighting themselves, supplying the costs of the war from their own resources, painfully making good the ensuing devastation, and, as the crowning evil, having to take upon themselves a burden of debt which will embitter peace itself and which can never be paid off on account of the constant threat of new wars.

Without democratic government, argued Kant, it is child's play to slide into war over and over again:

> But under a [despotic] constitution . . . it is the simplest thing in the world to go to war. For the head of state is not a fellow citizen, but the owner of the state, and war will not force him to make the slightest sacrifice so far as his banquets, hunts, pleasure palaces and court festivals are concerned. He can thus decide on war, without any significant reason, as a kind of amusement, and unconcernedly leave it to the diplomatic corps

(who are always ready for such purposes) to justify the war for
the sake of propriety . . . [The] glory of its ruler consists in his
power to order thousands of people to immolate themselves for
a cause which does not truly concern them, while he need not
himself incur any danger whatsoever.[1]

Since the examples of Stalin and Hitler and their less successful would-be imitators were not available to Kant (Napoleon was
just starting out), it must be admitted that his assessment of the
problem was prophetically precise. His solution was to advocate a
world federation of free countries strong enough to compel the
arbitration of disputes instead of war. As the League of Nations
and its successor, the United Nations, show, such federations fall
apart or are of limited use when they include dictators who have
the capacity to manipulate the organization in pursuit of their next
conquest.

The issue for democracies is therefore this: how to keep the
peace when they are engaged in conflicts with dictatorships. (For
obvious reasons there is far less need to ask how to keep the
peace when they are in conflict with another democracy.) The experience of the last two centuries tells us that it is indeed possible
to maintain peace under such conditions.

In the absence of the internal restraints that prevent democracies from going to war, the inclinations of dictatorship in this direction can nevertheless be controlled by the application of
external constraints. Even the most predatory of tyrants can be
deterred from using his state to wage war if it is clear to him that
he will lose power, land, honor, control of his country, and perhaps his own life if he persists in warmongering. Historically, this
idea has been given the name of "balance of power," and most recently, in the catchy slogan of the Reagan era, "peace through
strength." But the underlying idea is the same, and it is sound. As
long as you are faced with a dictatorial adversary, you must maintain sufficient strength to deter him from going to war. By doing
so, you can at least obtain the *peace of deterrence*. But if you let

down your defenses, or if it is even thought that you are letting them down, you invite war, not peace.

This was the tragic lesson of the first half of the twentieth century, and it has been carefully applied to Western policy in the second half. The basic difficulty for the democracies early in the century was in distinguishing the peace of democracies from the peace of deterrence, and the greatest tragedies of the century occurred when this distinction was not made. In 1925, the West pushed to have all military powers sign the Kellogg-Briand Pact, which outlawed war forever. The democracies seriously believed that they could refrain from maintaining their armed forces and that dictators would do the same. While Japan and Italy, and later Germany, ignored the treaty they had signed and pursued a military buildup that enabled them to invade other countries, the West continued to abide by its pledge until the eve of World War II.

In the face of Nazism, the democracies thus weakened themselves and strengthened their nemesis through a policy of appeasement that gave Hitler one military and political victory after another: rearmament, the Rhineland, Austria, the Sudetenland, Czechoslovakia. Not only did each triumph persuade Hitler even more firmly that the West would allow him the next victory, he gained immense physical resources with which to build his war machine: ten million more German citizens, a dramatically improved strategic position, vast new natural resources, and excellent industries, including weapons industries, all intact and ready to serve the Reich.

But most important were the psychological resources that Hitler amassed: His string of bloodless victories over the most powerful countries of the world allowed him to cast himself in the role of hero, as the champion and hope for the future of the oppressed Germans (and of other peoples, such as the Arabs). It was this image of genius and invincibility that made opposition to Hitler impossible, that robbed his opponents of their spirit to resist. At Nuremberg, German generals testified that in the early

years of Nazi rule they had planned to depose Hitler for fear that
he would ruin the country—but that his unbroken string of victories made it impossible to make this case to the German populace,
and they were forced to leave him in power.[2]

With the fall of Hitler's Germany and the rise of Stalin's Russia,
the West vowed not to make the same mistake again. The democracies promptly formed NATO, a powerful defensive alliance
against the Communist menace, which had just conquered Eastern Europe and taken over China. Ringing the Communist empire
with a chain of defense organizations, the American policy of "con-
tainment" was reviled as being warlike, intransigent, and an obstacle to peace through successive administrations from Truman to
Johnson to Reagan. But it was nothing of the kind. The unflinch-
ing American stand of the 1950s stopped the Communist jugger-
naut in its tracks and reduced it to a seesaw battle of ultimately
fruitless skirmishes for toeholds in the Third World. It was the
staunch American stand of the 1980s that ultimately convinced the
Soviet leadership to give up all hope of a triumph over the West
and to forge peace with it instead. In dealing with tyrants, capitulating to their whims often accelerates the descent into war. Standing firm in the face of dictatorial demands is not an obstacle to
peace, only to aggression.

Of course, since the fall of the Communist system and the democratization of the European republics of the former Soviet bloc,
the peace of deterrence between the eastern and western parts of
Europe is rapidly being replaced with the peace of democracies.
As soon as the Warsaw Pact was dismantled, NATO began to
change its form accordingly. There is talk of orienting it toward a
more political and a less military role, and to the extent that it re-
tains its military functions its members do not rule out incorporating into it the countries of Eastern Europe, even the former
Soviet Union itself. Furthermore, disarmament efforts, which previously had advanced at a snail's pace under the totalitarian Soviet
regime, are now hurtling along with such speed and scope that
some arms experts even suggest slowing the pace a bit. For a de-

mocratizing Russia need not be coerced into making such concessions; it *wants* to make them and readily volunteers to accelerate the process.

We can see the same principle at work in the former totalitarian regime of Germany, and in its relations with France, its principal antagonist since the 1800s. In the period between 1906 and 1945, France and Germany fought four of the bloodiest wars in history (the Napoleonic Wars, the Franco-Prussian War, World War I, and World War II). Millions of French and Germans died. The border between Germany and France was fortified, with standing armies facing each other. Yet today it is an open border, shorn of any physical barrier. This development is often held as evidence that peace is possible between antagonists of long standing. Indeed it is. But the question we must ask is, *when* did such a peace become possible? It was realized only after the last despotism in Germany, the Nazi regime, was destroyed and replaced with a democratic government. Once this occurred, Germany and France reverted automatically to the first kind of peace, the peace of democracies. All the fortifications, troops, and weapons disappeared from the Franco-German border, and after half a century of solid German democratic institutions, they have not come back. I hazard to say that things will stay that way as long as German democracy displays firmness and vitality, unlike the weak and vacillating experiment of the Weimar Republic between the two world wars. But should there be a weakening of German democracy in the future and a concomitant rise of antidemocratic forces in an increasingly powerful Germany, the peace of Europe and of the entire world will surely be threatened. I do not use Germany as an exclusive example. The same can be said of Japan, of Korea, and of any other country with a despotic past and a powerful economic, and hence political and military, future. Similarly, whether the newly liberated peoples of the former Soviet Union will be able to avoid escalating their nationalist antipathies and territorial grievances against one another into overt wars—as has happened in Yugoslavia—will depend in no small measure on their abilities to genuinely democratize. If they produce authoritarian or dictatorial regimes instead, the chances of enduring armed conflict among them will grow accordingly.

What we have learned in the twentieth century is that there are two radically different policies that will work to achieve peace and sustain it, depending on which kind of peace is at stake. In a society of democracies, such as Kant envisioned, it is possible to work to strengthen all states simultaneously, because the cooperation and goodwill of each state will in the long run work to the benefit of all. This is the situation that pertains in North America and Western Europe and that may now be spreading to parts of Eastern Europe as well. International relations in these areas consist almost entirely of devising cooperative schemes by which the peoples of the respective states will benefit. In such a context, concessions and appeasement toward friends are interpreted as signs of good faith, under the principle of "one good turn deserves another."

But since the policy of concessions does exactly the opposite when dealing with dictatorships, encouraging dictators to demand more, a different policy must be pursued toward such regimes. In these cases only the peace of deterrence is possible, and the only means of achieving it is *to strengthen the democracies and weaken the dictatorships*.

Here, in a nutshell, is the main problem of achieving peace in the Middle East: Except for Israel, *there are no democracies*. None of the Arab regimes is based on free elections, a free press, civil rights, and the rule of law. Further, they show absolutely no sign of democratizing, thereby bucking the almost universal trend toward liberalization evident in Eastern Europe, the former Soviet Union, Central and South America, Asia, and parts of Africa (which many predicted could never democratize). In an era when even such hitherto cloistered despotisms as Mongolia and Albania are undergoing democratic revolutions, the stubborn refusal of the Arab world even to contemplate genuine democratization, let alone implement it, should send a warning signal to the champions of democracy in Western Europe and America that for now this region is capable only of the peace of deterrence.

But alarmingly, no such signal is being received in the West. While the United States had a decisive role in pressuring the dictatorships of Latin America to democratize, as well as some of the African governments such as the Mobutu regime in Zaire; and while both America and Western Europe put enormous pressure (from trade sanctions to public protest) on the Soviet bloc and South Africa to observe human rights and allow pluralism, no such pressure, *none whatsoever*, has been placed on the Arab world. It seems that the crusading zeal of the democracies stops at the Sahara's sandy edge.

The first order of business for those in the West who are seeking a *Western-style peace* for the Middle East is to press the Arab regimes to move toward democracy. By this, I mean not only the tolerance of political parties or even of majority rule but the introduction of such novel concepts as individual rights, constitutional constraints on power, and freedom of the press. These run completely contrary to the bogus calls for "democratization" from the Islamic fundamentalists, whose first act upon coming to power would be to crush such freedoms, as was done in Iran.

I, for one, summarily reject the view that Arabs are incapable of democracy. Israel's Arab citizens (much like Arab-Americans in the United States) have adopted the country's democratic norms, practicing democratic politics in the town councils and municipal and national elections with all the feistiness of Israeli politics and with none of the violence characteristic in the Arab world. Yet similar norms cannot and will not develop in the Arab countries without intense and systematic encouragement from the West.

But if the West is unprepared to agitate for democracy in the Arab world, it should at least bolster the deterrent capacity of the Middle East's democracies (there is only one) and work to weaken the power of the more radical tyrannies. This is in line with the basic principle of building the peace of deterrence: firmness toward tyrants, friendship toward democracy. Yet so often when it comes to this part of the world, the hard-learned distinction between the two kinds of peace evaporates, and the West instead does precisely the opposite: pressuring Israel for concessions, and feverishly appeasing the tyrants with every conceivable weapon and resource. The most obvious example is Saddam Hussein, to whom the American government insisted on supplying loan guarantees a few *days* before his invasion of Kuwait.[3] In the subsequent war, the Americans had to fight weapons systems that had been supplied by firms from France, Italy, Britain, Austria, and Greece and tried to bomb Saddam out of fortified bunkers that had been built by Belgians and to gird its troops against poison gas supplied by German and Swiss companies.[4] Now the United States is trying to ferret out of Iraq the multiple hidden nuclear weapons projects that Saddam has built and continues to build, using technologies sold to him by the West. His current ill repute, of course, seems to have induced some of his Western suppliers to switch to selling their products to Syria, which was rewarded for its passive support of the American war against Syria's arch-enemy Saddam.

Not only does the West build up Arab dictators, it refuses to link granting them favors to any sort of democratic reforms or to an end to human rights violations. When it *does* bother to think of criticizing oppression in the Middle East, the West focuses on Israel, the solitary democracy in the region, whose record compares more than favorably with that of other democracies that have faced similar circumstances. Often enough, Western officials will even stoop to asserting that because of its behavior, Israel cannot be considered a democracy. But such condescension merely displays the speaker's ignorance: of riot control in Los Angeles and Detroit, of antiterror tactics in Northern Ireland, of the postwar Allied military administration in Germany and Japan. Israel is a democracy *at war*, and its behavior compares favorably with that of any democracy under such circumstances.

Even a cursory glance at events in the Middle East in recent years reveals that the Arab governments obey the rules of the peace of deterrence to the letter. In 1975, when the Shah of Iran was at the height of his power, Saddam Hussein signed a nonaggression pact with Iran *because* the Shah was so strong that there was nothing that Saddam could gain by aggression. But after the fall of the Shah and the collapse of his once-formidable army, Saddam tore up the agreement and invaded Iran, starting the nine-year Iran-Iraq War. It was only after the first years of fighting, when he realized that Iran would not be beaten, that Saddam sued for peace. But at this point the Iranians under Khomeini—no democrats either—thought that *they* could win and refused to call off the war. It was only after Saddam had managed to beat back the Iranian counterattack for several years that Iran too sued for an end to the fighting, and the peace of deterrence was restored along the original border.

Kuwait, too, lacked the capacity to defend itself against Iraq's aggressive designs and perished until an American-led invasion brought it back to life. Predatory Arab regimes are limited in their aggression either by deterrence (the two largest predators, Iraq and Syria, have never actually warred with each other because of mutual fear) or, when deterrence fails, by someone with superior force physically rolling back their conquests. This was the case with Libya's invasion of Chad, which the French intervened to repel in 1985, much as the British had helped Yemen repel the Egyptian invasion in the early 1960s.

In other words, peace in the Middle East means "peace through strength." One way the West does acknowledge this fact is through its massive arms sales to the nonradical Arab regimes. But this policy is chimerical, as all the weapons in the world cannot transform flimsy Kuwait and Saudi Arabia into nations capable of fending off a military state like Iraq, which has an army twenty times the size of theirs. They can be armed to the teeth, but they have no teeth—as the need for direct American protection of these states in the Gulf War has proved.

What the arms-sales policy does do, on the other hand, is

build the arsenals for the future fanatics who may one day over-throw the existing rulers—as Qaddafi overthrew the pro-Western King Idris of Libya, and as Khomeini deposed the Shah of Iran. Similarly, Arab tyrants may acquire weapons that their neighbors gained, through pillage (as Saddam did in Kuwait) or through pressure of other sorts to put the weapons at their disposal. In the Arab world, therefore, the destination of massive infusions of weapons today is not necessarily where they will end up tomorrow; nor is their purpose today necessarily the purpose for which they will eventually be used.

The only certain effect of these huge arms transfers is to bolster the conviction of the Middle East's radicals that the wherewithal to destroy Israel *does* exist in the Arab world. The more weapons the Arabs receive, the clearer it becomes to them that the only thing standing in the way of victory over the Jewish state is Arab disunity itself. Many people in the Arab world are well aware that Israel cannot possibly compete against the arms buildup currently under way. To them, the only thing lacking is the right strongman to concentrate all this power in his hands and bring it to bear. The policy of massive sales of advanced weapons to governments in the Arab world is thus an inducement for adventurers such as Saddam to make a bid for forcible unification. It is therefore a policy that works directly to undermine deterrence—and as such is diametrically opposed to peace.

The Arabs justify this policy by insisting on Israel's "aggressive" nature, a claim that they attempt to support by pointing to the fact that Israel has gone to war several times since 1948. It is hard to believe that anyone in the West could swallow this line, especially after the Gulf War. Night after night, Iraq dropped missiles on the civilian populations of Israel's largest cities, while Israelis huddled in rooms sealed against chemical attack, waking their children to place them in protective plastic tents and gas masks. The attacks were unprovoked, but at the request of the United States and in the hope of depriving Saddam of an excuse to deflect the Allied war effort, Israel did not retaliate—even when attacks on Tel Aviv caused the deaths of Israeli citizens. There can be no more graphic a demonstration of how serious the "Israeli threat" is and how "aggressive" Israel is.

Notwithstanding the false Arab claims, the United States has provided Israel with generous military assistance ever since the Six Day War. This has helped the cause of Arab-Israeli peace a great deal by contributing to the gradual Arab recognition of the fact that Israel will not be so easily destroyed. Reinforcing this perception and transmitting it to Arab regimes and organizations that have not yet assimilated it are the keys to achieving a sustainable peace between Israel and the Arabs.

We can see precisely this kind of process occurring slowly but surely in Israel's relations with the Arab states. In 1948 the Arab states thought they would have no difficulty in wiping out six hundred thousand Jews on their thin sliver of land. In 1967 that sliver was still tempting, and Syria and Jordan joined Egypt in trying to strangle Israel. But this attempt, too, failed. The Six Day War immeasurably improved Israel's strategic position. The addition of the mountainous buffer of Judea and Samaria for the first time removed Israel's population centers and airfields from the possibility of direct ground attack. When Egypt and Syria attacked Israel on Yom Kippur in October 1973, Jordan had to consider whether to join the fray. Faced with the prospect of fighting across the Jordan Valley and up the steep escarpment of the Israeli-held Samarian and Judean mountains, Jordan chose to sit out the war, sending only a token contingent to join the Syrian forces on the Golan.

Hence, while in 1948 *five* Arab armies invaded Israel and in 1967 *three* Arab armies fought, in 1973 only *two* Arab states attacked. And in the 1982 campaign against the PLO in Lebanon only *one*, Syria, entered into a limited war with Israel. Further, in the Gulf War in 1991, it was only Iraq, having promised to "burn half of Israel," that struck with missiles, but it did not attempt any ground engagements—promoting one observer to describe it as "the half-effort of a half-country."

This represents a promising trend, provided we understand what forces brought it about. (If we do not, we could easily bring about its reversal.) Why has this decline in the number of countries attacking Israel taken place? It certainly has not happened because the Arab world as a whole has changed its opinion of Israel. Yet King Hussein's willingness to go to war in 1967 stands in sharp contrast to his unwillingness to do so just six years later. Whether or not he went to war was determined by which side of Israel's protective wall (the West Bank) his army was on when the war broke out. Likewise, the results of the Yom Kippur War strongly influenced Anwar Sadat in his decision to make peace with Israel. He may have restored Arab "honor" (by not losing to Israel for a couple of weeks), and he may have even earned the opportunity to speak of the Egyptian "victory" in that war, but he knew full well that despite the surprise attack on Israel that was launched on the holiest day of the Jewish year, the Israeli army soon turned the tables and reached the outskirts of Cairo and Damascus within twenty-one days.

The declining number of warring Arab states reflects the underlying reality: Peace between Israel and its neighbors is the second kind of peace, the peace of deterrence. The probability of achieving it is directly proportional to Israel's ability to project a strong deterrent posture—the stronger Israel appears, the more likely the Arabs will be to agree to peace. There is nothing surprising about this. It is the classic doctrine of deterrence. It was not lack of desire that prevented the Soviet Union from attacking the West but the Soviet fear of retaliation. Similarly, what has decreased the likelihood of a joint Arab assault on Israel is not the absence of hostility but the fear of failure.

This deterrent effect not only prevents those Arabs who are in a state of war with Israel from actually going to war, it helps keep those Arabs who are in a state of peace from reneging on it. This is why the single peace treaty between Israel and an Arab country, the Camp David Accords, provides for a larger buffer space between Israel and Egypt. The demilitarized Sinai is sufficiently vast that if Egypt were to violate the peace with Israel, Israel would have time to mobilize its defenses and counterattack.

In the Middle East, security is therefore indispensable to peace; a peace that cannot be defended is one that will not hold for very long. The relationship between security and peace is often presented in reverse—for Israel alone, of course. Nobody would dream of telling Kuwait that its security lies in having peace treaties with Iraq. It *had* such treaties, and they were totally useless when Iraq came to believe it could swallow Kuwait whole. But those who confuse the peace of democracies with the peace of deterrence nonetheless tell an Israel beleaguered by heavily armed dictatorships that it can take inordinate risks with its security for the sake of "peace" because "peace is the real security." On this Henry Kissinger has remarked that all wars start from a state of peace. This is especially true of the Middle East, which is littered with inter-Arab peace treaties and friendship accords, not one of which ever prevented a war.

If over the next generation the Arab world internalizes the fact that Israel is here to stay, this might produce a psychological shift in its attitude toward Israel's *right* to exist. The Arabs, like other people, will not bang their heads against a stone wall forever. But if the wall itself is dismantled, if Israel's most vital defenses are suddenly stripped away, the great progress that has been made toward peace over recent decades could be reversed at once.

In one of his books, Max Nordau described a well-known experiment that the German zoologist Karl August Möbius designed to study the relationship between predator and prey. The experiment was conducted with two fish:

> An aquarium was divided into two compartments by means of a pane of glass; in one of these a pike was put and in the other a tench. Hardly had the former caught sight of his prey, when he rushed to the attack without noticing the transparent partition. He crashed with extreme violence against the obstacle and was

hurled back stunned, with a badly battered nose . . . He repeated his efforts a few times more, but succeeded only in badly
hurting his head and mouth.

Slowly, wrote Nordau, the pike began to realize

that some unknown and invisible power was protecting the
tench, and that any attempt to devour it would be in vain; consequently from that moment he ceased from all further endeavors to molest his prey. Thereupon the pane of glass was
removed from the tank, and pike and tench swam around together . . . All [the pike] knew was this: he must not attack this
tench, otherwise he would fare badly. The pane of glass, though
no longer actually there, surrounded the tench as with a coat of
mail which effectually warded off the murderous attacks of the
pike.[5]

No matter how compelling the reasons, there is no point in attacking where there is no hope of success. This elementary understanding is no less applicable to human behavior. It is precisely
such an understanding that has been slowly evolving in the attitudes of the radical Arab regimes toward Israel. But it cannot be
said that they have reached the stage of having fully assimilated
the reality of Israel's existence. Deprived of its equivalent of the
glass partition, Israel might become the target once again of
pouncing predators. This partition, Israel's defenses, is made up
of several important elements: the physical and human resources
available to protect the country, and the material and psychological assets deployed for the common defense. But without a doubt,
central among them is the physical partition that separates Israel's
cities from the vast eastern-front armies of Syria, Iraq, Iran, and
Saudi Arabia. The separation consists of a wall: the dominating
heights of the Golan and the mountains of Samaria and Judea,
commonly known to the world as the West Bank, whose military
value I now turn to discuss.

7

THE WALL

On October 6, 1973, I was in my second year as an undergraduate at the Massachusetts Institute of Technology. Although this was Yom Kippur, the news traveled fast, reaching Cambridge by early afternoon.

"Haven't you heard? War's broken out. Egypt and Syria have attacked."

Several of us, Israeli students studying at MIT and Harvard who were reserve officers in the Israeli army, said good-bye to our friends and quickly drove to Kennedy airport in New York to catch the first plane back. But that did not prove to be simple. Israeli reservists were streaming to Kennedy from all corners of the United States and Canada. The first Boeing Jumbo had already left, every seat taken. There was fierce competition to go on the second plane. I used all the pull and connections at my disposal (what we in Israel call *protektsia*), calling Motta Gur, Israel's military attaché in Washington, and everybody else I could think of. Since I had served for five years as a soldier and officer in the special forces, I was finally able to get on board. The plane was bursting at the seams with doctoral students, computer specialists, physicians, and physicists, some of whom I knew but had not seen for years. For too many of them, this would be their final trip.

On the plane, there was a serene confidence that within a few days, a week at most, the war would be over with an Israeli victory. But things did not turn out that way. The Egyptians and Syrians achieved impressive initial gains with their surprise attack. Syria sliced through the entire width of the Golan Heights, and the forward Syrian tanks almost reached the bridges across the Jordan and into the Galilee. The Egyptian army in the south crossed the Suez Canal, overran the fortified Bar Lev Line, and reached as far as the foothills of the Mitla and Gidi passes, some twenty miles east of the canal. Worse, both armies were equipped with new and unfamiliar antiaircraft and antitank missiles, which took a punishing toll from Israel's air force and a less severe but nonetheless frightening toll of Israel's armor.

In Israel everything was in confusion. Two days into the war, the reservists had not yet been fully mobilized—and some of the troops were still arriving from abroad. By the time I reached my unit, it had already scrambled to the two fronts. We formed a makeshift force of "returnees," equipping ourselves with armed vehicles and jeeps, and made our way to the front facing the Egyptian army. When we reached the front the hemorrhage had been stanched and the lines stabilized, in preparation for the counterattack across the Suez Canal that was to come days later under General Ariel Sharon.

Our job was to protect the armored formations at night from Egyptian heliborne commandos. We alternated between reconnoitering for marauding helicopters and guarding the perimeter of the tank encampments. Inside the perimeter the tank crews, exhausted from the fighting and from the endless job of tending to the tanks, would get a few hours of fitful, grimy sleep. On one occasion, in the pitch darkness that was enforced in the camp, I literally bumped into a buddy I hadn't seen in years, and wild rejoicing ensued. But more often I learned, usually from news delivered in hushed tones, of friends who had been killed in the first spasm of fighting. I remembered many of them as children, and I wondered if their families had received the news. Many more were to die in the counterattack, including soldiers from my own unit whose framed photographs would later fill up the memorial wall in the unit's modest library. But these were early days, and there was soon a tense lull across the front, the kind that comes after the first violent exchanges in any firefight.

In the Golan Heights, where we were next taken, we found much the same thing. In fierce fighting, the Israeli units, outnumbered ten to one by the advancing Syrians, had managed to hold the line until the reserves arrived. The Israeli command of the Golan at Nafah had to vacate the sea to open terrain when Syrian tanks reached the fenced perimeter. Crews were having their tanks shot out from under them, and the surviving soldiers jumped into new tanks to continue the fighting. Entire brigades were wiped out. The officers were the first to be mowed down as they exposed themselves above the turrets in order to direct the battle. In several brigades the command reverted to sergeants and corporals, who joined the remnants of other units to fight with incredible, desperate tenacity, trying to ward off what Moshe Dayan warned could be "the fall of the Third Temple." Later, the ashen-faced survivors—the regulars just out of their boyhood and the reservists who were clerks, teachers, and farmers in private life—would describe the feeling that at once overwhelmed and sustained them, that they held the weight of Jewish history and the very fate of the Jewish people in their hands. If they were to lose here, all would be lost. The line held.

Once the other reserves had arrived in full, the Israeli armor went onto the offensive and quickly rolled into Syria. On the southern front, the Israeli columns that had counterattacked and crossed the canal encircled and trapped the Egyptian Third Army. Here the Arabs pleaded with the Soviets and the Americans to stop the war, which they did with a Security Council ultimatum. At war's end, the Israeli army was twenty-five miles from Damascus and eighty miles from Cairo.

Israel had achieved a stunning reversal. But the cost was staggering: In the pulverizing battle to keep the front from collapsing entirely in the face of overwhelming numbers, the army had sustained 2,552 dead—the worst losses since the War of Independence. This was proportionately as though the United States had taken three times the losses of the eight-year Vietnam War in a period of three weeks.

There was an important lesson here for both Israelis and Arabs. On both the Egyptian and Syrian fronts, the Arabs had managed to penetrate as much as twenty miles before Israeli forces finally checked them. If the war had begun not on the post-1967 lines but on the pre-1967 lines, and if the Arab armies had advanced the same distances, Israel would have ceased to exist. The Egyptians would have reached the outskirts of Tel Aviv from the south; the Jordanians (who no doubt would once more have caved in to the temptation to join in the attack) would have reached the sea, splitting the country in two; and the Syrians would have cut deep into the Galilee.

Israel's army was able, albeit by a hair's breadth, to prevent defeat in the face of a surprise attack under the most auspicious conditions the Arabs could muster, including their throttling of the Western economies with an Arab oil embargo. By hiking up oil prices and denying the world economy the fuel it needed to run, the Arabs had mounted extraordinary international pressure on Israel, and Israel's relations with dozens of nations were severed for two decades. When the United States sought to airlift emergency assistance to Israel during the three weeks of the war, it could not find a single country in Europe that would let the American supply planes land and refuel there. (In the end, Portugal agreed to allow the planes to refuel in the Azores Islands.)

But despite such enormous advantages, the Arabs were routed within the month. That they had so little to show for an onslaught stacked so decisively in their favor was a crucial factor in inducing Anwar Sadat finally to come to terms with Israel. And indeed, in the aftermath of the Yom Kippur War, Israel and Egypt ultimately negotiated the Camp David Accords of 1979, the first peace agreement between an Arab state and Israel. While Israel returned the Sinai to Egypt, it was agreed that the Sinai would remain for the most part demilitarized, with the bulk of Egyptian forces staying on the western side of the Suez Canal. Three zones were established in the Sinai delineating permissible Egyptian troop levels. An elaborate monitoring system was established, including a multinational observer force, to ensure that the demilitarization was observed.

The fact that the Sinai is so large (more than twice the size of Israel and the West Bank combined) meant that any violation of the demilitarization agreement on the part of Egypt would leave Israel with sufficient time and depth to intercept an incoming Egyptian force before it reached the border. Since the only kind of peace that can endure in the Middle East is a peace that can be defended (the peace of deterrence), the only kind of peace treaty that can be sustained is one that allows adequate defense against its possible violation. Because of the availability of the Sinai as a buffer, it was relatively easy to achieve such conditions along the Egyptian border, Israel's southern front. On other fronts, however, the situation was much more complicated.

To understand the prerequisites for keeping peace on Israel's eastern front, facing Syria, Jordan, and Iraq, one must first understand the building blocks of Israel's military defense. Israel's ability to deter aggression depends on three central factors: its *military strength* relative to that of the Arabs; the *warning time* it has to mobilize its forces; and the *minimum space* that its army requires to deploy in the face of potential threats.

With regard to Israeli *military strength*, the Arab advantage in armaments has been mounting steadily against Israel for years. Since the Yom Kippur War the Arabs have spent more than $150 billion on arms and military facilities.[1] Saudi Arabia alone annually spends as much on its military as a major industrialized nation such as Great Britain.[2] Syria now has more tanks than the German army used when it invaded Russia.[3] To this arsenal are added the F-15S, AWACs planes, and Sidewinder missiles of Saudi Arabia, and the Hawk missiles and advanced artillery of Jordan—all supplied by the United States. To be sure, Israel has morale, training, and other qualitative edges over the Arabs, but with the vast purchases of weapons by the Arab regimes, the Middle East is fast reaching a point beyond which Arab quantity translates into quality.

Military strength is also a function of manpower. In 1999, Israel's population is roughly six million, as opposed to thirty-five million for the eastern front states of Syria, Iraq, and Jordan. This advantage in population allows the Arab regimes to field larger armies, and it means that they can afford to keep most of their forces on active duty—unlike Israel, most of whose army consists of reservists who must be called up to fight. On the eve of hostilities in 1973, Israel's usual contingent of sixty tanks on the Golan was bolstered by the arrival of the Seventh Armored Brigade, bringing the total to 177 tanks. The Israeli force was nonetheless vastly outnumbered by the Syrian active-duty force of 900 tanks. Israel's defense therefore requires a capability of deterring or defending against an attack in which its troops are initially outnumbered by a margin of five or seven to one. This enormous Arab advantage in arms and manpower, which Israel cannot possibly match, makes the two remaining factors in Israel's security equation even more critical.

For Israel, *warning time* is a precondition of survival. Israel needs sufficient time to mobilize the civilian reserves that make up the bulk of its army. This consists of calling them up from their homes all over the country, assembling them in units, issuing them weapons and ordnance, briefing them, and then transporting them to the lines. To mobilize several hundred thousand soldiers simultaneously in this way is a herculean task, and it cannot be performed in less than forty-eight to seventy-two hours. (The Syrians have no analogous problem because their standing army is almost as large as Israel's entire reserve force,[4] and they therefore need only a few hours' notice to go to war.) Until mobilization is completed, the survival of the entire country is literally in the hands of the few thousand soldiers on active duty on the front at any given time. If they were to fail to hold the front until the arrival of reinforcements, the battle would sweep into the streets of Israel's towns and cities.

The situation in the air is even worse. For a jet fighter, the flight time between Jordanian air bases and Israeli population centers is five minutes, and it is only ten minutes from Syrian bases—while the absolute minimum time required to scramble an interceptor is three minutes, assuming that it is waiting in a condition of highest alert. This means that without advance warning of an attack, Israel's coast and airfields could be bombed without a fight. Such a scenario is so fearsome and so plausible that during the Gulf War, Israel was forced to keep a large portion of its fighter force *in the air*. In many parts of Israel during the Gulf War, you could step out of your house and see combat aircraft circling overhead during prolonged periods—for an entire month and a half. Moreover, this was only possible because the Americans had announced in advance the starting date of the war. Such readiness is impossible against a surprise attack, so the air force relies heavily on surveillance installations that hope to shave seconds off the period before Israel becomes aware of an impending blow.

Among the most important surveillance positions in the entire Israeli defense system are the "early-warning stations" in the mountain peaks of Samaria. These bases are high enough to be able to monitor troop movements and air base activity over the mountains in Amman and the other major cities in Jordan. At the same time, the high ground interferes with surveillance efforts aimed at Israel. If a hostile country were ever to gain control of these mountains, the situation would be reversed: The Arabs would be afforded unlimited surveillance of the Israeli coastal plain, while Israel would lose much of what it has in the way of an early-warning system. In facing a potential threat from Saddam Hussein, for example, these stations are critical and irreplaceable. Today, Israel's surveillance positions on the crest of the Samarian mountain ridge can tip off Israel to an attack; if they were in Arab hands, the same positions would be reporting to Saddam about the activity of Israel's forces instead. (Jordan, for example, has regularly shared surveillance intelligence with Iraq.)

While airborne and satellite reconnaissance is improving, these sources of intelligence are notoriously vulnerable to bad weather and maintenance problems. They are still prohibitively expensive, and in the case of early-warning aircraft, they can be lost to enemy missile fire. No nation relies exclusively on airborne or space-based early-warning and this is true for Israel as well. For Israel, there is still no substitute for a good mountaintop.

During the critical first seventy-two hours of war, one of the most precious commodities the handful of defenders on the line can have is *space*. The Israeli army must have minimal physical room to deploy men and hardware at the outbreak of war. Already squeezed in the country's present boundaries, it could not do so effectively if Judea and Samaria were lopped off, leaving the army to deploy in the streets of Jerusalem and on the outskirts of Tel Aviv. Worse, almost the entire zone of mobilization and deployment would be subject to artillery bombardment, which can be effectively directed at most of Israel's major cities from the hills of the West Bank. Once astride this mountain range, an enemy could easily take aim at airfields, mobilization centers, crucial highways, power plants, and key industries. Such intervention at the outbreak of a war would spell substantial disruption of the entire mobilization network. By physically shielding the coast from attack, the wall of the West Bank is able not only to save the lives of the Israelis living below but to afford the Israeli army the time it badly needs to get the troops to the front (see Map 9).

This is the crucial point to understand about a military buffer space: *Space buys time*. The distance the enemy has to cover before it can enter Israel's populated areas, inflict enormous civilian casualties, and conquer its cities translates into the time that Israel has to mobilize. The farther the advancing column has to travel, the more likely it is that air harassment and resistance on the ground will be able to stem the advance and thereby purchase time for the mobilization and deployment of the reserves. The space available for such delaying tactics is called "strategic depth," and NATO's forces in Germany counted on a depth of *150 miles* for tank battles involving roughly the same number of tanks that Israel has to face along its eastern front.[5]

In addition, the topography of the Judean and Samarian mountains is particularly well suited for the delaying actions necessary for Israel's defense. To an invader from the east, this range is an extraordinary obstacle that must be overcome to reach the Israeli coastline. Such an invader enters the West Bank in the Jordan River Valley, which is the lowest point on earth, more than a thousand feet below sea level. He then has to fight his way up a cliff face that rises a daunting three to four thousand feet within a space of seven to nine miles. This is terrain that, with the exception of a few tortuous routes, is virtually impassable to tanks and other heavy equipment. No amount of electronic gadgetry can replace a stone wall thousands of feet high as an obstacle to war. The West Bank thus provides Israel not only with strategic depth but with strategic height.

In withdrawing from the Sinai, Israel took upon itself considerable risks, but not ones that immediately jeopardized its existence. For if the Egyptians were to violate the peace treaty by moving substantial forces into the Sinai, it would take these forces several days to cover the 120 miles from the Suez Canal to the border of Israel. This would give Israel sufficient time to mobilize its ground forces and intercept the Egyptian expedition in the desert before it reached the Israeli border. By contrast, the distance from the West Bank to the Mediterranean is only ten miles. Were Israel to vacate the West Bank, hostile forces could cover these distances in a matter of hours.

It is often difficult for non-Israelis to grasp just how tiny Israel is and what kind of military odds it faces. I suppose this difficulty arises from the string of Israeli victories, extracted from the teeth of extinction. These tend to obscure the fact that one defeat for Is-

rael means the last defeat. Further, because of their lack of familiarity with Israel's geographical and topographical realities, people
in the West have a great difficulty understanding that Israel's position vis-à-vis the Arabs could change from one of relative strength
to one of extreme vulnerability by shifting the border "just a few
miles."

How is it possible that the physical circumstances of the country that the press and television crews of the entire world cover
perhaps more than any other are so little understood by millions?
After all, the map of Israel appears routinely on the television
nightly news. But there's the rub: The map, with no reference to
scale, is usually designed to emphasize Israel and its "occupation"
of the West Bank, which the viewer naturally believes to be, not
thirty miles wide, but a substantial piece of real estate—like, say,
the west bank of the Mississippi, which stretches a thousand miles
to the Rockies.

American visitors to Israel are often astonished at its tininess.
In this they echo Mark Twain, who observed that "the State of Mis-
souri could be split into three Palestines, and there would then be
enough material left for part of another—possibly a whole one."[6]

It was only during the Gulf War, when the focus on Iraq required a larger map of the region that showed Israel to be the minuscule thumbprint that it is, that many Western viewers gasped
in amazement. But not even that conveyed Israel's microscopic
size compared with the Arab world. The territory of the Arab
countries is far larger than the land mass of the United States. Israel in the pre-1967 boundaries is smaller than the state of Maryland, and the West Bank is a quarter that size.[7] To put it another
way, if the Arab world were imagined as a football field, Israel
could easily fit between the goalposts on one end of the field. Its
population is six million, less than the population of greater Los
Angeles, as compared with over 150 million Arabs. Further, the
Arabs' fantastic petrodollar wealth has allowed them to invest unlimited funds in buying the latest weapons and building formidable arsenals. Consequently, Israel's army is one-sixth the size of

the combined armies directly facing it and one-seventh the size of those of the entire Arab world.[8] If ever in the history of nations there was a clear-cut case of David facing Goliath, this is it.

Israel has had to face enemies on its eastern front who in short order could field thousands of tanks, planes, artillery pieces, and rockets, and millions of men, reminiscent of the eastern front faced by NATO. But whereas the distance between the Warsaw Pact lines and the English Channel was a thousand miles, Israel's current width from its eastern front to the sea is forty miles. This is bad enough, but Israel is now being seriously asked to reduce that distance to ten miles. Against such odds, it could not survive.

I have a special kind of familiarity with these distances. It is an Israeli dictum that you get to know the country through your feet, a cliché immortalized by endless blisters that Israelis acquire during military service. When I was in the army, we used to hike the distance "from sea to sea" in a day's march. We'd fill up a canteen with sea water from the Mediterranean at five in the morning and empty it into the Sea of Galilee at five in the evening—twelve hours to cross the country on foot from west to east. This one-day trek crosses Israel in its *present* width. Its previous width lent itself to a brisk run, which is what we used to do when I entered the army a few weeks after the Six Day War. The paratroop base where I did basic training was situated right opposite Tuklarem, on the just-erased Jordanian border. We used to run from the base to the sea in a little over an hour.

How can someone living in America or Britain or France comprehend the vulnerability of a country of such minuscule dimensions? A plane trip from Montreal to Miami along the narrower north-south dimension of the United States takes three hours. I recently flew into Israel with the same kind of jetliner, which was flying east and circled back for the landing at Lod Airport, near Tel Aviv. From the time it crossed the Mediterranean shoreline to the moment it passed over the old border, two minutes had elapsed. By the time it reached the turn (coming up over Jerusalem), another minute had elapsed. If it had continued eastward it would have crossed into Jordanian air space two minutes later. In other words, compared to the three hours it takes to fly across America's narrower dimension, it takes five minutes to do so in Israel. A jet fighter can cover the distance in three.

How to defend such a speck of territory against forces that approach the size of NATO's is a tactician's nightmare. It is a question that was once asked of me in the heart of Africa. The head of an African state with which Israel had no relations had invited me on a private and unofficial visit. After graciously receiving me, the African leader explained that he was no enemy of Israel, but as he was a friend of the Palestinians, he wanted to know why we could not just give them the West Bank and be done with it. I took one of the paper napkins that were served with the coffee and proceeded to draw the country's dimensions, the West Bank, and the forces arrayed against Israel in the east. "Mr. President," I said, "you're a military man. Here, why don't you draw the minimal borders necessary for our defense?" He said he saw my point.

In fact somebody did draw a map. That somebody was none other than the American Joint Chiefs of Staff. On June 29, 1967, eighteen days after the Six Day War, the then U.S. secretary of defense, Robert McNamara, asked the joint chiefs to submit a position paper outlining the minimal territory Israel would need to protect itself, "without regard to political forces." The Pentagon proceeded to draw a map based on purely military considerations, well before political ones were introduced under Arab pressure to muddy up the simple military facts. The map is reproduced as Map 11, and the report accompanying it is in Appendix G. It recommends that Israel retain four-fifths of the territories (not counting the Sinai). This includes most of the West Bank and all of the Golan Heights. The only area that the Pentagon thought Israel could afford *not* to annex was the eastern slope of Samaria facing the Jordan River. This was the opinion of the objective, apolitical military planners of the U.S. Department of Defense.

Twenty-one years later, in 1988, *one hundred* retired U.S. generals and admirals petitioned the American administration, argu-

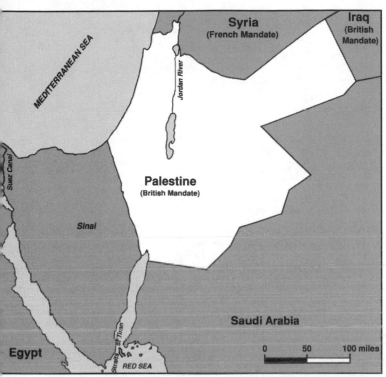

3. 1920
The Jewish
National Home
Under British
Administration

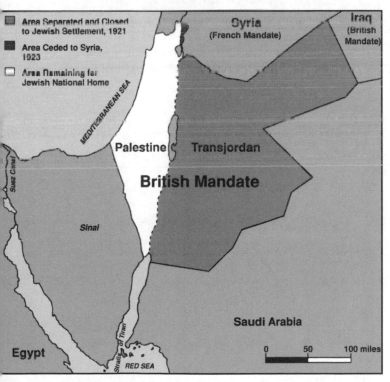

4. 1922
The Jewish
National Home
After Creation
of Transjordan

Area Separated and Closed
to Jewish Settlement, 1921

Area Ceded to Syria,
1923

Area Remaining for
Jewish National Home

**5. 1947
UN
Partition
Plan**

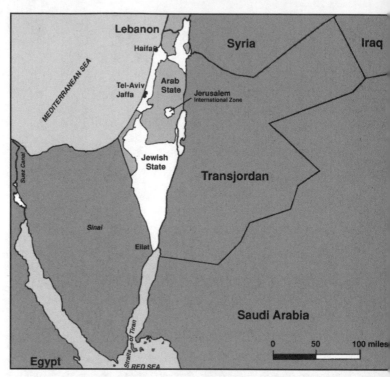

**6. 1949
Armistice Lines
After War of
Independence**

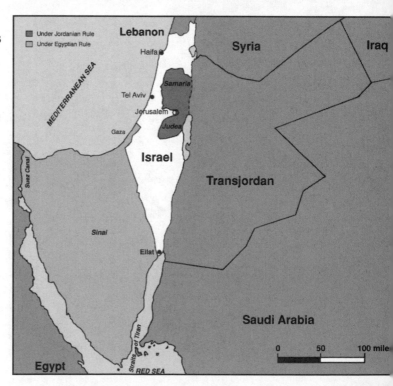

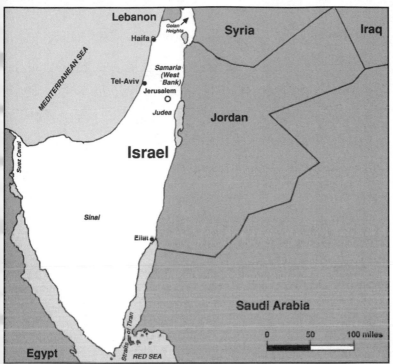

**7. 1967
Armistice
Lines After
Six Day War**

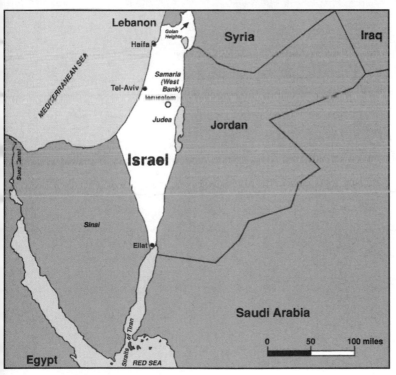

**8. 1992
Israel
Before the
Oslo Accords**

9. Israel's Strategic Vulnerability 1949–1967

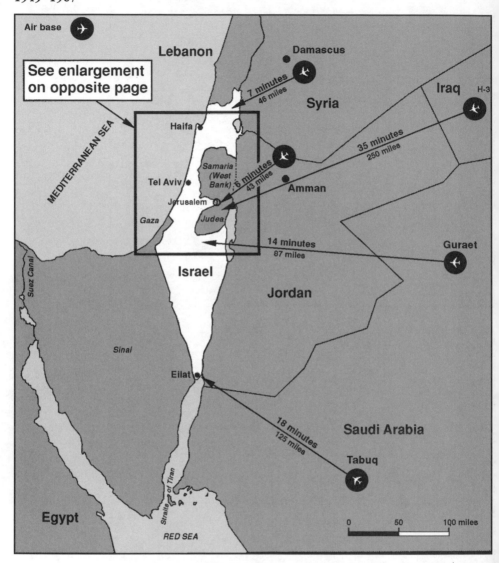

**10. Israel's Exposed Shoreline
1949–1967**

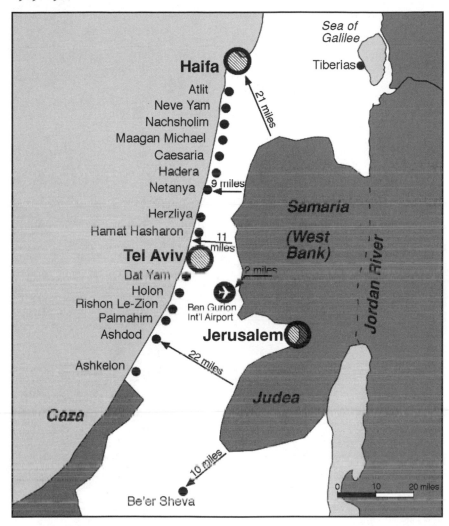

11. The Pentagon Plan for Israel's Security Needs
June 18, 1967

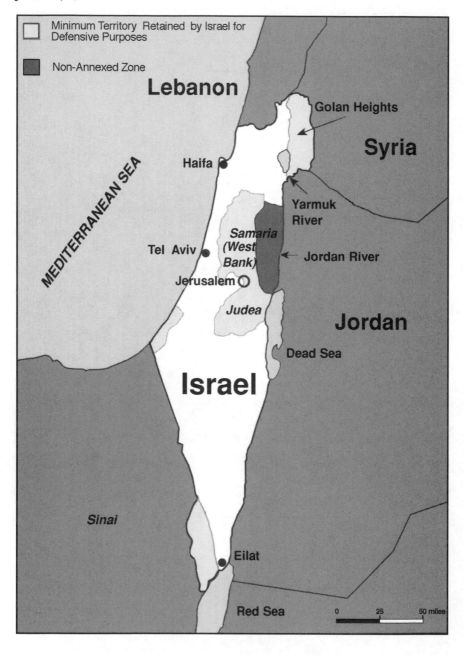

**12. 1999
Israel After the
Oslo Accords**

FULL PALESTINIAN
CONTROL

JOINT ISRAELI
PALESTINIAN CONTROL

FULL ISRAELI
CONTROL

0   Miles   50

MEDITERRANEAN SEA

Jenin

Tulkarm

Qalqilya   Nablus

WEST BANK

Ramallah

Jericho

Bethlehem

Hebron

Dead Sea

GAZA STRIP

Israel   Jordan

ing that the Pentagon's conclusion from 1967 "is even more valid today":

> [Without the territories, a] dwarfed Israel would then be an irresistible target for Arab adventurism and terrorism, and ultimately for an all-out military assault which could end Israel's existence. . . .
>
> If Israel were to relinquish the West Bank . . . it would have virtually no warning of attack. . . . Virtually all the population would be subject to artillery bombardment. The Sharon Plain north of Tel Aviv could be riven by an armored salient within hours. The quick mobilization of its civilian army . . . would be disrupted easily and perhaps irreversibly.[9]

The view of the generals was forcefully elaborated upon in November 1991 by Lieutenant-General Thomas Kelly, who had served as the director of operations for the Joint Chiefs of Staff during the Gulf War and who visited Israel later that year:

> It is impossible to defend Jerusalem unless you hold that high ground. . . . [I] look onto the West Bank and say to myself, "If I'm chief of staff of the Israel Defense Forces, I cannot defend this land without that terrain." . . . I don't know about politics, but if you want me to defend this country, and you want me to defend Jerusalem, I've got to hold that ground.[10]

Of course, the position of successive administrations in Washington has not been based on such cold strategic calculations. The U.S. government cannot escape the intense politicization of the issue that has taken place since 1967, and the version of Israel's defense needs to which the United States is officially committed is skewed accordingly. This is why a great many American officials insist on ignoring their generals and asserting that an Israel ten miles wide can count portions of the Mediterranean in its tally of the strategic depth available for its defense, evidently believing that the Israeli army can walk on water. But there is a limit to the number of miracles an army can perform, and Israel's soldiers have performed more than most. No country should ask its army to continue to do the impossible, especially since it would be hard pressed to perform even the ordinary military tasks that security dictated while standing on the head of a pin.

This is obvious enough even to nonmilitary observers who have become acquainted with Israel's geography. Their common sense tells them what every military planner knows: Never pre-pare for the previous war. But here Israel is being asked to prepare to fight the Six Day War again, a conflict that preceded the previ-ous war by several wars—except that the conditions that prevailed before June 5, 1967, and that allowed Israel to escape death then are gone forever. For one thing, a repetition of the surprise Israeli air strike that demolished all the Arab air forces in 1967 is impos-sible, because since 1968 Arab military aircraft no longer sit on open runways but are sheltered underground in fortified bunkers. For another, after 1969 the Arabs acquired highly effective antiair-craft missiles, which took a deadly toll of Israel's air force in 1973. And with the improvement of Arab battle strategy, the long hesi-tation that allowed Israel the time to mobilize its troops, which was the fatal error of the Arab coalition on the eve of the Six Day War, will certainly not occur again. Further, the Arab armies have increased three- and four-fold in size. Their slow-moving infantry divisions of the past have become rapidly moving armored and mechanized formations. Arab artillery is no longer towed but is self-propelled.

But whereas the Arabs have plenty of space to deploy their massive armies around Israel's borders, a truncated Israel would find it extremely difficult to field its army, which has also been en-larged since 1967, in the small stretch of space between the edges of Tel Aviv's suburbs and the border. It is therefore absurd to as-sume that since Israel survived a previous attack from the bound-aries of the Six Day War, it could necessarily do so again.

One way I have tried to get this point across to foreign visitors is by flying with them from Sdeh Dov, the small airport on the Tel Aviv beach, to the pre-1967 border a few miles to the east. The helicopter traverses the suburbs of Tel Aviv and reaches the last house of the last suburb, Kfar Saba, in minutes. From there it flies over a small field, then reaches the Arab town of Kalkilya across the old border. Before the 1967 war, the distance between Kfar Saba and Kalkilya used to be a number of miles. But Kfar Saba has grown, and so has Kalkilya. "That," I say, pointing to the few hundred yards that currently separate the last house in Kfar Saba from the first house in Kalkilya, "is what most of the world intends to be Israel's strategic depth."

Beyond Kalkilya, we can see the wall rise up: the mountains of Samaria, which from the air look like a castle fortress looming up over the coast. Then I ask the pilot to fly due west to the coast, heading directly for embassy row on Tel Aviv's beachfront Hayarkon Street. If the visitor is American, the pilot flies us over the American embassy; if British, over the British embassy, and so on. The round trip takes all of ten minutes. When the visitor is a diplomat from a country that is particularly dogmatic about having Israel "return the West Bank," he can easily imagine himself working in an embassy all of five minutes' helicopter flight from the new border that his government insists Israel should have.

On one occasion I was explaining the significance of this tiny distance to an American senator. The pilot became very excited and joined in on my side of the discussion. It turned out that he was the brother of a prominent civil servant who was identified with Israel's dovish Labor party.

"Tell him who you vote for," I said to the pilot, guessing.

"Labor," he answered. "But what's the difference? We all want to live."

While this determination never to return to the pre-1967 borders is shared by most Israelis, a small minority has emerged that does not have the same qualms about withdrawing to these lines. Since this minority exercises considerable influence in Israel's media and politics (it is very potent in the left), its argument should be paid due attention. To counter the menacing geographic reality, the members of this school of thought argue that in the age of missiles the amount of territory Israel holds does not matter. For if the Arabs possess projectiles that can fly over a territorial defense and hit Israel's cities and military bases, what use is territory? This simple formulation has great appeal and is receiving much currency. After all, wasn't Israel attacked by Iraqi Scud missiles fired from a thousand miles way? What difference does it make whether it controls or does not control the West Bank?

However appealing, this argument is based on a fallacy. Missiles do not win wars. They can do damage, even terrible damage, but they do not conquer territory. The intense bombing of North Vietnam by the United States caused considerable destruction, but since the American army did not invade North Vietnam and take possession of its territory, the United States could not win the war. Similarly, the devastating American air strikes against Saddam's troops in Kuwait and Iraq, with everything from smart bombs to cruise missiles, could not by themselves win the war. Ground action remained indispensable to physically drive Iraq's army from Kuwait. Israel might be attacked from the air, but it cannot be overrun and conquered without being physically overrun and physically conquered. And this can be done only by armies possessing tanks, mobile artillery, and mechanized infantry that can move into a territory and take possession of it. The distance they have to cover and the terrain they must negotiate at the start of the fighting are vital factors in determining the outcome of battles. Distance may not make much difference to missiles, but to an armored division it makes a world of difference whether it must cover 12 miles or 120 miles to reach its target, and whether the ground it must cross is flat or mountainous. (In point of fact, larger distances do diminish the effectiveness of missiles as well, though in a different way. The same Scud missiles that were fired at Israel from distant Iraq are now in the possession of nearby Syria, which would be able to pack twice the explosive payload into each warhead because of the shorter distance the missile must travel to reach its target.)

The physical barrier that the West Bank places before incoming divisions is of particular value in the age of missiles. Israel must mobilize the bulk of its army to ward off a threat, but in the age of missiles we must assume that the time needed for such mobilization will *increase*. For missiles, even unsophisticated ones like the Iraqi Scuds, can hit population centers with ease, thereby disrupting the flow of Israeli civilians to their mobilization centers. As one Israeli reserve officer told me, "If missiles rain down on my city, I'll rush to my daughter's school to see if she's alive before I head for my unit." And as the missiles get more deadly and more accurate, they can be pinpointed on the mobilization bases themselves and on the road intersections that lead to them, thus further delaying the deployment of Israeli troops toward the front. If, during such an aerial bombardment, enemy ground troops were to advance toward Israel's borders, Israel would be hard pressed to bring the reserves to the front to oppose them. Initial terrain conditions would therefore be even more vital for Israel's small standing army as it seeks to hold off the assault of the far larger Arab forces until the arrival of reinforcements. Israel would need more rather than less space to absorb an attack and buy for itself the precious time it needed to regroup. Thus, the protective wall of the West Bank provides invaluable time and space.

The age of missiles has introduced not only long-range missiles but also short-range missiles. For these weapons, too, territory is a vital consideration. I am referring to such weapons as SAM-7s and shoulder-fired American Stinger missiles that can down helicopters and fighter aircraft with devastating effectiveness. Just how effectively they can do this had been seen in the war in Afghanistan by the mid-1980s. The mujahideen had been all but crushed by the Soviet army and air force when the United States decided to supply them with Stingers. This was the turning point of the war. A few years later, Soviet air power in Afghanistan was almost obliterated by peasants firing sophisticated missiles from mountaintops. Israel has recently had to contend with thousands of youngsters throwing stones on the hills of Samaria. Imagine the situation if those youngsters were replaced by thousands of PLO fighters carrying not rocks but rockets, which could shoot down Israeli military and civilian aircraft. Israel's international airport, after all, is two miles from the West Bank, and all except one of the Jewish state's military airfields are within range of various short-range missiles that could be easily placed on the West Bank, crippling Israel's military precisely as the mujahideen crippled the Soviet military. Of course, such weapons were not available to the Arabs when they controlled the West Bank twenty-five years ago. Today, courtesy of years of Soviet supplies, they are a key component of their arsenals. And there is a growing fear in the West that the deadly Stingers that were supplied to the Afghanis, Kuwaitis, and others have been making their way into the hands of terrorists—such as the PLO.

The lesson for a small country like Israel is this: *In the age of missiles territory counts more, not less.* Long-range missiles increase the need for mobilization time, and short-range missiles can destroy strategic targets within their reach. For both reasons, the control of a contiguous buffer area becomes more, not less, important. This is the conclusion of the Jaffee Center for Strategic Studies, whose left-leaning sympathies stand in sharp contrast to its military recommendations:

> Leaving politics aside for a moment, we can maintain that though surface-to-surface missiles cannot be stopped by territory, . . . we do have to recognize that missiles cannot win a war. . . . Territory is especially vital when it permits our forces to "buy" time: in case of a surprise attack, this enables us to mobilize our reserves and bring them to the front lines before the aggressor succeeds in taking any part of our vital area.[11]

Israel does not ask for additional territory, only that the present strategic depth (and strategic height) of the West Bank be left intact. Of course, for a country the size of the United States, ceding even a large parcel of territory, like a corner of North Dakota, would not appreciably endanger the country's security. There would be plenty of spare strategic depth left (and yet Americans find it impossible to imagine ceding any part of America to anyone). But imagine an enemy state across the Potomac, within sniper range of the capital—and you begin to understand why Israelis feel that territory contiguous to strategic targets is vital as well (see Map 9).

We can now understand the full danger that a Palestinian state on the West Bank would pose. Such a state could certainly have weapons, including sophisticated ones, brought into it. How could Israel prevent it? The common response that advocates of Israeli territorial concessions make is that the areas vacated by Israel will be "demilitarized." But traditional concepts of demilitarization cannot be applied here, for two reasons. First, demilitarizing the area against the introduction of smaller weapons is impossible. Unless Israel physically controls the entrances to the West Bank, it cannot possibly prevent the smuggling of missiles and other weapons the size of a suitcase. These can be brought in by trucks or even cars, or flown in by civilian aircraft. Even today, when Israel fully controls access to the West Bank and strip-searches the vehicles entering it, it cannot prevent the smuggling of various weapons into the territories. Imagine what would happen if it were to vacate the territories and such controls were removed. In an open, empty, unpopulated area like the Sinai, demilitarization can be enforced against the entry of tanks or artillery pieces into an area, and if small weapons were somehow smuggled in, they would be too far away from any target to be effective. But demilitarization is woefully ineffective against the miniaturized weapons of today and tomorrow, which can be smuggled into a populated territory such as the West Bank with relative ease, threatening vital Israeli ground and air installations. Demilitarization of the territories is therefore not an answer. Where hostility is so deeply rooted, arms so readily available, and distances so compressed, a "demilitarized zone" is wishful thinking.

Second, demilitarization could not be relied upon to protect Israel for political reasons. For it is clear that any space from which Israel withdrew would rapidly be filled by a PLO state, no matter what political figleaf were chosen to obscure the fact (such as "confederation" with Jordan). The advocates of the demilitarization of the West Bank are therefore talking about *demilitarizing an entire sovereign state*—something unheard-of in the annals of nations, and for good reason: It cannot be sustained. Demilitarization in certain *zones* is hard enough to maintain for prolonged periods. For example, the demilitarization of the German Rhineland following World War I was intended to protect France against future German aggression. But as neither Britain nor France was prepared to go to war to *enforce* it, demilitarization proved to be no barrier to remilitarization when Hitler chose to abrogate the commitment.

The fate of past promises of partial demilitarization by Arab states is no more encouraging. King Hussein of Jordan had agreed to American conditions that he not deploy on the West Bank the Patton tanks, which the United States had supplied him, but in the weeks before the Six Day War these very tanks were moved into position facing Jerusalem anyway. Similarly, Egypt broke its arms-control agreement with Israel not to move antiaircraft batteries to the Suez Canal prior to the Yom Kippur War. Since dictators have no qualms about violating demilitarization as the need arises, it makes no sense to agree to demilitarization in cases in which a sudden *remilitarization* would jeopardize the country's security.

Yet none of these efforts at partial demilitarization compares to the demilitarization of an entire country. Israel could not strip-search every truck and every car that went into a hypothetical Palestinian state on the West Bank. Nor, obviously, could it intercept every civilian plane that came from Libya or Afghanistan, landing it first in Tel Aviv, then taking it apart piece by piece before letting it continue on its way. What country would allow such gross interference with its international commerce and transport? The Palestinian state would claim the right that every state claims to control its borders. Furthermore, it would demand the right of self-defense—without which it would immediately fall prey to the intrigues and intimidation of other Arab states and terror organizations—which would very soon mean the establishment of its own army. Further still, it would demand the removal from its soil of any encampments or enclaves of a neighbor's army.

Is there any doubt that a Palestinian state would have the backing of the entire Arab world and of many in the international community for such demands? The fervent desire by some to abandon the West Bank cannot be a substitute for clear thinking, and the first order of clarity is to recognize that the concept of demilitarization may sound like a useful panacea to offer an Israel anxious about its security (some Israelis are willing to prescribe it for themselves), but it cannot hold over time, indeed not even for a short time. Even if some Palestinian Arabs could be persuaded initially to accept demilitarization, this commitment is not one that could be expected to last long, and Israel would find itself unable to reassert its military authority in the area. Crossing into the West Bank in reaction to a violation of demilitarization would mean crossing an *international* frontier that could well be guaranteed by other powers. Israel would then risk triggering a full-scale Arab-Israeli war and international sanctions.

The impossibility of maintaining demilitarization is even more evident when one considers the strategy of the PLO's Phased Plan: Get a PLO state, arm it, launch terrorist attacks from it to provoke an Israeli response, prod the Arab world into defending Palestine, and thereby set off the decisive confrontation. In addition to the Palestinian forces that would fire rockets from the mountaintops on a vulnerable Israel below, one cannot rule out the entry of Arab troops from across the Jordan to assist their brethren. They might even be flown into the West Bank hilltops in helicopters *before* the actual outbreak of hostilities. If this were done at night in communication silence, as was the case in the Yom Kippur War, Israel could find itself with a second "October surprise." This time, how-ever, the Arab starting lines would not be on the relatively distant Suez Canal or on the Golan, but a few miles from Israel's cities.

How Israel would avert such a disaster from the pre-1967 lines is not obvious. If Israel were to completely withdraw from the West Bank, it would have to field a much larger standing army, since the length of pre-1967 Israel's convoluted border with the West Bank is more than 3.5 times the length of the present straight border along the Jordan River.[12] The resultant financial cost of fac-ing a greatly extended front would add a crushing burden to Is-rael's economy and deprive it of much-needed manpower. But even then there is no certainty that, in the stitch of space between a Palestinian state and Israel's cities, the Israeli army would find sufficient territory to deploy and fan out for battle. A PLO state on the West Bank would be like a hand poised to strangle Israel's vital artery along the sea. No wonder the overwhelming majority of Is-raelis reject it and see in it a mortal threat to their country.

When advocates of an Israeli withdrawal are presented with all these facts, they usually fall back on one final argument: Israel can always unsheath a nuclear sword, thereby ending all threats to its existence. But Israel has promised not to be the first to introduce nuclear weapons into the Middle East, and even if it were to change its policy and introduce them, it is unclear how even this would serve as a deterrent. Considering the tiny distances in-volved, every movement of Palestinian troops could constitute a serious threat to Israel. But would Israel really be willing to threaten nuclear war every time a Palestinian battalion changed its position? Would nuclear weapons be used if an Arab column crossed into Israeli territory on the outskirts of Petah Tikva, or would they be reserved for the actual arrival of such a force in downtown Tel Aviv twenty minutes later? Israel's hypothetical nu-clear deterrent would suffer from lack of credibility, for who would start a nuclear war over a border crossing? But at the same time, it would require a dangerously sensitive hairline response, for in a ten-mile strip, every border crossing would threaten to snuff the country out of existence.

The idea of reducing Israel to an indefensible strip along the Mediterranean would mean that it would have to resort to non-conventional means to defend itself, for it would be left with precious few options. It is not an accident, therefore, that even the most extreme territorial doves are nuclear hawks (they cannot conceive of any other defense once they part with the territory), while the territorial hawks are nuclear doves. Naturally, I prefer to be counted among the latter. The idea of laying a nuclear tripwire along Israel's borders so that it and it alone is the real guarantor of Israel's security is sheer folly. Further, what would you bomb? Nablus? East Jerusalem? Besides the horrible devastation that such an attack would unleash, the radioactive fallout would poison the entire region, killing Arabs and Jews alike. Atomic radiation does not recognize the "Green Line," Israel's pre-1967 border.

The threat of Arab dictatorships armed with nuclear weapons is a real and growing one, to Israel and everyone else. There are policies that Israel can pursue to reduce that threat and to deter would-be attackers from making good on it. They merit the detailed discussions they receive inside Israel's defense establishment, but I will refrain from going into such matters here. It is, however, important to dispel one patch of fog: There are those who argue that in an age of nuclear weaponry, conventional military concepts such as strategic depth become irrelevant. This position is flawed and dangerous. The fact that Israel may face a *nonconventional* threat to its life is no reason for it to leave itself open to a *conventional* threat as well. The fact that a country may have to defend itself against one possible danger that may destroy it does not mean that it should subject itself to intolerable danger on another front. In the heyday of the Cold War, the United States did not disarm its massive conventional forces facing the Warsaw Pact, even though it had plenty of nuclear missiles to destroy the Soviet Union if the need arose. The wisdom of this policy was amply demonstrated by the fact that in all the various wars that the United States has fought since World War II, nuclear weapons were never once used—and traditional conventional factors determined the outcome every time.

Although by no means universal, the broad consensus in Israel is therefore that the army must retain military control of the defensive wall of the West Bank. It is fashionable to claim that many of Israel's generals, or at least those who lean to the left, disagree with this conclusion. While there are a handful who do, most emphatically do not. Like other Israelis, they may support Israel's withdraw from politically controlling the Arab population, but almost all favor an Israel military presence. This contradiction was captured in a round-table discussion with eight left-leaning former Israeli generals in the newspaper *Ha'aretz* in 1988. Each of the generals explained in turn that he favored withdrawal from the territories, but he insisted that the IDF would have to retain control of some aspects of the terrain so that his own particular branch of the service could function effectively in case of war. By the time the generals were finished itemizing what Israel would need to keep to defend itself, there was little left to negotiate, and the correspondent for the newspaper, not exactly known for its hawkish tendencies, had no choice but to point this out:

All of you favor withdrawal, but the conditions are [retaining] air space, early-warning stations, the right to hot pursuit, the Jordan River Valley, Israeli cantons. . . . What Arab partner would be willing to enter into negotiations at all with conditions like these?[13]

Indeed, the truth is that for Israel to protect its cities, it must retain military control over much of the territory west of the Jordan River. The Joint Chiefs had it right in 1967. They reported the unvarnished truth.

Only in the case of Gaza is the principal danger for Israel political rather than strategic. Whereas the West Bank and the Golan are high ground that completely dominates the country below them, Gaza is flat and small. It was used, and could be used again, as a base for terrorist attacks and Katyusha bombardment, but this danger would be reduced if the Sinai remained demilitarized and Egypt remained faithful to the peace. Consequently, the principal danger in the case of Gaza is that if Israel were to simply walk away from it, the vacuum would be filled instantly by a PLO ministate—which would use this toehold to press for application of the Palestinian Principle to the Arabs of the West Bank and the Negev Bedouin community just across the fence. What this means in terms of future peace arrangements is discussed in Chapter 9. Suffice it to say here that for Israel to defend itself it must keep effective military control of the area west of the Jordan River, as the Pentagon planners said in their political survey.

Can military control be separated from political sovereignty for very long? This is the difficulty with all the proposals put forward on behalf of relinquishing the territories. The debate between Israel's left-wing and right-wing generals over the question of territorial compromise is ultimately not a *military* debate. There is a rough strategic consensus as to what kind of military presence must be retained in the territories in order to make Israel defensible. Rather, the debate is one over *political* judgment: What kind of sovereign arrangements must exist on the ground in order to make Israel's defense workable? Some have asserted that one could have an Israeli military presence on sovereign Arab soil. But the Egyptians refused to allow the retention of a single Israeli air base in the Sinai, and there is no reason to expect that any other Arab government would behave any differently. Similarly, some have asserted that Israel could permanently control their space over an Arab country. All such schemes would break down in the face of Arab domestic pressure—just as American control over the Panama Canal and British authority in Suez broke down in the face of Panamanian and Egyptian pressure—leaving Israel hopelessly vulnerable to powerful neighboring armies. If you wish to control a territory as minuscule as the West Bank, where the strategic points and the population centers are in close proximity to one another, you have to control it *both* militarily and politically.

If you give up political control, you will ultimately have to give up military control. This is the challenge and difficulty of reaching peace with *added* security with the Palestinians. They should have all the political powers to run their lives but none of those political powers that could threaten Israeli security and survival.

In addition to such defense-related issues, there are other security issues that must be taken into account. One of the most critical of security arguments pertaining to Judea and Samaria is seldom, if ever, discussed in the foreign media: water. No country can survive without water, and in the Middle East there is not much of it to go around. Like its neighbors Egypt, Syria, and Jordan, Israel is a country that is in severe water deficit, annually consuming substantially more water than is replenished from natural sources. The situation is worst in Syria, whose capital, Damascus, is often without running water at night.[14] A real peace in the region would require regional efforts to conserve water and develop alternative sources. Without such efforts, the only thing that is likely to come of the severe and worsening crisis is more conflict. This has been most evident in the case of the Tigris and Euphrates, which carry fresh water from the mountains of eastern Turkey to Syria and Iraq downstream. Turkish moves to dam and otherwise develop the headwaters have met with outraged and bellicose reactions from its southern neighbors in recent years, and the prospects look no more promising for the future.[15]

In Israel's case, fully 40 percent of the available fresh-water resources consists of ground water drawn from aquifers wholly or partially under Judea and Samaria. This is a supply without which Israel would be brought to the brink of catastrophe, and no "solution" to the dispute over the territories can be resolved without this possibility being forestalled. The question is how? The problems that would be caused by having the most vital of all resources under the control of an enemy do not stop at water blackmail, a frightening enough scenario in itself. The underground water supply could be contaminated in ways that could spread epidemics and even destroy the aquifer permanently, either on purpose or by accident. Given that one of the weapons of the intifada was the burning of forests all over Israel, and that Saddam was willing to fight America by pouring millions of barrels of crude oil into the gulf and setting oil wells afire, Israel cannot rule out the possibility of deliberate diversion and pollution of its water supply. (Significantly, the first attacks that Yasser Arafat's Fatah ever launched in the 1960s were attempts to destroy the National Water Carrier, the Israeli pipeline that provides water from the Golan and Galilee to parched communities and farms all over Israel.)[16]

But accidental poisoning is no less a concern. The improper treatment of sewage and other industrial and urban waste-disposal problems have an immediate impact on the fresh-water reserves under the ground. Poorly sealed sewers are capable of leaking toxic wastes into the aquifier for years without detection, as are factory disposal sites. Preventing such deadly seepage requires both a high level of governmental and public awareness, and the dedication of substantial funds to inspection, monitoring, and repairs. If it is difficult to muster the necessary concern over environmental poisoning in the most advanced countries in the West, it is clear that handing such fearsome responsibility to an impoverished and hostile Arab regime on the West Bank would be an act of unalloyed foolishness, and no Israeli government could seriously be expected to do it.

When one considers the crucial factor of strategic depth and height, the topographical and geographical obstacles to invasion, and the control of the precious water resources offered by this vital mountain ridge known as the West Bank, one thing becomes apparent. It is the same stark conclusion that one reaches on a clear day standing on the ridge of the Samarian mountain of Ba'al Hazor, seeing at once the entire breadth of the country, with the Jordan River Valley to the right and the Mediterranean to the left: that western Palestine, the present territory under Israel, is *one* integral territorial unit, dominated by one mountain range that overlooks one coastal plain. For any nation this would constitute a tiny physical platform on which to build and protect its physical life. To subdivide this land into two unstable, insecure nations, to try to defend what is indefensible, is to invite disaster. Carving Judea and Samaria out of Israel means carving up Israel.

The considerations of strategic depth, geography, and water are also crucial in considering the future of the Golan Heights, and they render concessions on that front extremely dangerous as well. The Golan, which dominates the headwaters of the Jordan River and the Sea of Galilee, controls *another* 40 percent of Israel's water supply. Like the West Bank, it too constitutes a natural barrier shielding Israel, rising nearly four thousand feet above the farmland in the Hula Valley of northern Israel. The Golan is also similar to the West Bank in that it is tiny—no more than sixteen miles at its widest point—as opposed to the Sinai, whose 120-mile expanse offered relatively flat approaches to Israel and not a drop of water. Thus, while Israel could afford to be extremely generous in ceding the Sinai in its peace with Egypt on the western front, there is no margin for similar concessions in the Golan and the West Bank on its eastern front.

This becomes readily apparent when one considers that the conventional military threat to Israel's existence can come from three potential sources: the large and powerful armies of Egypt, Syria, and Iraq. The well-armed Egyptian army is separated from Israel by the Sinai desert, which affords Israel sufficient strategic depth should Egypt ever choose to violate the peace treaty with Israel. The Iraqi army, although reduced in strength after the Gulf War, remains a substantial threat and is in the process of being rebuilt. It is separated from Israel by a buffer area roughly the same size as the Sinai—the Jordanian desert. Although the Jordanian army that patrols this empty waste is a good one, it is too small to constitute a serious threat to Israel on its own. Israel has always said publicly that it considers the entire territory of Jordan to be a buffer area, and that it would under no circumstances allow "foreign forces" to enter Jordan—a warning with which King Hussein was never too unhappy, since it shielded him from his Arab neighbors, just as it protected Israel itself. Thus during the Gulf War,

Israel issued repeated warnings that if the Iraqi army entered Jordan for any reason, this would be considered an act of war. (A similar Israeli warning to Syria in 1970 caused the invading Syrian army to withdraw from Jordan.)

Most Israelis oppose the insertion of a PLO state on the West Bank because they do not want a state allied with Iraq and the most radical forces in the Arab world on their doorstep. Such a state would nullify the whole value of the buffer area on Israel's eastern front.

But whereas Israel presently possesses sufficient strategic depth against potential threats from the south (Egypt) and east (Iraq), it has no such strategic depth in the case of the Syrian threat in the north. It must be remembered that the Syrian army is one of the largest and best equipped in the world. It is permanently deployed on the broad plateau between Damascus and the Golan Heights, a mere sixteen miles from the Israeli breadbasket of Galilee, and another thirty miles from Haifa and the Israeli coastal plain. While the Egyptian and Iraqi armies face a journey of days to reach Israel from their current emplacements, the Syrians could reach the first Israeli population centers in a matter of hours. The only military obstacle in their way is the necessarily far smaller Israeli force that is entrenched on the superior terrain of the Golan Heights. For ever since the Six Day War in 1967, Israel has looked down *at the Syrians*, rather than the other way around. From the precipices of Mount Hermon and Mount Avital, Israeli soldiers can observe the Syrian installations spread out beneath them. It is these commanding positions that make up for the lack of strategic depth. This is the reason that the Labor government of Yitzhak Rabin fought bitterly to retain this terrain in the 1974 disengagement agreement with Syria—much to the consternation of the U.S. administration, which found it difficult to understand what difference "a few miles" made.

Yet Israel is often told that, its security and water requirements notwithstanding, it is bound by international agreement to cede the territories to the Arabs. The Arabs invoke UN Security Council Resolution 242, which was adopted in the wake of the Six Day War and to which Israel has always been a full subscriber. This resolution, it is often claimed, expresses the will of the international community that Israel withdraw from Judea and Samaria, the Golan and Gaza. By now the actual wording of the text and the intentions of its authors have for the most part been forgotten. As in so many other things, the version of the resolution frequently discussed by "experts" on television has more to do with the intent of Israel's adversaries than with fact.

As written, Resolution 242 was originally about peace. It called for an immediate "termination of all claims or states of belligerency"; for the "acknowledgement of the sovereignty, territorial integrity, and political independence of every state in the area"; and for the recognition of the right of those states "to live in peace within secure and recognized boundaries free from threats or acts of force." (The full text can be found in Appendix F.) Thus the bulk of the resolution is a demand by the international community that the Arab states make peace: by ending the state of war against Israel, recognizing Israel's right to exist, and assuring that Israel's borders will be secure ones. That this was the central concern of the resolution was confirmed by Arthur Goldberg, the U.S. ambassador to the UN, who was one of the authors of the resolution:

> It calls for respect and acknowledgement of the sovereignty of every state in the area. Since Israel never denied the sovereignty of its neighboring countries, this language obviously requires those countries to acknowledge Israel's sovereignty.[17]

It took twelve years for Egypt to comply with the Security Council resolution. In explicitly refusing to make peace with Israel, other Arab states flout the dictates of Resolution 242 to this day. Yet with unsurpassed hypocrisy, they reverse causality yet again and claim that it is *Israel* that is in violation of a resolution with which they themselves have yet to make the slightest gesture of compliance. Their accusations are based on an additional clause in Resolution 242, which calls for "withdrawal of Israeli armed forces from territories occupied in the recent conflict." Israel, claim the Arabs, has never obeyed the directive to withdraw from "the territories." Why should they make peace, when Israel is still in possession of the West Bank, the Golan and Gaza? They conveniently choose to forget that *any* Israeli withdrawal was supposed to follow the signing of peace agreements, which the Arab states adamantly refuse to sign.

Viewed through the distorting prism of Arab propaganda, it is indeed possible to believe that the intention of the UN was unmistakably to oust Israel from "*the* territories," and that the resolution says only "territories" (leaving out the word *the*) due to a printer's error. In fact, as the very people who drafted the resolution attest, evacuating Israeli forces from the territories was not the central issue, and the *the* was left out on purpose so that Israel could negotiate to *keep* a portion of the land for security reasons. Hence Arthur Goldberg: "The notable omissions in regard to [Israeli] withdrawal are the word 'the' or 'all' . . . the resolution speaks of withdrawal from occupied territories, without defining the extent of the withdrawal."[18] This is also the view of Lord Caradon, the British ambassador to the UN, who co-authored the resolution with Goldberg:

> We didn't say there should be a withdrawal to the [pre-]1967 line. We did not put the "the" in. We did not say all the territories, deliberately. . . . We all knew that the boundaries of [pre-]1967 were not drawn as permanent frontiers, they were a cease-fire line of a couple of decades earlier. . . . We did not say that the [pre-]1967 boundaries must be forever.[19]

Eugene Rostow, who was U.S. undersecretary of state for political affairs when the American administration took the initiative to draft the resolution, confirms the position of the authors:

Security Council Resolutions 242 and 338 . . . rest on two principles. [First,] Israel may administer the territory until its Arab neighbors make peace. And [second,] when peace is made, Israel should withdraw to "secure and recognized borders," which need not be the same as the Armistice Demarcation Lines of 1949.[20]

But *has* Israel withdrawn from "territories occupied in the conflict"? It certainly has. The Sinai Peninsula, returned in the context of Israel's 1979 peace treaty with Egypt, is on the Israeli scale a very substantial piece of property: twenty-five thousand square miles on which Israel had built major airfields, developed luxury hotels, and discovered oil. In all, the Sinai—ten times bigger than Judea and Samaria—constituted no less than 91 percent of the territories captured by Israel in 1967. Nor does the resolution say in any of its clauses that Israel should have to withdraw on every front (Sinai and Gaza, the Golan, and the West Bank). This was left, precisely as intended by the framers of the resolution, for negotiation between Israel and its Arab neighbors.

Yet all of this misses what is surely the major moral principle embedded in the diplomatic wording of Resolution 242: that the *Arabs* should make concessions for peace. That is, if the resolution recognized an Israeli right to secure borders and furthermore did not necessarily expect Israel to return to the borders from which the war had started, this means that the framers of the resolution thought it was reasonable for the Arabs to sacrifice some of *their* territorial ambitions for the sake of a secure peace.

And why not? What kind of a "compromise" is it for one side to renounce one hundred percent of its claims and the other side to renounce zero percent? What kind of a moral position is it to say that the failed aggressor should be given back all the territory from which he launched his attack? And what kind of deterrence could Israel be expected to maintain if the negative consequences of Arab aggression against it were found to be nil for the Arab countries? Indeed, the position underlying Resolution 242 is as refreshing as it is just. Untouched by the propaganda of the decades that followed it, it states what any rational person would have said from the start: that peace benefits both sides, and so both sides have to share the costs. Secure boundaries for Israel are a prerequisite for peace in the Middle East. The Arabs have demonstrated again and again that the ten-mile strip on which Israel lived before 1967 could not constitute a secure boundary. This means the Arabs have to give something up for peace. There has to be an Arab leader courageous enough to be willing to forgo some or all of the Arab claims to the remaining land. So far none has been found. With the support of most of the world, the Arabs continue to demand every inch of the territories from which they attacked Israel.

Arab military strategy is simple: Squeeze Israel into the pre-1967 armistice lines, subjecting it once more to a state of intolerable vulnerability. Arab political strategy is to harness a forgetful West to this cause. But as President Lyndon Johnson said shortly after the Six Day War: "We are not the ones to say where other nations should draw lines between them that will assure each the greatest security. It is clear, however, that a return to the situation of June 4, 1967, will not bring peace."[21]

Whatever their differences, nearly everyone in Israel—whether Labor or Likud, government or opposition—agrees that Israel must not go back to these boundaries, and that it must not relinquish strategic control of Judea and Samaria.* This point was made forcefully by Labor's Moshe Dayan in August 1967 (two months after the capture of Judea and Samaria) at a ceremony commemorating those who fell in the desperate defense of Jerusalem in 1948—when the Arab armies occupied the strategic wall surrounding the city and starved and bombarded the city of Peace without mercy: "Our brothers, we bear your lesson with

---

*Not quite everyone. In March 1999, Nabil Shaath of the Palestinian National Authority revealed that Yossi Beilin, a senior member of the Labor party leadership, had reached an agreement with Arafat's deputy Abu-Maazen, under which Israel would hand over 95 percent of Gaza and the West Bank, thereby effectively returning Israel to the pre-1967 boundaries.

us. . . . We know that to give life to Jerusalem, we must station the soldiers and armor of [the Israeli army] in the Sh'chem mountains [Samaria] and on the bridges over the Jordan."[22] Thus, whatever views Israelis may have as to how to establish a modus vivendi between Arab and Jew in the territories, few question the necessity for continued Israeli military control of this vital space.

In those parts of the world where peace is the norm, borders, territories, and strategic depth may appear unimportant. In the Middle East they are of decisive importance. Given the specifics of the West Bank, the slogan "land for peace" is singularly inappropriate: To achieve a sustainable peace, Israel must maintain a credible deterrent long enough to effect a lasting change in Arab attitudes. It is precisely Israel's control of this strategic territory that has deterred all-out war and has made eventual peace more likely.

8

A DURABLE PEACE

Of late, a new "villain" was introduced into political discussions about the future of the Middle East. There are those who said that the responsibility for a thousand years of Middle Eastern obstinacy, radicalism, and fundamentalism has now been compressed into one person—namely, me. My critics contended that if only I had been less "obstructionist" in my policies, the convoluted and tortured conflicts of the Middle East would immediately and permanently have settled themselves.

While it is flattering for any person to be told that he wields so much power and influence, I am afraid that I must forgo the compliment. This is not false modesty. The problem of achieving a durable peace between Israel and its Arab neighbors is complicated enough. Yet it pales in comparison with the problem of achieving an overall peace in the region. Even after the attainment of peace treaties between Israel and its neighbors, any broader peace in the region will remain threatened by the destabilizing effects of Islamic fundamentalism and Iran and Iraq's fervent ambition to arm themselves with ballistic missiles and atomic weapons.

Let me first say categorically: It is possible for Israel to achieve peace with its Arab neighbors. But if this peace is to endure, it must be built on foundations of security, justice, and above all, truth. Truth has been the first casualty of the Arab campaign against Israel, and a peace built upon half-truths and distortions is one that will eventually be eroded and whittled away by the harsh political winds that blow in the Middle East. A real peace must take into account the true nature of this region, with its endemic antipathies, and offer realistic remedies to the fundamental problem between the Arab world and the Jewish state.

Fundamentally, the problem is not a matter of shifting this or that border by so many kilometers, but reaffirming the fact and right of Israel's existence. The territorial issue is the linchpin of the negotiations that Israel must conduct with the Palestinian Authority, Syria, and Lebanon. Yet a territorial peace is hampered by the continuing concern that once territories are handed over to the Arab side, they will be used for future assaults to destroy the Jewish state. Many in the Arab world have still not had an irreversible change of heart when it comes to Israel's existence, and if Israel becomes sufficiently weak the conditioned reflex of seeking our destruction would resurface. Ironically, the ceding of strategic territory to the Arabs might trigger this destructive process by convincing the Arab world that Israel *has* become vulnerable enough to attack.

That Israel's existence was a bigger issue than the location of its borders was brought home to me in the first peace negotiations that I attended as a delegate to the Madrid Peace Conference in October 1991. In Madrid, the head of the Palestinian delegation delivered a flowery speech calling for the cession of major Israeli population centers to a new Palestinian state and the swamping of the rest of Israel with Arab refugees,[1] while the Syrian foreign minister questioned whether the Jews, not being a nation, had a right to a state of their own in the first place.[2] (And this at a peace conference!) Grievances over disputed lands and disputed waters, on which the conference sponsors hoped the participants would eventually focus their attention, receded into insignificance in the face of such a primal hostility toward Israel's existence. This part of the conference served to underscore the words of Syria's defense minister, Mustafa Tlas, who with customary bluntness had summed up the issue one year earlier: "The conflict between the Arab nation and Zionism is over existence, not borders."[3]

This remains the essential problem nearly a decade later. The fact that the Syrians place such immense obstacles before the resumption of peace talks with us, and the fact that the Palestinians resisted for more than a year my call to enter fast-track negotiations for a final settlement, underscores their reluctance to make a genuine and lasting peace with us. To receive territory is not to make peace. Peace requires that you also give something in return, namely arrangements not to use the land that is handed over to you as a future staging area for attacks against Israel. Equally, peace requires that our Arab partners educate their people to an era of mutual acceptance, something we have failed to see in many parts of the Arab world.

To begin resolving the Arab-Israeli conflict, one must begin here. The Arabs must be asked forthrightly and unconditionally to make their peace with Israel's existence. The Arab regimes must move not only to a state of nonbelligerency but to a complete renunciation of the desire to destroy the Jewish state—a renunciation that will gain credibility only when they establish a formal peace with Israel. This means ending the economic boycott and the explosive arms buildup, and signing peace treaties with Israel. The Arab states must resign themselves to something they have opposed for so long: not merely the fact but the right of Israel's permanent presence among them. This necessarily means that they will have to accept mutual coexistence as the operating principle in their relations with the Jewish state.

A policy of coexistence between the United States and the Soviet Union was of course promulgated in the heyday of the Cold War, and we have become so used to hearing the phrase that we are inured to its profound importance. For even at a time when the Communists were possessed by doctrines of global domination, they were saying that they understood that there was a higher interest, higher even than the Marxist cause: the survival of their own society and of the planet as a whole.

This is a rational attitude since it allows warring societies to live, evolve, and eventually resolve the antagonisms between them. The crucial idea of mutual coexistence is setting limits to conflict. Yet for close to a century Arab society and Arab politics have been commandeered by an anti-Jewish obsession that has known no limits: It harnessed the Nazis, promoted the Final Solution, launched five wars against Israel, embarked on a campaign of global terrorism, strangled the world's economy with oil blackmail, and now, in Iraq and elsewhere, is attempting to build nuclear bombs for the great Armageddon. This obsession must be stopped not only for Israel's sake but for the sake of the Arabs themselves and for the sake of the world.

It will not do to obscure the primacy of this existential opposition to Israel as the driving force of the Arab-Israeli conflict. Such obfuscation is fashionable in current commentaries on Israel and Arabs, in the form of a neat symmetry imposed on their respective needs and desires. These commentaries hold that Israel's demand for Arab recognition of its right to exist should be met in exchange for various Arab demands, especially for land. Yet to treat these demands as symmetrical, as the two sides of an equation, is to ignore both history and causality. Worse, it sets a price tag on the lives of millions of Jews and their nation.

To see this clearly, imagine the situation in reverse. Suppose Israel refused to recognize Syria's right to exist and threatened to destroy the entire country unless Syria were to evacuate a swatch of territory controlled by Syria that Israel claimed as its own. This would be widely and correctly viewed as lunacy. Yet the Arabs' refusal to recognize Israel's right to exist unless it caves in to their territorial demands for lands from which they have attacked Israel is accorded serious consideration, even respect, in current diplomacy. What is overlooked is that Israel's right to exist is no more negotiable than is the right of Syria or Egypt to exist.

The Arabs often say that the wrong done to the Palestinians is so great that they cannot come to terms with Israel's existence until it is set aright. But this argument, too, is intended only to confound the issue. The Palestinian Arabs were offered a state by the United Nations in 1947, and they rejected it. So did the Arab states, which not only unanimously opposed Palestinian statehood but sent their armies into Palestine to grab whatever they could—for themselves. Further, when the West Bank and Gaza, which Jordan and Egypt captured in 1948, were in Arab hands, barely a whisper about Palestinian statehood was ever heard in either place. Thus, there is no shred of a historical connection linking the demand for Palestinian statehood to the Arab refusal to recognize Israel.

The issue of the Palestinian Arabs requires a fair and forthright solution that takes into account their full situation and the question of their civil status, alongside the cardinal issues of Jewish rights and Israeli security. But one thing must be said clearly at the outset: The grievances of the Palestinian Arabs, real or imagined, cannot be a loaded gun held to Israel's temple. Today, after five major wars, Egypt and Jordan have signed peace treaties with Israel and some of the other Arab states are prepared to recognize Israel, but only in exchange for a Palestinian state bordering Tel Aviv that would obviously jeopardize Israel's existence. This prerequisite, which is now demanded in nearly every corner of the Arab world, shows the distance that the Arabs must still travel in permanently reconciling themselves to the presence of a Jewish state in their midst.

This is not surprising if one considers the enormous anti-Israel propaganda that has been directed at the Arab and Moslem masses, in which 150 million people have been endlessly told that a tiny country in their midst has no place under the sun, that it must be "excised like a cancerous tumor" and "thrown into the dustbin of history," as I heard my Iranian counterpart at the UN say in 1984. When this notion is repeated again and again, day in and day out, for half a century, there is no reason why the Arab masses should alter their hostility toward Israel. To be sure, the Madrid Conference, despite its disappointments, also offered some glimmers of hope. Haltingly, awkwardly, Arabs and Israelis began a direct, face-to-face dialogue that started a process that may lead to peace. But Teheran had been touched by none of the stirrings toward change. Instead, it tossed up a resolution, signed by delegates from all over the Moslem world, including representatives of various PLO factions, calling once again for the annihilation of Israel.[4]

This is a symptom of a political pathology. Its essence, like that of certain psychological pathologies in the individual, is an escape from reality and the summoning of violence to act out irrational impulses. The first requirement of peace is that this fanaticism not be brooked. It should be condemned and excoriated in most vigorous terms wherever it appears. (The Islamic conference in Teheran received hardly a murmur of protest from any of the Western capitals.) It cannot be dismissed as posturing because, if left unchallenged, it contaminates the views of the pragmatists and realists among the Arabs and further inflames the passions of the "Arab street" of which the realists must be continually wary.

While there are many in the West who are prepared to admit the moral necessity of Arab recognition of Israel, there is also a widespread acceptance of the Arabs' utterly utilitarian rejoinder: What's in it for us? If not territorial concessions from Israel, then what do the Arabs get out of peace? Setting aside momentarily the issue of disputed territory (I will soon return to it), the Arabs have plenty to gain from the state of peace in and of itself.

First, they can avoid the escalating costs of war. As the Gulf War showed, war is becoming extremely expensive and exceedingly destructive. With the advance of military technology, precision bombing, laser-guided missiles, and the sheer firepower packed in today's artillery and tanks, an Arab leader bent on war could find his army destroyed, his capital in ruins, his regime threatened, and if he is not lucky, his own life in jeopardy. Saddam, after all, was very lucky. What could he have possibly put up against Norman Schwarzkopf's divisions if the American general had received the order to march on to Basra and Baghdad? At best he himself could have sought a hiding place in Iraq or escaped the country altogether, as Mengistu of Ethiopia did when his military collapsed (although given the skills in assassination of several of Saddam's Arab adversaries, it is not clear that he would have survived very long in hiding or exile).

But war today carries not only military and personal risks, it invites unparalleled economic desolation. The bombs may be smarter, but they are also more destructive. According to a UN report, the obliteration of Iraq's infrastructure of roads, bridges, railway lines, power plants, oil refineries, and industrial enterprises meant that "food . . . cannot be distributed; water cannot be purified; sewage cannot be pumped away and cleansed; crops cannot be irrigated; medicines cannot be conveyed where they are required." In short, the report concluded, Iraq had been "relegated to the pre-industrial age."[5] This may have been an exaggerated assessment, but it is nevertheless sobering to realize that this was a level of damage inflicted by an adversary that was *discriminate* in its use of force. Iraq—which was, to say the least, less discriminate in using force—exacted an economic toll from Kuwait estimated to be as high as $30 billion.[6] The pursuit of modern warfare therefore entails the triple risk of military, political, and economic devastation on a scale that is constantly escalating. Surely after the Gulf War the Arab leaders must ask themselves whether Israel would again sit back in the case of armed attack. And just as surely they must know that the answer is no. Further, if Israel were to face a threat to its existence, it would respond with awesome power—something that no sane person, Arab or Jew, could possibly desire.

As the cost of war rises, the benefits of avoiding war and establishing peace rise accordingly. Not only does peace allow a country to avoid devastation, it enables it to build on its existing economic foundation rather than devote several years and untold resources to rebuilding ruins. And it allows it to cooperate with its neighbors for mutual betterment.

Herein lie the greatest benefits of peace: the tremendous possibilities inherent in mutual cooperation between Arabs and Israelis. While this fact was always clear to Israel, it has yet to penetrate the thinking of most Arab leaders, to the obvious detriment of their societies. For the Arab world stands to gain as much from making peace with Israel as Israel stands to gain from making peace with the Arabs.

What would peace be like if the entire Arab world truly believed in it? There is no area of life that would not be affected. Take trade, as an obvious first example. Since the Six Day War, Israel's "open bridges" policy created a flourishing trade between Israel and Jordan across the Allenby Bridge over the Jordan River. The signing of the peace treaty between Jordan and Israel significantly expanded this trade. Such trade could be further expanded and its scope with Jordan and with other Arab countries substantially broadened. Equally, the Arab world could have access to Israel's ports on the Mediterranean and to technology and to other advances in the Israeli marketplace.

Water, too, looms large as a potential benefit of peace. This second precious liquid (the other is oil) will be the focus of much contention in the coming years. Agreements on water will be harder to achieve in an increasingly parched Middle East, whose growing populations will put mounting demands on a limited water supply. It is thus in everyone's interest to negotiate water agreements early on. The first to enjoy the benefits of peace in this regard has been Jordan. With only 150 cubic meters of water per capita per year (as compared to Syria's 2,000 cubic meters), Jordan is an exceedingly dry country. Israeli-Jordanian cooperation has increased the available water supply for Jordan, and enhanced cooperation could expand available water for both countries. This is especially true in the Arava region, the long valley connecting the Red Sea to the Dead Sea. The Arava is neatly divided down the middle between Israel and Jordan, and both countries draw waters from the wells dug into its sandy soil that exceed the capacity of the aquifer to replenish itself. This is leading to increasing salinization, endangering the future water supply. A coordinated policy could greatly ameliorate the situation. Israeli and Jordanian scientists could study the problem and devise a joint water policy for mutual benefit; after all, the subterranean water table does not recognize national boundaries. Equally, peace could enable Israel and Jordan to cooperate in the construction of a single desaliniation plant of appropriate scale on the Red Sea, a project that could prove far more economically sensible than separate, smaller Israeli and Jordanian facilities. Such an effort could be joined by another water-starved neighbor bordering on the Red Sea—Saudi Arabia.[7]

Syria, while on the face of it much more plentiful in water, nevertheless feels pressed by Turkey's plans to dam the Euphrates, which provides a sizable amount of Syria's water. This in turn has led to increased tensions among Syria, Jordan, and Israel over the existing division of the waters of the Yarmuk tributary to the Jordan River, which is bordered by all three countries. Peace agreements would of course require review of the Yarmuk arrangements originally negotiated by President Eisenhower's emissary, Eric Johnston, in 1955; but they could also assist Syria in using its other available water much more efficiently. Israel has devised methods such as drip irrigation to ensure that 85 percent of its irrigation water actually reaches the crops (15 percent is lost to evaporation and runoff). In Syria the efficiency is less than 40 percent. With the establishment of peace, Israel could teach Syrian farmers the techniques for more efficient water usage, just as it taught Arab farmers in Judea and Samaria to increase their irrigation efficiency from 40 percent to today's 80 percent. And Israeli engineers could also help Syria build the national projects it now lacks to carry water to arid sections of the country, just as Israel did in building its National Water Carrier.[8]

Among the other regional benefits of peace would be unfettered tourism and even broader access of Israel's medical facilities to the Arab states. This is one of the best-known yet least-discussed secrets in the Arab world. On any given day you can find in Hadassah Hospital in Jerusalem members of the Saudi royal family, Jordanian jet-setters, and patients from virtually all the rest of the Arab world who come for both routine and special medical treatment. What are now incognito sojourns for selected patients could become, especially if accompanied by training programs for doctors

from the Arab countries, an open service that could substantially improve health care throughout the region. The Israeli presence on
the West Bank has resulted in a significant improvement in this regard, dramatically reducing infant mortality and improving other
health indicators. Peace could bring overall effects like this to many
Arab countries, literally improving millions of lives.

This discussion of the benefits of peace remains largely theoretical because it assumes a genuine transformation of Arab attitudes toward Israel. But such a transformation is so difficult to
achieve that even the establishment of a formal peace with Egypt
has not produced it. Egypt continues to keep Israel at arm's
length, maintaining a "cold peace" consisting of a low-profile and
extremely circumscribed relationship that has prevented the realization of the full gamut of possibilities for both countries. If peace
with Israel could bring such enormous benefits to the Arab states,
why has virtually no Arab leader stepped forward to explain these
benefits to his people and obtain it for them? Could 150 million
people be blind, almost to a person, to something so obvious?

The answer is that they are not. In every Arab society there are
those for whom no explanation is needed concerning the urgent
need to end the state of war, recognize Israel, and get on with the
joint task of bringing the Middle East into the twentieth century before the twentieth century is out. But two obstacles stand in the way
of such realism. First, while the benefits of peace are understood by
isolated individuals, such a perspective is uncommon. Many Arab
leaders who profess a desire for "peace" think of it as a *means* to an
end, such as regaining lost territory or securing military supplies
from the West, rather than as an end in itself. (Such payoffs to Arab
governments should not be confused with the permanent benefits
that real peace would bring to every citizen.) For much of the Arab
world, peace is a coin with which one pays in order to get something
else. As such, it is expendable at a given moment and under the right
circumstances, and it need not last very long. Peace can be signed
one day and discarded the next, once the immediate payoff has been
pocketed—much to the astonishment of Westerners, including Is-

raelis, who have a completely different understanding of what it means to "make peace." (For Israelis, peace is the goal and everything else is a means to it.) Those few Arabs whose view of peace is more Western find themselves fighting against the tide in Arab countries that have never known this Western concept of peace from the day they gained independence, and which are much more familiar with the kind of peace occasionally offered by Arafat to Israel, the "peace of Saladin,"[9] which is merely a tactical intermission in a continuing total war.

A second obstacle facing the realists is that no Arab leader or representative wants to end up like Abdullah of Jordan, Anwar Sadat of Egypt, or Bashir Gemayel of Lebanon—or for that matter like the many thousands of moderate Palestinian Arabs whom the Mufti and the PLO have butchered over this century for "betraying" the Arab cause by trying to make peace with the Jews. For seventy years, ever since the heyday of the Mufti, every move and every gesture toward peace has been stifled by fear of the radical Pan-Arab nationalists and Moslem fundamentalists.

Those who are interested in something more than a pyrrhic peace in the Middle East must recognize the harsh reality that there is *always* a powerful Muftiot faction among the Arabs ready to veto peace. The Mufti's politics of terror is no less with us today. So long as this branch of Arab politics is powerful enough to terrorize other Arabs into playing by its rules, making peace will be an extraordinarily difficult business. When the radicals feel confident and powerful, the intimidated moderates run to snuggle within the tiger claws of the dictators, much as King Hussein of Jordan snuggled in Saddam's paws on the very eve of the Gulf War. Without suppressing the power of intimidation of the radicals, there can be no hope that moderates will emerge.

This principle was much in evidence in the case of Morocco. When Qaddafi was at the height of his power, having conquered most of Chad and terrorized much of the West with his threats, King Hassan of Morocco—as antithetical a figure to Qaddafi as one could conjure up in the Arab world—entered into a bizarre "marriage" between Libya and Morocco. Yet within months of the American bombing of Tripoli and the collapse of Qaddafi's forces in Chad, Hassan dissolved the union and invited Israel's foreign minister to an open meeting in Morocco. Similarly, when Syria came to realize in the wake of the Gulf War that the eclipse of its Soviet benefactor spelled a decline in its ability to resist American pressure, it suddenly permitted King Hussein and other Arabs to enter negotiations and even went so far as to sit at the same table with Israel itself. Pressing the radicals, curtailing their options to intimidate, and limiting their political and military clout are continual prerequisites for engaging in any realistic efforts for peace.

Any Israeli diplomat who has ever dealt with the Arabs can recount endless variations on this theme. My own experience with Arab diplomats has taught me how readily some of them would make peace if they were freed from the yoke of terror. When I was deputy chief of the Israeli mission in Washington, I used to meet regularly with one such diplomat, an ambassador from an Arab country with which Israel has no relations. On one occasion we had set a meeting in a small restaurant. I arrived five minutes late and asked the waiter whether a gentleman answering the description of my Arab colleague had been there.

"Yes," said the waiter. "He showed up, ordered something to drink, and left suddenly."

I called him up. "Ali, what happened?" I asked.

"I came to the restaurant at the time we'd agreed on. I sat down. Who do you think I saw at the next table? The Syrian ambassador. I walked out."

It is a sad commentary on the pace of political evolution in the Arab world that many years after this conversation took place, I am still unable to reveal the diplomat's real name and have had to substitute a false one to protect his identity.

This little vignette, set in a quiet corner of Washington, D.C., contains in microcosm the story of countless foiled peace attempts throughout the history of the Arab-Israeli conflict. The nonradicals might entertain the possibility of negotiating peace with Israel, but they fear the violent response of the radicals. This was painfully evident in the Madrid Peace Conference and in the subsequent talks in Washington. Once again, my Israeli colleagues and I found that even the most reasonable among the Jordanians and Lebanese were constantly forced to weigh every word for fear of the PLO and the Syrians, whose threatening gaze they felt even in the most private of conversations.

The West often aggravates this situation by strengthening the hands of the worst radicals. It is often so grateful for any reasonable gesture coming from these quarters that it proceeds to enter into economic and military agreements with them. It operates on the belief that such carrots will lure a radical regime to become a less radical one—a view whose full wisdom was revealed in the Western arming of Saddam in the 1980s. The fact is that the radicals should not be armed. There should be a curb on weapons sales to the moderates as well, for the simple reason that in the Middle East today's "moderate" could be tomorrow's radical, courtesy of a coup, an invasion, or mere intimidation.

So long as freedom of expression, the rule of law, and real representative government are absent from the Arab world, it will continue to be next to impossible for realist Arabs to have an enduring influence on Arab policies toward Israel. For this reason, there is a direct relationship between what the West does to press the Arab world to democratize and the chances of attaining a durable Middle East peace. In the cases of Germany and Japan, of Russia and the Ukraine, of Latin America and several African dictatorships, the powerful relationship between democratic values and the desire for peace has been obvious to American policymakers, who for years have tied American trade and other forms of assistance to domestic policy reforms and democratization. For example, the United States imposed sanctions on China after the massacre in Tienanmen Square that suppressed the movement for democratization in that country. Similarly, when the president of Peru suspended democratic institutions in 1992, the United States undertook a full-court press, including economic sanctions, in order to prevent backsliding to authoritarian rule in a Latin America it had tirelessly worked for decades to push into democracy.

Only the Arab states have been entirely exempt from such pressure—much to the dismay of a handful of reformist Arabs in exile in London who have seen their fellow Arabs abandoned to the unrelenting totalitarians of Syria, Iraq, and Libya, and to the unreconstructed dictatorships that form much of the rest of the Arab world; and much to the dismay of Israel, which must consider the possibility that these regimes will at any moment return to savaging the Jewish state alongside the treatment they mete out to their own people.

It might be argued that the West has been slowly inching toward broaching the subject of democracy with the Arab leaders. But in the wake of the Gulf War, which the United States waged to save a helpless Saudi Arabia from Saddam and to resurrect a Kuwait that he had conquered, it is clear that this is not the case. Never has a ruler been as helpless as was the exiled Emir Al-Sabah of Kuwait, sitting in Riyadh waiting to have the West extricate his country from Iraq's gullet. If ever there had been a moment to extract a commitment to basic human rights, or a constitution, or a free press, this was it. None was asked for.

Other than the fact that the Arab world possesses a good part of the world's oil supply, the West seems to have granted the democratic exemption to the Arab world for reasons virtually indistinguishable from those the British Colonial Office held at the end of World War I: a kind of smug condescension that the Arabs are "not ready" for democracy, that democracy is somehow incompatible with their Islamic heritage, that "their own traditional forms of government" should be considered "right for them," and so on— as though, for example, torture, amputation, slavery, a manacled press, and absolute rule by a family of a few hundred cousins is anything but a tyranny by any standard. Most bizarre are the attempts by Westerners to convince themselves that the Arabs should have their democratic exemption because what they already have is *as good* as democracy, as in the periodic journalistic accounts of Saudi Arabia as a quiet, gentle kingdom—a kind of Tibet in the sands.

Arab culture and Islamic civilization are no better excuses for an exemption from democracy than were Japanese culture in 1945 and Russian civilization in 1989—although neither of these had been democratic societies before. For an enduring peace to be built in the Middle East, America must stop coddling the various Arab dictators and autocrats and begin pushing them to adopt the most rudimentary guarantees that will allow those willing to live peacefully with Israel to come out of the closet, publish their opinions, organize political parties, and ultimately be elected to positions to make good on their beliefs. Some argue that democracy cannot be introduced into the Arab states because it will bring the Islamic fundamentalists to power. But of course the idea cannot simply be to establish majority rule, and thereby hand power to the tyranny of the mob. To advance democracy in the Arab world, the West must promote the concepts of individual rights and constitutional limits on governmental power, without which the existence of any genuine democracy is impossible. Without real and concerted steps in this direction, the perennial search for Arabs willing to make a permanent (as opposed to a tactical) peace with Israel will be ultimately futile.

I wrote the above before I was elected Prime Minister, and my views have substantially remained unaltered. But I have come to recognize that neither the United States nor the Western countries are likely to act toward the goal of democratization in the Arab world. Nor is it possible for Israel to do so, for any action on our part would be falsely interpreted as an attempt to destabilize neighboring regimes, changing one ruler with another—something we have absolutely no desire to do. Consequently, we must assume that for our generation and perhaps the next, the task of peacemaking is with the Arab world as it is, unreformed and undemocratic. The prevalence of radicalism in the Middle East—and the danger that, in the absence of any democratic traditions, a nonradical regime can turn radical overnight—means that peace in the Middle East must have security arrangements built into it. I have already noted that for the foreseeable future the only kind of peace that will endure in the region between Arab and Arab and between Arab and Jew is the peace of deterrence. Security is an indispensable pillar of peace for any resolution of the Arab-Israeli conflict. Ending the state of war is a must, but that will not end the possibility of a *future* war. An Israel lacking security would eventually invite an act of aggression that would destroy the peace. The question we must therefore ask is, what are Israel's minimal security requirements that can sustain its defenses and thereby sustain the peace?

This question need not be answered in territorial terms alone. The adoption of security arrangements between Israel and the Arab states, such as a hotline between Damascus and Jerusalem, or procedures to alert the other side to planned military maneuvers, can reduce the possibility of war. Buffer zones might be created to prevent the stockpiling of weapons next to particularly sensitive borders. Such zones would be free of heavy military equipment such as tanks and artillery and could be accessible to the officers of the other side. Of necessity, the configuration of these zones would have to take into account the tremendous disparity in the dimensions of Israel as compared with those of its Arab neighbors.

But however useful such devices may be, they cannot meet a contingency in which Israel's enemies decide to violate the rules and invade. In the case of Israel, as we have seen, military distances are so tiny and warning times so short that without minimal strategic depth to absorb an attack and mobilize its reserves, Israel's existence would be placed in jeopardy. Nor can its need for strategic depth be filled by international guarantees. Even if the guaranteeing powers summon the will to act—which, despite a formal promise, the friendly American administration did not do on the eve of the Six Day War—there looms the question of whether they could physically dispatch the forces in time. Kuwait, a country almost exactly the size of Israel (minus the West Bank), was overrun in a matter of six hours, but liberated only after a six-month buildup of huge forces shipped from West to East. Israel cannot be asked to play the role of Lazarus. It will not rise from the dead, to whose ranks its defeat would surely consign it. For unlike Arab Kuwait, no one doubts that if the Jewish state were ever conquered by Arab armies, it would be effectively, irredeemably destroyed. The problem with international guarantees for Israel is therefore exactly what Golda Meir said it was: "By the time they come to save Israel, there won't be an Israel."

Israel's defenses therefore must be entrusted to its own forces, which are willing and able to act in real time against an imminent invasion or attack. When seeking, as we must, a peace based on security, we must necessarily ask what secure boundaries for Israel would be. Clearly, the Six Day War boundaries are the boundaries not of peace but of war. But how much broader does Israel need to be? As we have seen, the crucial question is not only additional increments of strategic depth but the incorporation of the Judea-Samaria mountain ridge, which forms a protective wall against invasion from the east. It is not feasible for Israel to relinquish military control of this wall. A similar situation prevails for the Golan Heights, which dominate the north. When these territories were in Arab hands, the result was war, not peace. One simply cannot talk about peace and security for Israel and in the same breath expect Israel to significantly alter its existing defense boundaries.

Arab leaders' promises that the Palestinian Arabs would have the whole of Palestine in 1947, the whole of Israel in 1967, and the whole of Jordan in 1970 all proved to be impediments to resolving the problem of the Palestinian Arabs, each one leading to the rejection of rational compromises and to further calamity.

Jerusalem, too, has been the subject of renewed Arab demands. Arafat has long and often said that there will be no peace so long as the PLO flag does not fly over the city. The West has often taken this statement at face value, and every peace plan to date that Westerners have offered has been in some fashion gerrymandered to allow an Arab flag to fly over some section of Jerusalem—usually over what the media like to refer to as "Arab East Jerusalem." Of course, there is nothing exclusively or even mainly "Arab" about eastern Jerusalem. This part of the city consists of those portions of Jerusalem that the Jordanian Legion was able to tear away by force in 1948. Many Jews lived there at the time, but the Jordanians expelled them. Today these sections of the city have 150,000 Jewish residents and a similar number of Arab residents. (Unlike the Jordanians, who expelled the Jews when they conquered this portion of the city in 1948, Israel left the Arab population intact and offered it Israeli citizenship.)

Eastern Jerusalem includes the Temple Mount, the Western Wall, and the City of David. It was the capital of ancient Israel for twelve centuries, the very heart and soul of all Jewish aspiration to return and rebuild the Land of Israel. Israel could not under any circumstances negotiate over any aspect of Jerusalem, any more than Americans would negotiate over Washington, Englishmen over London, or Frenchmen over Paris. Israel is prepared to offer the Arabs full and equal rights *in* Jerusalem—but no rights *over* Jerusalem.

The tremendous significance of Jerusalem to the Jewish people—as well as the indelible physical facts of Jewish neighborhoods such as Gilo, Ramot, Ramat Eshkol, French Hill, Pisgat Ze'ev, and Neve Ya'akov built in eastern Jerusalem since 1967—make the notion that somehow Jerusalem will be redivided sheer fantasy. Yet it is not only Arabs who cling to this fantasy. In practically every foreign ministry in the West, including the U.S. State Department, there are maps that do not include East Jerusalem as part of a united Jerusalem under Israeli sovereignty. Indeed, most governments refuse to recognize even *West* Jerusalem as part of Israel, on the grounds that "the final status of Jerusalem remains to be negotiated," in the hope that it will be internationalized—this in recognition of its "special status," reflecting its unique importance not only to Judaism but to Islam and Christianity as well. But it is *only* under Jewish rule that Jerusalem has become a city open to all faiths, with the holy sites of all religions protected equally for the first time in history. The Jewish belief in the universal meaning of Jerusalem has made it today a truly universal city. To pry the city away from the one people that has ensured unimpeded access to it for all, to put it under a UN-type administration, would not

merely violate the historic right of the Jewish people to its one and
only capital. It would assure a descent into factionalism, where
shrill partisans of Islam like the followers of Khomeini and Qaddafi
would return the city to the divisions and sectarian strife that characterized it before 1967—something for which no rational person
could possibly wish. This is why Israel, within the context of a
peace agreement with the Arabs, is prepared to guarantee free access to Moslems wishing to make pilgrimages to their holy places
in Jerusalem, but will in no way alter Israel's ability to maintain
Jerusalem as a peaceful and open city under Israeli sovereignty.

It will be objected that in keeping sovereignty over Jerusalem
and the remaining territories, Israel is expecting the Arabs to renounce their claim to what they consider part of their domain.
This is precisely the case. An entire century of Arab wars has been
waged against the Jews because the Arabs have refused to in any
way temper their doctrine of never giving up what they claim to
be Arab lands. In fact, in its entire recorded history, the Arab nation has *never* given up a single inch of land willingly, for the sake
of peace or for the sake of anything else. This fact was confirmed
to the point of absurdity after the cession of the entire Sinai (more
than twice the size of all of Israel), when Egypt refused to recip-
rocate by ceding Israel a few hundred yards on which the Israelis
had partially built a luxury hotel—leading to a crisis of several
years that finally ended when Israel gave up the land in 1989.

But the time has finally come to recognize that peace will be
possible only when both sides are willing to strike a compromise
that gives each the minimum it needs to live. The Zionist movement
and the State of Israel are by now well acquainted with compromis-
ing on ideology for the sake of coexistence and peace, having done
so at least four times in this century. In 1919 the Zionists bitterly
gave up on their claim to the Litani River (now in southern
Lebanon), which was to have been the main water source for the
new Jewish state. In 1922 four-fifths of the Jewish National Home
was made off-limits to Jews so that there could be a territory, Jordan,
reserved for the Arabs of Palestine. This was much more painful, for

it meant giving up on a large portion of biblical Israel and agreeing that the Jewish state would be only forty miles wide. But for the sake of peace, the Jews have given up on this claim as well, and they asked the Palestinian-Jordanian state four times the size of Israel to give them nothing in return. In the 1979 treaty with Egypt, Israel compromised many of its most cherished principles for the sake of peace. In giving up the Sinai, it conceded vast lands, transferred thousands of Jews from their homes, razed houses, schools, and farms that had been built from the desert over fifteen years, and utterly renounced every one of the Jewish historical, strategic, and economic claims to land where the Jewish people had received the Law of Moses and become a nation. In 1989, Israel gave Taba, near Eilat, to Egypt for the sake of peace and once again, in the 1993 Oslo Accords, Israel ceded land to the Palestinians.

For three-quarters of a century the Jews have repeatedly compromised on substantive strategic, historical, and moral claims in order to placate their Arab neighbors in the hope of buying peace. It is impossible that peace should be attained by asking the Jews to compromise on everything and the Arabs to compromise on nothing. The Arabs, possessing lands over five hundred times greater in area than Israel's, must now do a small fraction of what Israel has done: For the very first time in their long history of expansionism and intolerance, they must compromise. For the sake of peace, they must renounce their claims to part of the four ten-thousandths—*.0004*—of the lands they desire, which constitutes the very heart of the Jewish homeland and the protective wall of the Jewish state. If the Arabs are unwilling to make even this microscopic one-time concession, if they are still so possessed by the fantasy of an exclusively Arab realm that they cannot bring themselves to compromise on an inch of land to make the Middle East habitable for the Jewish state, it is hard to make the case that they are in fact ready for peace.

But what about the other side, the question of the Arabs in the zones of Judea and Samaria? The fact that Israel is extremely circumscribed in the territorial compromises it is capable of making necessarily raises the question of the future of these people. By hanging on to territory, Israel, it is said, might gain the security inherent in better terrain, but it would encumber itself with a hostile population.

True enough. But this dilemma has been put behind us by the implementation of the early stages of the Oslo Accords. Israel transferred to Palestinian control most of the territory in the Gaza district, which encompasses *all* the Palestinian residents of that area. Further, in the West Bank, Israel transferred to Palestinian control the lands that encompass a full 98 percent of the Palestinian population (the remaining 2 percent are composed in part of nomadic Bedouin who move from place to place). Thus the question of Israel's retaining a hostile population has become a moot point. As of 1995 the Palestinian Arabs of Gaza and the West Bank live under Palestinian rule. The remaining issues to be resolved are not over the human rights of the Palestinians or their civil enfranchisement. That is an issue that they have yet to resolve among themselves: individual rights, freedom of the press, pluralism, and democracy are matters that the Palestinians have to resolve between themselves and the Palestinian Authority that rules them. Israel, however interested an observer, has no part in this debate. The Israelis and the Palestinians must resolve two pivotal questions:

(1) the disposition of the remaining territory of Judea and Samaria; and

(2) the political status of the self-governing Palestinian entity and its relationship to the State of Israel.

Resolving the territorial issue, though an extremely complex matter, has been made somewhat less difficult because of the fact that the remaining territories are largely uninhabited by Palestinians (more precisely, they are inhabited by Jews). This terrain includes, however, areas that are crucial for Israel's defense and vital

national interests. Accordingly, Israel seeks a final peace settlement with the Palestinians that would leave it with indispensable
security zones. First and foremost, it requires a land buffer that includes the Jordan Valley and the hills directly overlooking it and
that would extend southward to the ridges above the Dead Sea. At
its deepest point, this buffer will be about 12 miles wide, a minimal depth given the fact that Israel faces a threat from a potential
eastern front, which might include thousands of Iraqi, Syrian, and
Iranian tanks. During the Cold War, NATO's generals assessed that
they would need 180 miles of strategic depth to ward off a similar
threat from the east. Alas, Israel must live with strategic depth that
is less than 10 percent of that, but it cannot shrink this depth any
further. Second, Israel must have a zone of separation between
the Palestinian areas and the crowded coastline where most of its
population lives. This zone, whose widest point is a few miles, is
narrower than the eastern buffer, but is important in any future
arrangement for minimizing terrorist infiltration from the Palestinian areas to Israel's major cities. Furthermore, Israel must retain
a security cordon around Jerusalem to ensure that the city is not
choked by adjoining Palestinian areas. Israel must also keep its
early warning stations at the heights of the Samarian mountains,
facilities that offer indispensible warning against air and ground attacks from the east. In addition, Israel must maintain broad corridors of territory to facilitate movement from the coastline to the
Jordan Valley buffer in times of emergency. Those corridors, not accidentally, include much of the Jewish population in Judea-Samaria.
Israel must protect the Jewish communities and facilitate the citizens' ability to live and travel securely. Equally, Israel must make
sure that the main aquifer that supplies some 40 percent of the
country's water, running at the lower part of the western slopes of
the Judean and Samarian hills, does not come under Palestinian
control; it is, after all, impossible for the country to live with its
water siphoned off or contaminated by the Palestinian Authority. Israel must take into account other special security requirements,
such as controlling the areas abutting the Tel Aviv or Jerusalem air-

ports to prevent terrorists from firing at civilian aircraft from these positions. Finally, Israel must keep places sacrosanct to Judaism and the Jewish people within its domain and guarantee unfettered access to them as was done in the Hebron agreements, which left the Tomb of the Patriarchs under Israel's control.

These are Israel's minimal requirements to protect the life of the state. Obviously, full control of the West Bank, including the Palestinian areas, would have given Israel much greater security in an insecure Middle East. Yet retaining the minimal elements of defense enumerated above will enable Israel to transfer to the Palestinians additional areas that are not included in these categories, thereby expanding the Palestinian domain without significantly hurting Israel's security. Equally, Israel is prepared to make special arrangements facilitating safe passage of Palestinians through its own territory, thus enabling direct Palestinian travel between Gaza and the West Bank.

It is largely for these considerations that I negotiated the interim agreement at the Wye River Planation in 1998 with President Clinton and Yasser Arafat. My principal objective at Wye was to limit the extent of further interim Israeli withdrawals so as to leave Israel with sufficient territorial depth for its defense. As stipulated under the Oslo agreement, Israel was to withdraw in three successive "disengagements" from additional territory in Judea-Samaria, which would be handed over to the Palestinian Authority *prior* to the negotiations on a permanent peace agreement, or "final settlement."

The Palestinian side had already received 27 percent of the territory from the Labor government. Based on its experience of negotiating with that government, it expected Israel to cede in these withdrawals the bulk of the territory. As Arafat's deputy, Abu Maazen, explained to a senior official in my government upon the signing of the Hebron agreement in 1997: "What about the 90 percent of the territory you promised us?" The response was: "We didn't promise you anything of the kind." Whatever officials of the previous Labor government had whispered in Palestinian ears was irrelevant. What was relevant were the signed contracts we inherited from Labor, and these did not obligate Israel to such dangerous withdrawals. Indeed, since the Oslo Accords did not quantify the extent of redeployment, we proceeded to negotiate with the Palestinian Authority, or more specifically with the United States, on much smaller redeployments. Ultimately we agreed in Wye that the first two redeployments would amount to 13 percent of the territory. We also agreed with the U.S. that Israel would officially declare that the third redeployment, which the U.S. recognized as an Israeli prerogative not subject to negotiation, would not exceed an additional 1 percent.

Thus, instead of a process in which Israel would retreat to the virtually indefensible pre-1967 line even *before* final settlement negotiations were concluded, I sought and achieved a different result at Wye: that most of the West Bank would remain in our hands pending the start of these negotiations. Israel would retain some 60 percent of the territory with all the West Bank's Jewish population; the Palestinian Authority would have some 40 percent of the area with virtually the entire Palestinian population. Naturally, this is a much improved position for Israel to negotiate from; one that bolsters our defenses against external attack and the threat of terrorism, while leaving us in an advantageous position for the final settlement negotiations.

We aslo achieved a second objective at Wye: We incorporated the principle of *reciprocity* into the agreement. Palestinians would get 13 percent of Judea-Samaria (West Bank) territory in three successive stages only after they implemented their own commitments undertaken at Wye. No more free lunches.

The first stage in the implementation of Palestinian commitments involved mostly formalities, such as naming Palestinian delegates to various joint committees and issuing decrees against incitement and the possession of illegal weapons. The Palestinians met these obligations, and we promptly discharged ours: We withdrew from 2 percent of area C and transferred 7 percent of area B, hitherto under joint Israeli-Palestinian security control, to full Palestinian control.

The second stage—which covered the next four weeks—was a different story. At this point the Palestinians were obligated to repeal the articles in the Palestinian Charter, which called for Israel's destruction, and take the first concrete steps against the terrorist infrastructure. On December 14, they repealed the charter—a genocidal document without parallel in today's world—in a Gaza gathering addressed by President Bill Clinton.

Many claimed that from a strictly legal viewpoint the repeal was invalid. According to the charter's own provisions, it can be amended only in a special session of the Palestinian National Council by a vote of two-thirds of the membership—conditions that were not met in Gaza. But the purpose of the exercise—to make the rejection of the charter irreversible—was achieved. After renouncing the charter in a public display before the world's cameras and in the presence of the U.S. president, it would be impossible to claim that it was still a valid document.

But the Palestinians seemed to feel that rejecting the charter was all they had to do. And they expected us not only to reward them for disavowing genocide, but to ignore their failure to discharge their other obligations.

To us, the other commitments undertaken at Wye were at least as pertinent, for they constituted the first concrete steps to be taken by the Palestinian Authority against the terrorist organizations. The Palestinian Authority was supposed to arrest wanted terrorists and have representatives of the U.S. verify their incarceration; implement the law prohibiting membership in terrorist organizations; collect illegal weapons held by civilians and hand over such prohibited weapons as mortars, anti-tank missles, and land mines held by the Palestinian Authority police; cease daily incitement to violence; stop organizing anti-Israeli riots; submit a report on the number of Palestinian Authority police in excess of the 30,000 permitted by the Oslo agreement; and maintain "comprehensive, intensive, and continuous" cooperation with Israel on security matters.

The Palestinian Authority complied with none of these commitments. They did, to be sure, display a few assault rifles and handguns, presumably confiscated from civilians, and they detained some wanted terrorists and Hamas political leaders. But after Arafat himself asserted that there were at least 30,000 illegal weapons in Gaza alone, the collection of a few illegal guns for the benefit of network cameras appeared to be little more than a public relations exercise. And the arrest of Hamas operatives was of little consequence. Some of the most notorious participants in planning and executing suicide bombings against Israeli civilians (some of whom were American citizens) were among the scores of Hamas detainees released by the Palestinian Authority within weeks after their arrest.

Adhering to the principle of reciprocity, the Israeli government announced that there would be no further withdrawals until the Palestinian Authority complied with the aggrement. This was the guiding principle of my policy from the day I formed the government in 1996, and I was not about to abandon it at this crucial time.

Insistence on reciprocity became particularly pertinent after the Wye conference, because Arafat and other Palestinian leaders took to threatening to unilaterally declare a state on May 4, 1999, regardless of what happened in the negotiations. By thus predetermining the result of the Oslo process, they made a mockery of the negotiations.

To hand over territory under such circumstances would have been an act of national irresponsibility. The Palestinians' refusal to combat the terrorist groups ensured that the relinquished land would be used to facilitate attacks against us and to shelter terrorists. And their threat to declare a state—which by the very manner of its establishment would be hostile, dangerous, and unbound by any agreement with us—rendered the forfeiture of territory on our part nothing short of reckless.

I made it clear that Israeli redeployment could only follow the faithful and complete implementation of Palestinian obligations, and that conclusive negotiations over territory would have to await the final status talks.

The negotiations over territory will be the most complex and difficult in Israel's history. They will involve balancing Israel's national interests, foremost of which is security, with the Palestinians' wish to increase their own territorial domain. These negotiations will determine whether Israel will have the territorial bulwarks necessary to defend itself and safeguard a future peace. But they are only one of the two crucial issues for permanent peace negotiations with the Palestinians. The second is the question of the status of the Palestinian entity. Many in the world have blithely accepted the notion that the Palestinians must have their own independent state. They have not asked themselves what powers would accrue to such unbridled Palestinian self-determination. Could the Palestinian state make military pacts with Iran, Iraq, or Syria? Could it be allowed to place troops from these countries on the hills above Tel Aviv? Could it build an army of its own? Could it arm itself with the most sophisticated weapons, such as ground-to-air missiles that can shoot down the planes of the Israeli air force, thereby endangering Israel's very existence? Could it bring in untold numbers of Arabs, nonrefugees as well as refugees, under the banner of the "right of return," position them along the seamline with Israel, and begin to infiltrate the country? Clearly, a Palestinian entity with all these powers is a recipe not for peace but for disaster.

My view of an equitable and secure arrangement for the status of a Palestinian entity is based on a simple principle: The Palestinians should have all the powers to run their lives and none of the powers to threaten Israel's life. This means that the Palestinian entity can enjoy all the attributes of self-government, which include its own legislature, executive, judiciary, passports, flag, education, commerce, tourism, health, police, and every other power and institution controlling the collective and individual life of Palestinians within the Palestinian entity. In fact, the Palestinians have by now received nearly all of these things in the first two stages of the Oslo Accords. What remains to negotiate are those few powers relating to *external* security. In a permanent peace settlement, the Palestinians should have all the powers to administer Palestinian life; some should be shared with Israel, such as those relating to the environment (since mosquitoes, for example, do not recognize territorial divisions), and still a few other powers, primarily those relating to external security, should be retained by Israel. Thus, the Palestinian entity should not be able to form military pacts with sovereign states, or build and arm a standing army, or import weapons without Israel's consent. Israel must maintain control of the airspace, vital for its very survival, and the international entry points through which dangerous arms and terrorists could penetrate into the Palestinian areas and from there into Israel itself. The issue of the Palestinian refugees must be settled responsibly. The overwhelming majority should be given full rights and rehabilitation in the respective Arab countries where they reside. Israel should not be put at risk of being flooded with refugees sworn to its destruction.

These arrangements would leave the Palestinian entity with considerable powers, and certainly all the ones necessary for self-government. Yet they are not compatible with the idea of unlimited self-determination, which is what many normally associate with the concept of statehood. Statehood has a dynamic of its own, which implies powers that self-government does not necessarily warrant. Among other things, it will enable the Palestinian Arabs to join the United Nations, where they will easily receive the support of most governments and quickly free themselves of any limitation that they may contractually assume to obtain our consent. That is why when I am asked whether I will support a Palestinian state, I answer in the negative. I support the Palestinians' ability to control their own destiny but not their ability to extinguish the Jewish future. As I have indicated earlier in this book, I believe that this functional solution, giving the Palestinians all the powers necessary for self-administration and Israel those essential powers necessary to protect its national life, is a model for the kind of solution that could be replicated in many similar disputes around the world. It offers the only reasonable alternative between two unacceptable options: military subjugation on the one hand, and unbridled self-determination on the other. The first option is morally unacceptable, the second a prescription for catastrophe. But at the heart of the solution that I advocate is not only a fair and durable division of territory and powers but also a reasoned hope that the Palestinians will recognize that no other solution will be acceptable to the overwhelming majority of Israelis;

and that this realization in turn would foster over time a gradual, if grudging, reconciliation with the permanence of Israel's existence and the need to come to concrete terms with it. It nullifies the hope of using the Palestinian areas as a base to launch the future destruction of the Jewish state, while offering the Palestinians a life of dignity, self-respect, and self-government.

But it is not only Israelis and Arabs who have roles to play in bringing a lasting peace to a region so important to the entire world. As the Camp David Accords demonstrated, the moral, strategic, and financial assistance of the West can play a decisive role in making peace possible. An important step was taken with the commencement of multilateral talks under the auspices of the peace talks begun in 1991. This international support was later reaffirmed and expanded under the Oslo Accords. Foreign involvement in areas such as the development of water resources and protection of the environment would be of major significance to the region, and it would alleviate some of the sources of tensions that could easily contribute to renewed hostility and war.

In particular, there are two areas demanding substantial commitments from Western governments, without which the possibility of achieving peace would be seriously, and I believe irrevocably, impaired. The first is the resettlement of the remaining Arab refugees. As we have seen time and again, the various refugee districts scattered throughout the Middle East are the breeding ground for misery and hatred. Without them the PLO would have a hard time even existing, and a major source of instability would have been removed from the region. In this effort, the continuation of the problem is not a matter of disinterested morality to the states of the West. They too have a stake in dismantling the camps as a step toward ending the long campaign of terror that the rulers of the camps have waged against Israel and the West. Western assistance will be necessary to undertake the large-scale construction of housing projects and infrastructure necessary to transform the camps into towns, as well as educational projects and investments in businesses intended to raise the standard of living. The Western countries should also offer to absorb those refugees who prefer a new home in North America or Europe to continuing to live in Israel or the Arab states. Among them, the Western countries could handily absorb even the entire refugee population if necessary, settling the matter once and for all.

It is true that the Arab states possess sufficient funds to easily pay for this effort themselves, but given their past record of refugee relief (the entire Arab world contributes less than one percent of UNRWA's budget*), it will be a triumph if they can be prodded into assisting at all. Such Arab involvement in the resettling of refugees should be demanded, both because the Arab states are responsible for originating and sustaining the refugee problem and because their participating in resolving it would signify a real commitment to ending the conflict with Israel.

But the West, including the United States, has so far refused to put its foot down even on a matter as straightforward as ending the Arab fantasy of one day implementing the "right of return." When asked if the United States still supported UN Resolution 194 from December 1948 (in the middle of the War of Independence), which called for the return of the refugees, the United States couldn't muster the simple word *no*. It stammered for three days and finally came up with a circumlocution ("The Resolution is irrelevant to the peace process")[10] that leaves the Arabs still with the hope of one day thrusting upon Israel the burden of absorbing the hundreds of thousands of people whom the Arab regimes have cruelly maintained as lifelong refugees. On the refugee issue, as with other outdated or unjust UN resolutions (like the 1947 UN Partition Plan allotting the Jews only half of the present-day Israel, and the reso-

---

*The West has continued to contribute generously to support the Palestinian Arab refugees: The United States in 1990–91 had pledged $62 million, Sweden $22 million, Japan $17 million, Italy $12 million, and Britain $11 million. The figures for the Arab states, including the fabulously wealthy ones, are abysmal in comparison: Saudi Arabia's $1 million, Kuwait's $1 million, and Jordan's $365,000 are the only contributions worth mentioning. The contributions from the other eighteen Arab governments are each under five digits—less than the donation made by the Swedish Save the Children fund.[11]

lution calling for the internationalization of Jerusalem), the United States and European nations must alter their formal positions and flatly declare the resolutions to be null and void.

An essential area for international development is in the field of nonconventional arms development in the Arab countries. Nearly a decade after the victorious assault against Saddam Hussein, nuclear weapons facilities are *still* being found in Iraq, and there are probably plenty more where these came from. As the request to clean out Iraq has proved, it is exceedingly difficult to strip a country of the know-how and technology to build weapons of mass destruction once it has them. The only possible way of forestalling the day when Arab states will have the capacity to wipe out Israeli cities (and those of other countries) at the touch of a button is to secure a real, enforced moratorium on the transfer of such weapons and expertise to Iran and the Arab world—and this means the imposition of sanctions on countries that are found to be in violation of the ban. Without such concerted international action and in the absence of the democratization of Middle Eastern regimes, it will only be a matter of time before one of the dictatorships in the region acquires nuclear weapons, imperiling not only Israel and the Middle East but the peace of everyone else on the planet.

It is possible to present all of these steps as a peace plan comprised of three tracks: bilateral measures between Israel and Arab states; international measures taken by the nations of the world (including assistance to joint projects involving Israel and the Arab states); and measures taken to improve the conditions under which Jews and Arabs live side by side in peace with each other. Each of these elements obviously requires careful articulation and much elaboration, which only painstaking negotiations can produce. Such negotiations understandably might alter certain components and possibly add others. Nevertheless, I am convinced that the approach described in this chapter ought to serve as a blueprint for the achievement of a realistic and enduring peace between Arabs and Israelis.

In addition to the proposals for a resolution of the question of the disputed areas, a comprehensive approach to an Arab-Israeli peace must include formal peace treaties between the Arab states and Israel; security arrangements with the Arab states to protect Israel from future attacks and to enable all sides to monitor compliance with the agreements; normalization of relations (including an end to the Arab economic boycott of Israel); cessation of official anti-Semitic and anti-Zionist propaganda in Arab schools and government media; an international regime to ban the sale of nonconventional weapons or matériel to the radical regimes of the Middle East; internationally assisted refugee housing and resettlement projects; and regional cooperation for water development and environmental protection.

This is the path to an Arab-Israeli peace in the Middle East as it really is—turbulent, undemocratized, and as yet unreformed of its underlying antagonisms. Those antagonisms will be extremely slow to disappear. This is why a genuine reconciliation, in addition to having buttresses of stability, security, and cooperation built into it, must contain a strong element of gradualism. Such a graduated approach would allow both sides to alter their conceptions about achieving peace, should the basic political and military conditions of the region undergo a substantial transformation—for the better, one would hope.

While endless ink has been spilled in calling for various futile resolutions to the ongoing strife between the Jewish and Arab peoples over the disposition of Palestine, the proposal made here takes full account of Israel's security needs, while granting control over their own needs to the Arabs living in Judea, Samaria, and Gaza. Though it is certain to arouse furious opposition from irredentists in the Arab camp, as well as from purists on the Israeli left and right, I believe that it offers a real hope of a lasting peace—and one in which any realist in any camp can wholeheartedly believe.

9

THE QUESTION OF
JEWISH POWER

n 1987 I visited Poland, then still under Communist rule. I
landed at a military airport near Krakow and was then taken by
car to the drab countryside. We soon came across a dilapidated
village whose only mark of distinction was a sign that startled me:
"Auswiescen." Auschwitz. There were actually people who lived
there.

A few minutes beyond the village, we reached the gates of the
camp, inscribed with the infamous promise: *Arbeit macht frei*
("Work makes you free"). As I soon learned, the barracks of
Auschwitz were not the actual place where the great part of the
destruction of some two million Jews occurred. Although many
thousands died there, Auschwitz was used primarily as headquarters for the German staff for interrogation and for torture. But the
actual work of liquidation was done elsewhere. I marched with fellow Knesset members and Jewish youngsters from Israel and
other countries along the railroad tracks leading from Auschwitz
to nearby Birkenau. The tracks led through another infamous
gate, coming to an abrupt end at a white ramp several hundred
yards into the camp. On either side was a crematorium, now partially in ruins. The trains would stop at the ramp each day, de-

positing thousands of Jews who were quickly dispatched to the gas chambers. Soon there was nothing left of them but ashes.

Until I stood there at Birkenau, I never realized how tiny and mundane the whole thing was. The factory of death could have been put out of operation by one pass of a bomber. Indeed the Allies had been bombing strategic targets a few miles away. Had the order been given, it would have taken but a slight shift of the bomber pilot's stick to interdict the slaughter. Yet the order was never given.

Many people visiting Birkenau assume that the Allies were unaware of the fact that all of Europe's Jews were being systematically annihilated. I knew differently. For a year and a half during my tenure at the United Nations, my colleagues and I had waged a campaign to open the secret archives where the UN records on Nazi war criminals were kept. When we finally obtained access to the files, we saw that the Allies War Crimes Commission, established by Britain in 1942 and staffed by the officials of seventeen countries, had been receiving accurate and comprehensive information about what was going on in Birkenau, Chelmno, and Dachau in early 1944, a year and a half before the ovens were put out of commission by Germany's collapse. Had the Allies acted on this information, untold numbers of Jews could have been saved. But they knew, and did nothing. European Jewry was doomed.

How did the Jews come to this point of utter helplessness? How did an entire people arrive at a state where they were herded quietly to the slaughter, unable to resist this monstrous assault on their persons and on their collective existence? And how is it that they were able to do nothing to elicit even an ounce of action from their would-be saviors?

The question of Jewish powerlessness is central to the traumatic experience of the Jewish people, and it is the obverse side of the question of Jewish power. It is between these two poles that Jewish history has oscillated in modern times. Certainly in the last one hundred years, the period that is the primary focus of this book, the Jewish people has experienced the most extreme shifts of circumstance from one pole to the other. The pogroms in Russia, the Dreyfus trial, the gathering storm of anti-Semitism and its seismic explosion in the Holocaust, along with Great Britain's cynical obstruction of the Jewish national movement's efforts to bring the Jews of Europe to a safe haven—these are the tragic steps in a people's descent to utter impotence. Similarly, the resurrection of Israel, the rebirth of Jewish military power, and its spectacular successes against adversaries far superior in numbers and matériel signify a movement in the contrary direction.

Yet as dramatic as this oscillation has been during the last century, I believe that the rise of Israel can only be understood in a much broader historical perspective, a millennial one. For the Jews are one of the oldest nations on earth, and they are distinguished by their capacity for remembrance. In its essence, the rise of Israel has been a conscious attempt to wrest redemption from the grip of unrelenting agony and to do so by weaving into the future the enduring threads of collective will and purpose originating in a heroic past.

To fully understand the interplay between power and powerlessness in the history of the Jews, therefore, requires an examination of the Jewish position over a much longer period than the modern era. Of necessity, such a perspective must begin with the position of the Jews in antiquity, for it is in that period that the decisive experiences in the life of the nation took place, shaping many aspects of the Jewish character, Jewish attitudes, and Jewish expectations of the future.

As opposed to the image of the Jew during most of the modern period, Jews in ancient times were not known as docile victims. To the contrary, they were renowned for possessing the exact opposite qualities of national character. Biblical records attest to this, as do Hellenistic and Roman sources. The Jews may not have been loved in antiquity, but they were respected for their determination and capacity to resist assaults on their rights and liberty. In fact, it is hard to find a people that resisted so persistently, for so long, and against such overwhelming odds. Although the Jewish land was successively conquered by the Assyrians, Babylonians, Persians, Macedonians, Romans, Byzantines, and Arabs, the Jewish people resisted conquest, occupation, and exile for nearly twenty centuries.

In this first long phase of their history, the Jews produced a succession of remarkable military and political figures to lead their protracted struggle, a list that has few if any rivals in the history of nations: Moses, Joshua, Gideon, Samson, Debora, Saul, Jonathan, David, the Kings of Israel and Judah, Nehemia, the Maccabees, Bar Kochba, Elazar ben Yair, Judah of Galilee, Simon bar Giora, and other lesser-known Jewish leaders of the successive revolts against Rome and Byzantium.

Furthermore, Jewish resistance characterized the Jewish Diaspora of the ancient world as well. From the second century B.C.E. through the end of the Roman period, the Jews of Egypt, Syria, and Rome evinced a capacity to resist politically and militarily the pogroms, massacres, and violations of their rights by the non-Jews among whom they lived. "You know what a big crowd it is, how they stick together, how influential they are," pouted Cicero, seeking to avoid undue confrontation with the Jews of Rome.[1] Against Rome and Byzantium, the Jews of Judea stood utterly alone in the face of a superpower that had vanquished most of the civilized world, waging a seemingly hopeless resistance for six centuries.

If there is one quality that emerges from Jewish history in antiquity, it is the obstinate refusal of the Jews to defer their religious and political independence to other peoples, as well as their readiness to wage an unrelenting struggle against their would-be oppressors. They sometimes succeeded, although more often they did not. But they never gave up the struggle, which preserved in itself their identity and values and prevented them from assimilating and disappearing like the numberless other nations that succumbed to the power of empires.

How did this capacity to resist vanish, to be replaced by the image and reality of the defenseless Jew? This did not happen overnight. Conquered, subjugated, and exhausted, the Jews nevertheless continued the struggle to assert control over their fate, sometimes requiring long decades to replenish their collective will. Certainly the protracted and tragic struggle against Rome drained the nation of much energy. But contrary to popular notions, this series of defeats failed to root out the Jewish will to resist, as shown by the later Jewish revolts against Rome and Byzantium *after* Bar Kochba. For as long as the Jewish people lived on its land, it possessed a clear capacity for military and political action, demonstrated as late as the beginning of the seventh century with the Jewish alliances first with and then against the Persian invaders of the land.

Yet once the Jews were driven into exile and became a collection of dispersed communities in the medieval world, they were gradually deprived of all the conditions necessary for self-defense Although in the cities of the Middle Ages the Jews lived in their own fortified quarters, they slowly lost the power necessary to sustain such defenses. Most notably in the states of medieval Germany, the Jews were stripped of the right that others had to carry weapons for self defense, despite the fact that (or perhaps because) it was the Jews who often faced the most wanton assaults. If you cannot carry a sword, you soon forget how to use one altogether; both the physical and psychological preparedness to resist eventually atrophy. Step by step, the Jews were consigned to the status of a minority dependent on the protection of its hosts—that is, if the hosts were inclined to protect it in the first place. In some cases it took many centuries for the Jews to be reduced to a level of such perfect powerlessness. As late as fourteenth-century Spain, for example, there are records of Jewish armed resistance against attacks. But by then, such resistance had become an aberration. The Jewish people had effectively lost control over its destiny.

A condition of inherent defenselessness necessarily invites aggression. This was especially true in the case of the Jews, who uniquely combined economic success and endemic weakness, making them an irresistible target and producing an escalating cycle of pogrom and displacement. Tossed out from one land, the Jews would find a haven in another, usually striking an arrangement with the sovereign and the nobility only to be brutally attacked when their allies and protectors were toppled or weakened. The Jewish people became a people that other people killed, often with relish, generally with impunity. A direct line leads from the massacres of Jews in the Crusades in the eleventh century, to the mass killing in Spain in 1391, to the great bloodletting in the Ukraine in the seventeenth century, to the pogroms in Russia in the nineteenth century, to the Holocaust in Europe in our own time. And as the technology of destruction improved, the horrors became even more horrible.

The first result of the atrophy of Jewish resistance was physical destruction on an unimaginable scale. No other people has paid such a price for being defenseless. But there was a second fateful consequence: Slowly and surely, through the centuries of exile, the image and character of the Jew began to change. For non-Jews, the glorious Jewish past faded into dim memory and irrelevance. The word *Jew* became an object of contempt, derision, at best pity. It became synonymous with the word *coward* in a hundred different tongues. The adjective *wandering* was affixed to it, signifying the rootlessness and precariousness of Jewish existence. Not a trace could be found of the grudging admiration that the peoples of antiquity had harbored for Jewish courage and tenacity.

Worse, a substantial segment of Jewish opinion assimilated this disparaging image of the Jew, and many Jews came to view themselves as others had come to view them. This took on a particularly pernicious twist in the modern era. As the doctrines of modern pacifism emerged, many Jews rushed to embrace them, pretending they could transform into a universal virtue what had always been a unique vulnerability of the Jews. That the Jews "would not" (could not) resort to arms, that they would not "demean" themselves by "stooping to violence," was taken to be a clear sign of their moral superiority over other peoples who were not similarly constrained. Once leading segments of Jewish opinion in Europe had transformed Jewish weakness into a positive good, the Jewish people's chances of escaping its fate reached a new low.

Of all Zionist leaders, Jabotinsky was virtually alone in seeing where all this was leading. Throughout the 1930s, he sounded the alarm of impending danger. In Warsaw in 1938, on the Jewish fast day of Tisha B'av (marking the destruction of the Second Temple in Jerusalem by the Romans), he said to Poland's three million Jews, almost none of whom were to survive the war:

> For three years I have been imploring you, Jews of Poland, the crown of world Jewry, appealing to you, warning you unceasingly that the catastrophe is nigh. My hair has turned white and I have grown old over these years, for my heart is bleeding that you, dear brothers and sisters, do not see the volcano which will soon begin to spew forth its fires of destruction. I see a horrible vision. Time is growing short for you to be spared. I know you cannot see it, for you are troubled and confused by everyday concerns . . . Listen to my words at this, the twelfth hour. For God's sake: let everyone save himself, so long as there is time to do so, for time is running short.

But Jabotinsky also saw a glimmer of light in the blackness:

> And I want to say something else to you on this day, the Ninth of Av: Those who will succeed in escaping this catastrophe will live to experience a festive moment of great Jewish joy: the rebirth and establishment of the Jewish State! I do not know whether I myself will live to see it—but my son will! I am certain of this, just as I am certain that the sun will rise tomorrow morning. I believe in it with all my heart.[2]

Even a year before the outbreak of the war, few could see the catastrophe coming, and fewer still could share in Jabotinsky's note of hope. For those who could see the danger clearly, the Jewish people was approaching the end.

A scene at the close of Claude Lanzmann's haunting documentary, *Shoah*, captures this hopelessness. *Shoah* ends with the testimony of one of the survivors from the Warsaw ghetto. He describes how in the last desperate days of the fighting, when the ghetto was being pulverized by the German forces, he was sent to seek help from the Polish Resistance. Lowering himself into a sewer, he made his way through the German lines to the "Aryan" section of Warsaw. The Poles refused his request, and after doing what he could, he decided to go back. He reentered the sewer and surfaced in the midst of darkness in the heart of the Warsaw ghetto. He was greeted by utter silence. Everyone was dead. The survivor remembers saying to himself: "I'm the last Jew. I'll wait for morning, and for the Germans."[3]

His assessment about being the last Jew was not so far off the mark. In 1942, the rulers of Nazi Germany had met in a villa in the Berlin suburb of Wannsee to design the Final Solution. As was later learned from the Wannsee Conference documents, the Nazis planned to annihilate every Jew in Europe, from Britain to the Soviet Union. They drew up detailed lists for the liquidation of eleven million human beings, down to the two hundred Jews of Albania scheduled for destruction.[4] The original German plan dealt only with European Jewry, but when the Nazi armies reached North Africa, they began deporting the Jews of these lands to the death camps as well. They, like the Jews of Russia, were saved only by Hitler's defeat.

It seemed this was to be the inevitable consequence of the long, horrible transformation of the Jews: The sons of the Maccabees had become the ultimate victims, destined to vanish from the earth.

Yet at this lowest of lows in Jewish history, the Jews were beginning to experience a second great transformation: They were rediscovering the capacity to resist, a rediscovery that had begun slowly in the previous century. The huge citizen-armies of Europe after Napoleon had begun to train a Jewish soldiery, and by World War I hundreds of thousands of Jews were under arms and fighting with distinction on both sides. In World War II such Jewish strength was committed to the Allied cause. But the most telling sign of a transformation was occurring at the very bottom of the abyss itself. In the Warsaw ghetto, as in Treblinka and in Sobibor, Jews were undertaking the most heroic resistance in the annals of man. In rising up against the Nazis in the most desperate and impossible of circumstances, they were showing that the ancient thread that ran through the fabric of their character had not been severed after all.

This resurrection of the Jewish capacity to resist had been fashioned as a deliberate policy only within the Zionist movement. As early as World War I, the Zionists had set out to reconstruct, after many centuries of neglect, the elements of Jewish military power, starting with Jabotinsky's Jewish Legion during World War I, through the makeshift Hashomer units in the 1920s, Orde Wingate's Special Night Squads in the 1930s, and the Jewish Brigade in the British Army during World War II. From these sprang the various underground forces, the Hagana, Irgun, and Lehi, which in turn paved the way for the establishment of the Israel Defense Force on the eve of Israel's independence.

With the founding of the State of Israel, the majority of Jews quickly came to understand the critical importance of military power—a change far more abrupt and spectacular than the gradual loss of this understanding had been. For if the rendering of the Jews from a militant to a docile people had taken place over many centuries, here in the space of only a few years a reborn Jewish sovereignty rediscovered the art of soldiering. Israel devoted an enormous part of its economy and the finest of its youth to the task of militarily defending the state. Much to the amazement of the world, the Jewish state was soon producing fighters second to none and an army that proved itself capable of routing far larger and better-equipped fighting machines again and again. Furthermore, in the war against terrorism Israel's soldiers showed a demoralized and paralyzed world that civilized societies could fight this scourge: In countless raids and special operations culminating in the rescue mission at Entebbe, Israel proved that terrorism could be fought and beaten.

All this not only changed the condition of the Jews of Israel, enabling the Jewish people to successfully resist assaults aimed at its annihilation for the first time in centuries. It also changed the image of the Jew in the eyes of non-Jews. The respect for Israel's military prowess against overwhelming odds did not necessarily mean that the anti-Semitic stereotypes of the Jews were replaced everywhere and in every way; in some cases, the anti-Semites, encouraged by the Arabs, created a strange amalgam of the cowardly, mercenary Jew bedecked in a storm trooper's uniform. But notwithstanding these grotesque distortions, most of the world was keenly aware that the Jewish people was experiencing in Israel a great transformation. As in antiquity, many marveled at the resolve, resourcefulness, and audacity shown by the Jewish army, changing for millions their conception of the Jews, or at least of some of them.

But the change in the way the Jews viewed themselves was even more dramatic. It had begun as early as the 1890s. Visitors to Palestine at the time noted a change in the first generation of Jewish youngsters who had been raised on the land outside the enclosed ancient Jewish quarters of Safed and Jerusalem. Unlike their Orthodox brethren, these young Jews, mostly sons and daughters of recent immigrants, cultivated the land, rode horses, learned to shoot, spoke a revived Hebrew, and were capable of befriending or confronting the Arabs, earning their respect if not their love.

A quintessential example of this new breed was the Aaronsohn family of Zichron Ya'akov, which gained renown both in Palestine and abroad after the turn of the century. Well-to-do farmers, they received international acclaim through the achievements of the family's eldest son, the strong-willed Aaron Aaronsohn. Aaronsohn was a multifaceted personality: a talented agronomist whose experimental work was crucial in convincing many that the barren land could indeed be brought back to life and successfully cultivated, a political thinker of great sagacity, a hard-headed organizer and leader of men. As such, he was totally committed to driving out the Turks by helping the British liberate Palestine. He, his equally strong-willed sister Sarah, and a band of young Palestinian Jews that included the colorful adventurer Yosef Lishansky and the sensitive romantic Avshalom Feinberg organized an espionage ring that transmitted signals to British ships from the family's estate on the cliffs overlooking the Mediterranean. Each of these extraordinary figures of the "Nili" group, as it was later known, was to die tragically: Sarah, by her own hand while being tortured during interrogation by the Turks; Avshalom, murdered by Bedouins in the sands near Rafah while he was en route to British lines in Egypt; Lishansky, hanged by the Turks in Damascus after he was caught in the north of the country; and Aaron, lost at the age of thirty-nine when his plane mysteriously disappeared over the English Channel after the war. Nonetheless, the audacity and courage shown by these young Jews, the special spirit they exuded, combining worldliness with fierce pride and an equally fierce determination to overthrow the Ottoman occupation of the Jewish land, shaped the ethos of generations of young Palestinian (and later Israeli) Jews. It also influenced the non-Jews who came into contact with them, most notably the remarkable Colonel Richard Meinertzhagen (described in Chapter 2), who as General Allenby's intelligence officer worked with Aaronsohn's group and as a result reversed his previous opinion of the Jews.

This essential transformation of the Jew occurred with great rapidity on the soil of Palestine over the first half of the century. By the eve of Israel's independence, a distinctly different Jewish character had emerged, ready to take up the struggle to deliver the nation. Fifty or sixty years may be like the blink of an eye in the collective life of an ancient people, but in the lives of individuals it can seem like an eternity: What is true in a person's own life and in his or her parents' lives comes to seem as though it has been true forever. By the time the second or third generation born and bred into the change reached adulthood, the Jews of Israel had begun to lose their awareness of what it meant to be a Jew in the ghettos of Europe or Yemen. Sometimes it would take an unexpected event to awaken this understanding anew.

This was very much my own experience. One of the young Israeli recruits whom I met in an elite military unit for which we had both volunteered was Haim Ben-Yonah. Haim was a good half a head taller than the rest of us, and he stood out in other ways as well. A self-effacing smile disguised an inner toughness, wedded to a basic integrity that made him the first of our induction to be sent to officers' school. If ever there were a person exemplifying so many of the things that we valued in the Israeli character, Haim was that person. This was obvious to all of us from our first days in the army together. Our induction into our unit entailed a twenty-four-hour, eighty-mile march, some of it over grueling terrain, and all of it during one of the worst winter storms in years. Early in the march, when the officer leading Haim's team twisted his ankle and had to be evacuated, he asked Haim, then a raw recruit like the rest of us, to take command—which Haim did calmly, almost matter-of-factly. And while the position of leadership Haim assumed naturally distanced him somewhat from the others in the unit, his habitual reserve did not prevent him from opening up when it was needed. I remember in particular the friendship he struck up with a young recruit whose family had come from Allepo in Syria. The youth found himself on perpetually unfamiliar ground in dealing with the clannish kibbutzniks, but Haim was undeterred, spending hours speaking Arabic with him using what little of the language he had managed to pick up on his kibbutz and sending both of them into paroxysms of laughter over the absurdities of his pronunciation.

One dark night in 1969, as the unit was carrying out a counterstrike across the Suez Canal after deadly Egyptian raids on the Israeli side, Haim was killed in a burst of gunfire. His body fell into the waters of the canal and disappeared. We searched for him fruitlessly that night and the next, and his body was finally returned to us days later by the Egyptians. It was at the end of a long row of cypress trees at Kibbutz Yehiam in the western Galilee, Haim's home, that he was buried. It was there also that I met Haim's mother Shulamit and discovered that Haim had been born shortly after she and his father had been freed from the death camps of Europe. Had he been born two years earlier, this daring young officer would have been tossed into the ovens, one of the million nameless Jewish babies who met their end in this way. Haim's mother told me that while she felt a great deal of pain, she felt no bitterness. At least, she said, her son had died wearing the uniform of a Jewish soldier defending his people.

I was nineteen years old then, and these words had a profound effect on me. I found myself thinking again and again about the possibility that Haim might not have lived even the short life that he did live. Or, eerily, that he might have outlived the war, but in a world in which Israel had not come into being. Would Haim have come out the same way in another land—a Hungarian-speaking version of the same dauntless Israeli youth, sure of his place in the world, possessed of the same inner calm? For me this was an unsettling question, and I was not at all sure of the answer. I had been born into the Jewish state and therefore believed that the values and attitudes with which I and my generation had grown up were natural, long abiding, and even shared by all, or most, Jews.

But this was not the case. A distinguishing feature of many Jews raised in Israel is the absence of the sense of personal insecurity that accompanies many Jews in the Diaspora, even the most successful ones. While Israel itself may come under periodic attack, the sense of *being* a Jew in Israel seldom does. There are occasional existential musings, limited to tiny fringe groups in the society, about the purpose of it all and whether the Diaspora was not really preferable to all this, but these are sharp aberrations from the norm: In the deepest personal sense, the overwhelming majority of Israelis feel completely and naturally at home in Israel, notwithstanding its many problems. There are, of course, quite a few Jews who feel at home in America as well, but a few sharp incidents of anti-Semitism may deprive them of this sense of security. When non-Jews sense this vulnerability in Jews, some wrongly ascribe it to cowardice. I could not fully understand until much later in life the view of the Jew as a pusillanimous creature because, although I had certainly met some noteworthy cowards in my childhood and youth in Jerusalem, I had also seen the very opposite qualities in the young Israelis who grew up with me. In any case, the issue here is not individual courage or lack of it, but the inner sense of belonging that produces in turn a personal sense of security about one's place in the world. This was the other great result of the Return. In addition to the physical ingathering of the Jews, it stimulated a spiritual ingathering where feelings and attitudes that had been lost in the dispersion were retrieved.

The speed with which a new generation raised in Israel had developed and absorbed this old-new ethos was one of the most remarkable transformations in the history of any culture and of any people. No doubt it could take place so rapidly because the Jewish people maintained the memories of its life in antiquity and preserved intact its desire not only to restore its independence as a nation but its integrity as individuals. This is why what was happening in Israel radiated to the farthest corners of the Diaspora and affected the self-perception of many Jews around the world. In particular, the victory after the Six Day War stiffened Jewish pride and made many Jews speak out and declare their activism and commitment to the Jewish people and the Jewish state. It was anything but coincidental that the great awakening of Soviet Jews, buried under half a century of Communist amnesia, took place after Israel's victory in the Six Day War in 1967, as Natan Sharansky and others have testified. The reestablishment of the State of Israel and the rediscovery of the Jewish capacity to resist dramatically transformed the objective and subjective condition of the Jewish people worldwide.

*   *   *

But this was not a complete transformation. Indeed, it could not have been complete. For the Jewish people, having lived outside politics for so long, having not wielded power for so many centuries, could not adapt to an independent existence all at once. If your fate has been entirely determined by others for centuries, it is difficult to internalize the idea that not only can others bend you to *their* will, but that *you* can shape the actions of others to conform to *your* needs. A culture that is truly political assumes that the mustering of support and the periodic exercise of political power is a natural and inevitable part of the ongoing struggle to survive.

But for the Jews, even reimplanting an understanding of the elementary need for *military* power entailed a bitter battle to overcome the entrenched view that Jews ought to have nothing to do with armies. The calls by Theodor Herzl, Vladimir Jabotinsky, and others to challenge this state of helplessness by creating Jewish military and political power met with derision even from many Jews and were dismissed as irrelevant absurdities or fascistic fetishes. Jewish critics from all quarters warned that the establishment of Jewish military might would throw the Jews into the arms of militarism and extreme nationalism, as though the act of wielding arms were in and of itself morally repugnant. If the Allies fighting the Nazis had adopted such a view, it would have doomed humanity. Yet in rejecting the Zionist message to organize political and military resistance, the Jews of Europe wasted a full four decades in which they could have obtained arms, allies, and escape routes to save themselves. The result was Auschwitz.

The persistent refusal of most of the Jews to see the need for something as obvious as the capacity for self-defense seems incredible today. It was indeed incredible, the result of over a thousand years of nearly complete detachment from political and military realities. Of course, after the catastrophe of World War II, many Jews came to understand the need for military power quickly enough; they understood the stark fact that the absence of a Jewish ability to physically resist the Nazis had permitted a third of their people to be slaughtered. This understanding they translated into the Jewish army of Israel, without which, they knew, another Holocaust would have befallen them at the hands of the Arabs.

But even many Israeli Jews, who have come to accept the need for and the possibility of resistance, balk when it comes to sustaining this resistance into the indefinite future. Perhaps because of the agonized odyssey of the Jewish people, the Jewish mind seeks a way out of coping with this incessant political and occasional military struggle, stretching out into foreseeable time. When will it all end? many Israeli and non-Israeli Jews ask. Will we go on struggling forever? Will the sword forever devour its makers?

For Israel, such questions are never fully answerable. One cannot prophesy an endless succession of wars, nor predict the scope of battles or their outcomes. Whether wars break out, whether they are defused by diplomacy or stopped by deterrence, are questions no one can answer with certainty. But what is a safe assumption is that political conflict in the Middle East is not about to disappear under any predictable circumstance—that is, unless one accepts the idea that history will soon come to its end and we shall reach the millennium. Not coincidentally, this thought is of Jewish origin as well, although the visions of Isaiah and the other Jewish prophets were principally intended to teach us what to strive for—and not necessarily what to expect next week. But whereas many other peoples have been able to distinguish between the ideal vision of human existence and the way the affairs of nations must be conducted in the present, the Jewish people has had a harder time accepting this separation. The Jews have such an acute sense of what mankind *should* be that they often act as though it is virtually there already.

Nowhere is this penchant for seeing it all come to a speedy and satisfactory end more sharply felt than in Israel itself. A country besieged time and again by armies calling for its destruction, whose eighteen-year-old sons and daughters give years of their youth to serving in the army, and whose adult men do reserve duty for another twenty-five years, naturally develops a powerful longing for peace. As a result, broad swaths of Israel's population have developed simplistic, sentimental, and even messianic views of politics.

I recall, for instance, the attitudes of many people in Israel following the defeat of the Arabs in the Six Day War. A widespread view was that the Arabs would sue for an immediate end to the conflict. I remember that even as an eighteen-year-old I found inanely childish this notion that the Arab leaders would pick up the phone and call the whole thing off any moment now. Yet it is remarkable how many in Israel actually believed this at the time, making no allowance for the possibility that the Arabs would pursue the war against Israel by other means until they were ready for the next military round; nor did they make any allowance for the time and experiences that would be needed for an evolution in the Arabs' deeply held beliefs about Israel.

This approach was partly rooted in the tendency to ascribe to the Arabs the same sentiments that we felt in Israel, with a total disregard for the differences in culture, history, and political values. Many Israelis believed that the Arabs loathed war as much as they themselves did and that, given a proper explication of Israel's peaceful intentions, the Arabs would embrace and welcome us. This cloyingly sentimental approach was espoused in the 1920s by the Brit Shalom (Alliance for Peace) movement led by the American rabbi Judah Magnes, who had settled in Jerusalem and became chancellor of the Hebrew University. Magnes believed, in decidedly American terms, that the Arab campaign against the Jews was a product of a failure to communicate. The Mufti, he believed, could be reasoned with, pacified, and appeased. Under no circumstances should the Jews take up arms and retaliate, for this would merely heighten the Arabs' hostility. It is difficult to believe how many of the leading intellectuals of the Jewish community in Palestine continued to cling to this view, not only in the face of murderous anti-Jewish passions incited by the Mufti but even in the period when he was an active partisan of the Nazis. The successor-believers in this view are still very much with us today, ignoring the realities of Arab political life, dismissing the intentions of those bent on destroying Israel, or inverting logic by suggesting that they must be appeased rather than resisted.

Though the great majority in Israel shuns this simple-minded attitude toward the Arab world, it is nonetheless strongly influenced by a current of thinking that encompasses surprisingly numerous segments of the population, left and right. This current derives from the relentless Jewish desire to see an end to struggle. In its essence it is a nonpolitical, even antipolitical, approach to the life of nations. Basically, it holds that history, or more precisely Middle Eastern history, will have a finite end. We will arrive at a state called "peace" in which history will simply stop. Wars will end, external conflicts will subside, internal conflicts will vanish, Israel will be accepted by the Arabs, and the Jews will be forever content. At this end of days, Israel will become a kind of blissful castle in the clouds, a Jewish never-never land in which the Jews will be able finally to find a respite from struggle and strife.

It is a view that I remember well from my childhood. The illustrated textbooks of Israel's geography had drawings of rolling hills and cultivated fields, in the center of which was a cluster of little white houses with red-tiled roofs and a water tower in the background, presumably signifying some idyllic kibbutz or moshav. The idea was that we each were destined to have our own version of this idyll, with our own little house, a stretch of grass next to it, and a leafy tree shading it—as though we did not live in the middle of a sandstorm, as though the swirling dust of fanaticism and war were not enveloping us, as though we were living in the Midwest and not in the Mideast. This fantasy view of Israel's situation, including its fairy-tale denouement, was broadly prevalent in the education of generations of youngsters both before and after the establishment of the state.

But after the creation of Israel, with the successive attacks and the continuing absence of the long-hoped-for peace, the gap between the idyll and the reality grew greater and greater, creating an ever-increasing sense of frustration that was felt most acutely at the extremes of the Israeli political spectrum. According to the views prevalent in these quarters, the problem was not that the idyll was misplaced or in need of revision, but that we had strayed from the path of righteousness and were being punished for our sins by the Arab refusal to accept us. If we would only correct our ways, we could reach the hoped-for pastoral state of bliss, the desire for which is embedded so deeply in the Israeli psyche.

On the left, this messianic belief focuses today on the "sin" of Israel's conquest of the territories during the Six Day War. The proponents of this view look nostalgically back to the nineteen years in which Israel lived in a vulnerable, embryonic condition. Somehow they manage to remember not the terrible danger to which the country was subjected but only the relative degree of national unity that this danger produced.

In this leftist revision of history, the incorporation of the territories into Israel during the Six Day War was the beginning of all evil. Israel became smug and self-satisfied, insensitive and inhuman, repressing the Palestinian Arabs and tarnishing the Israeli soul in the process. To save Israel's soul, we must amputate part of the body. If only the nation were to rid itself of the territories, its economy would improve, Israelis would have to serve less reserve duty, and there would be jobs for new immigrants and money for building safer highways. This strain of argument occasionally spills over into the foreign press in articles about the ill effects of the "tensions produced by the occupation," which are supposed to lead to such things as increased child abuse and wife-beating. The essential thesis of this view is: Give up the territories and be saved. The true believers are certain that we are at salvation's gate but have simply been too blind or too foolish to go in.

A mirror image of this messianism is found on the religious right, where it is believed that the act of settling the land is in and of itself sufficient to earn divine providence and an end to the country's woes. If Israel were merely to hang tough and erect more settlements, it could dispense with world opinion and international pressures. A variation on the religious right's view is the idea advanced by a segment of the nonreligious right that Israel could achieve lasting stability if only it could get rid of the Arabs living in its midst. That is, the left believes that getting rid of the territories would cure all of Israel's ills, the right believes that keeping the territories would achieve the same effect.

These are all quick fixes that are neither quick nor able to fix. For what needs fixing is the underlying problem of Arab hostility— a problem that may or may not disappear with the passing of several generations. Both of these fantasies evidence a fundamental immaturity in Israeli political culture, a desperate search for an escape from the difficult struggle that Jewish national life among the Arabs has engendered throughout this century, and that Israel will have to face in the next century as well.

True, continuing struggle does not necessarily mean perpetual war, but it does mean an ongoing national exertion and the possibility of periodic bouts of international confrontation. Ending the state of war with the Arab states and establishing formal peace with them would substantially reduce the degree and the intensity of the conflict, but it can never fully eliminate the possibility of *future* wars and upheavals, just as the end of the Cold War did not constitute an end to all conflicts or to history itself, as some had inanely believed. You cannot end the struggle for survival without ending life itself.

It is this that Jews in general and Israelis in particular find so difficult to accept. A nation of idealists and closet idealists, still lacking the experience of political sovereignty needed to sharpen political perspicacity, they have found it difficult to adjust to the realities of international politics. The escapist tendencies to Israeli politics stem from this Jewish inability to reconcile oneself to the permanent need for Jewish power.

Of course, after many decades most Israelis have come to terms with the idea that the military is, at least for the time being, the indispensable foundation of Israel's security. But the evident successes of the Israeli army in protecting the country and its citizens have obscured a crucial truth: Military strength is not enough to ensure the nation's survival. Just as the Jews had earlier failed to grasp the significance of military power, a great many Jews, including many Israelis, now fail to understand the significance of, and the need for, other types of power—and the totality of strength that derives from a nation's military, economic, and political resources.

Thus, in contrast to their new-found willingness to defend themselves against *military* attacks, many Israelis show a marked and disturbing tendency toward conceding at the first sign of serious international *political* and *economic* pressure. Who are we, they ask, to resist the entire world? If this is the will of the powers that be, what choice do we have but to go along? That it is sometimes—and in the case of Israel, often—necessary to dissent from and resist prevailing opinion seldom crosses their minds. That dissent is *possible* is believed even less frequently. In the realm of political power, the habits of passivity and submissiveness acquired in exile are still very much with us.

Yet the twentieth century has shown better than any other age that political power is no less important than military might in international conflicts. This is a lesson that no one, regardless of his ends, can afford to forget. The Czechs neglected this lesson and allowed Hitler, who understood it well, to paint them into a political corner in Munich, forcing them to surrender their country's defenses without firing a shot. But it is not only victims of aggression who pay the price for underestimating the importance of political power. Sometimes the perpetrators of aggression forget it as well. Saddam Hussein, for one, did not take it into account in his bid to rule Kuwait. His army had overcome all Kuwaiti resistance within hours, but the battle that Saddam was unprepared to fight was the political battle, over the next six months, to persuade international opinion that his cause was just, and that the governments of the world should not embark on embargo and war to pry

Kuwait from his grasp. He could have prepared the ground in advance by conducting a full-scale campaign in the West to obscure his designs under a cloud of palatable arguments: that the Kuwaiti rulers were corrupt oppressors of their own people, that Kuwaitis were an integral part of the Iraqi people, that they welcomed his populist rule, and so on. But having failed to fight on this battlefield, Saddam lost ignominiously. He was completely isolated internationally, with virtually no one to come to his assistance or broker an elegant, face-saving compromise. He was saved only by American timidity in the closing hours of the war.

As Saddam learned the hard way, to win militarily you must also win politically; to win politically, you must win over public opinion; and to win over public opinion, you must convince the public that your cause is just.

This chain of imperatives, culminating in the need to muster public support on a vast scale, is not a luxury that nations may choose to forgo. The advent of democratic ideals and democratic terminology, along with the rise of the mass media, have elevated international public opinion into the crucial arena in which political struggles are waged. It matters little if your cause is just or unjust, moral or immoral. Anyone engaged in political or military conflict in this century must seek to persuade international audiences that his cause is just. Indeed, Hitler and Churchill were quintessential examples of political leaders who understood the logic of this new necessity. Hitler and Goebbels perfected the techniques of the propaganda blitz, disguising their aggressive intentions in appeals to justice and self-determination. Although these were outrageous parodies of the truth, they were nonetheless accepted at the time as plausible explanations of Nazi actions (and as excuses for Western inaction). Churchill recognized that his first task as war leader was to mobilize the entire Western world by appealing to its most cherished values of freedom and human dignity. His main weapons, his speeches, were carefully constructed toward that end, as were those of his ally, Franklin

Roosevelt, who pioneered the systematic use of broadcasting as a device to rally public opinion.

To see the power of public opinion in the age of mass communication, one need only compare the electrifying effect of Churchill's speeches, broadcast to millions over radio, with the virtual initial noneffect of Lincoln's Gettysburg Address. That address, though at least as inspiring as any that Churchill wrote, was heard by only a handful of people, and it played almost no immediate role in determining the course of the Civil War.[5] The millions who were swayed by its poetry and power became familiar with it only later, and not in the midst of the great events that had led Lincoln to compose it. It could be argued that even if Lincoln had had broadcasting available to him, his weak voice would not have carried the message, as Churchill's stentorian delivery did. All this serves simply to underscore the new realities of the century: that the effect of a powerful message powerfully delivered and powerfully broadcast to public opinion has become an indispensable element in the waging of political and military struggles.

Many of the century's chief antagonists in international disputes have understood this principle. Stalin applied it enthusiastically, presenting himself as the world's savior and changing democracies into despotisms in the eyes of hundreds of millions of people. This legacy of the big lie hugely told has been bequeathed by Hitler and Stalin to an endless array of lesser dictators, from Nasser to Ho Chi Minh to Fidel Castro, who have used their techniques on their victims and on their victims' allies to weaken resistance to their aggression.

Take the North Vietnamese as an example. They pursued the propaganda war with great success against South Vietnam, presenting themselves as a paragon of goodness while vilifying the South, whose government was anything but pristine but was certainly not guilty of the mass killings and uprooting of entire populations that the North habitually practiced. The relentless North Vietnamese propaganda campaign aimed at American public opinion made an important contribution to sapping the American will to pursue the war. To the understandable question of why American boys should be fighting in a far corner of Asia was added the corollary: especially when America's ally is so corrupt and evil. With repetition of the question, the answer became increasingly obvious, paving the way to North Vietnam's victory.

But notwithstanding the success of the North Vietnamese, I believe that in the postwar era the preeminent masters of translating propaganda into political pressure have been the Arabs. The Arab regimes and terror organizations have understood the importance of this instrument as it applied to their particular objective: the destruction of Israel. They saw that to reverse Israel's military victory of 1967 they would have to defeat Israel politically, that this meant defeating it on the battleground of public opinion, and that this in turn meant defeating it in the appeal to justice. They consequently proceeded to weave an elaborate patchwork quilt of falsehoods: the false Theory of Palestinian Centrality, the false Reversal of Causality, the false image of PLO Congeniality. Above all, the Arabs sought to rob the Jews of every aspect of the historical case that suggested the justice of their cause, constructing an extraordinary distortion of Jewish history and substituting in its place a fictitious Palestinian one: The Arabs took the place of the Jews as the natives in the land, and the Jews took the place of the Arabs as the invaders; the horrible Jewish exile into a hundred lands was exchanged for a Palestinian Arab "exile" (into the neighboring Arab states); the atrocities committed against the Jews were denied and dismissed, while any hardship encountered by the Arabs was inflated into a miniature Holocaust. All this was meant to persuade the peoples of the world, especially those of the United States and Europe, that Israel had committed a grave injustice, which the Arabs were merely trying to correct, and that decent people everywhere were obligated to help them correct it.

While the Arabs were exceptional in waging the battle for public opinion so long and so systematically, the Jews of Israel were unique in abandoning the field for so long. For as we have noted, the Israelis have been encumbered by the great debilitation stem-

ming from the long Jewish absence from international political life
and the renewed emphasis on military power. The majority felt
there was no *need* to counteract Arab propaganda. Had not the Israeli Defense Forces extricated Israel from destruction in 1948 and
again in 1967? Were they not capable of doing so again? And if the
Arabs kept prattling away at the UN, in the media and in universities of the West—what of it? Surely Israel did not have to concern
itself with such trivial carpings, as long as it possessed the military
power to defend itself. As David Ben-Gurion bluntly informed a
young nation in the 1950s: What matters is not what the *goyim*
(Gentiles) say, but what the Jews do. He was half right, of course.
Without resolute Jewish actions, the building and fortification of
the Jewish state could not take place. But he was flat wrong in dismissing the importance and power of public opinion—he found
out later, when Israeli forces responded to Egyptian-sponsored
terror attacks by entering the Sinai in 1956. At the time, Ben-
Gurion announced that Israel would not leave the Sinai for a thousand years. But Israel's failure to win support for its action in the
American administration, the Congress, and with the public in
order to dampen Eisenhower's opposition resulted in a hasty Israeli retreat within months.

It took several decades for the majority of Israelis to acknowledge the force of public opinion. And though by now there are
many who lament Israel's ongoing lack of activity in this area, most
still do not see in sharp focus how much real damage is caused to
their country by its negative portrayal, and how much more difficult it makes the job of securing alliances, without which no small
nation can survive.

Ironically, it is precisely the common Israeli belief in the para-
mountcy of military power that has reduced Israel's ability to secure such alliances. A reigning assumption that military power
alone suffices to guarantee the security of a nation will inevitably
breed complacency with regard to the political side of national
power. Alliances that are not cultivated are alliances that do not
come into being, and the absence of reliable allies in turn fosters

an enervating fatalism about the political world: that Israel is irrevocably doomed to an unsplendid isolation; that the entire world is inevitably against it; and that there is nothing that it can do other than to muster the force, exclusively physical in nature, to withstand the pressures.

That this has sometimes been the case does not make it always the case. For the nations of the world form their alliances and their antipathies according to their changing interest and, in an increasingly democratic world, according to their public opinion. Israel could therefore act on both these fronts of interest and opinion to persuade governments and their citizens alike about the advisability and the justice of siding with it. This might not get everyone on Israel's side and it might not even get most on Israel's side, but it would get *some*, and it would reduce the antagonism of others.

This was precisely Herzl's conception when he successfully sought to obtain the support for Zionism among the rulers of Britain, Germany, Russia, Turkey, and others, but it cannot be said that his followers understood his conception or applied it very well. Perhaps it was because Herzl, who understood political power and public opinion so intuitively and applied them so brilliantly, died so young. It is a fact that most of the Zionist leadership after his death accepted with only minor resistance the great injustices that the British heaped upon them between the two world wars, believing they were powerless in the face of a great power—even though British public opinion, like American opinion later, could be made sympathetic and susceptible to Zionist appeals.

The one student of Herzl who understood the importance and the possibility of political resistance was Jabotinsky. In addition to stressing the need for Jewish military force and a territory on which the Jews could build their state, Jabotinsky put forward what he called the theory of public pressure:

> For there is no friendship in politics: There is pressure. What
> tips the balance one way or another is not whether the ruler is

good or bad, but the degree of pressure exerted by the subjects. If pressure is exerted solely by our opponents, with no counter-pressure applied by us, then whatever is done in Palestine will be against us, even if the head of the government will be called Balfour, or Wedgwood, or even Theodor Herzl!

Politics does not suffer a void; and if one side presses another with political and propaganda pressure while its opponent does nothing, the passive party will ultimately have to yield to the pressure. Therefore the only way for the Jewish people to resist this kind of coercion, Jabotinsky thought, was to apply the counter-pressure aimed at influencing foreign governments and their publics. And to do this, no less than on the military battlefield, the Jews would have to be willing to fight:

For no reformation in national conditions is attained without pressure and struggle. And whoever lacks the stamina, courage, ability, and desire to fight, will not be able to achieve even the smallest adjustment [of these conditions] on our behalf.[6]

Like Herzl, Jabotinsky was little understood. He too died relatively young—actually, in the course of attempting to launch such a campaign in 1940 to win over American public opinion to the cause of a Jewish state. The majority of his followers grasped very well his military and territorial ideas, but only a few fully appreciated the third, political element of his conception of national power—the need for an unrelenting international effort of persuasion and pressure to protect Jewish interests.

This is why the successive Likud governments that emblazoned Jabotinsky's teachings on their ideological flag in fact often proceeded to act on the international scene in direct contravention of his principles. They frequently took actions that were justifiable in themselves, but they made absolutely no effort to persuade the world that this was the case. Likud governments emphasized the pride Jews should take in acting firmly, rather than the prudence of ensuring that the action was understood to be correct and just. The need to win over public opinion was simply not perceived to be a priority (or even a possibility), and as a result no capability was developed to see it realized on the world scene.

Hence the Israeli military strike on the Iraqi reactor in 1981, to take one obvious example, was met with near-universal opprobrium, since Israel did next to nothing to counter Arab propaganda and Western censure, both of which would have been relatively easy to refute in this case. And when Israel entered Lebanon in 1982, this error was compounded: Rather than fighting the political battle, Israel did the *opposite*, imposing an information blackout for the first crucial days of the war—the chief effect of which was to ensure that the Israeli side of the story went virtually unreported. Completely left out of the picture was the fact that Israel's northern cities had been tormented by PLO rocket and terror attacks for a decade, as children grew up in bomb shelters and urban populations dwindled from year to year. Also left out was the preceding decade's history of PLO murder, rape, and looting in South Lebanon and the fact that even the Shi'ite Moslems there greeted the Israeli soldiers as liberators. The PLO took full advantage of this vacuum to flood the world media with fabricated reports of Israeli atrocities. It succeeded, for example, in convincing the media for a time that Israel's attack had left six hundred thousand people in South Lebanon homeless— more than the entire actual population of the region. By the time Israel lifted the blackout, much of the PLO's depiction of events had been accepted as truth, and even Israel's staunchest friends abroad had trouble explaining why Israel should be supported. The political battle had been lost.

But it was worse than lost. For if there is one thing for which the Lebanon campaign is remembered internationally, it is the massacre of several hundred Palestinian Arabs by Christian Lebanese allied with Israel in the refugee camps of Sabra and Shatilla outside Beirut. This horrifying massacre was not perpetrated by Israeli forces but by *Arabs* seeking to avenge the assassination of Lebanese President-elect Bashir Gemayel (who was a Christian). It was yet another bloody chapter in a civil war in which Palestinians and Christians had massacred each other again and again since the early 1970s. Israeli forces did not participate in the massacre, did not enable it, did not even know about it. In fact, Israel's judicial commission of inquiry, the Kahan Commission, recommended the resignation of Defense Minister Ariel Sharon in the wake of the massacre *because* he knew nothing about it, and, according to the commission, should have *foreseen* that the Christians would slaughter the Palestinians and should have acted to preempt the massacre. Yet skillful Arab propaganda, combining with the Israeli media paralysis, left its indelible impression that Israel, having launched a pointless war of aggression, had sunk to the level of massacring Arab innocents.

The consequences of this were all too real. Instead of being understood as a decisive blow against international terror, the Israeli campaign was received in the West as unreasonable and unjust, even in the United States and Britain, which were to bomb Libya only three years later in response to terrorist attacks that affected them. The result was mounting Western opposition to the Israeli operation and mounting pressure to stay Israel's hand and prevent the PLO, trapped in West Beirut and surrounded by the Israeli army, from being destroyed. The West, whose airliners had been blown out of the sky, its citizens kidnapped, and its diplomats murdered by terrorists dispatched from the PLO's lair in Lebanon, now fought to save the organization that had committed these crimes from the Israeli onslaught. In the end Western pressure prevailed, and the PLO's ten thousand gunmen were escorted out of Beirut, rifles in hand, and spirited away to the safety of the PLO's bases in Tunisia and other Arab states.

During the Lebanon campaign, nothing more dramatically underscored the importance of the political battle than the incident of President Ronald Reagan and the armless Palestinian girl. The Israeli Defense Force had achieved a complete military victory, destroying the PLO presence everywhere in southern Lebanon. Only West Beirut, the last PLO stronghold, remained, and the Israeli army was selectively bombarding PLO strongholds in the hope of forcing a surrender and preventing the higher casualties that would be involved in a direct assault. At the height of the siege, President Reagan was handed a photograph of a little Palestinian girl who, he was told, had lost her arm in the Israeli bombard-ment. Moved to anger, the president picked up the telephone and told Israeli prime minister Menachem Begin that the bombard-ment had to stop. Begin complied.

At the time, I was posted to Washington as Israel's deputy chief of mission. When I saw the photograph, I asked if it could be enlarged. The more the picture was enlarged, the less it looked like a fresh photo taken after that summer's operation. We pored over it. Finally, I managed to establish telephone contact with the Israeli headquarters in Beirut and suggested that the military try to find the girl. A few days later, the Israeli army succeeded in lo-cating her. Her arm had indeed been damaged, but years earlier during the Lebanese civil war; she had been the victim of Arab and not Israeli fire. But by then it was too late. The notion of Israel's brutality had penetrated a notch deeper into the consciousness of the American leadership and public.

Nevertheless, the fact that policy and the explication of policy have become inseparably intertwined has still not penetrated into the consciousness of many in Israel, as it has in Western countries. The President of the United States and most other world leaders do not make decisions that are independent of the way in which these decisions will be received by international opinion (and ob-viously, domestic opinion). In fact, an integral *part* of making a de-cision is addressing the question of how it will affect public opinion and what needs to be done to make its message more palatable and effective to international audiences. This is a need that very large states may sometimes forgo, though they seldom do. But a small country, much more dependent on international climate, simply does not have the luxury of ignoring the principle that a policy and its presentation are inseparable.

Having rediscovered its military capabilities, Israel is now in the midst of discovering the political capacities it needs to survive in a swiftly changing world. These capacities require, I believe, a major overhaul in Israel's abilities to present its case and its policies before world audiences. This must be understood to be a central pillar of policy and be treated accordingly, necessarily changing both the formulation of Israel's messages to the world and the quality of its messengers.

Contrary to conventional wisdom, the issue here is not just what kinds of pictures will flicker across the television screen. It is the crafting of argument and image through language, which is always the decisive first step in political debate, and usually this takes place in print before broadcasting. I have found over the years, again contrary to the popular wisdom, that occasionally one word can be worth a thousand pictures, rather than vice versa. For example, the word *occupation*. Or the expression *homeless people*. Or *Arab land*. Or *land for peace*. In countless newspaper pieces, journal articles, and books, the Arabs have devoted untold intellectual resources to framing the argument in such a way that it frames Israel. Israel will have to devote an even greater intellectual effort to extricating itself from the trap into which it has so readily entered. Above all, this will require clearly written words, powerfully tying together arguments and facts that must be disseminated in journals, periodicals, and newspapers of the West— and now those of the East as well, especially in Russia and Japan. Israel must explain to world audiences the basis of the Jewish right to the land, the history of the Arab-Israeli conflict, the goals and tactics of its adversaries, and the prerequisites for genuine peace in the region.

By arguing for the need for written rebuttals to the Arab defamation of Israel, I do not wish to imply that spoken words should be neglected, especially those spoken on television. As the Gulf War showed, international crises are increasingly televised exchanges, and the protagonists and antagonists do much of the exchanging before the viewers' eyes. During the Gulf War, for leaders and public alike, the main source of real-time information—and what is more important, real-time impressions of the unfolding situation—was the new international news networks. What George Bush was seeing on his screen in the White House was seen by Saddam Hussein in his bunker in Baghdad, by Mikhail Gorbachev in the Kremlin, and by Yitzhak Shamir in the prime minister's office in Jerusalem—as well as by every other government in the world. What was said over this medium immediately and directly influenced the perceptions of the world's leaders, in addition to influencing the respective publics to which these leaders are ultimately accountable in democratic societies. If public opinion was of decisive importance in shaping political outcomes during the first half of the century, it is now, at the close of the second half of the century, assuming an importance not even imaginable thirty or forty years earlier. And Israel, which is at the eye of so many political storms, simply will not be able to continue to go about its political or diplomatic business as usual, as though none of this existed.

Astonishingly, some hold the view that Israel should actually give up the battle for public opinion. Thus, an Israeli daily in the early nineties explained that the Labor government then ruling Israel considered Israeli diplomats to be "discharged from the burden of aggressive public relations"; the government, it said, is "declaring a unilateral cease-fire in the media war" and "promises not to be dragged into responding to the provocations of the Arab spokesmen."[7] How effective a strategy this is was demonstrated in December 1992 when the new Labor government deported over four hundred Hamas Islamic fundamentalist organizers and inciters to Lebanon—making no provision whatsoever to stave off the public relations disaster that ensued when the deportees encamped themselves on a hillside near Israel's border and before the cameras of the world. Essentially, an Israeli media cease-fire amounts to capitulation: doing away with the presentation of realities and simply expressing Israel's peaceful intentions in the hope that this will suffice to protect the country politically. This view fails to grasp the significance of the ceaseless campaign of vilification aimed at Israel by the Arab regimes, regardless of which party is in power in Jerusalem. The absence of a credible effort to explain Israel's position to the world over the last few decades has led to one political defeat after another, and as long as only the Arab side is doing the explaining, the situation can only go from bad to worse.

As for Israel's messengers, its ministers, parliamentarians, and diplomats will have to become adept at communicating with international audiences. The diplomats, in fact, ought to be chosen in the first instance with these capacities in mind. Israel will have to recruit the sharpest minds and most eloquent pens to refute the many lies hurled at it and to present the truth. In the technical sense, this requires an overhaul of the government ministries involved, defining differently, for example, the job of a diplomat and recruiting candidates accordingly. It also requires a radically different level of staffing and funding to engage in research, publication, broadcasting, and press relations. Such reforms of Israel's information apparatus can take place only with the political reforms that will make available the authority needed to sweep clean the existing information barns.

Of course, to some Israelis and perhaps to some non-Israeli readers of this book, all this is not necessary. Israel, they believe, will be coddled by the world when it pursues the *right* policies. Presumably this means getting rid of the hateful "territories," since, these people believe, all of Israel's ills stem from the fateful days in June 1967, when it took possession of these lands. They forget the terrible campaigns of terror and warfare launched against the Jews and the Jewish state by the Arab world half a century before the Six Day War. They erase from their minds the peril in which Israel found itself on the eve of that war and the fact that it was from these very mountains that the attack was launched. They forget, too, that the demands placed on Israel will not end with the evacuation of the West Bank (as they did not end with the evacuation of the Sinai). After pocketing the territories, the Arabs

could go back to demanding eastern Jerusalem, the "right of return," autonomy (and later independence) for the Arabs of the
Galilee and the Negev, and more—demands that would place Israel in even greater danger, and against which Israel would still
have to struggle on the world scene to defend itself. The need for
waging a worldwide public information campaign is not going to
disappear with changing political circumstances.

In a world that has been conditioned to see Israel as the heavy,
every Israeli retreat from positions under dispute with the Arabs
will naturally be applauded. Israel will be patted on the back and
congratulated as long as it continues to make unilateral concessions. But once an Israeli government decides, as it inevitably
must, to draw a line beyond which it cannot retreat, the international applause will cease—and pressure will begin again. Hence
the test of Israeli diplomacy is not whether it can gain short-term
sympathy by sacrificing Israel's vital interests, but whether it can
protect these interests while securing international understanding
and support. To yield to pressure for the sake of ephemeral international praise is as tempting as it is short-sighted. To be firm
about vital matters and to earn the respect of nations for this
stance is much more difficult, but ultimately more prudent and responsible. The school of thought that holds that Israel's public relations problem would end with the establishment of a Palestinian
state is wrong. In such a case Israel would be faced with an existential threat *and* a public relations nightmare, as Arab irredentism turns its focus on the Arab population within the remainder
of Israel. Resisting an outcome so reminiscent of 1938 Czechoslovakia, or of Lebanon and the Balkans today, is critical for the continued existence of the Jewish state. Israel must direct the current
of public opinion rather than agree to being swept along by it toward the political cataract downstream.

Many of those Israelis who believe that influencing public
opinion is unimportant do so because they have adopted a significant portion of the Arabs' revision of the truth: They have come
to accept that the reason Israel has been attacked by the Arab

world since 1967 is because of its victory in the Six Day War. This is the ultimate in siege mentality: If I am besieged, I must have done something wrong. And if my enemy tells me to lower the drawbridge or else he will continue the siege, I must surely do as he says and relieve myself of the burden of his disapproval. (There are various rationalizations for this course of action: The enemy is not an enemy, the siege is not a siege, the protecting wall does not protect, and so on.) Moreover, argue the rationalizers, the situation on the outside has dramatically changed. Has not the world transformed itself, with old enemies becoming new friends everywhere? Why should Israel be the sad exception to this happy rule? Let us lower our defenses, embrace our adversaries, and live in everlasting tranquillity with one another.

The fact that many parts of the world may indeed be changing for the better does not mean that Israel's immediate vicinity is doing the same. Despite the good news that a regime such as Syria has been brought to the negotiating table as a result of the collapse of its Soviet sponsor, the fact remains that in many ways the neighborhood has been changing for the worse. It has certainly not improved. Has Saddam really changed for the better? Has Qaddafi? Is there an Iraqi Lech Walesa in the wings? An Iranian Václav Havel? The Middle East's numerous predator regimes remain unreformed, Arab arms purchases from West and East continue to escalate, and there is no longer a need to look for Soviet approval before embarking on the next adventure. Worse, Islamic fundamentalism continues to gather momentum. Worse still, the development of nuclear weapons by Arab states and Iran continues at a feverish pace. Yet none of this seems to matter to those who readily dismiss these problems as nitpicking, spoiling the picture they so desperately want to see outside the wall.

Sometimes these same Israelis offer a variation on their recipe for despair. What's the use of resisting Arab demands, they ask, if the United States and the other powers of the world are irredeemably committed to supporting those demands? How will Israel ever secure American favor if it does not comply with American conditions? It does not cross the minds of these advocates of capitulation that the task of Israel's leaders is to try to *convince* the American government that it is in the interest of the United States to follow policies that cohere with Israeli interests, not vice versa. This, after all, is the basic purpose of foreign policy for any country—to pursue one's own interests, not those of others.

Curiously, the advocates of this submissive posture fail to recognize that the United States is a vibrant democracy in which various forces affect the shaping of policy: the administration, the Congress, and especially popular opinion. Each of these audiences is *eager* to hear a variety of viewpoints and is very much open to persuasion. American policy toward Israel is ultimately determined by the synthesis of all these forces, and Israel has every fair opportunity to try to convince each of them of the justice of its case. Even those who have *no* case make this effort, and Israel cannot afford not to. As in the 1930s, when the Jews were paralyzed and did not make the case against the aspects of British policy so inimical to their interests and had forgone the attempts to appeal to a public and a parliament still very much favorable to them, so today there exists in Israel and in parts of the Jewish world elsewhere a faction that abhors the idea of an activist opposition to the policies dangerous to Israel that may come out of Washington, in the belief that such opposition would itself endanger Israel's relationship with the United States.

This is preposterously circular reasoning. It is not to Israel's advantage to sacrifice its most vital interests for a relationship that is meant to *safeguard* those interests in the first place. Furthermore, this thinking does not take into account the appreciation in Washington, as in many other places, of a sound argument cogently made and powerfully backed by resolute will. The weak and timid may do well for a while, but not for very long. In international politics, in fact in domestic politics too, strength attracts and weakness ultimately repels.

This is true not only in the battle for public opinion (in which a powerful presentation attracts support and a weak one does not) but also in enhancing the possibility of obtaining the support of governments even before the factor of public opinion is introduced. There is a tendency to forget that substantial foreign aid to Israel was not forthcoming between 1948 and 1967, when Israel was perceived as being fragile and endangered. The dramatic rise of American support for Israel began only *after* the Six Day War, when Israel resoundingly defeated the Arabs, captured the territories against terrific odds, and proved beyond a doubt that it was the preeminent military power in the Middle East—an assumption that was confirmed in September 1970, when Israeli power was used to prevent a Syrian takeover of Jordan. Those who constantly plead for a return to the eggshell borders of pre-1967 never seem to take these facts into account, ironically claiming that possession of the territories will jeopardize American aid. In fact, nothing is more likely to jeopardize American support for Israel than the return of Israel to a condition of chronic vulnerability. No nation in the world will choose to ally itself with Israel because it has returned to parading the virtue of Jewish powerlessness.

The same applies to economic powerlessness. An economically weak Israel inspires no desire for alliances, either economic or political. But an Israel that shakes off the political and bureaucratic manacles that have shackled its economy is being quickly transformed into a significant economic power that others would seek to join, much as Taiwan and South Korea were able to overcome their political isolation by demonstrating substantial economic strength. Moreover, since American aid to Israel is in any case going to be greatly reduced in the coming years due to domestic forces unrelated to the Middle East, Israel's economic focus should be on attracting American investments rather than American philanthropy. The result would be an increased American interest in Israel, even greater than the one that existed during the years of American-Soviet rivalry. This is the policy that I embarked on, for the first time actually reducing Israel's dependence on American financial support, while rigorously privatizing and liberalizing Israel's economy.

Some believe that the fact that the Soviet Union has collapsed and poses no more threat to American and Western interests in the region has irrevocably altered Israel's importance to the United States and to the West. I do not share this view. The collapse of the Soviets has merely replaced one type of threat with another. The Soviets were very careful to control the aggressive impulses of their clients, and they always knew when to pull back from an engagement that might escalate into a direct confrontation with American military power. Further, they were exceptionally careful not to allow any Soviet nuclear technology to reach the regimes allied with them, perhaps because they were fully acquainted with the terrible dangers that such technology in such hands might pose. But this is precisely the danger that the world faces today. Iraq, Iran, and Syria are now all vying to develop nuclear weapons and the missile systems to deliver them. The demise of the Soviet Union has enabled the unrestrained growth of the militant regimes in the Middle East, with no one in the region to continually check either their ambitions or their obsessive plans for armament—no one, that is, other than Israel, which is both willing and able to act in its own defense and thereby safeguard the broader interest of peace. The international community is not likely to station a permanent countervailing military force in the region anytime soon, even if the Arabs were to allow it, and the need for such a force is not going to disappear. In many ways Israel serves this purpose. Were it not for Israel, Jordan certainly would have been swallowed by its neighbors in short order, and the radical regimes of Syria and Iraq would now have little to obstruct their advance—unless the United States is prepared to reprise its performance in the Gulf War every few years.

A strong Israel introduces a measure of stability into an ultimately unstable region. A weak Israel does not. Consumed at every moment by the need to devote all its resources to protect its own fragile borders, it will not be able to contribute its part to deterring armed attacks from radical states in the region, or to reducing their capacity to launch international terrorism or interdict the sea lanes. These are real dangers that have not passed from the world with the disappearance of Soviet power; in fact, they may actually increase in the coming years. Israel shares a common interest with many other countries to ward off these threats, and such common ground can be the basis of important political alliances that can be formed in the future.

But the Soviet collapse has already brought to the surface other, previously suppressed areas of mutual interest. A host of countries that had broken off relations with Israel after the Six Day War and the Yom Kippur War have reestablished relations with Israel: China, Russia, India, Nigeria, and nearly thirty others in the years between 1988 and 1992. There were several reasons for this change (among them the democratization of Eastern Europe), but a principal force behind the seemingly endless procession of diplomats and heads of state to Jerusalem in recent years has been that many of these governments believe Israel possesses special capacities to influence American policy in what, for a while at least, promises to be a unipolar world. It matters little whether this assessment is correct; it matters a great deal that it is held. For those who argued that Israel was doomed to international isolation unless it gave up the territories, this was particularly sad news. Some exponents of this view wrote lugubrious articles in Israel's leading papers lamenting the narrow views of these foreign governments driven by considerations of power and self-interest alone.

In fact, this is not exactly the case. Unlike public opinion, many governments do tend to be concerned first with power, and only then with virtue or the appearance of virtue. This is exactly why a campaign to influence public opinion, which in turn influences government policy, is often so essential. Nowhere is this more important than in the United States. American support for Israel is not rooted exclusively, or even mainly, in the question of interest. The United States, more than any other country, shapes its policies in accordance with the climate of its public opinion, and the climate that has ruled for a very long time finds in Israel a society that treasures values shared with the United States. Nurturing these feelings, and the values Americans share with the Jewish state, should be a top priority of every Israeli government.

Nevertheless, I firmly believe that at the point of testing, a weak Israel would elicit a great deal of American sympathy but not much else. This is not mere theory. It was tested before the Six Day War in the life-threatening siege imposed by Nasser's coalition, when a highly sympathetic U.S. administration stood on the sidelines. This same lesson was taught once more by the terrible events that unfolded in the ruins of Yugoslavia in 1992. Although the Bosnians may have been able to muster all the sympathy in the world, a ground war intervention against the Serbs was nonetheless an option too costly, too dangerous, and too short on clear political benefits for any nation in the world to do more than sympathize, even as the slaughter raged on for years. If you lack the power to protect yourself, it is unlikely that in the absence of a compelling interest anyone else will be willing to do it for you. Air support, yes. Ground war action with its attendant casualties is much slower to come, if at all.

What emerges is this: Power is the cornerstone of the effort to attract and maintain alliances. Yet without a campaign to secure international sympathy, even the most formidable accumulation of military or economic power is simply insufficient to assure enduring support. Equally, the accumulation of international sympathy is no substitute for self-defense. The Jewish people must forcefully resist the jejune notion of the Israeli left that an Israel stripped of its physical defenses will be so morally strong as to inspire everready and everlasting protection from the mighty. Weakness buys you nothing. It is not a prescription for securing the support of governments, or for their acting on your behalf. On the contrary, it is the one sure way of securing their indifference.

But Israel must resist the equally immature conception of the Israeli right that nothing we will do or say will make a difference to an implacably hostile world. Actions invariably speak louder than words, assert the self-declared Spartan "realists" of the right, so let us do without the words. They are wrong. Support among the nations, especially in the great democracies of the West, can be bolstered, cultivated, and protected by an incessant campaign to win over the public. If the Jewish people had understood this principle during the couse of this century, it could have activated others to assist it in times of peril rather than having the very opposite happen. And had Israel understood this principle, it certainly would not have allowed Arab propaganda, including all the gross distortions detailed in this book, to capture the high ground of international opinion.

It may puzzle some that after all the depredations Jews suffered in the last one hundred years, all this is not self-evident. Yet there are many people who might glimpse pieces of a puzzle and reach totally different conclusions about the whole. For example, there are some in Israel who, sensing that military power is not enough, proceed to say that it is therefore unnecessary. Others question the wisdom of Herzl's vision by arguing that attacks against Jews still persist in the form of attacks against the Jewish state, just as they did when the Jews lived as a collection of dispersed communities. They miss the point. A Jewish state was not expected to eliminate all attacks on the Jewish people, merely to enable an effective *defense* against such attacks. Herzl viewed the establishment of a Jewish state as the prerequisite instrument by which the Jews could resurrect their capacity to resist the ill fortunes heaped on them by a history of dispersion and the baser instincts of mankind.

And indeed, what a difference the Jewish state has made for Jewish fortunes. It has rescued beleaguered Jewish communities, bringing them, as from Yemen and Ethiopia, on the wings of eagles to the soil of their ancient homeland. It beckons as a haven and resting place for millions of Jews in Russia, the Ukraine, and elsewhere, who look over their shoulders at the spectre of anti-Semitism. What these Jews have is what the Jews of Europe half a century ago did not: the knowledge that they are not alone, that they have a place to go, that there is a country that not only wants them but will intercede for their safety and their well-being.

In another powerful scene in *Shoah*, a minor official of the Polish government-in-exile, a non-Jew, describes how during the Nazi annihilation of Polish Jewry, he was approached by a delegation of

Jews from Warsaw begging for Allied assistance—for military action, for arms for the Jewish fighters in the ghetto, at least for public pronouncements of support. No one was listening, and so they had to come to him, they said. "We understand we have no country of our own, we have no government, we have no voice in the Allied councils. So we have to [seek help from] . . . little people like you . . . Will you approach . . . the Allied leaders?" But there was of course little he could actually do.[8]

No more succinct a statement could be made about the significance of the rise of Israel. For if there had been an Israel earlier in this century, there surely would have been no Holocaust. There would have been a country willing to take the Jewish refugees when America, Britain, and the other nations refused. There would have been a country to press for their departure. And there would have been an army ready to fight for them. If the past was lacking in this regard, the future is not: The Jews are no longer helpless, no longer lacking the capacities to assert their case and to fight for it. It is an uncontestable fact that the establishment of the Jewish state has retrieved for the Jews the ability to again seize their destiny, to again control their fate. And if that ability is still in the making, if the Jewish people needs time to shed its apolitical habits of thought and behavior acquired in years of exile, this process will have to be substantially accelerated. The Jewish state is at the center of an international maelstrom, and it needs much political ingenuity to maneuver on the international scene. Somehow Israel will have to compress the long decades required to produce the political statesmanship it so badly needs. It cannot wait to become politically mature. It must skip its adolescence and become politically adult. The Jewish people underwent this kind of rapid transformation in the case of building military strength, and it will now have to do the same in re-creating its political abilities.

But this is not a change that Jews alone find difficult to assimilate. Israel encounters difficulties in explaining its position that no other nation encounters. No other country faces both constant threats to its existence *and* constant criticism for acting against such threats. I do not believe that the international obtuseness in grasping Israel's predicament is grounded solely in the successes of Arab propaganda and Israel's ineffectual response to it. This explanation may remove the topsoil of attitudes toward the Jewish state, but it does not get to the psychological bedrock underneath. That rock, I believe, consists of a basic difficulty in accepting the revolutionary change in the status of the Jews.

The entire world is witnessing the historical transformation of the Jewish people from a condition of powerlessness to power, from a condition of being unable to meet the contingencies of a violent world to one in which the Jewish people is strong enough to pilot its own destiny. For a world accustomed to seeing the Jew as the perennial victim, suffering endless atrocities at the hands of a succession of persecutors, this is a jarring shift in reality that has barely begun to make sense. This is certainly true for the opponents of the Jews, who believe that Jewish power is nothing more than a passing aberration, and that the Jewish state will fall sooner or later to a combination of political and military forces.

But the inability to adjust to the reality of Jewish power is equally true of those who are sympathetic to Jewish suffering and wish to see it end. Many philo-Semites have come to appreciate the Jews as a persecuted people and therefore as a people that cannot be morally in the wrong. For one who has no power over anyone else, or even over himself, cannot be blamed for the harm that befalls others. For such sympathizers, it is no easy thing to watch the Jews become a people wielding power. Power inevitably means moral responsibility, and sometimes it means making mistakes as well. Once the Jews have an army and a state, it is all too easy to blame them for their actions—and to look back wistfully upon the perfect morality of the defenseless Jew.

This is an important part of the secret of the success of Arab propaganda: It appeals to a world that has not yet accustomed itself to the sight of Jewish strength, military and political. It implicitly urges philo-Semites to yearn for a "purer" age when Jews were beyond reproach because they were beyond succor. This is the root of the infamous, twisted standard by which the Arabs remain completely blameless for expelling hundreds of thousands of people—as Saudi Arabia did to its Yemenis in 1990 and Kuwait did to its Palestinians in 1991—while Israel is excoriated for deporting a cadre of terrorists; or by which Israel is condemned for maintaining the presence of a few hundred soldiers in a six-mile sliver of Lebanon while Syria annexes almost the entire rest of the same country; or by which Saudi and Jordanian apartheid laws forbidding Jewish residence went unnoticed for many years, while Israel, whose Arab citizens are freer than those of Arab states, is still accused of racism for quelling riots. All of this and much worse emanates not from Israel's opponents but from many of its sincerest sympathizers—who genuinely believe in the idea of the Jewish state but cannot bring themselves to accept the reality accompanying that idea: that such a state, in order to actually survive in practice, may have to resort to buffer strips, deportation of subversives, or riot control. It appears that attitudes evolved over centuries are difficult to change for non-Jews, too.

Yet there is, with all this, a profound desire in modern society, influenced as it is by biblical values, to see the Jewish people's odyssey through. I encountered that attitude on a drizzly morning in 1986, when I visited the Arch of Titus in Rome, which the Romans erected to mark their victory over the Jews in 70 C.E. I stood underneath the arch peering at the decaying Forum below. A group of Japanese tourists was vacating the space to a group of Scandinavians. The tour guides pointed dripping umbrellas at the engraving of the sacred Jewish candelabrum being taken into captivity on the shoulders of the triumphant Romans, looking as freshly cut in the stone as it had 1,900 years earlier, when the Romans had celebrated the razing of the Jewish Temple in Jerusalem.

A Jew's thoughts, or those of some Jews anyway, tend to turn introspective at moments like this. The destruction of the Temple was one of the two greatest catastrophes of a Jewish history teeming with catastrophes. But what struck me most that morning was the easy comprehension that I recognized on those Japanese and

Scandinavian faces. They nodded their heads, they pointed, and said the word *Israel* several times. Perhaps they sensed what many who have visited this arch sensed: that the candelabrum etched on its wall was a potent symbol of overturning the laws of history.

Writing in the early eighteenth century, the Italian philosopher Giovanni Battista Vico put forth what appeared to be an iron-clad historical sequence: Nations go through a predictable cycle of birth, adolescence, maturity, and death. Students of history from Hegel to Arnold Toynbee adopted this idea, pointing to the Assyrians, Babylonians, Persians, Egyptians, Greeks, Romans, and even their later counterparts such as the Incas and the Aztecs—civilizations that flowered, shriveled, then died. If you wait long enough, the historians assure us, the blows of time will eventually do their work on everyone. But the Jews were a problem: They received more blows than any other nation, yet they refused to die. Or more accurately, as one of Hegel's Jewish disciples, Rabbi Nachman Krochmal, explained, they suffered a decline as did all other nations, but each time they avoided death with a new birth, beginning the cycle anew. They refused to give up the dream of their salvation and the attainment of justice. Perhaps this is why when Frederick the Great asked his physician to adduce proof of God's existence, he was satisfied with the reply: "The proof that God exists is that the Jews exist."

This is the great mystery that made the story of the Jews so captivating to Rousseau and Byron, Balfour and Wilson, and to countless millions the world over. Speaking for these, Mark Twain wondered:

> The Jews constitute but one percent of the human race. It suggests a nebulous dim puff of stardust lost in the blaze of the Milky Way. Properly the Jew ought hardly to be heard of; but he is heard of, has always been heard of. He is as prominent on the planet as any other people. . . . He has made a marvelous fight in this world, in all the ages; and has done it with his hands tied behind him. . . . The Egyptian, the Babylonian, and the Persian rose, filled the planet with sound and splendor, then faded to dream-stuff and passed away; the Greek and the Roman fol-

lowed, and made a vast noise, and they are gone; other peoples have sprung up and held their torch high for a time, but it burned out, and they sit in twilight now, or have vanished. The Jew saw them all, beat them all, and is now what he always was . . . All things are mortal but the Jew; all other forces pass, but he remains. What is the secret of his immortality?[9]

This fascination has only grown since the rebirth of Israel. One could point to the scattered fragments of other ancient peoples in other parts of the world, the sparks of great firmaments dispersed to other lands. Only in the case of the Jews did these embers not die out when the home fire had ceased to burn. And only in the case of Israel did these sparks come together to rekindle a new flame.

But now the Jews have entered a new phase in their history. Since the rise of Israel, the essence of their aspirations has changed. If the central aim of the Jewish people during its exile was to retrieve what had been lost, the purpose now is to secure what has been retrieved. It is a task that has barely begun, and its outcome is of profound import not only for the fate of the Jews but for all mankind. In the hearts of countless people around the world burns the hope that the Jews will indeed be able to overcome the insurmountable obstacles that are strewn along their journey's path, ford the stormy river between annihilation and salvation, and build anew their home of promise. If, echoing the words of the prophet Amos, the fallen tent of David has indeed risen again, its resurrection is proof that there is hope for every people and every nation under the sun. The rebirth of Israel is thus one of humanity's great parables. It is the story not only of the Jews, but of a human spirit that refuses again and again to succumb to history's horrors. It is the incomparable quest of a people seeking, at the end of an unending march, to assume its rightful place among the nations.

CHRONOLOGY:

Zionism and the Rise of Israel

1881	Widespread pogroms in Russia reinforce Jewish national awakening.
1882	Publication of Leo Pinsker's *Auto-Emancipation*, calling for the establishment of a Jewish state.
1882	Beginning of the first wave of Zionist immigration to Palestine.
1894	Theodor Herzl attends the trial of Alfred Dreyfus in Paris and witnesses outpouring of French anti Semitism.
1896	Herzl's *The Jewish State* published.
1897	Herzl convenes First Zionist Congress in Basel.
1904	Herzl dies.
1915	Joseph Trumpeldor founds Zion Mule Corps of British army in World War I, the first Jewish fighting unit in centuries.
1917	Balfour Declaration commits Britain to supporting a Jewish National Home in Palestine.
1917	British forces under General Sir Edmund Allenby liberate Palestine from the Turks. Jewish Legion

participates in freeing Galilee, Samaria, and
Transjordan.

1919   Versailles Peace Conference. Wilson argues for self-
determination of peoples. Jewish-Arab accord: Jews
claim Jewish home in Palestine; Arabs claim Arab state
from Iraq to Yemen (excluding Palestine).

1920   San Remo Conference grants Britain Mandate over
Palestine with the aim of encouraging immigration and
settlement of Jews and establishment of a Jewish
National Home.

1920   British officials instigate Arab riots in Palestine. Rioters
demand end to Jewish immigration and incorporation
of Palestine into Syria.

1920   Vladimir Jabotinsky founds Hagana, the Jewish self-
defense force, in Palestine.

1921   British decide to install Abdullah in Transjordan
(eastern Palestine).

1921   Arab riots in Palestine.

1922   League of Nations officially ratifies British Mandate over
Palestine with aim of building Jewish National Home.

1922   British cut away Transjordan from Palestine.

1929   Arab riots in Palestine. Massacre of Jews in Hebron and
Safed. Arabs demand end to Jewish immigration.

1930   British White Paper limits Jewish immigration to
Palestine.

1933   Hitler comes to power in Germany.

1936–39 Campaign of Arab violence in Palestine. Arab rioters
murder five hundred Jews and thousands of Arabs,
demanding an end to Jewish immigration.

1937   British Peel Commission asserts that Jewish National
Home cannot be built in Palestine. Recommends
repartition of Palestine into tiny Jewish state (5 percent
of total area) and Arab state in remainder. Peel plan is
rejected by both Arabs and Jews.

1938   Munich Conference and betrayal of the Czechs. Hitler is given the Sudetenland.

1939   Chamberlain White Paper announces end to Jewish National Home and promises control of immigration into Palestine to the Arabs within five years. British blockade Palestine against "illegal" Jewish immigration.

1941   Mufti relocates to Berlin. Meets with Hitler, announces intention of creating "fascist" Arab state, and agitates for the destruction of world Jewry.

1942   Nazi conference at Wannsee decides on destruction of all Jews in Europe.

1945   World War II ends. Liberation of the death camps where six million Jews died. Arabs demand end to Jewish immigration to Palestine.

1945   "Illegal" smuggling of Holocaust survivors into Palestine by Jews. Increase of Jewish underground actions against British blockade and British administration in Palestine.

1947   Britain announces withdrawal from Palestine. United Nations announces partition into Jewish and Arab states. Jews accept partition; Arabs reject it.

1948   Invasion of Arab forces aimed at preventing the establishment of the Jewish state.

1948   Declaration of independence of the State of Israel. David Ben-Gurion first prime minister.

1948–49 War of Independence. Arab armies from five countries invade Israel. Jordanian forces occupy Judea, Samaria, and eastern half of Jerusalem, including Old City and Temple Mount, destroying all Jewish settlements. Egypt occupies Gaza. War of Independence ends in Jewish victory.

1948–52 800,000 Jews expelled from Arab countries. Most flee to Israel and are absorbed. 650,000 Arabs flee from Israel to Arab states and are confined to refugee camps.

1951   Yasser Arafat of the Husseini clan begins organizing
Palestinian radicals in Cairo and recruits Abu Iyad, Abu
Jihad, and other future leaders of the PLO.

1952–56 Terrorist raids into Israel from adjoining Arab states,
including Egyptian-sponsored fedayeen raids from
Gaza. Israeli army adopts policy of reprisals.

1956   Sinai Campaign, Oct. 29–Nov. 5. Gamal Abdel Nasser
nationalizes Suez Canal and blocks Israeli shipping.
Israel captures Sinai from Egypt. Terrorist bases in Gaza
dismantled.

1956   U.S.-Soviet pressure forces Israeli withdrawal from
Sinai without peace treaty. Dwight Eisenhower
guarantees protection of Israeli shipping.

1964   PLO is founded in Cairo with aim of "liberating"
Palestine. PLO Charter calling for Israel's destruction
adopted. Campaign of terror attacks across Israel's
borders escalates.

1967   Egypt floods Sinai with troops and blockades Israeli
shipping in the Red Sea. American guarantee to protect
Israel fails to take effect.

1967   Six Day War, June 5–10. Israel defeats combined forces
of Egypt, Syria, Iraq, and Jordan. Captures Sinai and
Gaza, Judea and Samaria, and the Golan Heights.
Jerusalem is reunited. Jewish settlements in eastern
Jerusalem, Judea, and Samaria reestablished.

1969–70 War of attrition. Egypt and Syria launch campaign of
continuous attacks along Suez Canal and Golan
Heights. PLO steps up terror attacks across Jordan
River. Heavy Israeli retaliation brings war to an end.

1970   Nasser dies and is succeeded by Anwar Sadat.

1970   PLO attempts to take over Jordan. King Hussein
massacres Palestinian Arabs and expels PLO in "Black
September."

1971–75 PLO relocates to Lebanon and establishes de facto state
on its territory, which becomes base for all

international terror organizations. PLO campaign of massacres in northern Israel.

1972   Munich massacre of Israeli Olympic athletes earns PLO international notoriety.

1973   Yom Kippur War, Oct. 5–24. Egypt and Syria launch surprise attack against Israel. Despite heavy casualties, Israeli army reverses tide and advances toward Cairo and Damascus. Israel negotiates disengagement agreements with Egypt and Syria, setting cease-fire lines in the Sinai and the Golan.

1973   Arab oil embargo is imposed. International oil prices rise dramatically.

1975   United Nations passes resolution defaming Zionism as racism.

1975   PLO control of Lebanon is challenged, and full-scale civil war erupts between Moslems and Christians.

1976   Syria invades Lebanon and sets up permanent control over more than half of that country.

1976   Israeli raid on Entebbe airport in Uganda, July 4, frees 103 hostages held by PLO.

1977   Likud government elected in Israel. Menachem Begin is first Likud prime minister.

1977   President Anwar Sadat of Egypt responds to Begin's invitation and visits Israel.

1978–79 First wave of Jewish emigration from Soviet Union as result of Soviet-American détente reaches peak. All told, 200,000 Soviet Jewish immigrants arrive in Israel.

1979   Egypt and Israel sign Camp David Accords. Israel agrees to return Sinai.

1981   Sadat is assassinated.

1982   Israeli ambassador is shot in London by PLO. Israel invades Lebanon with aim of dismantling terror bases. PLO is expelled from Lebanon and forced to relocate in Tunis.

1984   U.S. and Israel sign strategic cooperation agreement formalizing alliance.

1985   Israel withdraws from Lebanon and establishes security zone north of Israeli-Lebanese border.

1986   U.S. takes lead in war against terror after PLO hijacks *Achille Lauro* cruise ship. Midair interception of terrorists by U.S. fighter planes.

1987   PLO banned in U.S. by law for terrorist activities.

1989–91 Collapse of Soviet Union. Second wave of Soviet immigration to Israel brings 400,000 in two years.

1990   Israeli airlift brings most of Ethiopian Jewry to Israel.

1990   Saddam Hussein of Iraq invades Kuwait.

1991   Madrid Peace Conference among Israel, Syria, Lebanon, and a Jordanian-Palestinian delegation. Bilateral and regional peace negotiations launched.

1991   United Nations repeals Zionism-racism resolution.

1992   Labor returns to power in Israel. Yizhak Rabin becomes prime minister.

1993   Oslo Accords between Israel and the PLO signed. Israel agrees to cede most of the Gaza district and parts of the West Bank to the control of a Palestinian Authority, headed by Yasser Arafat, in exchange for recognition of Israel and an end to Palestinian terrorism.

1995   Peace treaty between Israel and Jordan is signed.

1994–95 Wave of terrorist bombings emanating from Palestinian areas ravages Israel's cities and claims over 200 lives.

1996   Yitzhak Rabin assassinated. Shimon Peres becomes prime minister.

1996   Benjamin Netanyahu elected in Israel's first direct elections for prime minister.

1997   Hebron Accords signed between Israel and the Palestinian Authority.

1998   Wye River Accords signed between Israel and the Palestinian Authority.

APPENDIX A

The Arab-Jewish Agreement at Versailles

AGREEMENT BETWEEN EMIR FEISAL AND
DR. CHAIM WEIZMANN, JANUARY 3, 1919

His Royal Highness the Emir Feisal, representing and acting on behalf of the Arab Kingdom of Hedjaz, and Dr. Chaim Weizmann, representing and acting on behalf of the Zionist Organisation, mindful of the racial kinship and ancient bonds existing between the Arabs and the Jewish people, and realising that the surest means of working out the consummation of their national aspirations is through the closest possible collaboration in the development of the Arab State and Palestine, and being desirous further of confirming the good understanding which exists between them, have agreed upon the following Articles:

ARTICLE I

The Arab State and Palestine in all their relations and undertakings shall be controlled by the most cordial goodwill and understanding, and to this end Arab and Jewish duly accredited agents shall be established and maintained in the respective territories.

ARTICLE II

Immediately following the completion of the deliberations of the Peace Conference, the definite boundaries between the Arab State and Palestine shall be determined by a Commission to be agreed upon by the parties hereto.

ARTICLE III

In the establishment of the Constitution and Administration of Palestine all such measures shall be adopted as will afford the fullest guarantees for carrying into effect the British Government's Declaration of the 2d of November, 1917.

ARTICLE IV

All necessary measures shall be taken to encourage and stimulate immigration of Jews into Palestine on a large scale, and as quickly as possible to settle Jewish immigrants upon the land through closer settlement, and intensive cultivation of the soil. In taking such measures the Arab peasant and tenant farmers shall be protected in their rights, and shall be assisted in forwarding their economic development.

ARTICLE V

No recognition nor law shall be made prohibiting or interfering in any way with the free exercise of religion; and further the free exercise and enjoyment of religious profession and worship without discrimination or preference shall forever be allowed. No religious test shall ever be required for the exercise of civil or political rights.

ARTICLE VI

The Mohammedan Holy Places shall be under Mohammedan control.

ARTICLE VII

The Zionist Organisation proposes to send to Palestine a Commission of experts to make a survey of the economic possibilities of the country, and to report upon the best means for its development. The Zionist Organisation will place the aforementioned Commission at the disposal of the Arab State for the purpose of a survey of the economic possibilities of the Arab State and to report upon the best means for its development. The Zionist Organisation will use its best efforts to assist the Arab State in providing the means for developing the natural resources and economic possibilities thereof.

ARTICLE VIII

The parties hereto agree to act in complete accord and harmony on all matters embraced herein before the Peace Congress.

ARTICLE IX

Any matters of dispute which may arise between the contracting parties shall be referred to the British Government for arbitration.

Given under our hand at London, England, the third day of January, one thousand nine hundred and nineteen.

Chaim Weizmann.

Feisal ibn-Hussein.

RESERVATION BY THE EMIR FEISAL

If the Arabs are established as I have asked in my manifesto of January 4th addressed to the British Secretary of State for Foreign Affairs, I will carry out what is written in this agreement. If changes are made, I cannot be answerable for failing to carry out this agreement.

Feisal ibn-Hussein.

APPENDIX B
Feisal-Frankfurter Correspondence

DELEGATION HEDJAZIENNE,
PARIS, MARCH 3, 1919.

DEAR MR. FRANKFURTER:

I want to take this opportunity of my first contact with American Zionists to tell you what I have often been able to say to Dr. Weizmann in Arabia and Europe.

We feel that the Arabs and Jews are cousins in race, having suffered similar oppressions at the hands of powers stronger than themselves, and by a happy coincidence have been able to take the first step towards the attainment of their national ideals together.

We Arabs, especially the educated among us, look with the deepest sympathy on the Zionist movement. Our deputation here in Paris is fully acquainted with the proposals submitted yesterday by the Zionist Organization to the Peace Conference, and we regard them as moderate and proper. We will do our best, in so far as we are concerned, to help them through: we will wish the Jews a most hearty welcome home.

With the chiefs of your movement, especially with Dr. Weizmann, we have had and continue to have the closest relations. He has been a great helper of our cause, and I hope the Arabs may soon be in a position to make the Jews some return for their kindness. We are working together for a reformed and revived Near East, and our two movements complete one another. The Jewish movement is national and not imperialist. Our movement is national and not imperialist, and there is room in Syria for us both. Indeed I think that neither can be a real success without the other.

People less informed and less responsible than our leaders and yours, ignoring the need for cooperation of the Arabs and Zionists have been trying to exploit the local difficulties that must necessarily arise in Palestine in the early stages of our movements. Some of them have, I am afraid, misrepresented your aims to the Arab peasantry, and our aims to the Jewish peasantry, with the result that interested parties have been able to make capital out of what they call our differences.

I wish to give you my firm conviction that these differences are not on questions of principle, but on matters of detail such as must inevitably occur in every contact of neighbouring peoples, and as are easily adjusted by mutual good will. Indeed nearly all of them will disappear with fuller knowledge.

I look forward, and my people with me look forward, to a future in which we will help you and you will help us, so that the countries in which we are mutually interested may once again take their places in the community of civilised peoples of the world.

Believe me,

Yours sincerely,

(Sgd.) Feisal.
5TH MARCH, 1919.

APPENDIX C
The League of Nations Mandate
July 24, 1922

MANDATE FOR PALESTINE

The Council of the League of Nations:

Whereas the Principal Allied Powers have agreed, for the purpose of giving effect to the provisions of Article 22 of the Covenant of the League of Nations, to entrust to a Mandatory selected by the said Powers the administration of the territory of Palestine, which formerly belonged to the Turkish Empire, within such boundaries as may be fixed by them; and

Whereas the Principal Allied Powers have also agreed that the Mandatory should be responsible for putting into effect the declaration originally made on November 2nd, 1917, by the Government of his Britannic Majesty, and adopted by the said Powers, in favour of the establishment in Palestine of a national home for the Jewish people, it being clearly understood that nothing should be done which might prejudice the civil and religious rights of existing non-Jewish communities in Palestine, or the rights and political status enjoyed by Jews in any other country; and

Whereas recognition has thereby been given to the historical connection of the Jewish people with Palestine and to the grounds for reconstituting their national home in that country; and

Whereas the Principal Allied Powers have selected His Britannic Majesty as the Mandatory for Palestine; and

Whereas the mandate in respect of Palestine has been formulated in the following terms and submitted to the Council of the League for approval; and

Whereas His Britannic Majesty has accepted the mandate in respect of Palestine and undertaken to exercise it on behalf of the League of Nations in conformity with the following provisions; and

Whereas by the afore-mentioned Article 22 (paragraph 8), it is provided that the degree of authority, control or administration to be exercised by the Mandatory, not having been previously agreed upon by the Members of the League, shall be explicitly defined by the Council of the League of Nations;

Confirming the said mandate, defines its terms as follows:

ARTICLE 1.
The Mandatory shall have full powers of legislation and of administration, save as they may be limited by the terms of this mandate.

ARTICLE 2.
The Mandatory shall be responsible for placing the country under such political, administrative and economic conditions as will secure the establishment of the Jewish national home, as laid down in the preamble, and the development of self-governing institutions, and also for safeguarding the civil and religious rights of all the inhabitants of Palestine, irrespective of race and religion.

ARTICLE 3.
The Mandatory shall, so far as circumstances permit, encourage local autonomy.

ARTICLE 4.
An appropriate Jewish agency shall be recognised as a public body for the purpose of advising and co-operating with the Administration of Palestine in such economic, social and other matters as may affect the establishment of the Jewish national home and the interests of the Jewish population in Palestine, and, subject always to the control of the Administration, to assist and take part in the development of the country.

The Zionist organisation, so long as its organisation and constitution are in the opinion of the Mandatory appropriate, shall be recognised as such agency. It shall take steps in consultation with His Britannic

Majesty's Government to secure the co-operation of all Jews who are willing to assist in the establishment of the Jewish national home.

ARTICLE 5.

The Mandatory shall be responsible for seeing that no Palestine territory shall be ceded or leased to, or in any way placed under the control of, the Government of any foreign Power.

ARTICLE 6.

The Administration of Palestine, while ensuring that the rights and position of other sections of the population are not prejudiced, shall facilitate Jewish immigration under suitable conditions and shall encourage, in co-operation with the Jewish agency referred to in Article 4, close settlement by Jews on the land, including State lands and waste lands not required for public purposes.

ARTICLE 7.

The Administration of Palestine shall be responsible for enacting a nationality law. There shall be included in this law provisions framed so as to facilitate the acquisition of Palestinian citizenship by Jews who take up their permanent residence in Palestine.

ARTICLE 8.

The privileges and immunities of foreigners, including the benefits of consular jurisdiction and protection as formerly enjoyed by Capitulation or usage in the Ottoman Empire, shall not be applicable in Palestine.

Unless the Powers whose nationals enjoyed the afore-mentioned privileges and immunities on August 1st, 1914, shall have previously renounced the right to their re-establishment, or shall have agreed to their non-application for a specified period, these privileges and immunities shall, at the expiration of the mandate, be immediately re-established in their entirety or with such modifications as may have been agreed upon between the Powers concerned.

ARTICLE 9.

The Mandatory shall be responsible for seeing that the judicial system established in Palestine shall assure to foreigners, as well as to natives, a complete guarantee of their rights.

Respect for the personal status of the various people and communities and for their religious interests shall be fully guaranteed. In particular, the control and administration of Wakfs shall be exercised in accordance with religious law and the dispositions of the founders.

ARTICLE 10.

Pending the making of special extradition agreements relating to Palestine, the extradition treaties in force between the Mandatory and other foreign Powers shall apply to Palestine.

ARTICLE 11.

The Administration of Palestine shall take all necessary measures to safeguard the interests of the community in connection with the development of the country, and, subject to any international obligations accepted by the Mandatory, shall have full power to provide for public ownership or control of any of the natural resources of the country or of the public works, services and utilities established or to be established therein. It shall introduce a land system appropriate to the needs of the country, having regard, among other things, to the desirability of promoting the close settlement and intensive cultivation of the land.

The Administration may arrange with the Jewish agency mentioned in Article 4 to construct or operate, upon fair and equitable terms, any public works, services and utilities, and to develop any of the natural resources of the country, in so far as these matters are not directly undertaken by the Administration. Any such arrangements shall provide that no profits distributed by such agency, directly or indirectly, shall exceed a reasonable rate of interest on the capital, and any further profits shall be utilised by it for the benefit of the country in a manner approved by the Administration.

ARTICLE 12.

The Mandatory shall be entrusted with the control of the foreign relations of Palestine and the right to issue exequaturs to consuls appointed by foreign Powers. He shall also be entitled to afford diplomatic and consular protection to citizens of Palestine when outside its territorial limits.

ARTICLE 13.

All responsibility in connection with the Holy Places and religious buildings or sites in Palestine, including that of preserving existing rights and of securing free access to the Holy Places, religious buildings and sites and the free exercise of worship, while ensuring the requirements of public order and decorum, is assumed by the Mandatory, who shall be responsible solely to the League of Nations in all matters connected herewith, provided that nothing in this article shall prevent the Mandatory from entering into such arrangements as he may deem reasonable with the Administration for the purpose of carrying the provisions of this article into effect; and provided also that nothing in this mandate shall be construed as conferring upon the Mandatory authority to interfere with the fabric or the management of purely Moslem sacred shrines, the immunities of which are guaranteed.

ARTICLE 14.

A special Commission shall be appointed by the Mandatory to study, define and determine the rights and claims in connection with the Holy Places and the rights and claims relating to the different religious communities in Palestine. The method of nomination, the composition and the functions of this Commission shall be submitted to the Council of the League for its approval, and the Commission shall not be appointed or enter upon its functions without the approval of the Council.

ARTICLE 15.

The Mandatory shall see that complete freedom of conscience and the free exercise of all forms of worship, subject only to the maintenance of public order and morals, are ensured to all. No discrimination of any kind shall be made between the inhabitants of Palestine on the ground of race, religion or language. No person shall be excluded from Palestine on the sole ground of his religious belief.

The right of each community to maintain its own schools for the education of its own members in its own language, while conforming to such educational requirements of a general nature as the Administration may impose, shall not be denied or impaired.

ARTICLE 16.

The Mandatory shall be responsible for exercising such supervision over religious or eleemosynary bodies of all faiths in Palestine as may be required for the maintenance of public order and good government. Subject to such supervision, no measures shall be taken in Palestine to obstruct or interfere with the enterprise of such bodies or to discriminate against any representative or member of them on the ground of his religion or nationality.

ARTICLE 17.

The Administration of Palestine may organise on a voluntary basis the forces necessary for the preservation of peace and order, and also for the defence of the country, subject, however, to the supervision of the Mandatory, but shall not use them for purposes other than those above specified save with the consent of the Mandatory. Except for such purposes, no military, naval or air forces shall be raised or maintained by the Administration of Palestine.

Nothing in this article shall preclude the Administration of Palestine from contributing to the cost of the maintenance of the forces of the Mandatory in Palestine.

The Mandatory shall be entitled at all times to use the roads, railways and ports of Palestine for the movement of armed forces and the carriage of fuel and supplies.

ARTICLE 18.

The Mandatory shall see that there is no discrimination in Palestine against the nationals of any State Member of the League of Nations (including companies incorporated under its laws) as compared with those of the Mandatory or of any foreign State in matters concerning taxation, commerce or navigation, the exercise of industries or professions, or in the treatment of merchant vessels or civil aircraft. Similarly, there shall be no discrimination in Palestine against goods originating in or destined for any of the said States, and there shall be freedom of transit under equitable conditions across the mandated area.

Subject as aforesaid and to the other provisions of this mandate, the Administration of Palestine may, on the advice of the Mandatory, impose such taxes and customs duties as it may consider necessary, and take such steps as it may think best to promote the development of the natural resources of the country and to safeguard the interests of the population. It may also, on the advice of the Mandatory, conclude a special customs agreement with any State the territory of which in 1914 was wholly included in Asiatic Turkey or Arabia.

ARTICLE 19.

The Mandatory shall adhere on behalf of the Administration of Palestine to any general international conventions already existing, or which may be concluded hereafter with the approval of the League of Nations, respecting the slave traffic, the traffic in arms and ammunition, or the traffic in drugs, or relating to commercial equality, freedom of transit and navigation, aerial navigation and postal, telegraphic and wireless communication or literary, artistic or industrial property.

ARTICLE 20.

The Mandatory shall co-operate on behalf of the Administration of Palestine, so far as religious, social and other conditions may permit, in the execution of any common policy adopted by the League of Nations for preventing and combating disease, including diseases of plants and animals.

ARTICLE 21.

The Mandatory shall secure the enactment within twelve months from this date, and shall ensure the execution of a Law of Antiquities based on the following rules. This law shall ensure equality of treatment in the matter of excavations and archaeological research to the nationals of all States Members of the League of Nations; (1) "Antiquity" means any construction or any product of human activity earlier than the year 1700; (2) The law for the protection of antiquities shall proceed by encouragement rather than by threat. Any person who, having discovered an antiquity without being furnished with the authorisation referred to in paragraph 5, reports the same to an official of the competent Department, shall be rewarded according to the value of the discovery; (3) No antiquity may be disposed of except to the competent Department, unless this Department renounces the acquisition of any such antiquity. No antiquity may leave the country without an export licence from the said Department; (4) Any person who maliciously or negligently destroys or damages an antiquity shall be liable to a penalty to be fixed; (5) No clearing of ground or digging with the object of finding antiquities shall be permitted, under penalty of fine, except to persons authorised by the competent Department; (6) Equitable terms shall be fixed for expropriation, temporary or permanent, of lands which might be of historical or archaeological interest; (7) Authorisation to excavate shall only be granted to persons who show sufficient guarantees of archaeological experience. The Administration of Palestine shall not, in granting these authorisations, act in such a way as to exclude scholars of any nation without good grounds; (8) The proceeds of excavations may be divided between the excavator and the competent Department in a proportion fixed by that Department. If division seems impossible for scientific reasons, the excavator shall receive a fair indemnity in lieu of a part of the find.

ARTICLE 22.

English, Arabic and Hebrew shall be the official languages of Palestine. Any statement or inscription in Arabic on stamps or money in Palestine shall be repeated in Hebrew and any statement or inscription in Hebrew shall be repeated in Arabic.

ARTICLE 23.

The Administration of Palestine shall recognise the holy days of the respective communities in Palestine as legal days of rest for the members of such communities.

ARTICLE 24.

The Mandatory shall make to the Council of the League of Nations an annual report to the satisfaction of the Council as to the measures taken during the year to carry out the provisions of the mandate. Copies of all laws and regulations promulgated or issued during the year shall be communicated with the report.

ARTICLE 25.

In the territories lying between the Jordan and the eastern boundary of Palestine as ultimately determined, the Mandatory shall be entitled, with the consent of the Council of the League of Nations, to postpone or withhold application of such provisions of this mandate as he may consider inapplicable to the existing local conditions, and to make such provision for the administration of the territories as he may consider suitable to those conditions, provided that no action shall be taken which is inconsistent with the provisions of Articles 15, 16, and 18.

ARTICLE 26.

The Mandatory agrees that, if any dispute whatever should arise between the Mandatory and another Member of the League of Nations relating to the interpretation or the application of the provisions of the mandate, such dispute, if it cannot be settled by negotiation, shall be submitted to the Permanent Court of International Justice provided for by Article 14 of the Covenant of the League of Nations.

ARTICLE 27.

The consent of the Council of the League of Nations is required for any modification of the terms of this mandate.

ARTICLE 28.

In the event of the termination of the mandate hereby conferred upon the Mandatory, the Council of the League of Nations shall make such arrangements as may be deemed necessary for safeguarding in perpetuity, under guarantee of the League, the rights secured by Articles 13 and 14, and shall use its influence for securing, under the guarantee of the League, that the Government of Palestine will fully honour the financial obligations legitimately incurred by the Administration of Palestine during the period of the mandate, including the rights of public servants to pensions or gratuities.

The present instrument shall be deposited in original in the archives of the League of Nations and certified copies shall be forwarded by the Secretary-General of the League of Nations to all Members of the League.

Done at London the twenty-fourth day of July, one thousand nine hundred and twenty-two.

SECRETARY-GENERAL.

APPENDIX D

Ribbentrop Promise to Mufti to Destroy Jewish National Home

Ministry of Foreign Affairs

Berlin, April 28, 1942
Your Eminence:

In response to your letter and to the accompanying communication of His Excellency, Prime Minister Raschid Ali El Gailani, and confirming the terms of our conversation, I have the honour to inform you:

The German Government appreciates fully the confidence of the Arab peoples in the Axis Powers in their aims and in their determination to conduct the fight against the common enemy until victory is achieved. The German Government has the greatest understanding for the national aspirations of the Arab countries as have been expressed by you both and the greatest sympathy for the sufferings of your peoples under British oppression.

I have therefore the honour to assure you, in complete agreement with the Italian Government, that the independence and freedom of the suffering Arab countries presently subjected to British oppression, is also one of the aims of the German Government.

Germany is consequently ready to give all her support to the oppressed Arab countries in their fight against British domination, for the fulfillment of their national aim to independence and sovereignty and for the destruction of the Jewish National Home in Palestine.

As previously agreed, the content of this letter should be maintained absolutely secret until we decide otherwise.

I beg your Eminence to be assured of my highest esteem and consideration.

(Signed) Ribbentrop

To His Eminence
the Grossmufti of Palestine
Amin El Husseini.

APPENDIX E
The PLO Charter*

This Covenant will be called "The Palestinian National Covenant" (Al-Mîhâq Al-Watanî Al-Filastînî).

ARTICLE 1
Palestine is the homeland of the Palestine Arab people and an integral part of the great Arab homeland, and the people of Palestine is a part of the Arab Nation.

ARTICLE 2
Palestine with its boundaries that existed at the time of the British Mandate is an integral regional unit.

ARTICLE 3
The Palestinian Arab people possesses the legal right to its homeland, and when the liberation of its homeland is completed it will exercise self-determination solely according to its own will and choice.

ARTICLE 4
The Palestinian personality is an innate, persistent characteristic that does not disappear, and it is transferred from fathers to sons. The Zionist occupation, and the dispersal of the Palestinian Arab people as result of the disasters which came over it, do not deprive it of its Palestinian personality and affiliation and do not nullify them.

*Adopted in 1964 and revised in 1968.

ARTICLE 5

The Palestinians are the Arab citizens who were living permanently in Palestine until 1947, whether they were expelled from there or remained. Whoever is born to a Palestinian Arab father after this date, within Palestine or outside it, is a Palestinian.

ARTICLE 6

Jews who were living permanently in Palestine until the beginning of the Zionist invasion will be considered Palestinians.

ARTICLE 7

The Palestinian affiliation and the material, spiritual and historical tie with Palestine are permanent realities. The upbringing of the Palestinian individual in an Arab and revolutionary fashion, the undertaking of all means of forging consciousness and training the *Palestinian,* in order to acquaint him profoundly with his homeland, spiritually and materially, and preparing him for the conflict and the armed struggle, as well as for the sacrifice of his property and his life to restore his homeland, until the liberation—all this is a national duty.

ARTICLE 8

The phase in which the people of Palestine is living is that of the national (*Watanî*) struggle for the liberation of Palestine. Therefore, the contradictions among the Palestinian national forces are of a secondary order which must be suspended in the interest of the fundamental contradiction between Zionism and colonialism on the one side and the Palestinian Arab people on the other. On this basis, the Palestinian masses, whether in the homeland or in places of exile (*Mahâjir*), organizations and individuals, comprise one national front which acts to restore Palestine and liberate it through armed struggle.

ARTICLE 9

Armed struggle is the only way to liberate Palestine and is therefore a strategy and not tactics. The Palestinian Arab people affirms its absolute resolution and abiding determination to pursue the armed struggle and to march forward toward the armed popular revolution, to liberate its homeland and return to it, [to maintain] its right to a natural life in it, and to exercise its right of self-determination in it and sovereignty over it.

ARTICLE 10

Fedayeen action forms the nucleus of the popular Palestinian war of liberation. This demands its promotion, extension and protection, and the mobilization of all the mass and scientific capacities of the Palestinians, their organization and involvement in the armed Palestinian revolution, and cohesion in the national (*Watanî*) struggle among the various groups of the people of Palestine, and between them and the Arab masses, to guarantee the continuation of the revolution, its advancement and victory.

ARTICLE 11

The Palestinians will have three mottoes: National (*Wataniyya*) unity, national (*Qawmiyya*) mobilization and liberation.

ARTICLE 12

The Palestinian Arab people believes in Arab unity. In order to fulfill its role in realizing this, it must preserve, in this phase of its national (*Watanî*) struggle, its Palestinian personality and the constituents thereof, increase consciousness of its existence and resist any plan that tends to disintegrate or weaken it.

ARTICLE 13

Arab unity and the liberation of Palestine are two complementary aims. Each one paves the way for realization of the other. Arab unity leads to the liberation of Palestine, and the liberation of Palestine leads to Arab unity. Working for both goes hand in hand.

ARTICLE 14

The destiny of the Arab nation, indeed the very Arab existence, depends upon the destiny of the Palestine issue. The endeavor and effort of the Arab nation to liberate Palestine follows from this connection. The people of Palestine assumes its vanguard role in realizing this sacred national (*Qawmî*) aim.

ARTICLE 15

The liberation of Palestine, from an Arab viewpoint, is a national (*Qawmî*) duty to repulse the Zionist, imperialist invasion from the great Arab homeland and to purge the Zionist presence from Palestine. Its full responsibilities fall upon the Arab nation, peoples and governments, with the Palestinian Arab people at their head.

For this purpose, the Arab nation must mobilize its military, human, material and spiritual capabilities to participate actively with the people of Palestine. They must, especially in the present stage of armed Palestinian revolution, grant and offer the people of Palestine all possible help and every material and human support, and afford it every sure means and opportunity enabling it to continue to assume its vanguard role in pursuing its armed revolution until the liberation of its homeland.

ARTICLE 16

The liberation of Palestine, from a spiritual viewpoint, will prepare an atmosphere of tranquility and peace for the Holy Land, in the shade of which all the holy places will be safeguarded, and freedom of worship and visitation to all will be guaranteed, without distinction or discrimination of race, color, language or religion. For this reason, the people of Palestine looks to the support of all the spiritual forces in the world.

ARTICLE 17

The liberation of Palestine, from a human viewpoint, will restore to the Palestinian man his dignity, glory and freedom. For this, the Palestinian Arab people looks to the support of those in the world who believe in the dignity and freedom of man.

ARTICLE 18

The liberation of Palestine, from an international viewpoint, is a defensive act necessitated by the requirements of self-defense. For this reason, the people of Palestine, desiring to befriend all peoples, looks to the support of the states which love freedom, justice and peace in restoring the legal situation to Palestine, establishing security and peace in its territory, and enabling its people to exercise national (*Wataniyya*) sovereignty and national (*Qawmiyya*) freedom.

ARTICLE 19

The partitioning of Palestine in 1947 and the establishment of Israel is fundamentally null and void, whatever time has elapsed, because it was contrary to the wish of the people of Palestine and its natural right to its homeland, and contradicts the principles embodied in the Charter of the United Nations, the first of which is the right of self-determination.

ARTICLE 20

The Balfour Declaration, the Mandate Document, and what has been based upon them are considered null and void. The claim of a historical or spiritual tie between Jews and Palestine does not tally with historical realities nor with the constituents of statehood in their true sense. Judaism, in its character as a religion of revelation, is not a nationality with an independent existence. Likewise, the Jews are not one people with an independent personality. They are rather citizens of the states to which they belong.

ARTICLE 21

The Palestinian Arab people, in expressing itself through the armed Palestinian revolution, rejects every solution that is a substitute for a complete liberation of Palestine, and rejects all plans that aim at the settlement of the Palestine issue or its internationalization.

ARTICLE 22

Zionism is a political movement organically related to world imperialism and hostile to all movements of liberation and progress in the world. It is a racist and fanatical movement in its formation, aggressive, expansionist and colonialist in its aims; and Fascist and Nazi in its means. Israel is the tool of the Zionist movement and a human and geographical base for world imperialism. It is a concentration and jumping-off point for imperialism in the heart of the Arab homeland, to strike at the hopes of the Arab nation for liberation, unity and progress.

Israel is a constant threat to peace in the Middle East and the entire world. Since the liberation of Palestine will liquidate the Zionist and imperialist presence and bring about the stabilization of peace in the Middle East, the people of Palestine looks to the support of all liberal men of the world and all the forces of good progress and peace; and implores all of them, regardless of their different leanings and orientations, to offer all help and support to the people of Palestine in its just and legal struggle to liberate its homeland.

ARTICLE 23

The demands of security and peace and the requirements of truth and justice oblige all states that preserve friendly relations among peoples and maintain the loyalty of citizens to their homelands to consider Zionism an illegitimate movement and to prohibit its existence and activity.

ARTICLE 24

The Palestinian Arab people believes in the principles of justice, freedom, sovereignty, self-determination, human dignity and the right of peoples to exercise them.

ARTICLE 25

To realize the aims of this Covenant and its principles the Palestine Liberation Organization will undertake its full role in liberating Palestine.

ARTICLE 26

The Palestine Liberation Organization, which represents the forces of the Palestinian revolution, is responsible for the movement of the Palestinian Arab people in its struggle to restore its homeland, liberate it, return to it and exercise the right of self-determination in it. This responsibility extends to all military, political and financial matters, and all else that the Palestine issue requires in the Arab and international spheres.

ARTICLE 27

The Palestine Liberation Organization will cooperate with all Arab states, each according to its capacities, and will maintain neutrality in their mutual relations in the light of, and on the basis of, the requirements of the battle of liberation, and will not interfere in the internal affairs of any Arab state.

ARTICLE 28

The Palestinian Arab people insists upon the originality and independence of its national (*Wataniyya*) revolution and rejects every manner of interference, guardianship and subordination.

ARTICLE 29

The Palestinian Arab people possesses the prior and original right in liberating and restoring its homeland and will define its position with reference to all states and powers on the basis of their positions with reference to the issue [of Palestine] and the extent of their support for [the Palestinian Arab people] in its revolution to realize its aims.

ARTICLE 30

The fighters and bearers of arms in the battle of liberation are the nucleus of the Popular Army, which will be the protecting arm of the Palestinian Arab people.

ARTICLE 31

This organization shall have a flag, oath and anthem, all of which will be determined in accordance with a special system.

ARTICLE 32

To this Covenant is attached a law known as the Fundamental Law of the Palestine Liberation Organization, in which is determined the manner of the organization's formation, its committees, institutions, the special functions of every one of them and all the requisite duties associated with them in accordance with the Covenant.

ARTICLE 33
This Covenant cannot be amended except by a two-thirds majority of all the members of the National Council of the Palestine Liberation Organization in a special session called for this purpose.

APPENDIX F

Security Council Resolution 242, November 22, 1967

The Security Council,

Expressing its continuing concern with the grave situation in the Middle East,

Emphasizing the inadmissibility of the acquisition of territory by war and the need to work for a just and lasting peace in which every State in the area can live in security,

Emphasizing further that all Member States in their acceptance of the Charter of the United Nations have undertaken a commitment to act in accordance with Article 2 of the Charter,

1. *Affirms* that the fulfillment of Charter principles requires the establishment of a just and lasting peace in the Middle East which should include the application of both the following principles:

(i) Withdrawal of Israeli armed forces from territories occupied in the recent conflict;

(ii) Termination of all claims or states of belligerency and respect for and acknowledgment of the sovereignty, territorial integrity and political independence of every State in the area and their right to live in peace within secure and recognized boundaries free from threats or acts of force;

2. *Affirms further* the necessity

(a) For guaranteeing freedom of navigation through international waterways in the area;

(b) For achieving a just settlement of the refugee problem;

(c) For guaranteeing the territorial inviolability and political independence of every State in the area, through measures including the establishment of demilitarized zones;

3. *Requests* the Secretary-General to designate a Special Representative to proceed to the Middle East to establish and maintain contacts with the states concerned in order to promote agreement and assist efforts to achieve a peaceful and accepted settlement in accordance with the provisions and principles in this resolution;

4. *Requests* the Secretary-General to report to the Security Council on the progress of the efforts of the Special Representative as soon as possible.

APPENDIX G

The Pentagon Plan
June 29, 1967

JSCM—373–67

MEMORANDUM FOR THE SECRETARY OF DEFENSE
SUBJECT: MIDDLE EAST BOUNDARIES

1. Reference is made to your memorandum dated 19 June 1967, subject as above, which requested the views of the Joint Chiefs of Staff, without regard to political factors, on the minimum territory in addition to that held on 4 June 1967, Israel might be justified in retaining in order to permit a more effective defense against possible conventional Arab attack and terrorist raids.

2. From a strictly military point of view Israel would require the retention of some captured Arab territory in order to provide militarily defensible borders. Determination of territory to be retained should be based on accepted tactical principles such as control of commanding terrain, use of natural obstacles, elimination of enemy-held salients, and provision of defense in-depth for important facilities and installations. More detailed discussions of the key border areas mentioned in the reference are contained in the Appendix hereto. In summary, the views of the Joint Chiefs of Staff regarding these areas are as follows:

A. THE JORDANIAN WEST BANK
Control of the prominent high ground running north-south through the middle of West Jordan generally east of the main north-south highway

along the axis Jenin-Nablus-Bira-Jerusalem and then southwest to a junction with the Dead Sea at the Wadi el Daraja would provide Israel with a militarily defensible border. The envisioned defensive line would run just east of Jerusalem; however, provision could be made for internationalization of the city without significant detriment to Israel's defensive posture.

B. Syrian Territory Contiguous to Israel
Israel is particularly sensitive to the prevalence of terrorist raids and border incidents in this area. The presently occupied territory, the high ground running generally north-south on a line with Qnaitra about 15 miles inside the Syrian border, would give Israel control of the terrain which Syria has used effectively in harassing the border area.

C. The Jerusalem-Latrun Area
See subparagraph 2A above.

D. The Gaza Strip
By occupying the Gaza Strip, Israel would trade approximately 45 miles of hostile border for eight. Configured as it is, the strip serves as a salient for introduction of Arab subversion and terrorism, and its retention would be to Israel's military advantage.

E. The Negev-Sinai Border
Except for retention of the demilitarized zone around Al Awja and some territory for the protection of the port of Eilat, discussed below, continued occupation of the Sinai would present Israel with problems outweighing any military gains.

F. The Negev-Jordan-Aqaba-Strait of Tiran Area
Israel's objectives here would be innocent passage through the Gulf of Aqaba and protection of its port at Eilat. Israel could occupy Sharm ash-Shaykh with considerable inconvenience but could rely on some form of internationalization to secure free access to the gulf. Failing this, Israel would require key terrain in the Sinai to protect its use of the Strait of Tiran. Eilat, situated at the apex of Israel's narrow southern tip, is vulnerable to direct ground action from Egyptian territory. Israel would lessen the threat by retention of a portion of the Sinai Peninsula south and east of the Wadi el Gerafi then east to an intersection with the Gulf of Aqaba at approximately 29° 20' north latitude.

3. It is emphasized that the above conclusions, in accordance with your terms of reference are based solely on military considerations from the Israeli point of view.
For the Joint Chiefs of Staff
signed Earle G. Wheeler
Chairman, Joint Chiefs of Staff

DISCUSSION OF KEY ISRAELI BORDER AREAS

1. THE JORDANIAN WEST BANK
a. Threat.   The Jordan-Israeli border is 330 miles in length extending from the Gulf of Aqaba northward to the Dead Sea, thence following the armistice demarcation lines and the Jordan River northward to the Yarmuk River, thence along the Yarmuk River to the Syrian frontier. This border area has traditionally been lightly held by military forces and defenses consisted mainly of small, widely separated outposts and patrols and, therefore, afforded an area where launching of saboteurs and terrorists into Israel was relatively easy. During the period January 1965 to February 1967, a total of 53 incidents of sabotage and mining activity took place along this border. These activities resulted in three killed, 35 wounded, and damage to houses, roads, bridges, railroads, and water and electric power installations in Israel. Instances of exchange of small arms fire occurred quite frequently. The majority of these events took place from the Mount Hebron and Arabah areas where the Jordanian authorities did not take sufficient measures to protect against line crosses and saboteurs. The high ground running north-south through the middle of West Jordan overlooks Israel's narrow midsection and offers a route for a thrust to the sea which would split the country in two parts.
b. Requirement.   A boundary along the commanding terrain overlooking the Jordan River from the west could provide a shorter defense line. However, as a minimum, Israel would need a defense line generally along the axis Bardala-Tubas-Nablus-Bira-Jerusalem and then to the northern part of the Dead Sea. This line would widen the narrow portion of Israel and provide additional terrain for the defense of Tel Aviv. It would provide additional buffer for the air base at Beersheba. In addition, this line would give a portion of the foothills to Israel and avoid interdiction by artillery in the Israeli villages in the lowlands. This line would also provide a shorter defense line than the border of 4 June 1967 and would reduce the Jordanian salient into Israel. It also provides adequate lines of communication for lateral movement.

2. SYRIAN TERRITORY CONTIGUOUS TO ISRAEL

a. Threat. The border between Syria and Israel extends approximately 43 miles. It extends from a point on the Lebanese-Syrian border east to the vicinity of Baniyas, south to Lake Tiberias, then south along the eastern shore of the lake to the Syrian-Jordanian border. During the period January 1965 to February 1967, a total of 28 sabotage and terrorist acts occurred along this border. In addition, there were numerous shellings of villages from the high ground overlooking the area southeast of Lake Tiberias. Casualties were seven killed and 18 wounded. Control of the dominant terrain affords Syria a military route of approach into northern Israel; however, the greatest threat in this sector is from terrorism and sabotage.

b. Requirement. Israel must hold the commanding terrain east of the boundary of 4 June 1967 which overlooks the Galilee area. To provide a defense in-depth, Israel would need a strip about 15 miles wide extending from the border of Lebanon to the border of Jordan. This line would provide protection for the Israeli villages on the east bank of Lake Tiberias but would make defending forces east of the lake vulnerable to a severing thrust from Jordan to the southern tip of the lake. The Israelis would probably decide to accept this risk. As a side effect, this line would give the Israelis control of approximately 25 miles of the Trans-Arabian Pipeline.

3. THE JERUSALEM-LATRUN AREA

a. Threat. These areas have been the scene of intermittent trouble over the years as both Jordanians and Israelis have been illegally cultivating lands in the area between the lines. Only one serious incident occurred in this area during the period January 1965 to February 1967.

b. Requirement. To defend the Jerusalem area would require that the boundary of Israel be positioned to the east of the city to provide for the organization of an adequate defensive position. On the other hand, if Jerusalem were to be internationalized under the United Nations, a boundary established west of the city could be defended in accordance with the concept in paragraph 1, above.

4. THE GAZA STRIP

a. Threat. During the period 1949–1956, prior to the Suez war, numerous infiltrations and terrorist raids were mounted by Egypt from the Gaza Strip. However, with the establishment of the United Nations Emergency Force in 1957, based in the Gaza Strip and along the Sinai border, the situation has been quiet. Only three events of sabotage occurred in this area during the period January 1965 to February 1967. The Strip,

under Egyptian control, provides a salient into Israel a little less than 30 miles long and from four to eight miles wide. It has served as a training area for the Palestine Liberation Army and, despite the few incidents arising in this area of late, it is significant to note that one of the first actions by the Israelis in the recent conflict was to seal off the area from the Sinai.
b. Requirement. Occupation of the Strip by Israel would reduce the hostile border by a factor of five and eliminate a source for raids and training of the Palestine Liberation Army.

5. THE NEGEV-SINAI BORDER
a. Threat. This area has not presented any border problems since establishment of the United Nations Emergency Force in 1957. The demilitarized zone around Al Awja, containing the main north-south, east-west road junction in eastern Sinai and the major water source in the area, is the principal feature providing military advantage.
b. Requirement. Except for an adjustment of a portion of the boundary tied to the defense of Eilat, discussed below, and retention of the demilitarized zone around Al Awja, no need is seen for Israeli retention of occupied territory in the Sinai.

6. THE NEGEV-JORDAN-AQABA-STRAIT OF TIRAN AREA
a. Threat. There were only five incidents of sabotage in this area during the period January 1965 to February 1967. Israel's chief concern in this area is free access through the Strait of Tiran and the Gulf of Aqaba and protection of Eilat, Israel's chief oil port and trade link with the West African countries. Eilat, being at the apex of Israel's southern tip, is vulnerable to interdiction from Egyptian territory.
b. Requirement. To provide Israel with sufficient depth to protect the port, the boundary should be established approximately 20 miles to the west along the Wadi el-Girafi, south to its headwaters, then east to a point on the Gulf of Aqaba at approximately 39° 20' north latitude. In the event an international guarantee for free passage of the Strait of Tiran and the Gulf of Aqaba is not provided, Israel would feel compelled to occupy key terrain in order to control the entrance to the Strait.

APPENDIX H

Security Council Resolution 338, October 22, 1973

The Security Council,

1. *Calls upon* all parties to present fighting to cease all firing and terminate all military activity immediately, no later than 12 hours after the moment of the adoption of this decision, in the positions they now occupy.

2. *Calls upon* all parties concerned to start immediately after the cease-fire the implementation of Security Council Resolution 242 (1967) in all of its parts;

3. *Decides* that, immediately and concurrently with the cease-fire, negotiations start between the parties concerned under appropriate auspices aimed at establishing a just and durable peace in the Middle East.

APPENDIX I
The Phased Plan

TEXT OF POLITICAL PLAN APPROVED BY
THE PLO COUNCIL, JUNE 8, 1974*

On the basis of the National Palestinian Covenant and the PLO's political plan as approved at the 11th session (6–12 January 1973); and in the belief that a just and lasting peace in the region is impossible without restoration of the full national rights of the Palestinian nation, and first and foremost the right of return and self-determination on the homeland's soil entire; and after having studied the political circumstances as they developed during the period between its previous and its present session—the Council resolves as follows:

1. Emphasis of the PLO's position with relation to Security Council Resolution 242, which overlooks the national rights of our nation and approaches the Palestinian issue as a refugee problem.
   The Council therefore rejects any action on that basis on any level of Arab and international operation, including the Geneva Conference.
2. The PLO is fighting by every means, and primarily by the armed struggle, to free the Palestinian land and establish a national, independent and fighting government over every part of the soil of Palestine to be freed. This calls for a considerable change in the balance of forces, for the good of our nation and its struggle.
3. The PLO objects to any plan for a Palestinian entity at the price of recognition, peace (*sulh*), secure boundaries, surrender of national rights and deprivation of our nation's prerogative of return and of self-determination in its homeland.

*Broadcast on Saut Falastin Radio, Egypt.

4. Any step of liberation is a link in realizing the strategy of the PLO for the establishment of a Palestinian-democratic State, as resolved by the previous Councils.

5. It is necessary to struggle alongside the national Jordanian forces for the establishment of a national Jordanian-Palestinian front, with the purpose of forming a national democratic government in Jordan that will safeguard solidarity.

6. The PLO struggles to unify the efforts of the two nations and all the forces of the Arab liberation movements which subscribe to this plan.

7. In view of this plan, the PLO fights to strengthen national unity and raise it to a height where it will be capable of fulfilling its national missions.

8. After its establishment, the national Palestinian government will fight for the unity of the countries of confrontation, to complete the liberation of all the Palestinian land and as a step in the direction of overall Arab unity.

9. The PLO fights to strengthen its solidarity with the Socialist countries and the forces of liberation and progress, to frustrate all the Zionist reactionary and imperialist plans.

10. On the basis of this plan, the leadership of the revolution will formulate tactics that will enable these objectives to be realized.

NOTES

PREFACE

1. Letters from Jill W. Rhodes (Jan. 31, 1991), Marion Hitch (Feb. 11, 1991), and Judy T. Fulp (Jan. 20, 1991).

2. Mark Twain, *The Innocents Abroad* (New York: Literary Classics of the United States, 1984), pp. 385, 398.

INTRODUCTION

1. David Fromkin, *A Peace to End All Peace: Creating the Modern Middle East 1914–1922* (London: Andre Deutsch, 1989), p. 403.

2. See J.A.S. Grenville, *The Major International Treaties 1914–1945: A History and Guide with Texts* (London: Methuen, 1974), pp. 48–49.

3. Bernard Lewis, "The Palestinians and the PLO, a Historical Approach," *Commentary* (Jan. 1975), p. 32.

4. Bernard Lewis, *Semites and Anti-Semites* (New York: Norton, 1986), p. 169.

5. Ibid.

1. THE RISE OF ZIONISM

1. Anna Nordau, *Memoirs* (Jerusalem: Mitzpah, 1930), p. 159.

2. Alkalai's published calls for the establishment of Jewish colonies in the Land of Israel began to appear in 1834 in Semlin, the capital of Serbia, where he served as rabbi. One of his admirers was a fellow Semliner named Simon Loeb Herzl, grandfather of the founder of Zionism. Kalis-

cher's *Seeking Zion* (1862) was more widely read than Alkalai's writings, and it influenced not only the religious world but Hess's *Rome and Jerusalem* (1862), which quotes from it. Hess's book became a classic statement of Jewish nationalism, which is all the more astonishing because it was made by a prominent member of Germany's cosmopolitan intelligentsia.

Translated excerpts from all three authors can be found in Arthur Hertzberg, ed., *The Zionist Idea: A Historical Analysis and Reader* (New York: Atheneum, 1984), pp. 102–38.

3. Marvin Lowenthal, ed., *The Diaries of Theodor Herzl* (New York: Dial, 1956), pp. 267–73, 339.

4. *Encyclopaedia Judaica* (Jerusalem: Keter, 1971), vol. 14, pp. 352–53.

5. *Encyclopaedia Judaica,* vol. 9, p. 1312.

6. Jean-Jacques Rousseau, *Émile,* trans. Allan Bloom (New York: Basic, 1979), p. 304.

7. That millions of enslaved people were to be considered "free" because their oppressors were of their own kind was the fantastic creed foisted on a credulous Western intelligentsia during the second half of the twentieth century by an assortment of Communist and Third World dictators. They distorted beyond recognition Isaiah Berlin's ideas of positive and negative freedom (developed in his essay "Two Concepts of Liberty"), effectively leaving their subjects with no freedom of any kind. See *Four Essays on Liberty* (New York: Oxford, 1969).

8. Byron quoted in *Encyclopaedia Judaica,* vol. 4, p. 1549.

9. Adams quoted in Nahum Sokolow, *A History of Zionism 1600–1918* (Bombay: Longmans, Green and Co., 1919), vol. 1, p. 59.

10. Napoleon quoted in Peter Grose, *Israel in the Mind of America* (New York: Knopf, 1983), p. 8.

11. Shaftesbury quoted in Sokolow, *History of Zionism,* p. 123.

12. Palmerston quoted in Leonard Stein, *The Balfour Declaration* (London: Vallentine, Mitchell and Co., 1961), pp. 6–7.

13. A.W.C. Crawford, Lord Lindsay, *Letters on Egypt, Edom and the Holy Land* (London: Henry G. Bohn, 1858), p. xi.

14. George Gawler, *Tranquillisation of Syria and the East* (London: T. and W. Boone, 1845), p. 6.

15. Descriptions of the Zionist sympathies of prominent Britons and Americans can be found in Sokolow, *History of Zionism.* Also of interest are Fromkin, *Peace to End All Peace,* pp. 268–70; Grose, *Israel in the Mind of America;* and Samuel Katz, *Battleground: Fact and Fantasy in Palestine* (New York: Bantam, 1973), pp. 100–106.

16. George Eliot, *Daniel Deronda* (London: William Blackwood and Sons, 1876), vol. 3, book 6, p. 248.

17. Isaiah 11:12; Jeremiah 31:10; Ezekiel 36:24.

18. These Christian clergymen are quoted in Grose, *Israel in the Mind of America,* pp. 8–10.

19. Blackstone quoted in Ibid., p. 36.

20. Bliss quoted in Moshe Pearlman, *Digging Up the Bible: The Stories of the Great Archaeological Discoveries in the Holy Land* (London: Weidenfeld and Nicolson, 1980), p. 47.

21. Warren quoted in Ronald Sanders, *The High Walls of Jerusalem: A History of the Balfour Declaration and the Birth of the British Mandate for Palestine* (New York: Holt, Rinehart and Winston, 1983), p. 12.

22. Sokolow, *History of Zionism,* p. 299.

23. Edwin Sherwin Wallace, *Jerusalem the Holy* (New York: Arno Press, 1977), pp. 310, 355.

24. Balfour quoted in Grose, *Israel in the Mind of America,* p. 62.

25. Fromkin, *Peace to End All Peace,* pp. 270–75.

26. Churchill White Paper of 1922.

27. Rome did not officially annex Judea to the empire until 44 c.e. During the intervening decades it exercised control over the land through the client regime of Herod and his family.

28. Dio Cassius, *Roman History,* book 69, sec. 12.1, cited in M. Stern, *Greek and Latin Authors on Jews and Judaism* (Jerusalem: Israel Academy of Sciences and Humanities, 1980), vol. 2, p. 393.

29. Caracalla enacted the *constitutio Antoniniana de civitate,* which accorded Roman citizenship to "free residents" of the empire. See Salo W. Baron, *A Social and Religious History of the Jews* (New York: Columbia University Press, 1952), vol. 11, p. 109. See also *Encyclopaedia Judaica,* vol. 5, p. 157.

30. Katz, *Battleground,* p. 88.

31. Benzion Dinur, *Israel in the Diaspora* (Tel Aviv: Dvir, 1960; Hebrew), vol. 1, "From the Conquest of the Land of Israel by the Arabs to the Crusades," pp. 27–30. Prof. Dinur provides an exhaustive compilation of historical sources, mostly Arab and Jewish, documenting the condition of the Jews at the beginning of the Arab conquest, and its progressive decline as a result of Arab colonization policy.

32. According to Toynbee, "There is a thing in law, I think in all forms of law, the statute of limitations, which for the sake of producing the minimum amount of hardships and suffering, says that a legal claim does expire after such and such a time." "Selective Debates on Palestine," Kadhim Jawad, ed., *Baghdad Magazine* (1970), p. 74.

Furthermore: "[A]fter a lapse of 1800 years it could not be said that Palestine was the land of the Jews. Otherwise the United States of America should now belong to the Red Indians. . . . In my opinion, the Jews have no right in Palestine except their right to personal property. They do not have the right to establish a State. It is most unfortunate that a state is established on a religious basis." Shakil Ahmed Zia, *A History of Jewish Crimes* (Karachi: Ahmed Alam Khan, 1969), p. 231.

33. Jabotinsky quoted in Joseph Schechtman, *The Vladimir Jabotinsky Story: The Early Years* (New York: Thomas Yoseloff, 1956), p. 89.

34. Ruth 1:16; Psalms 137:5. The Shmoneh-esrei or Amidah, the central prayer in the traditional daily service, devotes six of its eighteen blessings to the subject of the Return to Zion.

35. The famous formula "Next year in Jerusalem" is recited at the end of the traditional service both on Passover, the holiday of national liberation, and on Yom Kippur, the day of atonement.

36. In J. Davidson et al., eds., *Prayerbook of Rav Saadiah Gaon* (Jerusalem, 1963), pp. 77–78. Cited in H. H. Ben-Sasson, ed., *A History of the Jewish People* (Cambridge: Harvard, 1976), pp. 446–47.

37. Solomon Grayzel, *A History of the Jews* (New York: New American Library, 1968), pp. 296–97.

38. Maimonides' "Epistle to Yemen" in Isadore Twersky, *A Maimonides Reader* (New York: Behrman House, 1972), pp. 456–57.

39. Nahmanides' commentary on Numbers 33:53.

40. Grayzel, *History of the Jews,* pp. 372–73.

41. Maharal, *The Eternity of Israel* (Prague, 1591), fol. 2r. Quoted in Ben-Sasson, *History of the Jewish People,* p. 709.

42. Hillel of Shklov, *Kol Hator* (B'nei Brak, Israel: Kol Hator Committee, 1968, Hebrew), p. 83.

43. *Encyclopaedia Judaica,* vol. 13, p. 216. For a brief survey of Jewish presence in the land during the centuries of the exile, see Katz, *Battleground,* pp. 89–100.

44. Franklin Delano Roosevelt, memo to U.S. Secretary of State, dated May 17, 1939, *Foreign Relations of the United States: Diplomatic Papers* (Washington, DC: U.S. Government Printing Office, 1955), vol. 4, p. 757.

45. Arieh Avneri, *The Claim of Dispossession: Jewish Land Settlement and the Arabs, 1878–1948* (New York: Herzl Press, 1982), p. 262.

46. Ibid., p. 261.

47. Ibid., p. 255.

48. Arafat address to the twenty-ninth session of the United Nations General Assembly, Nov. 13, 1974. Official UN translation published under the title "Palestine Lives" by People's Press—Middle East Project, p. 8.

49. By 1820–21, travelers such as Richardson, Carne, and Scholtz reported that Jews made up the largest ethnic group in Jerusalem. The first official public census, taken by the Turks in 1844, revealed a Jewish population of 7,120, as opposed to 5,760 Moslems. See Eliyahu Tal, *Whose Jerusalem?* (Jerusalem: Tal Communications, 1933), p. 51.

50. *The Journal of Henry Maundrell from Aleppo to Jerusalem, 1697* (London: Henry Bohn, 1848), pp. 428, 450, 477.

51. Thomas Shaw, *Travels and Observations Relating to Several Parts of Barbary and the Levant* (London, 1754), pp. 336–37.

52. Count Constantine F. Volney, *Travels through Syria and Egypt in the Years 1783, 1784, 1785* (London: Pater, Noster and Row, 1788), vol. 2, p. 36.

53. Alexander Keith, *The Land of Israel* (Edinburgh: William, Whyte, 1844), p. 465.

54. J. S. Buckingham, *Travels in Palestine* (London, 1821), p. 146.

55. Alphonse de Lamartine, *Recollections of the East* (London, 1845), pp. 268, 308. Cited in Katz, *Battleground,* p. 107.

56. Finn, letter to the Earl of Clarendon, Sept. 15, 1857, British Foreign Office Documents 78/1294 (Pol. no. 36).

57. Twain, *Innocents Abroad,* pp. 384, 403, 414, 442, 480, 485–86.

58. Arthur Penrhyn Stanley, *Sinai and Palestine* (London: John Murray, 1881), p. 118.

59. Alexander Scholch, "The Demographic Development of Palestine" in *International Journal of Middle East Studies,* vol. 17, 1985, p. 488.

60. Avneri, *Claim of Dispossession,* pp. 30–31. At the time of the granting of the Mandate, Transjordan's population was roughly three hundred thousand, half of whom were nomadic. Ya'akov Shimoni, *Political Dictionary of the Arab World* (New York: Macmillan, 1987), p. 254.

61. Kaiser quoted in Lowenthal, *Diaries of Theodor Herzl,* p. 292.

62. Jabotinsky in Hertzberg, *Zionist Idea,* p. 562.

63. Lewis, "Palestinians," p. 32.

64. British Royal Commission Report (1937), ch. 1, p. 6.

65. Felix Bovet, *Egypt, Palestine and Phoenicia: A Visit to Sacred Lands* (London, 1882), pp. 384–85. Cited in Michael Ish-Shalom, *Christian Travels in the Holy Land* (Tel Aviv: Am Oved, 1965; Hebrew), p. 714.

66. These Arabizations and hundreds more can be found in Michael Avi-Yonah, *Qedem Monographs of the Institute of Archaeology* (Jerusalem: Institute of Archaeology of the Hebrew University of Jerusalem and Carta, 1976).

67. Katz, *Battleground,* p. 114.

68. Smith quoted in Ibid.

69. Balfour quoted in Stein, *Balfour Declaration,* pp. 641, 643, 650.

70. Cited in Jill Becker, *The PLO: The Rise and Fall of the Palestine Liberation Organization* (New York: St. Martin's, 1984), p. 13.

71. Lord Cecil quoted in Stein, *Balfour Declaration,* p. 565.

72. Lloyd George quoted in Fromkin, *Peace to End All Peace,* p. 401.

73. Smuts quoted in Stein, *Balfour Declaration,* p. 627.

74. Benzion Netanyahu, ed., *Max Nordau to His People* (Jerusalem: Political Library, 1937), vol. 2, p. 59.

75. Churchill quoted in Fromkin, *Peace to End All Peace,* pp. 519, 520, 523.

2. THE BETRAYAL

1. Roosevelt quoted in Grose, *Israel in the Mind of America,* p. 134.

2. Horace Samuel, *Unholy Memories of the Holy Land* (London: Leonard and Virginia Woolf, 1930), pp. 6, 26.

3. Clayton quoted in Fromkin, *Peace to End All Peace,* p. 321.

4. Ibid., p. 318.

5. Ibid., p. 321.

6. Storrs quoted in Ibid., pp. 323, 325.

7. Jabotinsky quoted in Conor Cruise O'Brien, *The Siege: The Saga of Israel and Zionism* (New York: Simon & Schuster, 1986), pp. 135, 138–39.

8. Sanders, *High Walls of Jerusalem,* p. 651.

9. O'Brien, *Siege,* p. 139.

10. William Bernard Ziff, *The Rape of Palestine* (London: St. Botolph's, 1948), p. 14.

11. Sanders, *High Walls of Jerusalem,* p. 653.

12. Katz, *Battleground,* p. 61.

13. Sanders, *High Walls of Jerusalem,* p. 653.

14. Fromkin, *Peace to End All Peace,* p. 322.

15. Jabotinsky quoted in Sanders, *High Walls of Jerusalem,* p. 653.

16. Richard Meinertzhagen, *Middle East Diary, 1917–1956* (London: Cresset, 1959), p. 149.

17. Ibid., p. 67.

18. Ibid., p. 18.

19. Ibid., pp. 68, 132.

20. Samuel, *Unholy Memories,* p. 55.

21. Meinertzhagen, *Middle East Diary,* p. 56.

22. Ibid., p. 82.

23. Ibid.

24. Samuel, *Unholy Memories,* p. 57.

25. Ibid., p. 58.

26. Aref quoted in Meinertzhagen, *Middle East Diary,* p. 83.

27. Patterson quoted in Ziff, *Rape of Palestine,* p. 20.

28. Samuel, *Unholy Memories,* p. 68.

29. Samuel quoted in Sanders, *High Walls of Jerusalem,* p. 656.

30. Meinertzhagen, *Middle East Diary,* p. 97.

31. Ibid., p. 105.

32. Ziff, *Rape of Palestine*, p. 19.

33. Meinertzhagen, *Middle East Diary*, p. 116.

34. Fromkin, *Peace to End All Peace*, pp. 497–99.

35. Churchill quoted in Howard Sachar, *A History of Israel: From the Rise of Zionism to Our Time* (New York: Knopf, 1986), p. 110.

36. Balfour quoted in Ibid., p. 127.

37. Samuel quoted in Ziff, *Rape of Palestine*, p. 23.

38. *Times* quoted in Katz, *Battleground*, p. 54–55.

39. Arnold quoted in Ziff, *Rape of Palestine*, p. 79.

40. Sachar, *History of Israel*, p. 127.

41. Ziff, *Rape of Palestine*, p. 82.

42. Lloyd George quoted in Fromkin, *Peace to End All Peace*, pp. 504–505. The precise chronology of events surrounding the detachment of Transjordanian Palestine is provided by Becker, *The PLO*, p. 243: "On 24 April 1920 Britain was granted a mandate over the Palestine region by the San Remo peace conference. On 1 July 1920 Sir Herbert Samuel took over from the military administration and established a civil administration in Palestine on both sides of the Jordan River (see Viscount Samuel's *Memoirs*). . . . In March 1921 Abdullah was installed as Governor of 'Transjordan.' This decision to treat 'Transjordan' differently was not internationally sanctioned until it was confirmed as part of a text of the Mandate terms by the Council of the League of Nations on 24 July 1922 (Article 25 declared that in the 'territory lying between the Jordan River and the eastern boundary of Palestine as ultimately determined' the Mandatory might 'postpone or withhold' application of certain provisions of the Mandate). Only on 23 September 1922 did the League specifically approve a memorandum relating to Article 25 which specifically exempted the area of Transjordan from the original Mandate's requirements concerning the establishment of a Jewish national home."

43. Meinertzhagen, *Middle East Diary*, pp. 99–100.

44. Samuel, *Unholy Memories*, pp. 70–71.

45. Ziff, *Rape of Palestine*, p. 21.

46. Storrs quoted in Samuel, *Unholy Memories*, p. 73.

47. Storrs quoted in Fromkin, *Peace to End All Peace*, p. 215.

48. O'Brien, *Siege*, p. 151.

49. Fromkin, *Peace to End All Peace*, p. 524.

50. Ibid., p. 518.

51. Meinertzhagen, *Middle East Diary*, pp. 132–33.

52. Ziff, *Rape of Palestine*, p. 23.

53. Sachar, *History of Israel*, pp. 175–76.

54. Joseph Schechtman, *The Vladimir Jabotinsky Story: The Later Years* (New York: Thomas Yoseloff, 1956), p. 126.

55. Sanders, *High Walls of Jerusalem,* p. 661.

56. Meinertzhagen, *Middle East Diary,* p. 166.

57. Wingate quoted in Israel Beer, *Hagana as Britain's Ally* (Tel Aviv: Cooperative Press "Achduth," 1947).

58. Shuckburgh quoted in David Pryce-Jones, *The Closed Circle: An Interpretation of the Arabs* (New York: Harper and Row, 1989), p. 198.

59. Abram Sachar, *The Redemption of the Unwanted: From the Liberation of the Death Camps to the Founding of Israel* (New York: St. Martin's, 1983), p. 224.

60. David Wyman, *Paper Walls: America and the Refugee Crisis, 1938–1941* (New York: Pantheon, 1985), pp. 38–39.

61. Meinertzhagen, *Middle East Diary,* p. 171.

62. Halifax quoted in A. Sachar, *Redemption of the Unwanted,* p. 225.

63. Shuckburgh quoted in Ibid., p. 231.

64. Ibid.

65. Weizmann quoted in Ibid., p. 240.

66. Ibid., p. 210.

67. Ibid., p. 237.

68. Meinertzhagen commented on this incomprehensible, monomaniacal betrayal: "It is grossly unfair that the Jews are not allowed to bring in their own nationals, when the [Jordanian] Arab Legion, armed, equipped, financed, and officered by Britain, together with Army units from Iraq, Syria, Saudi Arabia, and Egypt are on the move into Palestine to attack them." Meinertzhagen, *Middle East Diary,* p. 223.

69. Pryce-Jones describes the rallying of the Arab leadership to the Germans in *Closed Circle,* pp. 199–206.

70. Quoted in Ibid., p. 202.

71. Husseini quoted in Ziff, *Rape of Palestine,* p. 111.

72. Niles quoted in A. Sachar, *Redemption of the Unwanted,* p. 318.

73. Crum quoted in Ziff, *Rape of Palestine,* p. 110.

74. David Wyman, *The Abandonment of the Jews: America and the Holocaust, 1941–1945* (New York: Pantheon, 1984), p. 159.

75. Kennan quoted in A. Sachar, *Redemption of the Unwanted,* p. 201.

76. Truman quoted in Ibid.

77. Saud quoted by Associated Press (Jan. 9, 1954). Cited in Henry Atkinson, *Security and the Middle East: The Problem and Its Solution* (New York: Ballantine, 1955) p. 26; proposals submitted to the President of the United States.

78. Hints of the land-for-peace discussions even made it into public discussion at the time. A major policy speech in 1955 by Secretary of State John Foster Dulles stressed that the armistice lines from the War of

Independence did not have to be permanent. Referring to the Negev, he complained that "territory which is barren has acquired a sentimental significance" for Israelis, making concessions unnecessarily difficult. British prime minister Anthony Eden was more forward, calling explicitly for territorial compromise. H. Sachar, *History of Israel,* p. 476.

79. Theodor Herzl, *Altneuland* (New York: Herzl Press, 1960), pp. 169–70.

80. Preamble: "Disregard and contempt for human rights have resulted in barbarous acts which have outraged the conscience of mankind. . . . Member states have pledged themselves to achieve, in cooperation with the United Nations, the promotion of universal respect for and observance of human rights and fundamental freedoms. . . ."

Article 28: "Rights and freedoms set forth in the Declaration cannot be enjoyed in a country under a reign of terror, nor in a world at war or in turmoil. . . . Only in a social and international order that is governed by the rule of law and the principle of mutual respect may human rights be fully observed." *The Universal Declaration of Human Rights: A Standard of Achievement* (New York: United Nations, 1948), pp. 1, 11.

81. By a vote of 111 to 25 with 13 abstentions, the UN General Assembly endorsed a resolution revoking the equation. *The Jerusalem Post,* Dec. 16, 1991.

82. Frederick Chary, *The Bulgarian Jews and the Final Solution 1940–1944* (Pittsburgh: University of Pittsburgh Press, 1972), p. 189; and Marshall Lee Miller, *Bulgaria During the Second World War* (Stanford: Stanford University Press, 1975), p. 96.

3. THE THEORY OF PALESTINIAN CENTRALITY

1. Shimoni, *Political Dictionary,* pp. 30, 165–66, 311–13.
2. Ibid., pp. 198, 514, 518–19.
3. Pryce-Jones, *Closed Circle,* p. 261.
4. *The Jerusalem Post,* Nov. 1, 1990, p. 4.
5. Shimoni, *Political Dictionary,* p. 229.
6. Ibid., pp. 295, 299.
7. Assad quoted in Kamal Jumblatt, *I Speak for Lebanon* (London: Zed, 1982), p. 78.
8. Shimoni, *Political Dictionary,* pp. 311–13.
9. Ibid., p. 23, 491–92.
10. Ibid., p. 230.
11. Ibid., p. 479.
12. Ibid., p. 101.
13. Atkinson, *Security,* p. 94.

14. Two hundred thousand Kurdish refugees fled to Iran in 1975 after the Shah of Iran stopped aid to the Pesh Perga Kurdish rebel forces. Shimoni, *Political Dictionary,* p. 287.

15. Atkinson, *Security,* pp. 95, 101.

16. Pryce-Jones, *Closed Circle,* p. 265.

17. *The New York Times,* Sept. 1, 1988.

18. Saddam poured two million barrels (84 million gallons) of crude oil into the gulf, producing a spill six times the size of the infamous Exxon *Valdez* spill in Alaska in 1989. *The Jerusalem Post,* March 11, 1991.

19. *Al-Gumhuria,* Oct. 19, 1984.

20. An excellent exposition of the Middle Eastern machinations of the rival British and French empires during World War I can be found in Fromkin, *Peace to End All Peace, passim.*

21. Pryce-Jones, *Closed Circle,* pp. 26–27.

22. Amir Shakib-Arslan, *Our Decline and Its Causes: A Diagnosis of the Symptoms of the Downfall of Moslems,* trans. M. A. Shakoor (Lahore, 1944). Excerpted in John Donohue and John Esposito, eds., *Islam in Transition: Muslim Perspectives* (New York: Oxford, 1982), pp. 60–62.

23. Anti-Defamation League pamphlet, "The Myth of Linkage," 1990.

24. *The New York Times,* Aug. 12 and 15, 1990.

25. Qutb quoted in Emmanuel Sivan, *Radical Islam: Medieval Theology and Modern Politics* (New Haven: Yale, 1985), p. 31.

26. Faraj quoted in *Al-Ahram* (Egypt), July 12, 1974. Cited in Sivan, *Radical Islam,* p. 20.

27. Pryce-Jones, *Closed Circle,* pp. 27–28.

28. Persecution of Jews in Arab countries began with the slaughter of the Jews of Medina by Mohammed in the year 625. The countless pogroms and massacres that punctuated the life of Jews under Arab Islam thereafter included those in Cairo (1012), Fez (1032), Marrakesh (1146), Baghdad (1333), Fez (1640), Basra (1776), Algiers (1801), Damascus (1840), Djerba (1864), Tunis (1869), Fez (1912), Constantine (1934), Damascus (1936), Baghdad (1941), Tripoli (1945), and cities across the Arab world in 1948 and 1967. A brief survey of Arab persecution of Jews can be found in Joan Peters, *From Time Immemorial* (New York: Harper, 1984), pp. 33–71.

29. After the destruction of the Temple in 70 c.e., this experience was encapsulated in the famous adage of the rabbis that the Jewish commonwealth was destroyed by gratuitous hatred among Jews. Talmud Yoma 9b.

A dramatic exception to the absence of Jewish political murder was the firing of Hagana troops on the ship *Altalena* bringing weapons and ammunition to Irgun troops immediately before the declaration of the state, in which eighteen members of the Irgun were killed. Another exception was the murder of Emil Greenzweig at an antiwar rally in February 1983. The murder was forcefully and universally condemned.

30. Shakib-Arslan, in Donohue and Esposito, *Islam in Transition,* p. 61.

31. Abdalla Laroui, *Contemporary Arab Ideology* (Paris: Maspero, 1967), p. 15, in Donohue and Esposito, *Islam in Transition,* p. 141.

32. Shakib-Arslan, in Donohue and Esposito, *Islam in Transition,* pp. 60–62.

33. Muhammad Nuwayhi, *Towards a Revolution in Religious Thought* (1970), in Donohue and Esposito, *Islam in Transition,* pp. 167–68.

34. Bitar, symposium of *Al-Ihya Al-Arabi,* Nov. 17, 1979. Cited in Sivan, *Radical Islam,* p. 157.

35. Pryce-Jones, *Closed Circle,* p. 235.

36. Cited in Ibid., p. 238.

37. Michel Aflaq, *In Remembrance of the Arab Prophet* (1972), in Donohue and Esposito, *Islam in Transition,* p. 111.

38. Muammar Qaddafi, *The Third Way,* in Donohue and Esposito, *Islam in Transition,* pp. 104–106.

39. Ghouri quoted in Becker, *PLO,* p. 18.

40. Charter quoted by Yehoshafat Harkabi, *Arab Attitudes to Israel* (Jerusalem: Keter, 1972), p. 70.

41. Nasser quoted in Pryce-Jones, *Closed Circle,* p. 253.

42. Quoted in Becker, *PLO,* p. 249.

43. Hussein quoted in Pryce-Jones, *Closed Circle,* p. 214.

44. Isurani in *Al-Qabas,* Oct. 27, 1986.

45. Arafat quoted in Saudi News Agency, Jan. 2, 1989.

46. During Henry Kissinger's shuttle diplomacy, Assad welcomed him beneath an oil painting of Saladin's victory over the Crusaders. Edward Sheehan, *The Arabs, Israelis, and Kissinger: A Secret History of American Diplomacy in the Middle East* (New York: Readers Digest Press, 1976), p. 95.

47. By 1963, so many Israeli farmers had lost their lives to Syrian fire from the Golan Heights that armored tractors had become standard equipment on Galilee farms. H. Sachar, *History of Israel,* p. 618.

48. Mubarak quoted in *The New York Times,* Sept. 16, 1990.

49. Sheikh Saud Nassir al-Sabah, Nov. 5, 1990. Cited in Anti-Defamation League pamphlet, "The Myth of Linkage," 1990.

4. THE REVERSAL OF CAUSALITY

1. Nasser quoted in H. Sachar, *History of Israel,* p. 633.

2. Radio Baghdad, May 31, 1967.

3. Algiers Home Service (in Arabic), June 4, 1967.

4. Radio Damascus, June 5, 1967.

5. H. Sachar, *History of Israel,* p. 633.

6. Amman Radio, June 7, 1967.

7. Actual strengths of Arab armies (Egypt, Syria, Jordan and Iraq) versus Israel: artillery 960 to 200; combat aircraft 682 to 286; tanks 2,330 to 1,000. Colonel Trevor Dupuy, U.S. Army, Ret., *Elusive Victory: The Arab-Israeli Wars, 1947–1974* (London: Macdonald and Jane's, 1978), p. 337.

8. The defense of Israel's shipping and the prevention of a blockade of the Straits of Tiran was central to the purpose of committing United Nations Emergency Force (UNEF) troops to the area in 1957. Dupuy, *Elusive Victory,* p. 221. Eisenhower confirmed this mission: "We should not assume . . . Egypt will prevent Israeli shipping from using the Suez Canal or the Gulf of Aqaba. If, unhappily, Egypt does hereafter violate the Armistice Agreement or other international obligations, then this should be dealt with firmly by the family of nations" (Feb. 20, 1957).

9. Dupuy, *Elusive Victory,* p. 247.

10. Jonathan Netanyahu, *Self-Portrait of a Hero: The Letters of Jonathan Netanyahu* (New York: Random House, 1980), p. 133.

11. International Documents on Palestine (1967), p. 62.

12. Ibid., pp. 62–63.

13. Ibid., p. 61.

14. Ibid., p. 100.

15. Charter of the United Nations, Article 2, Section 4. "All Members shall refrain in their international relations from the threat or use of force against the territorial integrity or political independence of any state, or in any other manner inconsistent with the Purposes of the United Nations."

16. Azzam Pasha quoted in Leonard David, *Myths and Facts: A Concise Record of the Arab-Israeli Conflict* (Washington, D.C.: Near East Report, 1989), p. 273.

17. *Filastin,* Feb. 19, 1949. Cited in Katz, *Battleground,* p. 16.

18. *Al-Hoda,* June 8, 1951. Cited in Katz, *Battleground,* p. 17.

19. *Al Difaa,* Sept. 6, 1954. Cited in Katz, *Battleground,* p. 18.

20. *Akhbar al-Yom* (Cairo), Oct. 12, 1963.

21. It is estimated that World War II uprooted 48 million people from their homes in Europe and another 31 million in Asia. Between 1945 and 1957, refugees created by forced population transfers, exchanges, and war totaled another 57 million. Israel Central Bureau of Statistics, "Immigrations to Israel, 1948–72," p. 72.

The Gulf War is estimated to have displaced another five million people, whose absorption by Jordan, Iraq, the Gulf states and other countries is taking place without any delays or fanfare. *The Jerusalem Post,* Aug. 8, 1991, p. 6.

22. Speech by Dr. Elfan Rees, reprinted in *Newsletter of the Anglo-Israel Association* 47 (Oct. 1957).

23. Atkinson, *Security,* p. 102.

24. Ibid., pp. 102–103.

25. Ibid., p. 102.

26. Arafat quoted in *Saut Falastin,* Dec. 9, 1980.

27. Mohsin quoted in *Trouw* (Netherlands), Mar. 31, 1977.

28. Official resolution from the Eighth Conference of the Palestine National Council, Mar. 1971.

29. Hout on Radio Cairo, May 30, 1967.

30. Arafat's speech before the United Nations, Nov. 13, 1974.

31. Hassan in *Al-Destour,* Feb. 5, 1970.

32. King Hussein on Egyptian television, Oct. 10, 1977.

33. King Hussein in *Al-Nahar Al-Arabi,* Dec. 26, 1981.

34. King Hussein in *Al-Anba* (Kuwait), Oct. 30, 1984.

35. Abu Iyad in *Al-Majallah,* Nov. 8, 1988.

36. Keitel quoted in William Shirer, *The Rise and Fall of the Third Reich: A History of Nazi Germany* (New York: Ballantine, 1950), p. 572.

37. Henlein quoted in Ibid., p. 440.

38. Ibid., pp. 488–89.

39. Ibid., pp. 524–26.

40. Ibid., pp. 493, 523–24.

41. Ibid., pp. 490, 519, 538.

42. Ibid., p. 489.

43. Ibid., pp. 522, 526.

44. Ibid., p. 527.

45. Ibid., p. 535.

46. Beneš quoted in Ibid., pp. 529, 564.

47. Hitler quoted in Ibid., p. 577.

48. *Times* editorial quoted in Ibid., p. 518.

49. Yitzhak Zaccai, *Judea, Samaria and the Gaza District, 1967–1987: Twenty Years of Civil Administration* (Jerusalem: Carta, 1987), pp. 14, 17, 25, 45, 84, 87, 96.

50. Quoted in Ze'ev Schiff and Ehud Ya'ari, *Intifada* (New York: Simon and Schuster, 1990), p. 18.

51. PLO Radio (Baghdad), Dec. 10, 1987.

52. Arafat in Riyadh, on Jan. 1, 1989. Quoted by a spokesman of the U.S. State Department at its daily press briefing on Jan. 19, 1989. A slightly different version was cited by the Kuwaiti News Agency on Jan. 2, 1989, but the sense is the same: "Any Palestinian leader who suggests ending the intifada exposes himself to the bullets of his own people and endangers his life. The PLO will know how to deal with them."

53. Leaflets of the Fatah, dated Jan. 21, 1991; Hamas, dated Mar. 5, 1989; United National Command of the intifada, dated Jan. 1, 1992.

54. Quoted on CBS, *48 Hours,* Feb. 9, 1988.

55. By mid-1992, the total number killed in clashes with the IDF stood at 776, while the number of slayings of Arabs by intifada activists stood at 698. Source: IDF spokesman, Aug. 23, 1992.

56. *The Jerusalem Post,* Nov. 27, 1992.

57. Ibid.

58. This figure includes all soldiers disciplined for unauthorized or excessive use of force through July 27, 1992, whether or not anyone was harmed as a result. Source: IDF spokesman.

59. Beirut Radio, Oct. 26, 1954.

60. *Al Difaa,* Apr. 19, 1957.

61. *Al-Nahar,* Apr. 25, 1963.

62. Reuters and *Al-Gumhuria,* Nov. 22, 1966.

63. *The New York Times,* March 2, 1987; The Associated Press, May 20, 1988.

64. *The Jerusalem Post,* May 3, 1992, p. 6.

65. *The Jerusalem Post,* July 22, 1990, p. 4.

66. "We do not believe there should be new settlements in the West Bank or East Jerusalem." *The New York Times,* March 9, 1990.

U.S. administration reports on settlement activity and the arrival of new immigrants in the territories have included East Jerusalem in their tallies, thus concluding that the 10 percent of Russian immigrants who move into Jewish neighborhoods in East Jerusalem are all "settlers." Ibid.

67. Zaccai, *Judea, Samaria,* p. 50; Department of Geography, Office of the Prime Minister of Israel.

68. Only an approximate estimate is possible. Source: Plia Albeck, State Attorney's Office.

69. Excerpted from Naomi Shemer, "Jerusalem of Gold," 1967. Translation mine.

70. J. Netanyahu, *Self-Portrait,* p. 238.

71. Dayan quoted in H. Sachar, *History of Israel,* p. 674.

72. I Maccabees 15. Simon not only claimed Judea and Samaria as Jewish land. Replying to the demand to return the cities of Joppa (today Jaffa, south of Tel Aviv, which Simon did not consider Jewish land) and Gazara (Gezer), Simon makes the argument from security: "As for Joppa and Gazara, which you demand, they were causing great damage among our people and to our land." Ibid.

5. THE TROJAN HORSE

1. Becker, *PLO,* p. 38.

2. Ibid., p. 42.

3. Official letter of the Bandung Commemoration Conference, April 24, 1985, entitled "Message from His Excellency Yasser Arafat, Chairman of the Executive Committee of the Palestine Liberation Organization, Commander in Chief of the Forces of the Palestinian Revolution, to His Excellency Mr. Soharto, President of the Republic of Indonesia, on the Occasion of the Commemoration of the Thirtieth Anniversary of the Asian-African Conference."

4. Pryce-Jones, *Closed Circle*, p. 199.

5. Ibid., p. 196.

6. Ibid., pp. 196–97.

7. Becker, *PLO*, p. 25.

8. Pryce-Jones, *Closed Circle*, p. 199.

9. Al-Banna quoted in Donohue and Esposito, *Islam in Transition*, p. 80.

10. Sami al-Jundi, *Al-Ba'th*, p. 27. Cited in Lewis, *Semites*, pp. 147–48.

11. Becker, *PLO*, p. 19.

12. Ibid.

13. Lewis, *Semites*, p. 150.

14. Ibid., p. 158.

15. Ibid., p. 151.

16. Ibid., pp. 152–53.

17. Ibid., p. 152.

18. Mufti quoted in Ibid., p. 155.

19. Ibid., p. 154.

20. Ibid., p. 156.

21. J. B. Schechtman, *The Mufti and the Führer: The Rise and Fall of Haj Amin el-Husseini* (New York: Thomas Yoseloff, 1965), p. 156.

22. Ibid., p. 157.

23. Ibid., p. 156.

24. Ibid., pp. 159–60.

25. Ibid., p. 160.

26. Lewis, *Semites*, p. 160.

27. Pryce-Jones, *Closed Circle*, pp. 206–207.

28. Hans Josef Horchem, "Terror in West Germany" in *Conflict Studien*, no. 185, 1985. Horchem was head of West Germany's Office for the Protection of the Constitution, whose responsibilities included the monitoring of left- and right-wing extremist groups.

29. Ibid.

30. Interviews with Abu Iyad in *Der Spiegel*, July 17, 1981, and *Die Tat*, July 19, 1985.

31. Source: Yigal Carmon, Prime Minister's Adviser on Terrorism, personal communication, Dec. 22, 1992.

32. Agence France Presse, May 21, 1986 and Reuters, July 4, 1986; for Abbas see *Liberation,* July 1, 1985 and *France Soir,* July 2, 1985.

33. *The London Observer,* Feb. 5, 1989.

34. Source: Yigal Carmon, personal communication, Dec. 22, 1992.

35. Ibid. Carmon has shown me photostats of captured PLO identity documents bearing such names.

36. Pryce-Jones, *Closed Circle,* pp. 206–207.

37. Sheehan, *Secret History,* p. 217.

38. Neil Livingstone and David Halevy, *Inside the PLO: Cover Units, Secret Funds, and the War Against Israel and the United States* (New York: William Morrow, 1990), p. 64.

39. O'Brien, *Siege,* p. 368.

40. H. Sachar, *History of Israel,* p. 342.

41. O'Brien, *Siege,* p. 476.

42. Arafat quoted in *Al-Destour,* Dec. 26, 1983.

43. Quoted in Becker, *PLO,* p. 53.

44. Ibid., p. 51.

45. "Those [Israelis] who survive will remain in Palestine. I estimate that none of them will survive." Shukeiri quoted in H. Sachar, *History of Israel,* pp. 633–34.

46. Becker, *PLO,* p. 66.

47. H. Sachar, *History of Israel,* p. 685.

48. The PLO estimated the toll at thirty thousand dead. Becker, *PLO,* p. 75. Israel offered medical treatment to casualties at Israeli hospitals. *The Jerusalem Post,* Sept. 23, 1970.

49. *The Jerusalem Post,* May 16 and June 7, 1982.

50. Raphael Israeli, *The PLO in Lebanon: Selected Documents* (London: Weidenfeld and Nicolson, 1983).

51. Livingstone and Halevy, *Inside the PLO,* p. 82.

52. *Al-Saeyasa* (Kuwait), June 2, 1990.

53. Jimmy Carter, *The Blood of Abraham* (Boston: Houghton Mifflin, 1985), pp. 112–13.

54. Arafat first approached the United States with a statement that he was willing to accept that "Israel is here to stay" in 1973, a full fifteen years before the supposed acceptance of Israel that prompted the U.S.-PLO dialogue. Arafat's original proposal to the Americans was that he would accept Israel if the United States would support a PLO state in Jordan. The Americans did not respond, in part because they believed that the PLO "was certain to be irredentist" and would not be satisfied only with Jordan. Henry Kissinger, *Years of Upheaval* (Boston: Little, Brown, 1982), p. 626.

55. *The Jerusalem Post,* March 26, 1973.

56. Harris Schoenberg, *Mandate for Terror: The United Nations and the PLO* (New York: Shapolsky, 1989), pp. 413–14.

57. *The New York Times,* Oct. 10, 1985. Cited in Livingstone and Halevy, *Inside the PLO,* p. 317.

58. Livingstone and Halevy, *Inside the PLO,* p. 259.

59. At an Arab League luncheon at the UN, at which the UN secretary-general was present; *The New York Times,* Dec. 4, 1985.

60. *The New York Times,* Nov. 13, 1988. Abbas continued: "It wasn't us who carried out this [*Achille Lauro*] operation, but the Americans. They are the ones who made this whole thing up. The Americans are trying to play the role of 'cowboy.' " *Al-Watan Al-Arabi* (Paris), Dec. 16, 1988.

61. *The Wall Street Journal,* July 26, 1979.

62. Nov. 8–11, 1987. *The Record of Events* called the conference "extraordinary" in that it was called to deal with the Iran-Iraq War rather than the usual agenda. "The Middle East and North Africa" (London: Europa Publications, 1991), 37th ed., p. 244.

63. Abu Iyad interviewed on BBC, Nov. 10, 1985.

64. Kaddoumi in *Quotidien de Paris,* Nov. 19, 1985.

65. The denial was issued by PLO spokesman Mahmoud Labadi. *The Jerusalem Post,* July 26, 1982.

66. Arafat's official text, Geneva, Dec. 13, 1988.

67. Arafat, in Ibid.

68. *The New York Times,* Jan. 19, 1989. Such reactions were based on the views of the State Department, whose spokesman announced that "things will never be the same again in the Middle East peace process." *The Washington Post,* Dec. 16, 1988.

69. Arafat on Austrian television, Dec. 19, 1988.

70. Za'anoun quoted in *Al-Anba* (Kuwait), Dec. 23, 1988.

71. Abu Iyad quoted in *Al-Rayah* (Qatar), Jan. 13, 1990.

72. Al-Hassan quoted in *Al-Rayah* (Qatar), Jan. 13, 1990.

73. Hawatmeh quoted by Jamahiriya News Agency (Libya), Apr. 19, 1989.

74. Abu Iyad on Radio Monte Carlo, March 4, 1989.

75. Kaddoumi quoted in *Politiken* (Denmark), May 18, 1989.

76. Abu Iyad quoted in *Al-Watan* (Kuwait), Feb. 11, 1989.

77. Habash quoted in the PFLP's *Al-Hadaf,* April 9, 1989.

78. Saudi Press Agency, Aug. 8, 1989.

79. Arafat and Qaddafi statement, Jana Libyan News Agency, quoted by Agence France Presse, Jan. 7, 1990.

80. Arafat on Radio Monte Carlo, May 2, 1989.

81. Arafat quoted by Agence France Presse, May 5, 1989.

82. Balawi interviewed with *Al-Sabbah* (Tunisia), quoted by Kuwait News Agency, May 6, 1989.

83. Abu Iyad quoted in *Al-Saeyasa* (Kuwait), June 1, 1989.

84. Abu Iyad quoted in *Ukaz* (Saudi Arabia), Jan. 23, 1989.

85. Natshe quoted in *Al-Watan* (Kuwait), Jan. 8, 1989.

86. Abu Iyad quoted in *Al-Anba* (Kuwait), Sept. 7, 1988.

87. Abu Iyad quoted in *Al-Yom Al-Sabi,* Nov. 28, 1988.

88. Abu Iyad quoted in *Al-Sapir,* Jan. 1988.

89. Abu Iyad quoted in *Al-Anba* (Kuwait), Dec. 18, 1988.

90. Abu Iyad quoted in *Dehira Ufales* (Kuwait), Jan. 6, 1987.

91. Abu Iyad quoted in *Al-Anba* (Kuwait), Sept. 7, 1988.

92. Abu Iyad quoted in *Al-Anba* (Kuwait), Dec. 6, 1988.

93. Abu Iyad quoted in *Al-Anba* (Kuwait), Dec. 12, 1988.

94. Arafat quoted by Libyan News Agency, May 1, 1990.

95. Kaddoumi quoted over BBC Arabic Service, Apr. 5, 1989.

96. Sayah quoted in *Al-Saeyasa* (Kuwait), Dec. 21, 1988.

97. Sayah quoted in *As-Shira* (Beirut), Aug. 22, 1988.

98. PFLP statement, Voice of the Mountain Radio (Lebanon), June 9, 1989.

99. PFLP's *Al-Hadaf,* Apr. 9, 1989.

100. Hawatmeh quoted by Agence France Presse, Jan. 1989.

101. Natshe quoted in *Al-Qabas,* Dec. 26, 1989.

102. *Al-Rai* (Amman), Nov. 12, 1992.

103. Dejani quoted in *Ukaz* (Saudi Arabia), Nov. 22, 1988.

104. Natshe quoted in *Al-Watan* (Kuwait), Jan. 8, 1989.

105. Danny Rothschild, Israel Government Coordinator for Judea and Samaria, Oct. 1991.

106. Hassan quoted in *Al-Watan* (Kuwait), Feb. 21, 1990.

107. Through Jan. 1, 1953. Atkinson, *Security,* p. 164. This amounts to more than $5 billion in 1992 terms.

108. Qaddafi on ABC, *20/20,* Jan. 27, 1988. Nasser said as much three decades earlier: "If Arabs return to Israel, Israel will cease to exist." *Züricher Woche,* Sept. 1, 1961; cited in Katz, *Battleground,* p. 31.

109. Arafat quoted in Qatar News Agency, Jan. 13, 1989.

110. Natshe quoted in *Al-Watan* (Kuwait), Jan. 8, 1989.

111. Arafat quoted by Middle East News Agency, Aug. 1, 1991.

112. Algiers Voice of Palestine, March 15, 1992.

113. Becker, *PLO,* pp. 175, 197.

114. Kaddoumi quoted in Ibid., p. 197.

115. As of Aug. 23, 1992, 698 "collaborators" had been murdered in the territories by the intifada committees. Source: IDF spokesman.

116. Arafat quoted in *People's Daily,* June 29, 1989.

117. Arafat quoted by Associated Press, Jan. 7, 1991.

118. Farouq Kaddoumi, on Radio A-Sharq (Lebanon), Aug. 20, 1991.

119. Voice of Palestine, Aug. 19, 1991. Predictably, within hours after the coup failed, Arafat issued a contradictory message of congratulations to Gorbachev and Yelstin. They were not pleased.

120. Mufti quoted in Schechtman, *Mufti,* p. 104.

6. TWO KINDS OF PEACE

1. Immanuel Kant, "Perpetual Peace," in Hans Reiss, ed., *Kant's Political Writings* (New York: Cambridge, 1970), pp. 100, 103.

2. Shirer, *Rise and Fall,* pp. 556–57.

3. Between 1989 and 1992, the U.S. government provided nearly $8 billion in unconditional loan guarantees to eight Arab governments, including $500 million in guarantees for Iraq approved immediately before its invasion of Kuwait. *Near East Report,* April 6, 1992.

4. Western European countries supplied Saddam with combat aircraft; assault, antitank, and reconnaissance helicopters; air-to-air, surface-to-air, and air-to-surface missiles and missile launchers; electronic systems for land and sea defense; military transports of various sorts; armored cars and antitank armored cars; mobile artillery; missile frigates and corvettes; and ammunition and explosives. Yedidya Atlas, "Where Did Saddam Get All Those Weapons?" *The Jerusalem Post,* Sept. 17, 1990. The recent revelations and accusations in Britain and the United States seem to indicate much more extensive Western involvement in creating the Iraqi menace than even the above list indicates.

5. Max Nordau, *Morals and the Evolution of Man,* Marie Lewenz, trans. (New York: Funk and Wagnalls, 1922), pp. 1–2.

7. THE WALL

1. Charles Perkins, *Arms to the Arabs: The Arab Military Buildup Since 1973* (Washington, D.C.: AIPAC, 1989), p. 5.

2. Saudi defense expenditures in 1990 totaled $31.9 billion, as compared with Britain's $38.5 billion. And Saudi expenditures in the coming years may include tens of billions of dollars in additional arms requested from the U.S. and other suppliers. International Institute for Strategic Studies, *Military Balance, 1991* (London: Brassey, 1991), p. 117.

3. The Germans had 3,350 tanks. Col. T. N. Dupuy, *A Genius for War: The German Army and General Staff 1807–1945* (Englewood Cliffs, N.J.: Prentice-Hall, 1977), p. 269. Compare this with Syria's 4,350 today. *Military Balance,* p. 120.

4. The Syrian standing army comprises 404,000 troops. Israel's active service comes to 141,000 men, and it can rely on 504,000 reserves. *Military Balance,* pp. 108, 120.

5. NATO forces arrayed against a possible Soviet assault were deployed across the entire depth of West Germany, affording 150 miles of defenses between East Germany and France at West Germany's narrow-

est point. David Isby and Charles Kamps, *Armies of NATO's Central Front* (London: Jane's, 1985), p. 194.

6. Twain, *Innocents Abroad,* p. 379.

7. The Arab states comprise 5.4 million square miles, while the United States is 3.5 million square miles. Maryland is 9,837 square miles, as opposed to 8,290 for pre-1967 Israel. The West Bank is 2,187 square miles.

8. A surprise attack by Syria, Jordan, and an Iraqi expeditionary force would have a six-to-one advantage in standing ground forces over Israel during the first forty-eight hours of the fighting. Aryeh Shalev, *The West Bank Line of Defense* (New York: Praeger Publishers, 1985), p. 42.

9. *The Washington Times,* Oct. 12, 1988.

10. *The Jerusalem Post,* Nov. 7, 1991.

11. *The Jaffee Center Study Group on War in the Gulf: Implications for Israel* (Boulder: Westview, 1992), p. 388.

12. The length of the West Bank's border with pre-1967 Israel is 361 kilometers, as opposed to 100 kilometers at present. Shalev, *West Bank Line,* p. 10.

13. *Ha'aretz,* July 22, 1988.

14. *The Jerusalem Post,* Nov. 12, 1986, and Apr. 5, 1987.

15. The Associated Press, Jan. 14, 1990.

16. Livingstone and Halevy, *Inside the PLO,* p. 68.

17. Arthur Goldberg, "The Meaning of 242," *The Jerusalem Post,* June 10, 1977.

18. Ibid.

19. Caradon on *The MacNeil-Lehrer Report,* Mar. 30, 1978.

20. Eugene Rostow, "The Truth About 242," *The Jerusalem Post,* Nov. 5, 1990.

21. Johnson, Address before the 125th anniversary meeting of B'nai Brith, Washington, D.C., Sept. 10, 1968. Reprinted in the *Department of State Bulletin,* Oct. 7, 1968.

22. Dayan quoted in H. Sachar, *History of Israel,* p. 674.

8. A DURABLE PEACE

1. "We, the Palestinian people, made the imaginative leap in the Palestine National Council of November 1988, during which the Palestine Liberation Organization launched its peace initiative based on Security Council Resolutions 242 and 338 *and declared Palestinian independence based on Resolution 181 of the United Nations, which gave birth to two states in 1948, Israel and Palestine"* (emphasis added). Head of Palestinian delegation, Haidar Abdel-Shafi, in *The New York Times,* Nov. 1, 1991.

2. "The claims invoked by Israel for the migration of world Jewry to it at the expense of the native Arab population are not sanctioned by any legal or humanitarian principle. If the entire world were to adopt such claims, it would have to encourage Christians to emigrate to the Vatican and all the Moslems to emigrate to holy Mecca." Syrian foreign minister Farouq Al-Shara, in Ibid.

3. Tlas quoted on Damascus Television Service, Mar. 7, 1990.

4. *The Jerusalem Post,* Oct. 22 and 23, 1991.

5. *The New York Times,* Mar. 22, 1991.

6. *The New York Times,* Mar. 18, 1991.

7. Telephone discussion with Eliyahu Rosenthal, Israel Water Authority.

8. Ibid.

9. Saudi News Agency, Jan. 2, 1989.

10. *The Jerusalem Post,* May 19, 1992.

11. Addendum to the report of the Commissioner-General of the United Nations Relief and Works Agency for Palestine Refugees in the Near East, "Financial Situation of UNRWA in 1990 and 1991 and Budget Estimates for 1992–93."

9. THE QUESTION OF JEWISH POWER

1. Cicero quoted in Stern, *Greek and Latin Authors,* vol. 1, p. 19.

2. Jabotinsky quoted in Benzion Netanyahu, *Jabotinsky's Place in the History of the Jewish People* (Haifa: University of Haifa Faculty of the Humanities Publications, 1981), p. 15.

3. *Shoah, An Oral History of the Holocaust: The Complete Text of the Film by Claude Lanzmann* (New York: Pantheon, 1985), p. 200.

4. Protocols of the Wannsee Conference, Jan. 20, 1942, in Yitzhak Arad, ed., *Documents of the Holocaust* (Jerusalem: Yad Vashem, 1981), p. 254.

5. In fact, many newspapers ridiculed the address. Carl Sandburg, *Abraham Lincoln* (New York: Harcourt, Brace, 1954), pp. 445–46.

6. Jabotinsky, in *Do'ar Hayom,* May 17, 1929. Cited in B. Netanyahu, *Jabotinsky's Place,* p. 7.

7. *Ha'aretz,* Aug. 27, 1992.

8. *Shoah,* p. 169.

9. Mark Twain, *The Complete Essays of Mark Twain,* Charles Neider, ed. (Garden City, N.Y.: Doubleday, 1963), p. 249.

Acknowledgments to
A Durable Peace

My friend Merv Adelson deserves all thanks for introducing me to Larry Kirshbaum of Warner Books, who persistently and doggedly pursued me to take time out from my schedule to complete the task of preparing this book for publication. Larry was not only successful in hunting his quarry (me), but also unusually generous with perceptive and invaluable editorial advice. At his suggestion, we touched as little of the original historical material as possible but updated the book to reflect the events of the last few years. Larry also brought with him excellent technical assistance in the person of his son Michael, who expertly manned the computer, kept up with my dictation, and proved that we are truly living in an electronic age. To both members of the Kirshbaum family, I extend my warmest thanks, as I do to David Bar Ilan, who applied his critical intelligence to the manuscript, old and new. As always, my wife, Sarah, put up with our impossible hours to complete the book with great understanding and even greater support.

Acknowledgments to
A Place Among the Nations

The task of writing this book would have been daunting enough in itself, but writing it in the midst of the turbulence of Israeli politics made it all the more so. A number of people helped me overcome what otherwise would have been insurmountable difficulties.

Dr. Dore Gold of the Jaffee Center for Strategic Studies at Tel Aviv University and Douglas Feith read the manuscript and suggested important revisions. My brother, Dr. Iddo Netanyahu, and my cousin, Nathan Mileikowsky, went over every word, steering me away from obscurity and toward what I hope is greater clarity and focus. The unwavering enthusiasm of Linda Grey and Ann Harris of Bantam Books was a constant source of encouragement, as were Ann's good-natured yet incisive editorial comments. Rami Elhanan and Jackie Levy calmly produced the maps and illustrations in the face of ever-changing demands. Esther Loewy, Avishai Cohen, and Ita Hanya verified facts and quotations, relentlessly weeding out inaccuracies and hunting down reliable information. Ralph Cwernan methodically tracked down material from some of my UN speeches, which I incorporated into the text. Above all, Yoram Hazony acted as an amalgam of researcher, editor, and typist, bringing a perceptive intelligence, as well as much patience and dedication, to work that often continued literally around the clock. To each of them I am deeply indebted, and to each I offer my thanks.

Last and most important, I owe an inestimable debt to my wife, Sarah, who gave me her clear insights into what was important and what was not, combining wise judgment with a profound sensitivity, while offering me her firm convictions and her courage.

BENJAMIN NETANYAHU

INDEX

A DURABLE PEACE